INSIGHT GUIDE

BALI

Part of the Langenscheidt Publishing Group

ABOUT THIS BOOK

Editorial

Managing Editor
Scott Rutherford
Editorial Director
Brian Bell

Distribution

UK & Ireland
GeoCenter International Ltd
The Viables Centre, Harrow Way
Basingstoke, Hants RG22 4BJ
Fax: (44) 1256 817988

United States
Langenscheidt Publishers, Inc.
46–35 54th Road, Maspeth, NY 11378
Fax: (718) 784 0640

Canada
Thomas Allen & Son Ltd
390 Steelcase Road East
Markham, Ontario L3R 1G2
Fax: (1) 905 475 6747

Australia
Universal Press
1 Waterloo Road
Macquarie Park, NSW 2113
Fax: (61) 2 9888 9074

New Zealand
Hema Maps New Zealand Ltd (HNZ)
Unit D, 24 Ra ORA Drive
East Tamaki, Auckland
Fax: (64) 9 273 6479

Worldwide
**Apa Publications GmbH & Co.
Verlag KG (Singapore branch)**
38 Joo Koon Road, Singapore 628990
Tel: (65) 865 1600. Fax: (65) 861 6438

Printing

Insight Print Services (Pte) Ltd
38 Joo Koon Road, Singapore 628990
Tel: (65) 865 1600. Fax: (65) 861 6438

©2002 Apa Publications GmbH & Co.
Verlag KG (Singapore branch)
All Rights Reserved
First Edition1970
Sixteenth Edition 1999
Updated 2001, reprinted 2002

CONTACTING THE EDITORS
We would appreciate it if readers
would alert us to errors or out-
dated information by writing to:
**Insight Guides, P.O. Box 7910,
London SE1 1WE, England.
Fax: (44) 20 7403 0290.**
insight@apaguide.demon.co.uk

NO part of this book may be reproduced,
stored in a retrieval system or transmitted
in any form or means electronic, mech-
anical, photocopying, recording or otherwise, without prior written permission of
Apa Publications. Brief text quotations
with use of photographs are exempted
for book review purposes only. Information has been obtained from sources
believed to be reliable, but its accuracy
and completeness, and the opinions based
thereon, are not guaranteed.

www.insightguides.com

This guide book combines the interest and enthusiasms of two of the world's best-known information providers: Insight Guides, whose titles have set the standard for visual travel guides since 1970, and the Discovery Channel, the world's premier source of non-fiction television programming. The editors of Insight Guides provide both practical advice and general background regarding a place's institutions, history, culture, and people. The Discovery Channel and its popular website, www.discovery.com, help millions of viewers explore their world from the comfort of their own home and also encourage them to explore it first-hand.

In this, the sixteenth edition of *Insight Guide: Bali,* we explore this Indonesian island that has reached mythical proportions. Who can deny the fantasies that swirl within the mind when one hears the word *Bali*? Exotic culture, lush scenery, and sand sifting through giddy toes more familiar with wingtips or nylons.

Travellers who have absorbed this myth may be shocked upon arrival. Much of southern Bali is developed like a chaotic suburb; Kuta is frantic and noisy. But fret not, for Bali has ample paradise yet to offer travellers.

EXPLORE YOUR WORLD®

DISCOVERY CHANNEL

Contemporary
Balinese art.

Using this book:

The Insight Guide format of informative and well-written text paired with exciting, evocative photography continues throughout this edition of *Insight Guide: Bali*. The guide is structured to convey a complete understanding of the island and its exceedingly rich culture, and to guide readers through the wide-ranging and diverse sights and activities found on Bali.

◆ The Features section, with a yellow colour bar, covers Bali's history and culture in lively and authoritative essays written by specialists.

◆ The Places section, with a blue bar, provides full details of all the sights and areas worth seeing. The chief places of interest are coordinated by number with specially drawn maps.

◆ The Travel Tips listings section, with an orange bar and at the back of the book, offers a point of reference for information on restaurants, accommodation, travel, and all other practical aspects. Information is located quickly using the index printed on the back-cover flap, which also serves as a handy bookmark.

The contributors

This latest edition of *Insight Guide: Bali* has at its core the first edition published in 1970. This updated edition was overseen by editor **Rachel Fox** in Apa's London office, and updated by **Debe Campbell**.

Contributors to earlier editions included **Sian Jay**, **Wendy Hutton**, **Ed Peters**, **Rachel Farnay**, **Hans Höfer**, **Leonard Lueras**, **Garrett Kam**, **Rucina Ballinger**, **John Darling**, **Fred Eiseman**, **Willard A. Hanna**, **David Harnish**, **Eric Oey**, **David Stuart-Fox**, **Made Wijaya**, **Paul Zack**, **Mary Zurbuchen**, **Jack Hollingsworth**, **Werner Hahn**, **Star Black**, **June Jacob**, **Sin Yoke Fund**, and numerous others.

Map Legend

— ·· —	International Boundary
— — —	Province Boundary
⊖	Border Crossing
—·—·—	National Park/ Nature Reserve
— — —	Ferry Route
✈	Airport
🚌	Bus Station
P	Parking
ⓘ	Tourist Information
✉	Post Office
†	Church/Ruins
	Mosque
✡	Synagogue
	Castle/Ruins

The main places of interest in the **Places** chapters are coordinated by number with a full-colour map (e.g. ❶), and a symbol at the top of every right-hand page tells you where to find the map.

CONTENTS

Topeng masks.

Travel Tips

AN ISLE OF IDYLL

Bali probably doesn't need an introduction.

Its name is a synonym for paradise, if not blissful exile

Agreat Javanese priest was forced to banish his dissolute son to the eastern tip of Java. The priest then drew a line with his cane across the sands to create a watery divide, and thus the island of Bali was created. The story points to a truth, for Bali was indeed once connected to Java. Less than 3 km (2 miles) wide, the strait that now separates the two islands reaches a depth of only 60 metres (200 ft). Yet on the opposite side of Bali, to the east between Bali and Lombok, surge some of the deepest waters in the 5,000-km (3,000-mile) long Indonesian archipelago.

Before the sea rose during the last glacial period, the present-day islands of Sumatra, Borneo, Java and Bali were all linked to mainland Asia. In the east, New Guinea was joined to Australia. Tectonic plates shifted and ocean levels changed, and the treacherous strait that separates Bali from Lombok is today the naturalist's divide between Asia and Australia, a transition zone of flora and fauna.

The earliest rumours of Indonesia to reach the West arose from the distant realities of this huge archipelago, surrounded by eight seas and two oceans. An immense region of 6 million sq. km (2 million sq. miles) encompassing land and sea, Indonesia continues to grow in size. One quarter of its 200 volcanoes, including two in Bali, are still considered active.

The mountains, not the ocean and distant horizons, are the source of life and wisdom for the Balinese. Mountains produce lakes and rivers, the source of the land's fertility. The lofty volcano Gunung Agung is the central abode of the island's deities.

Bali's volcanoes, stretching from east to west, divide the island in half. The northern region of Buleleng, a narrow coastal strip that quickly merges into foothills, produces Bali's main exports of cattle, coffee and copra. In the highlands are peanuts, cabbage, spices, and onions. On the volcanic slopes, lofty tree-ferns, elephant grass, and wild flowers hang from the cliffs hugging the roadside. Tall pines and cypress trees soar above the lower embankments. To the south of the volcanoes are the island's population centres and its rice-producing region. Much of Bali's celebrated cultural and aesthetic traditions are found in the south.

Like the majority of Indonesians, the Balinese are distant descendants of Malays and Polynesians. More recently, Balinese heritage has extended to central and eastern Javanese ancestors, perhaps with distant lineage to Indian and Chinese traders who long ago settled in the archipelago. Over the centuries, numerous groups of foreigners came to Bali, adding to the people's mix. The majority were Chinese, followed by Indians and Arabs. The Indians brought Hinduism,

PRECEDING PAGES: an ancient temple image; *wayang kulit*, or shadow-puppet play; ritual trance dance in a rural village; accompanying deities during Eka Dasa Rudra.
LEFT: rural Balinese tending his ducks.

which became the dominant belief on Bali, the only remaining stronghold of Hinduism in Indonesia. This Hinduism, including the belief in castes, has been melded with some of Bali's more traditional animistic beliefs. (In the interior, however, especially at higher elevations, several villages are inhabited by people known as Bali Aga, who live virtually untouched by Hinduism and social castes.)

Centuries of rule by a caste of aristocracy ended violently with the Dutch conquest of Bali at the turn of the 20th century. For half a century afterwards, Bali was a colonial island, yet it retained a considerable amount of its identity and culture. It is this culture, plus the exquisite landscape and ocean, that brings tourists to its shores and highlands. In 1970, fewer than 15,000 visitors came to Bali. By the year 2000, there were over a million visitors descending each year.

They come for the island's beauty and for its unique culture. Bali's location couldn't be more perfect. Even its relative remoteness nurtures the perception of escape and being far from it all, wherever it may be. Flanked by the Java Sea to the north and the Indian Ocean to the south, Bali is just eight degrees south of the equator and thus has reasonably consistent weather – that delightfully warm climate of the tropics so alluring to those living in the higher latitudes.

Tourism is always slammed by purists and even many tourists who fear the denigration of local culture. The commercial cauldron of Kuta is pointed at with evangelical fervour. Indeed, the first-time traveller expecting quiet and romanticism will be disillusioned by the sprawling infrastructure and often pushy commercialism of the southern tourist centres. But worry not. The cohesive bonds of religion, family and community life have given the Balinese a sound base from which to face problems and outside influences. Most of Bali is untouched by tourism's demands. In fact, it is probable that, in a significant way, tourism helped assure a cultural renaissance on the island. Tourism gave many communities the resources to restore temples and historic sites, and it provided the impetus to create new dance groups and centres of art.

For such a small isle – one of Indonesia's 17,500-plus islands – a relatively large number of people make the transoceanic journey each year to its embrace. There must be a good reason.

A note on names

In most cases, we use Bahasa Indonesian for geographical locations and points of interest. When possible and appropriate, the English translation appears in parentheses. Thus, Mount Agung is Gunung Agung. Similarly, Luhur Uluwatu Temple is Pura Luhur Uluwatu, and Kanginan Palace is Puri Kanginan. Thamrin Avenue is Jalan Thamrin.

Foreigners are sometimes confounded by Indonesian names. Some Indonesians use only one name, not a given and family name together. Also, there may be two ways of spelling a name. (The name of former president Soeharto is sometimes simplified to Suharto. Soeharto is more traditional and how he himself spells it.) Moreover, in Bali names are graced with reflections of one's caste and one's position in the family. *(See pages 68 and 70.)*   ❏

RIGHT: a captivatingly detailed *topeng* mask. **FOLLOWING PAGES:** raja of Gianyar with his wife and attendants, early 20th century.

Decisive Dates

Prehistoric years

1.7 million years ago: Hominids live in Java, the largest island in the archipelago.

40,000 years ago: Fossil records of modern humans *(Homo sapiens)* exist from this period in Indonesia.

5000 BC: Austronesian peoples begin moving into Indonesia from the Philippines.

3000 BC: Plain pottery pots and open bowls, together with shell bracelets, discs, and beads found in southwestern Sulawesi and eastern Timor.

500 BC–AD 500: Dong Son bronze age, including on

Bali. Characteristic of the period are the ceremonial bronze drums and axes, distinctively decorated with engraved geometric, animal and human motifs. This decorative style is highly influential in many fields of Indonesian art, and seems to have spread together with bronze casting techniques.

Indianised kingdoms

AD 400: Hindu kingdoms emerge in western Java and eastern Kalimantan (Borneo).

910: Political centre of Java moves to eastern Java; rise of Hindu kingdoms on Bali.

c. 1000: Airlangga succeeds to the throne in east Java after the Srivijayan forces depart. His reign influences culture in Bali.

Majapahit influences

1275: Ken Arok sends first successful naval expeditions against Srivijaya to wrestle control of the important maritime trade.

1284: Javanese kingdom of Singasari invades Bali.

1293: Wijaya founds kingdom of Majapahit and rules as Kertarajasa.

1343: Majapahit general Gajah Mada invades Bali.

1403–06: Struggle for control erupts into civil war.

1429: Country reunited; Majapahit loses control of the western Java Sea and the straits to a new Islamic power located at Malacca.

15th century: Islam on Java precipitates the fall of the Majapahit empire; much of the Hindu-Javanese aristocracy flees into exile on nearby Bali. The seeds of today's Balinese culture are sown. All trading ports of the western archipelago are brought within Malacca's orbit, including the important ports along the north coast of Java.

1515: Majapahit empire collapses.

Early 16th century: Islamisation of coastal kingdoms of Java begins. A unified Bali takes territories in eastern Java and also Lombok.

The Dutch years

1596: First Dutch ships drop anchor in Banten, Java.

1597: First Dutch arrive in Bali.

1602: The Dutch form the Dutch East Indies Company (VOC), a joint-stock corporation established to exploit Indonesia's wealth.

1641: Dutch capture Malacca from the Portuguese.

1799: Dutch financiers receive stunning news: the VOC is bankrupt. Indonesia becomes a colony.

1811–16: Brief period of English rule under Thomas Stamford Raffles.

1841: Dutch frigate *Overijssel* runs aground near Kuta and is salvaged by the Balinese. The Dutch are outraged both by the embarrassment of the *Overijssel*'s error and the Balinese plundering.

1846: The first Dutch military expedition lands in northern Bali; a few years later, the first Dutch regent establishes his headquarters in Singaraja. The Dutch institute laws banning slavery and *suttee*.

1882: Dutch unite Bali and Lombok into a single residency. Dutch control strengthens.

1894: Dutch troops invade Lombok.

1900: The raja of Gianyar asks for Dutch protection from the other Balinese regencies, who are fighting amongst one another.

1904: A Dutch trading ship, *Sri Kumala* runs aground near Sanur. Following local tradition, Balinese plunder the wreckage. The Dutch demand compensation, but are rebuffed by the raja of Badung.

1906: After two years of negotiations over the *Sri Kumala* incident, the Dutch take military action. The Dutch attack the royal palace in Denpasar. Dressed in white, the raja and his court walk directly into the Dutch bullets or commit ritual suicide in a *puputan*. About 2,000 Balinese men, women and children die.

1908: Indonesians attending Dutch schools form regional student organisations. On Bali, a *puputan* takes place in Klungkung. The Dutch control the entire island.

1910: Indonesian Communist movement founded.

1910–30: Turbulent period of strikes, violence and organised rebellions throughout Indonesia.

1917: Devastating earthquake hits Bali.

1927: First major political party with Indonesian

1946: In the village of Marga, I Gusti Ngurah Rai and 94 followers are killed while fighting the Dutch.

1949: The Dutch acknowledge Indonesia's independence and sovereignty. Bali becomes a province.

Late 1950s: Communist insurgency prompts Soekarno to declare martial law. Soekarno resurrects the "revolutionary" constitution of 1945.

1963: Gunung Agung erupts, killing thousands of people and destroying numerous villages.

1965: Blood-letting ensues after failed coup against Soekarno. The Chinese are the focus of anti-Communist attacks. Up to 500,000 people are killed, including from 100,000 to 200,000 on Bali.

1966: Soeharto replaces Soekarno.

independence as its goal is founded by Soekarno.

1933: Crackdown ensues; Soekarno and all other student leaders are exiled to distant islands for 10 years.

World War II and independence

1942: Japanese invasion of Java.

1944: Japanese promise independence in attempt to maintain faltering Indonesian support.

1945: Japan surrenders. Expecting to resume control, the Dutch return. Nationalists Soekarno and Muhammad Hatta declare Indonesia's independence as a republic on 17 August. The Dutch resist.

LEFT: ship of the Dutch East Indies Company.
ABOVE: body of Badung's raja after the 1906 *puputan*.

1986: Nusa Dua launched as a planned resort.

1996: Unrest ripples through Jakarta in response to the government's hard line against opponents.

1997: Economic recession throughout Southeast Asia. The rupiah collapses and riots begin.

1998: Price supports for fuel and other necessities are eliminated. Riots in Jakarta leave over 500 dead, but Bali is spared violence. Soeharto resigns.

1999: Indonesia's first democratic elections are conducted peacefully, bringing Abdurrahman Wahid to the Presidency.

2000: Wahid maintains tenuous control. Soeharto is charged with corruption, but is not brought to trial.

2001: Wahid faces corruption charges and is censured by Parliament. ❑

THE GOLDEN AGE

With the rise of its kingdoms and the influence of the Majapahit court on Java,
Bali's golden age flourished until Europeans started to meddle

The Balinese creation myth explains how Batara Guru (Great Teacher) and the god Brahma fashioned human figures out of clay. The first figures they baked in the oven were underdone and came out white. The second batch burned black. The last batch came out a perfect golden brown, and these last were given life by the two deities and became the ancestors of the Balinese.

The empirical evidence, however, suggests that the first ancestors of the modern Balinese was comprised of small bands of Austronesian hunter-gatherers who began moving into the archipelago some 4,000 years ago. These people had contacts – probably through trade – with other islands. There is evidence that by 2,000 years ago the Balinese had at least indirect trade links with India. Through contacts with other parts of Southeast Asia, the early Balinese learned the art of bronze and iron casting, and by AD 1,000 they were making beautiful bronze kettle drums.

Although we do not know for certain what kind of social system these late prehistoric Balinese had, certain clues about their society have been unearthed. Several different kinds of burial were practiced – jar burials, burials without coffins, and sarcophagi burials – which may reflect the existence of social stratification, with the sarcophagi probably for people of higher social rank. Some of these sarcophagi are carved with masks and anthropomorphic figures. Many of these burials included grave goods – jewellery, tools and pottery – indicating that these people were concerned with afterlife.

The only other clues we have about these ancient Balinese lie in megalithic remains that may be seen on the island: stepped or terraced structures, stone seats and *menhirs*. Many of these structures are still used today. They appear to be connected with the veneration of

PRECEDING PAGES: temple carving depicting hell.
LEFT: the Balinese cosmos, with turtle and two serpents, and Sanghyang Widi Wasa, the Supreme Being.
RIGHT: detail from Moon of Pejeng drum.

ancestors, and some of today's religious practices suggest a continuity of ideas related to this early belief system. The religious and social practices of the Bali Aga or Bali Kuna ("original" or "ancient" Balinese) who, until recently, were isolated communities living in the mountainous interior, may represent the present ves-

tiges of the prehistoric Balinese social system. Their religion centres on the veneration of natural deities and ancestors. Mountains and volcanoes, as well as water, play a central role in the beliefs of these people.

Indian influences

It is highly probable that Indian or Indianised traders were in contact with Bali at a very early stage in history. Whether these links were directly with India or with the Hindu-Buddhist kingdoms of Java is not known for certain. There is no doubt that Bali was part of the wave of Indian influence that spread throughout Southeast Asia from about the 7th century.

The key concepts introduced from India included ideas about a god-king, and it is during the early part of the first millennium that the idea of kingship evolved. Early inscriptions show that *candi* (shrines or temples) were erected for various rulers, and there are statues from this period that may portray royalty or other important people. The development of an Indianised – or rather, Hinduised – society came about when rulers recognised and adopted certain religious and administrative practices that served their purposes. India provided the literary, artistic and social models, as well as one of theology and politics.

However, the Balinese modified ideas to suit their own needs, retaining many of their indigenous beliefs and models. Hindu deities were adopted, especially Shiva (known as Siwa in Bali), but they often became identified with, or existed alongside, the older ancestral deities, so that Bali never became a carbon copy of Hindu India. Archaeological remains dating from this era include inscriptions written in Old Balinese on stone and copper, stone sculptures and bronzes.

Also from this period are ornamented caves, rock-cut temples and bathing places. These tend to be found near rivers and springs, and ravines and mountaintops, strongly suggesting that they were connected with ancient religious beliefs.

The role of the king was important, as he was seen as a reflection of the Divine and his *puri* (palace) was a miniature reflection of heaven. The king exercised spiritual and temporal power through a hierarchy of courtiers and priests. The priests held important and often powerful positions. It was believed that the kingdom and its people would prosper only as long as the king conducted himself properly in accordance with divine law. An evil or corrupt king could be – and sometimes was – replaced by a better one through the intercession of priests.

The historical period

More accurate historical records become available in the 10th century, although there remain large gaps in our knowledge. We know that at the end of the 10th century, in AD 991, the Javanese wife of the Balinese king gave birth to a son named Airlangga.

The links that existed between Bali and Java were strengthened when Airlangga married the daughter of the king of the Javanese kingdom of Sanjaya. When his father-in-law was murdered, Airlangga defeated the enemies of Sanjaya and ruled the kingdom of Sanjaya for the next three decades. His younger brother was installed as regent of Bali. Both brothers ruled with great skill, conforming to the ideals of Hindu kingship, and it was during this period that strong cultural and political links between Bali and Java were forged, beginning a long, if intermittent, Javanese cultural influence over Bali. It was at this stage that Javanese began to replace Old Balinese as the chancellery and probably the court language of Bali.

For the common Balinese at this time, life was focused on semi-autonomous villages centred on a core group from which a council of elders was elected. This is not dissimilar to the way that Bali Aga villages are structured today. Artists, craftsmen and traders, along with newcomers, lived outside this core alongside officials who were answerable to the king and who supervised taxation, corvée (unpaid serf labour) and trade matters. Groups of villages and temples came under the supervision of local lords, who in turn were directly answerable to the king. Society was hierarchical.

On Airlangga's death in 1049, Bali was again an independent kingdom for the next 235 years. There are numerous inscriptions bearing dates and connected with various Balinese rulers during these ensuing years. However, given that rulers often had more than one name, and that more than one ruler often shared the same name or title, a correct reading of the chronology becomes difficult. During this period of indepen-dence, the Balinese kings con-structed a series of rock-cut tombs at a place called Gunung Kawi (Poet's Mountain), along with a number of artificial med-itation caves. There is also evi-dence that Buddhism held an

BARBARIANS?

At a time when Bali was emerging as one of the most cultured and literate societies in the Indonesian archipelago, a Chinese text described a country called Bali as being inhabited by barbarians.

is claimed that Gajah Mada was sent to Bali to quell the cruel king Beda Ulu (the name means "different head"), who was noted for his super-natural powers. He was said to be able to decapitate himself, then restore his head to his neck. The god Siwa, offended by the king's audacity, caused the severed head to fall into a stream and be washed away. The king's minister replaced the king's head with that of a passing pig that he killed. The king decreed that no one must ever look upon his face again.

important role alongside Hinduism at this stage. At Goa Gajah, which dates from this period, Buddhist statuary has been found alongside Hindu relics.

While Balinese rulers became embroiled in dynastic rivalries, the great Javanese empire of Majapahit was expanding. From eastern Java, the short-lived kingdom of Singasari invaded Bali in 1284, ostensibly to pacify and reunify the island. Bali was again invaded in 1343 by Gajah Mada, the famous Majapahit general. It

LEFT: ancient carving depicting Airlangga as Wisnu (Vishnu) upon a *garuda*. **ABOVE:** modern visitors inside the cave at Goa Gajah.

When Gajah Mada was brought into the king's presence, he raised his head while drinking to see for himself if the stories about the king's appearance were true. So enraged was Beda Ulu that he was consumed by the fires of his own rage.

This allegorical tale mythicises the conquest of Beda Ulu's kingdom by Majapahit, which then proceeded to rule Bali through a series of puppet rulers. These rulers were surrounded by a group of Javanese nobles, called Aryas, who were given territories around the new capital, which lay near present-day Klung-kung. A Javanese-style court and court culture were introduced to Bali.

Village life also changed when the new Majapahit rulers broke up the old village structures and created units *(banjar)* that essentially grouped households according to corvée obligations, which were carried out under the supervision of a court-appointed official. The walled villages dividing the core members from the outsiders disappeared, and only individual household yards were walled – essentially the village structure of today. Those against the change fled to the mountains, ancestors of today's Bali Aga.

> **PACKED WITH PEOPLE**
>
> In 1597, Bali had a population density of 39 people per square kilometre, exceeding that of China (37) and India (32), and four times that of Europe.

Bali's Golden Age

The empire of Majapahit fell in 1515 to the new Islamic kingdoms that were beginning to emerge on Java. Reluctant to succumb to new religious ideas, the priests, nobles, soldiers and artisans of the Majapahit empire chose instead to flee to Bali, strengthening the Hindu culture that had already taken root there. The Balinese moulded the Majapahit influences to their own needs, reinventing the Balinese culture. In the process, they shaped the nucleus of contemporary Bali-

It was also at this stage in Bali's history that the Hindu caste system was introduced. At the apex were *Brahman* priests, followed by *Satria* (nobles), *Wesya* (land-holding nobles who were Aryas), and *Sudra*, comprising the rest of the population. Although the king, a *Satria*, ruled, it was the *Brahmans* who held real power. The state, a reflection of heaven, could only be held together by the performance of rituals and by the king conducting himself righteously. It was the task of the priests to ensure that this happened. Much of their power lay in an ability to use the complex sung poetry known as *kekawin*, which was written in Old Javanese, and in using metrical systems that came from India.

nese culture, so that much of the language, music, dance, sculpture and literature of today is derived from that time.

The 16th century marked what has come to be called the Golden Age of Bali. King Batu Renggong ascended the Balinese throne in 1550 and inherited the legacy of Majapahit. Among the refugees from Java was a *Brahman* priest named Nirartha, who was to become the ancestor of most Balinese high priests. He elevated to the major priestly group those priests who worshiped Siwa. The Majapahit rituals that he introduced were regarded as being more efficacious than those previously carried out in Bali, particularly the making of holy water, the key rite of the *Brahman* priests. Nirartha was also reputed to be a gifted writer and singer of *kekawin*, using the power of words and mystical knowledge to perform the rituals that were to keep the kingdom strong.

From his court in Gelgel, Batu Renggong, supported by Nirartha, welded the island into a strongly centralised kingdom, conquering Blambangan in east Java and colonising the neighbouring island of Lombok. He and his immediate successors became the epitome of the concept of a just ruler.

The 16th century also witnessed Bali's first encounter with Europe. The race of the Euro-

band's funeral pyre. This unfortunate image was long to colour the way that outsiders perceived the island. What the Dutch did not know was that they were observers of the height of the Balinese golden age, for soon after de Houtman's visit, Bali's court began its decline.

The first descriptions of Bali dwelt vividly on the lifestyle and culture of the court. The king was said to live in a palace enclosed by a four-metre-high wall with beautiful Chinese plates set into them. The doors were of carved wood covered with gold, and there were umpteen courtyards and pavilions for the royal slaves and concubines. At the centre of this vast

pean colonial powers to seize control of the so-called Spice Islands further east had begun, which ultimately ignored Bali. Although several European ships had sighted Bali and may have even landed there, the first substantial body of information to reach the West came from a Dutch expedition led by Cornelis de Houtman in 1597.

The Dutch were fascinated by what they observed, describing at great length the practice of widow sacrifice, or *sutti*, on her hus-

LEFT: 17th-century European illustration of raja in his chariot. **ABOVE:** widow of a raja leaping into her husband's funeral pyre in the rite of *sutti*.

complex lay the king's quarters and that of his principal wife, as well as subsidiary wives, which could number as many as 800. The palace represented the world in miniature. Within its confines were symbolic elements of the kingdom: gardens and ponds to represent forests and lakes, and all kinds of people, including albinos, dwarves and foreigners. These last represented the forces of diversity, constrained by keeping their potentially dangerous presence at the kingdom's centre.

The Dutch attempted to open trade agreements with the Balinese in 1601, but to little avail. For the next 200 years, encroaching European powers were largely to ignore Bali.

Decline of classical Bali

There began in Bali a long period during which new kingdoms rose and fell. The concept of a single ruler was replaced by that of many, and images derived from narratives such as the *Panji Tales* lent strength to the idea that a brave warrior could emerge out of nowhere and take a kingdom for himself.

The man credited with destroying the kingdom of Gelgel was the king's prime minister at the time. Although Balinese accounts have cast him as the villain, it is probable that he seized control in an effort to prevent the kingdom from being destroyed by two sons who were fighting

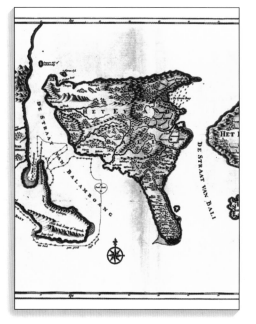

for succession. Whatever the truth, the floodgates were opened and other lords saw their chance to become kings of their own domains.

In northern Bali there emerged the kingdom of Buleleng, and in southern Bali a confusing number of kingdoms rose and fell. The two that were to survive into the 19th century were Badung and Mengwi. The Karangasem outpost in Lombok seized control of Lombok and succeeded in defeating the eastern Balinese kingdom of Klungkung, with whom it formed an alliance to conquer Buleleng in the north.

By the end of the 1700s, nine kingdoms had emerged out of the chaos, with Klungkung regarded as the highest kingdom. The other

rulers clung to their right to the title of king, but were prepared to recognise the existence of one kingdom of higher status. It meant that there was still the concept of Bali as a world, even if that world now consisted of several kingdoms instead of one.

One of the more negative images that was to emerge from Bali during this period was slavery. It was a demand for slaves on the part of the Dutch and the ability of the Balinese to supply them that enabled petty kings and princes to seize their moments of power. The victims of this situation were the common people. As wars were fought between rival kingdoms, the villagers were forced to fight alongside their lords, and they had a vested interest in ensuring that their lords won. If they did not, they and their families were sold into slavery.

We cannot know just how many Balinese were sold into slavery. However, it is estimated that during the 17th century, out of a slave population of 15,000 to 18,000 in Batavia (present-day Jakarta), 8,000 to 10,000 came from Bali.

Opium was another commodity upon which the Balinese rulers enriched themselves. The Dutch had introduced opium to the East Indies and held the monopoly. Balinese rulers, who after all did not come under Dutch rule, decided that they had a right to deal in opium. As well as buying and selling opium, the Balinese rulers and their courts became avid consumers of it. At a slightly later date, when opium smoking was freely indulged in the courts, the island of Bali was consuming 200 chests of opium a year, 20 to 30 chests being consumed by each of the island's kingdoms.

By the beginning of the 19th century, the rajas, drawing on the expertise of the brahman priests, were busy writing extensive genealogies that linked them to the ancient kingdoms of Java in an attempt to maintain their image as a separate nobility.

At the same time, many commoner families were beginning to increase their power. There had emerged many such families whose leaders held strong positions in the new kingdoms. When the Dutch turned their eyes towards Bali, it was ultimately the Balinese inability to present a united front against the enemy that was to lead to their downfall. ❏

LEFT: 17th-century map, possibly the first, of Bali.
RIGHT: niche for royal meditation near Gunung Kawi.

THE DUTCH CAMPAIGNS

First under the guise of treaties for friendship and commerce, the Dutch came to claim sovereignty over Bali, but only after the ritual suicides of its rajas

The beginning of the 19th century augured ill for the Balinese. In 1815 the volcano Tambora, on the neighbouring island of Lombok, erupted suddenly, sending out up to 180 cubic kilometres of ejecta. (Java's more infamous volcano, Krakatau, sent out only 50 cubic kilometres.) The initial explosion and shock waves killed over 12,000 people on Bali and Lombok. Bali was covered by 20 cm (8 inches) of volcanic ash that destroyed the harvest, and thousands of Balinese later died of starvation. In total, at least 25,000 people are believed to have died as a result of the eruption and its aftermath. Later, a mudslide at Buleleng that same year killed 10,000 people.

This disaster was followed by a series of mouse plagues that devastated the already meagre food supplies, causing further famine and disease. The second half of the century continued badly. There were seven epidemics of smallpox and five of cholera, four mouse plagues, and widespread dysentery outbreaks between 1850 and 1888. The smallpox outbreak of 1871 left between 15,000 and 18,000 Balinese dead.

Questions of trade

By the beginning of the 19th century, the Dutch had begun to look for ways to gain a foothold in Bali. To do so, they were convinced that it would be necessary to infiltrate traders on Bali and then assert sovereignty. By the end of the 1830s, the Dutch were openly discussing with the rajas of Bali the subjects of trade, politics, slavery and plunder – discussions that were veiled by treaties of friendship and commerce that would, in fact, recognise Dutch sovereignty and monopoly.

The Dutch were particularly suspicious of the Balinese dealings with the newly established British colony of Singapore. The ash deposits from the Tambora eruption soon cre-

ated a soil so fertile that the Balinese were exporting crops to Singapore. Instead of selling their people into slavery, as they had done previously, the Balinese rulers needed to keep them at work in the fields. In the early 1840s, the rajas of Badung, Buleleng, Klungkung and Karangasem were persuaded to sign treaties

that recognised Dutch sovereignty, although in fact the Dutch were more concerned with keeping the English out than actually administering Bali. The agreement, however, rested on a deceit, for the treaty was signed with the understanding that the Dutch would render military assistance in attack against the Mataram kingdom of Lombok, a promise the Dutch had no intention of fulfilling.

By 1840 two factors had convinced the Dutch that they should bring Bali under their influence. Firstly, they were concerned that another European power (especially the British) might become established there. Secondly, they wanted to put an end to the Bali-

---

PRECEDING PAGES: modern painting of the Balinese-Dutch conflict over the *Sri Kumala*. **LEFT:** Balinese warriors, 1880s. **RIGHT:** Dutch fighting the Javanese.

nese practice of plundering shipwrecks off the Balinese coast. It was this second factor that provided the Dutch with the excuse to intervene more directly in Balinese affairs.

In accordance with their principle of reef rights *(tawan mawan)*, the Balinese rajas had long regarded shipwrecks as a gift from the sea deity Baruna. The ship, cargo and everyone on board became the property of the raja, who shared the booty with those involved in the salvage. When the Dutch frigate *Overijssel* went aground

BATTLING AMOK

In battle, the Balinese attacked their enemies in a systematic formation. They were preceded by warriors high on opium or cocaine who ran amok among the enemy.

that. The other Balinese kingdoms chose not to get involved. The Dutch contingent numbered some 3,000 troops, and although the Balinese put up strong resistance, the Dutch won a swift victory. It was an empty victory, however, as they were still unable to impose their will upon the rajas, who were now firmly entrenched in the nearby hills.

A second expedition was less successful. The Balinese, with 16,000 men, fought off three Dutch attacks. It was during the third expedition, in 1849, that the Dutch were to encounter for

on Kuta reef in 1841, the Balinese, much to the anger of the Dutch, plundered it. The Dutch attempted to get the Balinese to sign another set of treaties, but were once more rebuffed.

"Never, while I live, shall the state recognise the sovereignty of the Netherlands in the sense in which you interpret it. Not by a mere scrap of paper shall any man become the master of another's lands. Rather let the *keris* decide", declared Gusti Ketut Jelantik of Buleleng's response to Dutch treaty proposals in 1841.

In 1846, the Dutch launched a punitive expedition against Buleleng, whose ruler was backed by Karangasem. The raja of Klungkung offered his blessing but could do no more than

BALINESE LITERACY

By the 1840s, Bali had one of the highest literacy rates in the archipelago. It was observed by one Dutch commentator at the time that "nearly all Balinese can read and write their language, even people of the lowest condition, as well as the greatest part of the women". These claims for almost universal literacy may be considered unique for the region. Later, early 20th-century reports suggested otherwise. However, it should be remembered that those compiling these reports – Europeans – would probably neither read nor speak Balinese and so were unaware of the literacy levels in that language.

the first time what one account described as "another kind of *amok*, which is wholly and exclusively peculiar to this nation."

The Dutch were confronted by Balinese troops who were dressed in the formal battle dress of warriors and assuming haughty stances. The raja of Buleleng and his brother, Gusti Ketut Jelantik, could be seen dressed in brilliant-red sarongs gathered up to reveal short, tight trousers underneath, with golden girdles nipped in at their waists. On their backs each displayed a huge, jewelled *keris* (dagger), the ornate handles extending above their shoulders, ready to be drawn. Their thick, flowing black

line of Dutch fire. All were cut down by Dutch bullets. The raja of Buleleng was killed, and Jelantik took poison. When the raja of Karangasem heard of the defeat, he killed his family and then himself.

Surrender was never an option for a Balinese raja staring at defeat. The only honourable course of action was to end his life in a ritual of self-sacrifice, displaying the courage that was expected of Balinese kingship. Similarly, his family and others within the court would do the same. The name of the ritual was *puputan*, which means "ending" or "finish", and in this context the end of an old way of life.

hair was bound up with white headcloths. This display of showmanship came to nothing.

It was to be another three weeks before the Dutch finally attacked the Balinese fortifications at Jagaraja, leaving thousands of Balinese dead. Dutch fatalities numbered 33. It was during this carnage that the Dutch witnessed a Balinese form of ritual suicide, which traditionally signalled the end of a kingdom. Jelantik's wife led a group of Balinese noblewomen – all in a state of near trance – directly into the

LEFT: Gusti Jelantik with Dutch expedition members, and Buleleng's royal court, c. 1880. **ABOVE:** raja of Karangasem and his grandson with *lontar*, c. 1900.

Bali in disarray

These tragic events left the Balinese resistance in disarray. A Danish trader named Mads Lange, who had lived in Bali since 1839, stepped in and negotiated a new agreement, which led to the installation of new rulers. Although the Dutch now regarded themselves as holding sovereignty, they did not interfere in the internal affairs of the kingdoms of southern and eastern Bali. However, when Buleleng rebelled in 1853, the Dutch took more direct control of Buleleng and Jembrana, introducing Dutch controllers who managed affairs through an appointed member of the royal family acting as regent.

Events in 1882 eventually brought matters to

a tragic and bloody conclusion. The Dutch united Lombok and Bali into a single Residency, essentially bringing northern Bali under direct rule. In spite of isolated outbreaks of Balinese resistance, Dutch control remained strong. They refrained, however, from interfering with the other kingdoms, which turned again to their own petty intrigues and conflicts. These rivalries and squabbles eventually led to all of Bali coming under Dutch control.

In 1891, Mengwi was defeated by Badung and Tabanan, and Mengwi's lands were taken over by Badung. Bali's fate then proceeded to unfold via events that took place on the neigh-

bouring island of Lombok. Throughout this period, the Balinese kingdom of Mataram on Lombok had enjoyed considerable influence and power. The rulers of Mataram, moreover, had been the overlords of Karangasem in eastern Bali since 1849, and it was through the actions of the Lombok rulers that Karangasem eventually came under Dutch control.

Although there was a sizeable Balinese Hindu population concentrated in western Lombok, the majority of the raja's subjects were Sasak Muslims, the indigenous inhabitants of Lombok concentrated in the central and eastern parts of the island. The Sasak had long

RAFFLES' VIEW OF BALI

Between 1811 and 1816, Sir Thomas Stamford Raffles administered Java on behalf of the Dutch government, who were in exile in London for the duration of the Napoleonic wars. A product of the European Enlightenment, Raffles came to view the Balinese as an enterprising and hard-working people, in contrast to the neighbouring Javanese. Although he also saw them as examples of the "noble savage", his view was that their rulers were not as despotic as those of Java.

His main interest in the Balinese, however, lay in the fact that he regarded them as representing the pre-Islamic civilisation of Java that had been destroyed with the arrival

of Islam. This sympathy was partly a reaction to the perceived threat of Islam, and the European prejudice of the time: that the Muslim Javanese had degraded their great civilisation.

Raffles quickly came to regard Bali as representing a continuation of the great achievements that had been lost on Java. It was a view that was to colour the attitude of the outside world towards Bali well into the 20th century. It was, moreover, a view that failed to recognise the considerable achievements made by the Balinese before the Majapahit era on Java, and the innate ability of the Balinese to incorporate and adapt outside ideas.

felt that they were treated less than fairly by their Balinese overlords, and when the raja tried to make his Sasak subjects fight in Bali, they rebelled. The alleged cruelty and discrimination towards the Sasak provided the Dutch with the excuse they needed to invade Lombok. In 1894, Dutch troops invaded the island and quickly conquered the capital at Mataram. Unchallenged, they marched into the heart of the island. At Cakrenegara they were suddenly attacked by Balinese warriors whose deadly rifle aim killed 98 Dutch and

RAZING THE PALACES

After the *puputan* in Denpasar and Klungkung, the Dutch then chose to raze the magnificent palaces of the dead rajas.

they rushed forwards into the fire of the Dutch troops. It was another *puputan*. The Dutch earned the victory by default, but the aftermath of these events were to leave deep scars on the Balinese soul and upon the Dutch conscience.

Worse was yet to come. The other rulers on Bali viewed the events that had taken place on Lombok with alarm, fearing that some minor incident would be all that was needed for the Dutch to launch another expeditionary force against them. Their fears were well-founded. In 1904, a Chinese-

wounded 272 in the first assault. The Dutch sent reinforcements and laid waste to the island. The raja took refuge in the village of Sasari, where he was eventually persuaded, along with son and grandson, to surrender.

However, the raja's nephew, Anak Agung Nengah, refused to surrender, and from his village hideout he and his followers chose the rite of *puputan*. As the Dutch advanced, Nengah led men, women and children towards them as if in a trance. If they did not die by the *keris*,

---

LEFT: Dutch artillery during the fighting against the Balinese. **ABOVE:** dead Balinese outside the Pemecutan palace in Tabanan after the 1906 *puputan*.

owned vessel, the *Sri Kumala*, struck a reef near Sanur, not far from the Badung-Gianyar border, and was plundered. The raja of Badung refused to pay compensation. He was supported by the raja of Tabanan to the west, who was embroiled in a crisis over a recent ceremony of *sutti*, which he had permitted despite Dutch protests.

That same year, the Dutch blockaded the coasts of Badung and Tabanan, and assembled a military expedition. In September of 1906, the Dutch launched perhaps one of the most shameful episodes in Dutch colonial history. The troops marched on Denpasar, only to find the town deserted and smoke rising from behind the palace walls, within which drums could be heard beating.

The Dutch watched as the palace gates opened and four bearers carried out the raja of Badung on a gold palanquin. He was dressed in white, wearing his finest jewellery and carrying a jewelled *keris*. Court officials, armed guards, priests, wives, children and retainers followed him, all similarly clothed in white and bejeweled. The party stopped 100 paces from the Dutch, and at his master's signal a priest plunged a *keris* into the raja's chest. This marked the beginning of one of the most horrific episodes of *puputan*. The raja's followers

turned their *keris* upon themselves, collapsing in a bloody heap on the ground, while more people surged out of the palace.

The Dutch fired into the crowds and the mound of bodies grew higher. The troops looted whatever they could from the corpses, and then they sacked the palace ruins.

That afternoon a similar scene was repeated at the smaller court of Pemecutan, in the district of Tabanan, where the old raja had died and his wives had elected to leap into his funeral pyre – the practice known as *sutti* – rather than surrender. The new raja and crown prince, too, committed suicide rather than surrender.

The *puputan* at Badung both fascinated and

horrified the Dutch, and it did much to turn the tide of Dutch public opinion against Dutch government policy in the East Indies.

Various eyewitness accounts provided the public back in the Netherlands with very graphic images of what had taken place.

"After the artillery fire stopped, the prince went there with his followers, women and children totalling around one hundred people, and there hidden from our view, they stabbed each other with *keris*. We found them together in a heap, the prince buried under the bodies of his faithful followers, as if to show that they wanted to protect him even in death, and the most beautiful young women we had seen in Bali lay lifeless next to their children", wrote one Dutch observer of the *puputan*.

If the Dutch had hoped that events would end there, they were mistaken. The kingdoms of Karangasem, Klungkung, Bangli and Gianyar reluctantly accepted Dutch authority, their will to resist having been sapped.

The end of an era

The final act of Bali's tragedy took place two years later, in 1908, when the raja of Karangasem objected to the Dutch imposition of an opium monopoly. Balinese rioted in Klungkung and the Dutch sent in troops. In Gelgel, Balinese killed a Javanese opium dealer and razed his store. The Dutch retaliated by killing or wounding 100 Balinese. The raja of Gelgel fled to Klungkung to take refuge.

The Dutch began their bombardment on Klungkung, witnessing a final *puputan*. The raja of Klungkung, followed by around 200 people, emerged from the palace, clad in white and carrying his ancestral *keris*. He thrust this into the ground. An old prophesy had stated that his magical *keris* would open up a chasm and swallow his enemies.

The prophesy proved to be false. A Dutch bullet killed the raja. Six of his wives knelt around his corpse and drove *keris* blades into their hearts. Then followers began the rite of *puputan*. The palace was burned, and on that day – 18 April 1908 – after 600 years of rule in Bali, the descendants of the great Majapahit empire of Java were wiped out. ❑

Left: nephew of the raja of Buleleng in royal dress, late 1800s. **Right:** detail from a modern painting by Budi of the Dutch assault on the Balinese.

CONTEMPORARY BALI

The Dutch ruled Bali for half of the 20th century. The second half, ignited by

Indonesia's independence, was of calamity followed by an idyllic image

Reports of the 1906 *puputan* reached the outside world, and protests began pouring into the Dutch colonial office condemning what were regarded as Dutch reprisals that were widely disproportionate to any known Balinese offences. There was guilt, too, on the part of the Dutch, who resolved to make amends by introducing certain reforms.

These reforms coincided with the introduction of what has come to be known as the Ethical Policy, after a group of Dutch academics and thinkers called the Ethici. They believed that the Dutch bore a certain responsibility towards people subjected to their colonial rule. It was also a period during which an increasing number of Dutch scholars went to Bali to study Balinese culture.

The Dutch reforms did go some way towards protecting the Balinese and their culture. Foreigners were excluded from owning land. The Dutch also opposed all efforts to open up tea or rubber plantations, and also sugar and tobacco estates, thereby protecting the Balinese from the exploitation that was taking place elsewhere in the region, especially in Java.

However, the Dutch reforms also took account of the scholarly writings that were being produced, writings that tended to focus on the knowledge of the *Brahmans*. As a result, they came to regard Bali as a museum of Hindu-Javanese culture, and the idea of Bali as a "living museum" came into being.

As such, there was little scholarly focus on the practical lives of most Balinese. The Dutch attitude was that if Balinese culture was to be saved (ultimately for the tourists who would play such an important part in modern Balinese history), then the Balinese were to be taught by their new colonial masters how to become more authentically Balinese.

Their crass misunderstanding of how Balinese society really worked also resulted in the

Dutch – again with the aid of the brahmans – "freezing" the caste system. This decision was to cause much strife amongst the Balinese themselves in decades to come.

With no real understanding of the caste system's inherent mobility and flexibility, the Dutch "fixed" the social positions and roles of

each Balinese individual. This rationalisation by the Dutch – not only of the caste system, but also of political units, labour, and rice farming – threw the traditional Balinese system into chaos. Moreover, the restructuring of society was greatly to the advantage of many of the upper-caste members, who became strong supporters of the Dutch.

Colonial creation of paradise

From the 1920s onwards, not only were increasing numbers of tourists visiting the island of Bali, but also a small but influential number of foreigners were choosing to live on the island, including artists, sociologists, econ-

PRECEDING PAGES: contemporary art depicting modern Balinese life. **LEFT:** detail from a contemporary Balinese painting. **RIGHT:** two rajas, c. 1930.

omists, dancers and musicians. Enticed by what they had seen and read about Bali, these individuals did much to contribute to the image elsewhere in the world of Bali as an island of paradise, both through their research and their writings aimed at the general reader.

What was more important, however, was that although they were keen to promote Bali, what they promoted was their interpretation of the "real" Bali. Their writing also implicitly supported colonialism. If the

BALINESE ROOTS

A Dutch scholar in Bali employed a young Javanese to copy manuscripts. This young man then married a Balinese *Brahman* woman and they had a son: Achmad Soekarno, Indonesia's first post-independence leader.

influenced the content of art are equally debatable. Rather, suggest some scholars, the Balinese simply adopted the introduced media and foreign styles into their own evolving aesthetic.

Those Balinese artists who were promoted and lauded in the early 20th century were generally those who fitted the aesthetic criteria of Europeans, like Bonnet, sometimes at the expense of those with greater talent. Adrian Vickers, a critic of the traditional colonial view of Bali's history, cites the Bali-

many writings on Bali that emerged during this period are to be believed, then without this European presence, the island would have amounted to little. These writings implied, for example, that the Balinese had little to do with the development and course of their own culture and history.

The question of how much influence foreigners had on Balinese art is a prime example. Artists like Walter Spies and Rudolf Bonnet are often credited with setting the tone for modern Balinese art. However, experimentation with new and different media and styles had been going on amongst Balinese artists since the 19th century, and claims that the Europeans

nese artist Pan Seken, who was "one of the best traditional artists of his generation", but did not feature in any of Bonnet's writings. Similarly, the artist Walter Spies is credited with developing the now famous *kecak* dance, when in fact the initiative came from the Balinese. Spies merely adapted it for a film.

Calamities near and far

While the resident Europeans continued to create an image of paradise, the Balinese lived with the reality. In 1917 a devastating earthquake struck the island, flattening villages and destroying some of the island's most important temples. More than 1,000 people were killed.

The earthquake was followed by a mouse plague that decimated the crops, followed by the worldwide Spanish-flu epidemic that claimed thousands of Balinese lives.

As if that was not enough, the Great Depression of the 1930s hit Bali, quartering the price of their major exports (pigs and copra) and halving the value of local currency. Members of the higher castes, especially the ruling houses, were able to buy up land from poor peasants forced to sell land because of hardship. Others changed to tenant farmers when they became indebted to the rajas, who took their land as collateral. If Bali was paradise for the rich and

deaths than all the earlier *puputan* combined.

Bali became an early target for the Japanese imperial army when in February 1942 it landed 500 troops on the beach at Sanur. They marched unopposed into Denpasar and assumed control of the island. The *kempetai*, or military secret police, lost no time in seizing Balinese who were seen as having associated or collaborating with the Dutch. As elsewhere in Asia, the Japanese occupation of Bali was brutal, harsh and unforgiving.

The Japanese proclaimed themselves fiercely anti-colonial (although their proposed replacement – themselves – was colonial and much

beautiful who sang the island's praises, it was less than perfect for the Balinese.

Throughout the first four decades of the 20th century, the alliance between the upper castes and the colonial government, together with the implementation of a rigid hierarchy, was increasingly challenged by educated commoners, who regarded education as being as important as old status titles. Tensions came to the foreground after the Japanese occupation during World War II, ultimately to lead to far more

LEFT: Walter Spies, a Dutch painter, and a *janger* performance, both during the 1930s. **ABOVE:** Dutch *controleur* arriving at his residence, 1930s.

more patronising), and part of this stance involved the ostensible promoting of Balinese culture. The Japanese also fostered feelings of nationalism among the Balinese, who hoped that Japanese promises would be backed up with arms for the struggle against the Dutch. When the Japanese surrendered in August 1945, Soekarno and Mohammad Hatta declared the independence of Indonesia from Dutch rule.

Between August and December of that year, when the Dutch returned to Bali hoping to reassert their position in the former colony, Bali was left with no real centre of power. An interim administration struggled to keep order and gain recognition, while the old kingdoms tried to reassert their importance. Some, like the raja of Klungkung, emerged as strongly pro-Dutch, while others were nationalists supporting an independent Indonesia. The Dutch imprisoned members of the anti-colonial administration, and the struggle for independence went underground. There ensued several years of bitter fighting, which left over 2,000 Balinese dead. This period also saw the emergence of various Balinese heroes.

A freedom fighter named I Gusti Ngurah Rai emerged as a charismatic hero and martyr during the Balinese fight for independence. His slogan was "freedom or death", a belief he put to the ultimate test. Ngurah Rai created the People's Security Force, which eventually merged with various other paramilitary movements. In the end, Ngurah Rai effectively commanded a Balinese people's army.

In 1946, Ngurah Rai assembled all available men in his army from western and southern Bali on the slopes of Gunung Agung, Bali's most sacred mountain, hoping to lure Dutch forces there. Dutch forces surrounded his encampment, but Ngurah Rai and his men escaped over the volcanic peak, crossing formidable mountain terrain to Tabanan, in southwestern Bali. There, in Marga, in November

AN EXPEDITION IN MUSICAL HISTORY

One of the finest historical collections of recordings of Balinese and other regional music now lies in the Library of Congress, Washington D.C. The music is valuable to researchers because it has not been influenced by Western culture, music, or tourism.

Two American brothers, Sheridan and Bruce Fahnestock, set off on their first scientific voyage to the Pacific in the 1930s to collect scientific samples for the American Museum of Natural History. In 1940 they set off on a second expedition, during which they recorded traditional music on Java and Bali by stringing cables from the recording equipment on their yacht to microphones on shore. (They also carried out intelligence and reconnaissance work for the US government, as war in the Pacific was imminent.) When their schooner sank off the Great Barrier Reef, they safely carried their recordings back to America.

Both brothers returned to the Pacific as soldiers after war with Japan broke out; Bruce was killed in New Guinea. Decades later, in 1986, his brother's widow found the long-forgotten recordings in the attic and donated them to the Library of Congress, which spent years restoring them. They are now available on compact discs.

1946, the Dutch again surrounded them. Rather than surrender, Ngurah Rai and his men engaged in a suicide attack – another *puputan* – upon the heavily armed Dutch. Ngurah Rai and 94 of his men were killed. The site of the Margarana Incident, as it came to be known, is now a national cemetery.

The Soekarno era

The years between 1946 and 1949, when the Dutch were finally forced to leave, epitomised Bali's colonial tragedy. The split between the pro-

was to change dramatically in the late 1950s.

Soekarno, then president of the Indonesian republic, always claimed empathy with the Balinese people because of his own Balinese background. However, he did little to enhance the spiritual and material welfare of his people, leaving on Bali little more than a collection of self-congratulatory monuments symbolising ill-chosen priorities. Rampant inflation and corruption under Soekarno did not help matters. Nevertheless, nationwide attempts at land reform went some way in

Dutch and nationalist factions was pronounced, with many nationalists – including leading artists – jailed, tortured and killed by other Balinese. These divisions were compounded by the split between feudal and modern forces, and tensions continued even after the Dutch departure. Members of the aristocratic castes moved increasingly into business, seeing this as a natural continuation of their traditional roles. Political affiliation was similarly divided between the nationalists and socialists, a situation that

LEFT: Soekarno, left, reads statement relinquishing power to Soeharto, right. **ABOVE:** Ida Bagus Nyoman Rai's impression of 1963 eruption of Gunung Agung.

loosening the grip that the raja landowners held over their tenants. When Soekarno banned the Socialist Party, many of its members became radicalised and joined the Communist Party instead. In Bali, Communist support was especially strong.

Bali has been described as being a place of tension and continual political rallies during the early 1960s. For many Balinese there were fears that the supernatural powers were being provoked, and that the gods would compel the Balinese to revert to the values of the past.

In 1963, the eruption of Gunung Agung during the Eka Dasa Rudra ceremony, staged only once a century, reinforced this fear. For four days the mountain threw out mud and rock, and then great rivers of molten lava poured down the mountainside. Smoke and ash blotted out the sun. Entire villages were destroyed. Thousands died in the eruption and the ensuing famine and disease.

Bloodbath in paradise

When an abortive coup (said to be Communist-inspired) took place in Jakarta in 1965, the floodgates were opened. A bloodbath followed. Whole villages were massacred, and up to 100,000 people – few were actually card-carrying Communists – were killed on Bali.

Old scores were settled between villagers, between castes, and between brothers.

Earlier in the 1960s, there had developed a great deal of support among the Balinese for the PKI, or Indonesian Communist Party. This popular support came about largely in response to the Communist push for land reform. Under the banner of "Peasants Unilateral Action", the Communist Party urged the Balinese to claim the majority of the farm land that was, at the time, owned by only a few hundred landowners. Support for the Communists came largely from some 18,000 Balinese people who were badly affected by the 1964 famine, which they believed would have been less severe had land

ownership been more equitably distributed.

There developed a marked split between supporters of the PNI (Nationalist Party of Indonesia) and the PKI, a split that was seen largely as a challenge to the old feudal and caste systems. Rallies were held throughout the island advocating the overthrow of the caste system. It was also a period during which art became tangled up with propaganda as the Communists encouraged traditional dance troupes to spread their proletariat message.

When news of the murder of six leading generals in Jakarta, supposedly at the hands of the Communists, reached Bali, the PNI and other anti-Communists took it upon themselves to destroy the PKI in Bali completely. The ensuing massacre ultimately had little to do with PNI and PKI politics and more to do with settling old scores. Whole villages of people were shot and the buildings razed. So bloody was the violence that ripped through Bali that General Sarwo Edhy, nicknamed the Butcher of Java, is reported to have said "in Java, we had to egg them on to kill Communists; in Bali we had to restrain them."

It is perhaps surprising to see how Bali has emerged from this tragedy, which few survivors are willing to talk about today.

An idyllic return

The history of Bali since the 1960s has been defined and propelled forward by tourism *(see opposite)*. Blessed with beautiful scenery and an appealing, vibrant culture, tourism has arguably been the making of Bali over the past decades. The Balinese have created a prosperous oasis that they intend to maintain, and their determination was apparent in the late 1990s.

After the deadly 1998 riots in Jakarta and elsewhere in Java that led to the ousting of Soeharto, busloads of angry Javanese were reported to be making for the island of Bali, which had emerged little affected by the political and street events elsewhere. Their intention was to burn and loot the properties – including several leading hotels – owned by the Soeharto family. Hundreds of Balinese, armed with *keris*, were waiting at the Gilimanuk ferry terminal and refused to let the Javanese disembark. ❑

LEFT: Soeharto and wife at Pura Besakih for 1979 Eka Dasa Rudra ceremony. **RIGHT:** tourism's gift to traditional Balinese culture.

Tourism's Legacy

From a trickle of a few hundred usually well-heeled tourists who began visiting Bali early in the 20th century, the island has now to contend with a flood of people each year. By the 1990s, over 1 million people were visiting Bali annually. The growth has been spectacular.

The Dutch Royal Packet Navigation Company (KMP), which built the Bali Hotel in Denpasar, had developed a basic tourism infrastructure in Bali before World War II. However, it was Soeharto's government, which came to power in 1967, that began to develop Bali's full tourist potential. In order to address a pressing national balance-of-payments deficit, Bali was identified as the best site to focus on tourism development in Indonesia. It was also seen as a means of creating jobs and wealth for the local community.

This decision was supported by the World Bank, which drew up a master plan for the development of tourism on the island. The World Bank proposed developing a huge luxury tourist resort at Nusa Dua, with a road network linking the site to the island's major tourist attractions. There were several advantages to this plan. Not only would it confine tourists to a single area, it also made use of an area largely unsuitable for agriculture.

Although the initial plan was that tourism would be confined to Nusa Dua and later to Sanur, the high-quality hotels tended to be owned by foreign and Jakarta-based companies; the overall benefits for the Balinese were initially questionable. However, local Balinese entrepreneurs did not hesitate to develop their own tourism centres – Kuta, Legian and Ubud – where local involvement and employment would be much greater. The Balinese took an active interest in the control of tourism, particularly as development threatened to get out of hand. Farmers began to sell off agricultural land to developers, and land prices soared. Seafront sites that previously had little commercial value were acquired for restaurants, and souvenir shops sprang up all along the streets of the developing resort areas. What became more alarming to many Balinese was that outside investors began moving in, particularly Javanese and Australians, putting additional burdens on existing infrastructure and frequently creating friction with local entrepreneurs. Today, in places such as Kuta or even Denpasar, one might easily conclude a loss of Balinese innocence.

Despite the negative effects of tourism, there are many who have pointed out the advantages of the industry in terms of the employment it creates.

There can be no doubt that tourism has helped to revitalise the island's craft and art industry and the many performing arts such as gamelan and dance-drama. Others would counter this claim by saying that what the Balinese are now producing is inferior tourist-quality souvenir art that has debased the true creativity of the Balinese artisan. This is not true. The Balinese produce crafts of a very high quality, but it depends on whether tourists are prepared to pay high prices. If you only want to spend a few rupiah, you can hardly expect

top quality. Moreover, although tourists may only see condensed versions of the dance-dramas and shadow plays (how many would wish to sit through a performance of several hours?) the same dances and plays are still performed in the villages.

Bangkal Kusuma, a Balinese anthropologist, notes a change in the nature of tourism: the emphasis that was formerly on the maintenance of traditional Balinese culture is now moving more towards a "McDonaldisation" of the culture, a result of the national government's decision on the course that tourism should take. However, with the advent of regional autonomy in 2001, the Bali government began to take control of the direction of tourism and of the future of the island. ❏

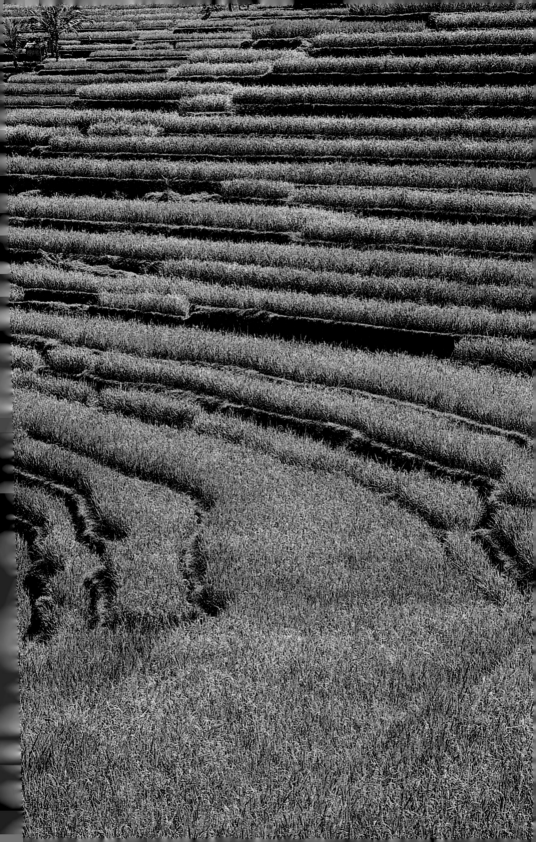

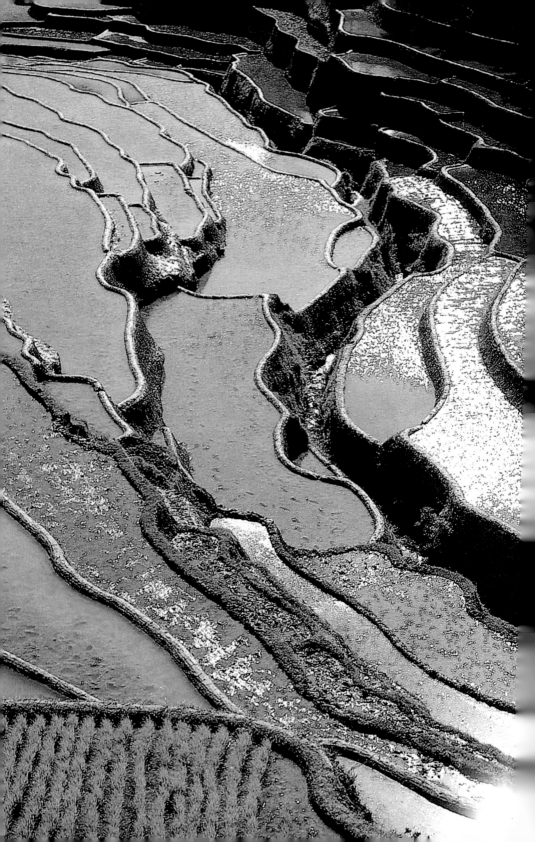

THE ISLAND'S GEOGRAPHY

Volcanoes punctuate this island of rain forests, rice paddies and monkeys.
Indeed, their presence is responsible for Bali's idyllic and fertile character

The island of Bali, one of the 17,508 islands that make up the archipelago of Indonesia, comprises just one-third of a percent of the country's total land area. Like a jewel in a necklace of islands, it lies at the westernmost end of Nusa Tenggara – the Lesser Sundas – part of a chain of volcanic islands that make up the nation's backbone.

Bali is 8 degrees south of the equator and is separated from Java to the west by the Straits of Bali, which are no more than 40 to 50 metres (160 ft) deep. During the last Ice Age, the sea level was much lower than it is today, and so Java and Bali were joined as a single land mass. To the east of Bali, the Strait of Lombok separates Bali from the island of Lombok and marks the point of a deep ocean trench that plunges steeply down to a depth of around 1,300 metres (4,200 ft).

Physical terrain

Lying at the core of the island itself are six volcanic peaks, all over 2,000 metres (6,500 ft) high. These mountains have been thrown up from the seabed over eons by volcanic activity. Bali lies at an unstable point on the earth's surface, over a major subduction zone where the southern Indo-Australian tectonic plate is forced under the more rigid northern Eurasian plate, often with explosive results.

The highest volcano on Bali is Gunung Agung, at 3,142 metres (10,308 ft) regarded as the abode of the gods by the Balinese. It is believed that it is the gods who cause the volcano's eruptions, so as to punish the Balinese for wrongdoing or for not showing due respect to the gods. But by the same token, the rich mineral soils – a result of those eruptions – nurturing the crops that feed the islanders are also believed to be the gift of the gods.

More than anything, Bali's active volcanoes have determined its landscape and the land's

use. The periodic eruptions of these smoking cauldrons, whilst wreaking havoc and destruction in their immediate aftermath, have also given rise to extremely fertile soils that enable Balinese farmers to harvest up to three crops a year. The high peaks catch the rain-laden clouds that drift in from the southern Indian Ocean and ensure a plentiful rainfall averaging 2,150 mm (85 inches) yearly. Most of Bali's 162 rivers and streams run from their source in the mountains southward to the Indian Ocean, cutting deep ravines through the soft volcanic rock.

Although vast areas of Bali have been altered by agriculture, it is still possible to see what the natural state of the island once was. Originally much of the island would have been covered by deciduous or monsoon forests, interspersed with savannahs and grasslands. Because monsoon forest is drier and much more open than tropical rain forest, it is more susceptible to fire, which usually leads to the spread of grass. It is likely that natural fires, coupled with human

---

PRECEDING PAGES: mist clinging to Gunung Batur, and terraced rice fields. **LEFT:** flooded rice terraces in central Bali. **RIGHT:** Bali is anchored by volcanoes.

action in historical times, led to the gradual disappearance of Bali's monsoon forests. Today, they may only be found in Taman Nasional Bali Barat, the national park in western Bali.

The extreme western part of Bali, Jembrana, is mainly forested, but because of its arid nature, few people live there. Many Balinese describe the region as only half civilised and not really Balinese. At the southern part of the island, Bukit Badung, a jagged plateau joined to Bali by a narrow isthmus, is geologically a dry and barren limestone area with sandy, infertile soils. The high limestone cliffs along its coastline stand in stark contrast to the beaches found

Animal life

Many kinds of wildlife live throughout the island. Lizards are found everywhere, including the insect-eating geckos. Snakes are also common. Of the large mammal species only the wild boar and deer remain; the Balinese tiger became extinct in the early 20th century.

In contrast, as tourists know only too well, monkeys may be found all over Bali, especially macaques. In the "monkey forest" at Sangeh, it is said that when Hanuman, the monkey general of the *Ramayana* tale, tried to crush the evil king Rawana with the peak of Mount Meru, some of his monkey army fell to

elsewhere on Bali, as does its scrub-like vegetation. Mangrove swamps line the coast.

A wide variety of plants may still be found on Bali. They range from many species of palm tree, bamboo, and beautiful flowering shrubs like frangipani, poinsettia, bougainvillaea and orchids. In nearly every Balinese village is a banyan tree with its hundreds of aerial roots. The pandanus, or screw pine, and even cacti grow in the dry Bukit Badung of southern Bali. Throughout the island, there are many exotic plants to look out for. Lofty tree ferns, elephant grass, and hundreds of wild flowers cling to rocks and cliffs. Tall pines and cypress trees soar above the ground.

WILD WESTERN RESERVE

The largest park on Bali is the Taman Nasional Bali Barat (West Bali National Park), where there are the remnants of montane forests, coastal swamps and beautiful, clear seas once found throughout Bali.

The park, established in 1984, provides visitors with a glimpse of a unique environment. It is home to the endangered Bali starling and to another rare species, the Javan buffalo, of which only a few remain on Bali. Also found in the park are several species of deer, including rusa deer, mouse deer and barking deer, and carnivores such as the leopard and civet cat, and several species of monkey.

earth on Sangeh when he threw the mountain.

Of the domesticated animals, the sway-back pig and Bali cattle are important, along with chickens and ducks. One animal that will be found wandering all over the island is the dog. Many of these, often mangy-looking and hungry-looking animals, are piebalds. Some people suggest that they represent the mongrel descendants of several dalmatians that were owned by the Danish merchant Mads Lange, who traded in Bali in the 19th century.

TREE RETREAT

One of Bali's earlier reserves is Kebun Raya Eka Karya Bali, a botanical garden near Lake Bratan and home to over 650 species of tree and over 450 species of wild and propagated orchids.

maximum temperature of 32°C (90°F) in March and an average maximum temperature of 29°C (84°F) in July. As one climbs higher up into the mountains, the temperature of course becomes cooler and less humid.

Finding water

Although there is more than enough water to grow crops, the Balinese have to divert it from the rivers to the rice fields. Because the steep and narrow valleys preclude damming, over the centuries Balinese farmers

Climate

Although hot and humid, Bali's climate is tempered by cool ocean breezes, and most visitors will find it a pleasant one.

It is the northwest monsoon that causes the greatest humidity levels – sometimes as high as 95 percent – in the rainy season, which lasts from November until April. The dry season, which falls between May and October, is generally much more pleasant and coincides with the peak tourist period. The average temperature at sea level is 26°C (79°F), with an average

LEFT: coast of Nusa Penida. **ABOVE:** scarecrow to shoo away the birds that feed on rice.

have devised an elaborate engineering system of channels and tunnels cut into the rock and have constructed bamboo aqueducts and pipes to carry the water. This is a centuries-old system, and an inscription dates one tunnel as being constructed in AD 944. Some of these tunnels are up to a kilometre long, and for the professional tunnellers who make and maintain them, an important skill is to ensure that they emerge where they should.

Because much of the terrain is steep, a system of terraces that utilises the land to its maximum efficiency has been built up, producing the classic Balinese landscape so beloved by artists. The water is taken to the highest terraces, and from there uses gravity to flow through the *sawah*, or paddy fields. Much of Bali's soil has a very fine texture, and water would normally drain quickly into the subsoil. But the farmers who may be seen all over the island trudging behind their ploughs, pulled along by a patient buffalo, are actually making the soil impermeable by their repeated ploughing, so that the soil holds the water until it is released through a sluice or cutting into the next sawah down the slope.

The irrigation system that is so important to every farmer, whether at the top of the mountain or in the valley, cannot operate success-

harvesting, and on a daily basis each farmer knows when he will receive water and when he must release it to the next *sawah*. Smaller water temples are found further down the system, along with water shrines where offerings are regularly made.

Strangely, for an island people, the Balinese have always avoided the surrounding ocean and its bounty, regarding it as a place – an underworld – of demonic forces. Treacherous currents have also persuaded the Balinese to concentrate instead on using the resources available on the land. Those who can avoid encountering the sea will do so.

fully unless water is shared. All farmers belong to a *subak* or irrigation society that unites the farmers who take water from a common source. The head of each *subak* makes sure that members maintain the system by mending dykes and dams, and in keeping channels free.

Heading the island's irrigation system are two lake temples dedicated to the goddess of the water, Dewi Danau. To the Balinese, water is a gift from the gods who must be properly acknowledged for their gift through offerings and prayer. Pura Batu Kau coordinates the irrigation system in western Bali, while Pura Ulun Danu oversees the north, east and south. The temple priests set the schedule of planting and

Over the centuries, the tendency has emerged for many poorer Balinese – those who cannot afford to buy or lease irrigated land – to make their living from the sea. Although fishing is practiced, a large part of the catch is destined for the restaurants and hotels catering to Bali's tourism industry rather than as a primary food source for the island's people. Another resource that has been utilised in recent years is seaweed farming. Its main use has been in the making of sweets, for seaweed contains substances that thicken or jellify liquids. Shrimp cultivation is also important, although most of it is exported to Japan, with less than one percent sold to the local tourism sector.

Rice and agriculture

Although rice is the island's most important crop, farmers usually rotate rice with cash crops such as peanuts, chilli peppers, onions and soya beans, among other vegetables. Non-rice food crops are called *palawija*, and they make use of the *sawah* in the dry season when there is less water available for wet rice. Still, rice is the pivot around which much of Balinese life revolves – the rice cycle determines the daily rhythm of village life and many facets of social organisation.

the watchful eye of their "shepherd", who keeps the feathered charges under control with a long stick that is used to gently nudge them back into line when they begin to stray.

Three basic varieties of rice are grown in Bali. The main ones are the white varieties *(baas)*, but Balinese also grow red *(barak)* and black *(injin)* varieties. During the 1970s, Indonesia underwent a "green revolution", which introduced a new high-yield variety of rice. Although the intention was to make Indonesia more self-

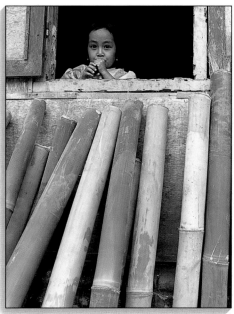

The wet-rice system, moreover, is a complete ecosystem in itself. By flooding the fields, the inflow of silt brings nutrients to the soil. The *sawah* not only supports the growing rice, but also algae, tiny fish, and insects, all part of an important food chain. One of the most endearing sights in Bali is the waddling march of flocks of ducks each day, in the company of a small boy or old man, making their way to the sawah. There, they feed all day on the insect and plant life that thrives in the fields, under

sufficient in the production of rice, this miracle rice was found to have several drawbacks. For example, this type of rice rapidly depleted the soil, so that large quantities of chemical fertilisers had to be used. Moreover, the use of limited varieties of rice narrowed the genetic base, which ultimately led to crops becoming more vulnerable to pest attack.

In 1974, the brown planthopper *(wereng)*, which damages rice plants by sucking the sap, devastated rice crops throughout Bali and Java. Chemical pesticides were used to kill the *wereng*, but the pesticides also destroyed the insects that were such an important component of the wet-rice ecosystem. Given the extra expense that

LEFT: flooded rice terraces use water allocated by irrigation societies. **ABOVE:** coffee bean before harvesting, north Bali, and the ubiquitous bamboo.

farmers had to bear in buying fertilisers and pesticides, coupled with the loss of important creatures in the rice ecosystem, it is hardly surprising that Balinese farmers are returning to the traditional rice varieties. Not only are these more friendly to the island's ecology, but the Balinese also claim the traditional rices taste much better.

The beautiful scenery of the rice fields is only part of the tale. The glistening lakes of silver water ready to be planted with seedlings; the fresh green shoots lifting their heads above the surface of the water; the golden yellow stalks bent gracefully by the weight of the grain; and then the bare, muddy ground waiting to be planted again are the result of careful agricultural and social planning.

In fact, however, the rice cycle relies as much on religious management as it does on nature and secular concerns. The growing rice is regarded as the personification of the goddess Dewi Sri, and throughout the growing cycle appropriate offerings must be made. When the grain appears on the stalks, the rice is described as being pregnant. When the grain is finally ready for harvesting, the women gather to cut the grain. They enter the drained fields carrying little finger knives called *ani-ani*, which lie concealed in the palms of their hands so that they do not frighten the souls of the rice goddess. Interestingly and tellingly, this traditional method of harvesting is today used only for Balinese varieties of rice, not introduced ones.

Other crops

Bali also produces a variety of other crops, many of which are exported to other parts of Indonesia and abroad. Many of the farmers have found a lucrative outlet for their crops through the numerous hotels and restaurants catering to the tourist industry.

In the temperate upland areas, where there is plentiful rainfall, around Bedegul for example, market gardens now produce an astonishing array of fruit and vegetables, including strawberries. Flower nurseries have also developed, and each morning *bemo*-loads of fresh cut roses, gardenias, lilies and other garden flowers are taken down to the plains.

To the north, the mountain range drops sharply down to a narrow coastal strip with black volcanic sands. This is one of Bali's driest regions, and there is less water available here, since many of the rivers flow only during the wet season. Thus, in the few northern areas where wet-rice can be grown, only one crop a year is possible, unlike the three common to the southern areas. More important in the north is the dry-land agriculture that produces vegetables, cocoa, peanuts, bananas, pineapples, papayas, mangos, and spices, including cloves, cinnamon and vanilla. Balinese coffee has become known the world over and is an important export crop for the island. ❑

LEFT: central Balinese village on the slopes of Gunung Agung. **RIGHT:** trees found within temple compounds are often revered, such as this one.

THE BALINESE

*Community and participation in honoured rituals that celebrate
the cycles of life give the Balinese an uncommon sense of roots and purpose*

Every Balinese individual is born into a community, and she or he remains part of the community from cradle to grave. The strong ties of the community – whether village, neighbourhood, irrigation society, temple or family – are a good measure of the Balinese world of caring and sharing.

The majority of Balinese still live in a village *(desa)*, which is typically centred upon three main temples *(pura)*: the origin temple *(pura puseh)*, the village temple *(pura desa* or *pura bale agung)*, and the death temple *(pura dalem)*. These temples form the core of every village community, and all villagers worship at the village's temples.

The village is run by an elected individual called a *klian*, who heads the village council. This is comprised of all the married men in the village who own land. The klian is responsible for the smooth running of village affairs. Today there is also an appointed individual, the *klian dinas*, responsible to the government.

The focus of a village

However, it is not the village that is the main foundation of daily life, but the *banjar*, the ward or hamlet into which every village is divided. Even in the larger urban centres, the *banjar* is the most important community unit. Banjar are essentially cooperative groups of neighbours who assist each other at festivals, family gatherings and in crisis. Membership in the *banjar* is compulsory for every married man. Like the village as a whole, every banjar has an elected leader, the *klian banjar*.

The people within a *banjar* usually own property in common, such as a meeting hall *(bale banjar)*, which contains all the cooking equipment for preparing community feasts, as well as the musical instruments of the *banjar*'s *gamelan* orchestra. Members of the *banjar* who belong to the music and dance clubs will have

---

PRECEDING PAGES: young schoolboys taking the easy way home after school. **LEFT:** young Balinese woman. **RIGHT:** harvesting the dry rice.

access to these and practise in the *bale banjar*. The *banjar* is, in turn, made up of the individual family compounds. These walled-off units enclose the sleeping quarters, family temple, kitchen, granary, pigsty and various pavilions that belong to the individual family.

In addition, any villager who owns rice fields

will belong to an irrigation society *(subak)* that controls water and ensures that all receive what they need. Membership in a *subak* is not tied to a village or *banjar* but rather to the location of one's rice fields and the source of water. Members of a *subak* draw water from the same source, and members may come from different *banjar* and different villages. An individual may also belong to more than one *subak*.

For all Balinese, membership in these units defines who he or she is. The worst punishment that can befall someone is to be banished from these organisations. To lose one's membership means that no help will be extended, property may be confiscated, and exile from the village may ensue. They may be declared morally dead, and upon actual death may be denied burial and eventual cremation.

This is the community structure into which every Balinese is born. Throughout her or his life, a Balinese will always have the sense of belonging, and it is rare indeed for an individual to feel lonely or isolated. There is always someone nearby who cares and who will help out. Even after death the individual is not separated from the community. The community will ensure that the soul is able to complete its journey to the next world. There it will stay for a while before being reborn on earth and back into the community.

From child to adult

From cradle to grave, the lives of the Balinese are punctuated with various rites of passage that mark the leaving behind of a former stage in the life cycle and the signalling of the individual's willingness to enter the next. Symbolic acts of shedding the old life – such as cutting hair or filing teeth – are typical elements of these rites of passage, which are often followed by carrying the individual undergoing the rite over a threshold of some sort or carrying them through the village in procession.

The Balinese adore children, and every new baby is welcomed into the family as a privileged individual. Children are considered to

have entered this world from a spiritual realm, so that the younger the infant, the closer its soul is to heaven. For this reason, a baby will not be allowed to touch the impure earth for the first three months, and is carried everywhere by its mother and as often as not by an older sibling. It is not unusual to see a tiny baby being carried on the hip of a young four-year-old sister.

At three months, a ceremony called *nelabulanin* is when the baby's feet will be placed on the ground for the first time. Even after this, the child will still be carried, and crawling is discouraged, as it is too much like the behaviour of animals. During this ceremony, white

---

A CASTE OF NAMES

Every Balinese – with the exception of the Bali Aga – is born into one of four main castes, a system traced back to India and introduced by the Hindu courts of the Majapahit empire, whose influence arrived in Bali during the 15th century.

The highest caste is that of the *brahman* or priests, who use the title Ida Bagus (male) or Ida Ayu (female). The *satria* are the higher nobility who were the former rulers of the island, and they are distinguished by titles such as Anak Agung, Dewa and Cokorde. The *wesya* are members of the former lower nobility and use the title of Gusti. These three castes comprise only three per cent of the Balinese. All other Balinese belong to the *sudra* caste, also known as *jaba*, or "outside the court". Most *sudra* are descendants of the pre-Majapahit Balinese. Some *sudras* seek to have castes abolished, arguing that it is not indigenous to the Balinese. *(See related box on page 70.)*

---

threads are placed on the baby's head to tie its soul to its body. This symbolises that the child has moved away from the more spiritual realm and has entered a new stage of life in the human community. It is only after the first tooth has fallen out, however, that the child is regarded as a real human being.

As the child grows up and begins to walk, she or he is free to wander about the village with other children. Balinese children are self-reliant at an early age, although there are nearly always adults around to keep an eye on them. No Balinese child is ever physically beaten, as that would damage the soul. Children learn through guidance and example, and it is this raising of children with independence and respect that accounts for a maturity and responsibility compared to Western children. It is rare to see Balinese children fighting or crying.

Puberty is marked for a girl by her first menstruation and for a boy by the deepening of the voice. A *Brahman*-caste girl must go into seclusion at this stage. She emerges after three days dressed in rich brocades to be purified by the priest. It is at this stage of life that adolescent girls and boys go through a tooth-filing ceremony. Uneven teeth, particularly the pointed canines, are considered to be too much like those of demons and witches. Filing them is

Every Balinese wishes to be married, and it is considered abnormal if a man or woman remains single. It is only on marriage that an individual becomes a full member of the village community. A man becomes a member of the village association and of the *banjar*. A woman usually moves to the compound of her husband, which may be in another village, and she will become incorporated into that community. Unmarried Balinese boys and girls mix freely with each other and frequently fall in and out of love. Amulets and various spells may be employed to make the person of one's choice take appropriate interest.

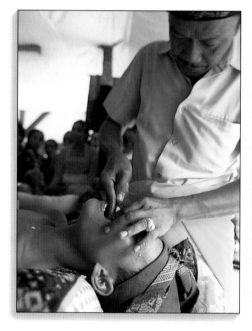

believed to diminish the six evil qualities of human nature: passion, greed, anger, intoxication, stupidity and jealousy. So they are ritually filed as a passage towards adulthood.

Because of the expense of holding a tooth-filing ceremony, it is not uncommon to defer it to just before marriage. Nor is it unknown for a corpse to have its teeth filed before the cremation, as it is feared that the soul will be denied access to the spirit world if it looks too much like a demon.

LEFT: children assume responsibilities early.
ABOVE: tooth-filing marks the transition to adulthood, and portrait of a Balinese man.

Marriage customs vary throughout Bali and from caste to caste. The two most common forms of marriage are by request *(mapedik)*, in which the parents of the boy officially approach the parents of the girl with offerings and gifts, and by *ngorod,* or elopement.

This latter form is considered more economical and far more entertaining by the Balinese, who enjoy the theatrical aspect immensely. The groom, who kidnaps the girl of his choice and flees with her to a friend's house to enjoy a pre-wedding honeymoon, is considered a far more heroic figure than the man who has his parents act as negotiators and proxy. In reality, however, *ngorod* is a carefully planned affair. It is fashionable nowadays to kidnap the girl by car, and she will be ready and waiting at the appointed time and place with bag already packed. Her father may display outrage when he finds her gone – even though he have known of the plan – but it is all part of the fun.

Meanwhile, the couple will go through a ceremony that makes the marriage official under customary law. A formal ceremony will be held later when a priest will bless the union, and offerings and prayers will be made to ancestors and deities of the house temple. She formally enters the man's family and becomes a member of his caste, family and clan.

The aim of marriage is ultimately to have children, and the wedding ceremony is full of symbolism suggesting this. The groom may stab a plastic bag filled with blood using a *keris*, or stir a pot with a stick, both objects being held by the bride. The sexual symbolism is obvious.

An ending to life

The human soul only borrows the physical body temporarily. Upon death, this body must be returned to the five elements, or *pancama-habhuta* – earth, wind, fire, water and ether – so that the soul may be released. Freed from all worldly attractions, the soul can then reunite

THE CONFUSION OF COMMON NAMES

Balinese names and language can be extremely confusing for outsiders, Indonesians and foreigners alike. Visitors often comment that there appear to be a lot of people with the same name.

If you ask to speak to Made or Ketut, you will invariably be asked which Made or Ketut. When it comes to personal names, many Balinese do indeed seem to share the same name. This is because among the ordinary Balinese there is a tendency to name the child according to the birth order. Hence, the oldest child may be called Wayan, the second Made, the third Nyoman, and the fourth Ketut. A similar system prevails for members of the higher caste. Here, the

eldest child is typically called Raha, Putu or Kompiang, while the second may be called Raj, the third Aka, and the fourth Alit. *(See box on page 68.)*

To compound the visitor's confusion, there are several levels to the Balinese language. The level spoken depends upon the caste, status, or social relationship between the speaker and the other. One has to choose between high, middle, or low Balinese. High Balinese is used when speaking to a superior, while the superior will use low Balinese in replying. Friends and equals will also use low Balinese. Middle Balinese is regarded as a polite form of speech and is used to address strangers.

with the Supreme Being. Hence, for the Balinese, death is regarded as a passage from this life to the next. When someone dies, that person's friends and family gather together to share feelings and memories, and to give comfort.

Ideally, the corpse should be cremated upon death. However, a cremation is the costliest of all life-cycle ceremonies, and the expense may mean that a family will have to wait several years. A group of families may then hold a joint cremation to spread the cost. In the meantime, the body is puri-

ROYAL COST OF DEATH

The cremation of the wife, mother and stepmothers of Gianyar Rajah Dr Ida Anak Agung Gede Agung in 1992 was reputed to have cost at least US$1 million.

has been buried, it cannot be returned house, but the deceased's soul must be called back from the graveyard. An effigy called a *sangah urip*, which contains some soil from the grave, is placed in a little pavilion and a lamp is hung outside to guide the soul home. The corpse should be washed before cremation, but this is done symbolically using a board with a drawing of a human figure on it if there is no corpse. Guests come and go and are lavishly entertained as though at a party.

Cremation should not begin

fied and buried in the village cemetery. A priest cannot be buried and will be cremated as soon as possible on an auspicious day.

Once a date for a cremation is set, the village comes alive with activity during the days beforehand, as everyone in the banjar, and even the village, helps with the preparations. It is at these times that the spirit of the community and of sharing is most apparent. An army of knowledgeable individuals and ritual specialists, together with priests, friends and neighbours, all mobilise in a flurry of activity. If the body

until after the sun has reached its zenith. When this time approaches, there is a sudden burst of activity as people begin the journey to the burning ground. The gamelan begins playing, and village men rush in and seize the effigy or the corpse. Participation demonstrates loyalty to the deceased. Outside is a high tower, a *wadah* or *bade*, made from wood or bamboo and sparkling with gold paper, mirrors and other ornaments.

This tower is a representation of the cosmos, and at its base is often a figure of the turtle entwined by two snakes, symbolising the foundation of the world. Above this is an open platform representing the space between heaven and earth and where the corpse or effigy is

LEFT: a Balinese wedding is a village affair. **ABOVE:** carrying the sarcophagi to the cremation ceremony.

placed. A body that has previously been buried – and thus had contact with impure earth – may not be placed in such an elevated place. There may be other figures depicted on the tower, such as Bhoma, the guardian of the upperworld, or a goose symbolising purity, for example.

The platform is covered by a series of tiered roofs representing the heavens. The number of tiers (always an odd number) is determined by the clan and caste of the deceased. A member of the *brahman* caste may have eleven roofs, a member of the nobility (*satria* or *wesya*) seven or nine, and *sudra* one, three or five. A priest, however, will have no roofs.

BALI AGA

On the slopes of the major volcanoes are villages of the Bali Aga or Bali Kuna, people who have retained old Balinese traditions from pre-Majapahit times, before Javanese and Hindu influences took root.

The Bali Aga exist outside of the caste system and retain their own autonomous structure. Their religion is ancestor focused, and therefore it excludes the Hindu Balinese. It is centred instead on the primacy of village origin and an internal social hierarchy. The Bali Aga conduct rituals that are exclusive to the community, and these, more than anything else, give the Bali Aga their autonomy from the rest of Balinese society.

A procession of women carrying the offerings will lead the way. Then the funeral tower is hoisted up on the shoulders of the eager men and a stampede to the cremation ground ensues. This is no solemn dignified procession. As many as 100 men may carry the tower, which sways and threatens to fall at any moment. They spin it round at crossroads so as to confuse the soul, important so that it cannot find its way back and return to disturb the living. A long, white cloth is attached to the front of the tower, representing the ties of the living to the dead. Members of the deceased's family hold this as they participate on the final journey.

The final rites

At the cremation ground, as the body or effigy is removed from the tower, a pair of birds is set free, symbolising the soul's release. The body will then be placed in a sarcophagus, which takes the form of an animal; the caste of the dead person determines which animal may be represented. A *brahman* may have a bull, whereas the other castes may have a lion or deer, for example.

Once the body (or effigy) is in the coffin, the shroud is opened and holy water is poured on the remains and the water pots smashed. Letters of introduction to the gods may be placed inside, along with money to pay Yama, god of the underworld. The coffin is then closed and the whole structure set ablaze.

No weeping or grief should be displayed during the journey from the house to the cremation. To do so would disturb the soul such that it will be unwilling to leave. Once the cremation fire has died down, the family will gather up the charred bone fragments and then pulverise them before placing them in a container. This will then be taken to the sea, or to a river, and cast into the waters. A ceremony to cleanse the pollution brought by death on the living is held three days later.

Twelve days after the cremation, a final ceremony will be held to release the soul from any thoughts or feeling still clinging to it. In practice this ceremony may be held years later. Once it is complete, the soul may be enshrined in the family temple. ❑

LEFT: bringing an offering to a cremation.
RIGHT: the sarcophagus is elaborate and richly endowed; a bull is usually used for a *Brahman*.

RELIGION

The combination of the introduced Hindu traditions from Java and Bali's own

animist beliefs has endowed the island with a spiritual richness and depth

Bali is the only island in Indonesia – the world's largest Islamic country – where Hinduism is the predominant religion. It was gradually introduced to the island from Java between the 8th and 15th centuries, incorporating many of the older beliefs and practices of the Balinese. The religion that is practiced by the Balinese is today officially called Agama Hindu Dharma but is also known by other names, especially Agama Tirta ("religion of the holy water"), as holy water plays a crucial role in many of the rituals. The Balinese have become increasingly conscious of the unique situation of their religion in modern Indonesia and so have become highly organised.

Introduction of Hinduism

Since early times the Balinese have regarded the universe as a structured entity in which everything, including gods, people and demons, each have their allotted place. The introduced Hindu idea of the universe as an ordered place fitted easily into this scheme. The positive, life-giving and life-sustaining deities *(dewa* and *batara)* live on the tops of mountains, while the demons and evil beings *(bhuta* and *kala)* who are dangerous to humanity dwell under the sea. The Balinese are one of the few island cultures that regard the sea with a sense of dread.

This scheme reflects the duality of all nature: high and low, right and left, day and night, clean and unclean, good and evil, life and death. Humans are caught between these opposing forces. In the Balinese context, order and harmony are personified by the gods and disorder by the demons. The deities residing on upper slopes of the mountains, and who include the deified ancestors, are the beings who bestow life on human beings. Demons dwelling in the sea seek humanity's destruction. Hinduism seeks a balance between opposing forces.

Offerings must be regularly made, acknowl-

edging the bounty of the gods. If this respect is not shown, they may punish humanity with volcanic eruptions, earthquakes and epidemics that will destroy those things that people have been given by the gods, so as to remind the Balinese of their duty. Offerings must also be made to demons and witches to keep them at

bay. But whereas those offerings given to the deities are beautiful creations that the Balinese may partake of after the gods have taken the essence, offerings for the demons are simple affairs that are cast on the ground where they may be scavenged by dogs.

The higher gods of Bali are all of Javanese-Hindu origin. The lower local deities, or *batara*, are said to be the descendants of the seven sons and daughters of Sanghyang Pacupati, who is the pre-Hindu high-god of Java.

Hinduism became much stronger in Bali in the 15th century when large numbers of *Brahman* priests fled from Java to escape the encroachment of Islam. It was they who intro-

---

PRECEDING PAGES: participants in a village's trance ceremony. **LEFT:** temple devotees. **RIGHT:** offerings *(banten)* on Nusa Penida.

duced the caste system to Balinese life, placing themselves at the top of the hierarchy.

The Balinese priest is a highly respected figure. There are two levels of priest. The *pedanda*
is a *Brahman* high priest. One of his chief
duties is to make and dispense the holy water.
The *pedanda* carry knowledge of Hindu theology, and through their ritual knowledge can
achieve unity with god, and thereby can absorb
divine power into the self to purify the water
that is needed for all rituals. The *pemangku* is a
temple priest and is usually a member of the
sudra caste. They are the priests who tend to
take a more active part in the temple cere-

One god from many

The Hindu believes first and foremost in the
existence of a god and its various manifestations. For the Balinese, there are many gods,
but ultimately only a pantheistic one, an idea
that many outsiders may find difficult to grasp.

Shivaism became the main focus of Balinese
worship; as the destroyer and reincarnator,
Shiva (Siwa in Bahasa Indonesia) had the most
direct relevance to the Balinese. He is often
manifested in the form of Surya, the sun god
whose throne may be found in the corner of
almost every Balinese temple. However, the
other two gods of the Hindu trinity, Brahma

monies, receiving the holy water, and generally supervising the proceedings.

One of the ways that Hinduism was introduced to the Balinese by the *Brahmans* was
through the shadow play, or *wayang kulit*, and
other theatrical performances such as the
masked dance; indeed, these fundamental arts
are common on Java. Knowledge of the Hindu
epics – *Ramayana* and *Mahabharata* – together
with their commentaries forms a very important element in Hindu teaching. The *Brahmans*
also introduced the basic doctrines of Hinduism, the Pancacradha or Five Beliefs, which
ultimately govern the everyday behaviour and
conduct of the individual.

and Vishnu (Wisnu), are also worshiped. In
many Balinese state temples there is a three-
seated shrine for these gods. When a ceremony
is to take place, this shrine will be decked out
with coloured banners: red for Brahma, white
for Siwa, and black for Wisnu.

In addition, the Balinese worship a host of
other beings – deities of fertility, and the
elements of the natural world, as well as the
deified ancestors. However, cutting across this
is the ultimate belief in a transcendental spiritual unity known as Sanghyang Widi Wasa.
Essentially the Balinese see the different deities
– male and female – as different aspects of a
singular supreme god. This god in the mani-

festation of rice is Dewi Sri, goddess of fertility, while the same god in the manifestation of the ocean is Dewa Baruna. Whenever the Balinese venerate one of these gods or an ancestor, they are indirectly honouring Sanghyang Widi Wasa.

A *Brahman* priest on Bali explains the concept of a singular supreme god and its manifestations like this: "As we are one person but use our eyes to see, our hands to work and our feet to walk, so Sanghyang Widi Wasa is one god. Yet in his power as creator he is Brahma, in his power as preserver he is Wisnu, and in his power to destroy he is Siwa."

The other aspects of the Pancacradha that are central to Balinese Hinduism include the belief in the permanent soul *(atman)* and the idea that every action will have its effect on the person *(karma phala)*. The belief in reincarnation *(samsara)* and the ultimate belief that the individual can achieve pure happiness through enlightenment *(moksa)* are also of central importance. And the understanding that the soul is permanent determines the way that the dead are treated. The soul will return and therefore it is the duty of the living to the dead to ensure that the soul of the deceased is able to pass to the next stage of existence before returning. In fact, the soul may be reborn many times, but ultimately it seeks to reach the blissful state where it is freed of all desire, so that it may become one with the prime mover of the universe.

Once it is recognised that every individual is an integral part of, and has his or her allot-ted place within, the universe, it becomes one's duty *(dharma)* to behave so that harmony will be maintained. It is *dharma*, therefore, that controls the way people conduct their lives. If behaviour is inappropriate it may lead to chaos, which can manifest itself in the form of desire, for example. A person's behaviour will determine his ultimate fate *(karma)*, being rewarded or punished both in this life and the next.

> ### HOLY WATER OF BALI
>
> Balinese religion is called Agama Tirtha, or the Religion of Holy Water, because holy water is a crucial element in the performance of religious rituals.

LEFT: a *pedanda,* or high priest, in meditation, and a female *pemangku.* **ABOVE:** symbolic image of Sanghyang Widi Wasa, and temple image.

Performance of rituals

A large part of correct behaviour is directed towards the correct performance of rituals *(yadnya)*. The Balinese divide their rituals up into five categories, each one being directed towards a different group. The *dewa yadnya* are performed for the deities, the *bhuta yadnya* for demonic forces, *pitra yadnya* for the dead or the ancestors, and *manusia yadnya* for the living. There is also a category of rituals directed at the priesthood, to consecrate them.

None of these rituals, however, is directed solely at one group. At a ceremony for the living – a wedding, for example – offerings will invariably also be made to the deities and ancestors to elicit their blessings. All rituals must be witnessed by the gods to make them spiritually legitimate. At a ritual directed towards the deities, offerings must be made to

the *bhuta* to keep them from disturbing the proceedings. Indeed, at any ritual, all forms of deities, good or evil, ancestor or not, are always deemed to be present.

The dark side

The Balinese believe that deities will protect and watch over them if they behave correctly and make the appropriate offerings at rituals. They also believe that if they treat the *bhuta* and *kala* appropriately, these evil spirits will not break through the invisible boundary that divides the world of demons from the world of men and women. However, there is another,

NAWA SANGA: THE DEITY IN ITS MANY FORMS

In Balinese thought, a supreme god, Sanghyang Widi Wasa, has various aspects, each with a different name. They are represented by nine gods (including the Hindu Trimurti) referred to as the *nawa sanga* and which inhabit the eight cardinal directions and the centre. The nine gods represent the fusion of different Balinese deities with Indian gods, a merging that came about through the long process of Hinduisation. Each of the nine gods has his own main public image and an associated colour and direction, as well as other characteristics.

The main temples on Bali associated with the nine Balinese gods of the nawa sanga are:

- Pura Lempung Luhur: Dewa Iswara
- Pura Goa Lawah: Dewa Maheswara
- Pura Andakasa: Dewa Brahma
- Pura Uluwatu: Dewa Rudra
- Pura Butukaru: Dewa Mahadewa
- Pura Pucak Mangu: Dewa Sangkara
- Pura Batur: Dewa Wisnu
- Pura Besakih: Dewa Sambu
- Pura Pusering Jagat: Dewa Paramasiva

In the above listing, *pura* means temple, while *dewa* refers to a deity.

more terrifying aspect of evil that is much harder to control and which is found in the midst of the human world.

Most Balinese will be able to tell stories of strange creatures they have encountered on the roads at night: monkeys with golden teeth, bald-headed giants, or perhaps just a strange ball of light hovering in the night sky. These manifestations are *leyak*, living humans who can change their spirits into another form, such as into a strange animal or a headless body. The human form

The Balinese accept that there are individuals who seek to study the black arts for evil purposes. Moreover, both constructive and destructive forces are necessarily present in the world. What is of paramount importance is that neither gets the upper hand. An individual who chooses to gain control over evil supernatural forces and uses them to harm others must study hard. The individual may expose him or herself to danger in the process. The powers that they will need to obtain are written in palm-leaf manu-

IN THE FAMILY

The victims of most *leyak* are more than likely to be members of their own family, and motives are seen as being revenge for simple affronts, jealousy, or greed.

of the *leyak* will remain asleep in bed, so it is difficult to know who the *leyak* are. The *leyak* should not be confused with either *bhuta* or *kala*, of course. These are also negative beings, but most Balinese will say that these are more bothersome – making children quarrel, or stealing a treasured possession – whereas the *leyak* are humans who use black magic to harm other humans. It is rare that a Balinese will speak openly about *leyak* and black magic for fear that such a practitioner – maybe a relative – will overhear and harm the speaker.

scripts, or *lontar*, where all sacred knowledge is preserved. To gain the knowledge needed to become a *leyak* takes many years of dedicated study in secret and considerable self-sacrifice.

White magic

There are various ways that the Balinese may protect themselves from *leyak*. Babies are most susceptible before their three-month ceremony, and all kinds of amulets and talismans may be utilised to protect the individual. The amulets may be obtained from a religious specialist called a *balian*.

It is likely that when a Balinese falls ill, the cause of the illness will be ascribed to either

LEFT: going to *odalan*, and a dressed temple image.
ABOVE: Rangda trance dancers outside a temple.

the black magic of a *leyak* or to the violation of a religious law or custom. In turn, they are likely to visit the traditional healer, or *balian*. A *balian* may well use traditional herbal remedies, but they are just as likely to use more esoteric knowledge to help people. Indeed, the *balian* may be called upon to help locate a lost object or to determine auspicious days.

The *balian* is, in many ways, the opposite of the *leyak*. Like the *leyak*, they have the ability to penetrate the spirit world, but they will use their ability or gift to help other people. The *balian*'s powers involve the use of mystical forces, and he or she is just as capable of using these pow-

ers to harm people should they choose. They usually have a spirit helper with whom they can communicate and who guides the *balian* in dealings with other humans. The relationship between a *balian* and the spirit world is, like that of the *leyak*, potentially dangerous, and it is one that has to be treated with great care and respect.

There are various ways that one may become a *balian*. Many are individuals who once suffered a serious illness and went to another *balian* for help. It is widely believed that certain kinds of sickness are caused by spirits and that the only cure is to learn to communicate with a particular spirit, who will not only neutralise the illness but will then work with that person on future occasions to help others. In return, the *balian* directs prayers and offerings to this helper spirit.

Magical energy

Different kinds of *balian* are known for different skills, some of which fall more into the sphere of traditional, rather than spiritual, medicine. A *balian tulang* specialises in setting broken bones, for example, while a *balian manak* is a midwife. Others, such as the *balian tenung*, specialise in divining and prophesying, while the *balian usada* is able to heal people with the help of *lontar* containing magical knowledge about medicine and healing. Although many *balian usada* are highly literate scholars who will be consulted because of their ability to interpret these manuscripts, it is the *lontar* itself that is believed to contain the magical energy.

One of the most common types of *balian* is the *balian taksu*, usually consulted on matters relating to sickness. Perhaps the illness is due to a curse placed by a fellow villager or a failure to observe a ceremony in the correct way, which leads to divine punishment. Or the family may wish to communicate with a deceased relative to find out if they are happy so that they will not haunt the family.

The *balian taksu* will begin a session by directing prayers and making offerings to their guiding spirit in front of a smoking brazier. Gradually they will slip into trance and once they have summoned their spirit, the spirit will speak through the *balian*, questioning the clients to find out what the problem is before revealing the cause and cure. ❑

A RELIGIOUS WAY TO LIVE

Religion governs the Hindu individual's social life. A person is expected to live according to his *dharma*. Ideally, one should follow certain rules, the most important of which are good conduct *(kakika)*, good speech *(wacika)*, and good thinking *(manacika)*. If one does this, the various prohibitions and obligations will follow naturally.

Prohibitions include the six internal enemies such as greed and jealousy, six bad behaviours such as arson and slander, and the seven darknesses such as beauty and physical strength. Obligations include such things as no stealing, no anger, and spiritual cleanliness.

LEFT: carving a demon image in *paras* stone.
RIGHT: priest reading a palm-leaf *lontar* manuscript.

BALINESE CEREMONIES AND FESTIVALS

The frequency of Balinese ceremonies and festivals means that most visitors will be able to attend at least one celebration during their stay

The Balinese believe in the eternal cycle of reincarnation and view their life on earth as just one stage in their continued existence. As part of these beliefs, a person's life is marked by rites of passage that are celebrated by the whole community.

The cycle of *manusa yadnya* ceremonies or rites of passage begin six months after conception. At birth, the baby's placenta is buried in a coconut shell in the family compound. Ceremonies continue, marking 12, 42, 105 and 210 days after birth, when teeth appear and fall out and at puberty. Tooth filing ceremonies precede marriage.

Marriage rituals in Bali are unique and often involve the families of the bride and groom in an elaborate mock drama.

The final and most important rite in the cycle of life is cremation. Cremation rituals are joyous occasions as they release the soul from earth so that it may start its journey to heaven before being reborn. The *Mukur* ceremony is held 40 days after a cremation to mark the entry of the person into heaven.

A three-day *odalan* festival takes place in a village every 210 days on the anniversary of the village temple's dedication, and is a time of great celebration. During the island-wide festival of Galungan, ancestors are thought to descend from heaven and enter the world. On the 10th day, Kuningan, the spirits ascend back to heaven. Nyepi, the New Year by the *saka* calendar, is usually celebrated in March.

△ **TOOTH FILING**
At puberty the canine teeth are filed to eliminate symbolically any demonic characteristics and to temper passions.

◁ **CHILDHOOD**
Children are not allowed to touch the ground until they are 210 days old, when their is hair is cut and they are given a name.

MARRIAGE CEREMONY
Wedding ceremonies take place 42 days after a staged abduction of the bride by the groom, during which time the marriage is consummated.

BARONG
The sacred Barong, imbued with magical properties, may travel from village to village to perform at temple celebrations.

CREMATION CEREMONY
At the cremation site the bones of the dead are put into a sarcophagus, which is then set on fire and the ashes scattered on the sea.

MELASTI FESTIVAL
Villagers gather at beaches for Melasti cleansing celebrations. Ritual bathing of temple artefacts precedes Nyepi, the day of silence.

TUMPEK: DAYS OF HONOUR

Tumpek are days that are set aside to honour deities who are guardians of special disciplines. Batari Dewi Saraswati, the Goddess of Learning and Knowledge, is honoured once a year when books are given to her to be blessed, and no reading or writing is done throughout the island. The Lord of the Crops, Batara Sangkara, is honoured on Wariga or Uduh Day by tying offerings around coconut palms. On the day devoted to the divinity of prosperity and financial success, no business is conducted. Landep Day honours metal objects, most importantly daggers *(keris)* but more conspicuously now cars and motorcycles. It is celebrated by decorating items with ritual offerings and palm-leaf ornaments. There is also the day of the "golden blessing", when offerings are made to all objects made from gold, silver and precious stones, and to the Lord of Gold, Mahadewa, guardian of the West. Uye or Kandang Day is reserved for offerings to domestic animals, and there is also the Krulut Day of honour for all types of musical instruments, dance costumes, and puppets.

DANCE-DRAMA

Balinese dance-drama can be staged for simple entertainment value,
or more substantially as serious storytelling of great epics and moral lessons

The dramatic or *bebali* genres of dance are narrative forms descended from the dance-dramas of the ancient Javanese empire of Majapahit, introduced to Bali and then furthered developed in the Balinese courts. They may also be danced in connection with the *odalan* – a temple's anniversary ceremony – to entertain both divine and human audiences, but they are not a necessary part of the ritual.

In addition to the traditional forms of dance-drama, there are also newer forms that have emerged during the past century. Many are derived from sacred forms but were adapted for secular situations, including tourist performances. The semblance of a sacred structure may remain, but the offerings and prayers have been removed. Moreover, some of the newer expressions of dance took on political themes, such as the *tari tani* (peasant dance), sponsored by the Nationalist Party. Other modern dance-dramas, such as the *sendratari*, were developed by students and teachers at the government high school for performing arts.

Gambuh

Of the dance-dramas, the formal and stately *gambuh* is the most important, as it is from this prototype that more modern forms of dance-drama have developed. Originally the *gambuh* would have been performed in the courts for entertainment, but it was also performed in connection with religious events. Today, the *gambuh* is regarded as indispensable for the success of a temple's *odalan*. Formerly, males would have performed all the parts. Today, women take on the female roles, and a woman may even dance the role of the male prince.

The stories that are enacted in the *gambuh* are drawn from the poetic romances of the Javanese cultural hero, known as *panji* or *malat*. In elaborate costumes and performing stylised choreographics, the dancers are accompanied by an orchestra of bamboo flutes, lutes, drums and percussion instruments. The dialogues are spoken in Kawi, the language of Old Java, with attendants and comic retainers providing translations for the audience. The repertoire of the *gambuh* consists of scenes with precise movements.

Wayang wong

The *wayang wong* is undoubtedly the most dramatic of the dance-dramas. The repertoire is drawn from the stories of the great Indian epic, *Ramayana,* that was performed as *wayang,* or shadow theatre. Instead of puppets, people *(wong)* perform. Certain adaptations had to be accommodated, of course. The stories were simplified, and the long dialogue of the shadow theatre had to be changed. On the other hand, abstract introductory dances adapted from the *gambuh* were added. With the exception of Pujungan, in Gianyar regency and where an abridged version of the entire epic is performed, most performances will deal with only a single

---

PRECEDING PAGES: young *baris* dancer. **LEFT:** *legong* dancer, early 1900s. **RIGHT:** boys and girls perform in a village *janger* dance.

episode of the *Ramayana*. The *wayang wong* is generally presented as a form of simple entertainment. However, in the village of Tejakula, in Buleleng, one of the most complete sets of *wayang wong* masks has been preserved, and villagers give performances every 210 days for *odalan* in the second courtyard of the village's temple. Performances are considered sacred, the masks spiritually powerful.

The *penasar*, or servant clowns, are very important in these *wayang wong* dances, not only as translators of Kawi, explaining what is happening, but as much loved comedians. Verbal punning and slapstick are important to the

performances. The play always finishes with a battle between the ogres and the army of monkeys, a dramatic display of movement and energy. In the *wayang wong*, Rawana, the evil king of the *Ramayana*, is never killed.

Legong

The *legong*, a dance genre said to have developed following a vision of a prince in Gianyar, may be described as the quintessence of femininity and grace. The original version, *sanghyang legong*, was a sacred dance and masks were worn. Young boys without masks danced a slightly later version. Today, however, it is the dance by three pre-pubescent

girls who tell a simple story through the performance that most travellers see.

The dance presents a range of delightful movements. Bound from head to toe with shimmering brocade, with flower-bedecked headdresses, the dancers must be able to move from one role to another, from maidservant to raven, from princess to prince, without disrupting the harmony of the dance.

The introductory solo dance demonstrates the full vocabulary of the *legong* style, while the vigorous duet that follows has two little dancers mirroring the other's movements. They flutter their fans, hands moving in a strange, jerky fashion as fingers tremble. They flick their eyes from side to side in a flurry of delightful and constant motion of synchronised movement before coming to an abrupt halt.

Kebyar

Another dance that has gained wide acclaim in Bali is the *kebyar* ("a flash of lightning"), a dance that was developed at the beginning of the 20th century. It started as a pure dance medium using young women dressed in men's clothing to interpret the music. This form was called *kebyar bebanchian* (neutered *kebyar*) and may be performed by men or women. While dancers presented a character study of young men, there is no story.

The *kebyar* was further developed in the 1920s by a talented young dancer, I Ketut Mario, into a form called *kebyar duduk*, which involved him playing the *tompong* (gong set) and flamboyantly twirling the sticks in between pure dance movements.

The dance expresses the emotions of a youth: bravery, shyness, and sadness through the interpretation of the music. Because the dancer is seated *(duduk)*, it is in the gestures and nuances of the wrists and elbows, and in the position of the fingers and the movement of the torso and the facial expressions, that the genius of the dance lies.

Arja

The *arja* is a folk opera that developed in the 19th century, and it is unique in that the dancers must be trained singers.

It is a technically demanding form of entertainment that draws its themes from the eastern Javanese romances of the Majapahit era, packed with sentimentality and melodrama.

Originally, it was performed by an all-male cast, but in the 1920s women replaced men. As the female voice is considered more beautiful than the male, this proved to be a popular innovation, and today female *arja* performers have even become radio stars.

Kecak

The *cak* or *kecak* dance is the well-known "monkey dance" that was developed by the villagers of Bededulu and popularised by Walter Spies in the 1920s. Originally derived from

Janger and prembon

The word *janger* means infatuation, and it is essentially a fun dance choreographed at the beginning of the 20th century with opposing male and female dance styles. It pulls in elements from Balinese, Indonesian and Western sources. The 12 girls who perform the dance wear traditional dance costumes, executing dance steps that display very slow, elegant movements displaying distinct influences from the *legong*. Dancers enter the stage singing a simple folk

PRACTISED AMATEURS

Although dance-drama performances are precise and practised, dancers – except at hotels – are not professionals, but just members of the community.

a sacred *sanghyang* dance, it has subsequently been added to and adapted, incorporating scenes from the story of the *Ramayana*. The *kecak* dance is an amazing cacophony of interlocking sounds – 100 men representing the *Ramayana's* monkey army sit in concentric circles and chant. Their arms are thrown up to the skies, fingers outstretched, but the sounds and gestures have no meaning other than to drive out evil, as was intended in the original *sanghyang* dance.

LEFT: night performance of *arja*, in Bangli.
ABOVE: I Ketut Mario, the originator of the *kebyar* dance. Photograph from the 1930s.

song in Balinese. The 12 boys, who appear after them, wear painted moustaches and their costumes often display wild flights of fancy such as sunglasses, tennis shoes and exaggerated epaulettes. The boys' dance forms a complete contrast to the girls with a series of jerks, twists and lunges during a period of frenzied activity and brisk shouts. The dance is usually performed as a prelude to dramatic performance.

The *prembon* is essentially a dance-drama made up of several genres. The term applies to the revue-style presentations that are performed for tourists, usually presented in a series of scenes from the *legong*, *kebyar* and several other dances, with no dialogue or story. ❑

SACRED DANCE

Trances and possession mark many of the Balinese sacred dances,
performed for the needs or purposes of the island's villages and deities

The most sacred Balinese dances are probably of indigenous origin, but with Hindu-Buddhist additions. This is suggested by the fact that many of the dances involve trance and the possession of the dancers by divine spirits. Some of these dancers are also closely associated with the Bali Aga villages.

Sacred dances may be divided up into those performed in the *jeroan*, the most sacred inner courtyard of the temple, and those performed in the second courtyard. Most are associated with particular cyclical rituals, especially *odalan*, the temple anniversaries held every 210 days.

Sanghyang

Perhaps the most notable of the sacred dances is the *sanghyang* group – *sanghyang* referring to the divinity that will possess the dancer during the performance. The *sanghyang dedari-dedari* dance, for example, is performed to ward off an epidemic or disaster, and so it is performed when community needs require.

Two pre-pubescent girls, who invite the *widedari* (demi-goddesses) into their bodies, perform the dance.

At Kintamani, the *sanghyang deling* is a variant of this dance, in which the two girls hold the two ends of a string on which two dolls are suspended. As the goddesses descend, the dolls begin to dance and vibrate, apparently without help from the girls.

The next stage of the dance follows as the girls begin to dance on glowing embers. If they really are entranced, they will not burn their feet. The girls are then lifted onto the shoulders of two men who, apart from holding the children's ankles, will provide no other support. The men carry them to the four corners of the village and to the central crossroads. Here the girls – all the while dancing with their torsos in graceful swaying and bending movements – will make gestures to repel the demons who have caused the sickness. When they return to the temple, the girls are placed on the ground and brought out of trance with the aid of holy water and prayers.

There are other kinds of possession that occasionally may be witnessed, in which the demons causing an epidemic are chased away by men possessed by animal spirits. In parts of Denpasar, for example, the *sanghyang jaran* is performed by a man possessed by a horse spirit. He runs, neighing, through the streets and prances barefooted on burning coals to scare the demons away. Similar dances are the *sanghyang bojog* and *sanghyang celeng*, which involve possession by a monkey and a pig spirit, respectively.

Rejang and baris

Most of the other sacred dances occur in the period surrounding the *odalan* festivals. On the day preceding the *odalan*, for example, dances to present offerings to the deities visiting the temple may be performed. These dances are called the *gabor* and *mendet*.

On the actual day of the temple festival, women and girls – who do not necessarily have to be trained dancers – perform a very simple but lovely dance called the *rejang*. Whereas the dances that are performed the day before are a means of presenting offerings to the visiting deities, the *rejang* dance itself is regarded as an offering to entertain the deities. A long line of dancers made up of girls and women of all ages will enter the temple courtyard from the outer precincts. They divide into four lines and move slowly towards the visiting gods, holding their sashes out at waist height and waving their fans gracefully.

BARIS BASICS

The *baris* dancer's face must convey fierceness, disdain, pride, acute alertness, and equally important, compassion and regret – a noble's characteristics.

just before or after the *rejang*. There are numerous versions of the *baris* dance performed in both sacred and secular contexts. Distinctive, triangular headdresses bristling with decorations top the magnificent costumes of the four to over 60 dancers. They carry old heirloom weapons, which must all be of the same type.

The villagers at Batur in Bangli are famed for their local version of this dance, called *baris tumbak* (*tumbak* means lance). Each of the dancers carries a lance as they march into

A more unusual form of *rejang* – *rejang sutri* – is performed in Batuan village, in Gianyar. This version is performed as an exorcistic dance at the Usaba Nini festival, which is held to ward off the danger of epidemics.

The men also dance on the festival day, when they are regarded as the bodyguard of the visiting deities. The dance form is called *baris gede* (*baris* means line, and *gede* means great) and refers to the lines of magnificently attired men who perform the dance, which is danced

LEFT: the *sanghyang jaran* assists in a village's well-being. **ABOVE:** Barong and Rangda performances are stories of good and evil.

the temple precinct, shouting in unison to the accompaniment of the village's old *gamelan*. At a given signal, the dancers kneel and pray in front of the deities for about five minutes. This is followed by the dance, which consists of stylised fighting between two groups who face each other, the "fighting" consisting of coordinated group action.

Another version of the *baris* is *baris dadap*, performed at cremations. The dancers carry shields made from the wood of the *dadap* tree, but in this instance the shields represent boats, not weapons, and are a symbolic reference to ancient beliefs whereby the souls of the dead are carried to the afterlife in boats.

Topeng

A form of dance called *topeng pajegan* also belongs to the sacred *(wali)* dance category. These *topeng* (mask) dances are sometimes also called *topeng wali* because they share some of the features of the *wali* dances. At an *odalan* such a dance may be performed in the *jeroan*, but it may also be seen at weddings, tooth filings, and other rituals of passage. The *topeng pajegan* is a remarkable form of sacred dance-drama.

One dancer, who changes masks as he assumes the part of each character, portrays all the roles. The stories are all drawn from the

chronicles of Balinese history, dealing with the adventures of semi-legendary Balinese kings along with their ministers and high priests. The story presented will be chosen depending upon the occasion or community needs.

Barong kedingking

In the village of Madegan, in Gianyar, a masked dance is performed in one of the village temples every six months. The dance is held to protect the villagers from disease and has its origins in the 17th century, when a plague that threatened the village was averted by the performance of this masked dance.

The masks all represent monkeys. A priest

usually dances the part of the monkey king. The movements of the dance mimic those of monkeys, and the dance is performed to present offerings to temple deities and to the demons that may cause sickness. Once the offerings of roast pork and a live pig, to be sacrificed, have been made, the monkeys enter village houses and cause havoc and climb trees to shake the branches and scare off evil spirits.

Barong and Rangda

There is a category of sacred dance that is performed as exorcistic dances to chase away demonic forces. The Barong is a mythical lion-like animal with the power to chase away evil, and an elaborate Barong mask will be regularly danced round the village to keep away evil.

If Barong epitomises the power of good over evil, the mask of Rangda, the widow-witch who rules the evil spirits and who haunts graveyards, represents evil. The struggle between the forces of good and evil are played out periodically in the form of a dance, often within the framework of a popular story, such as an episode from the *Mahabharata*.

When the Barong appears, he is snapping his huge jaws and swishing his tail. He has come to protect the audience and the village. Then Rangda enters with her long claw-like fingers, her flaming tongue, and a necklace of human entrails that hang down over her pendulous breasts. She waves a white cloth, which wafts her evil magic as she stalks the Barong. A group of men with their *keris* sit nearby, representing the community. They see the threatened Barong and rush to attack Rangda. She casts a spell upon them so that instead of stabbing her they turn their *keris* upon themselves.

But the power of the Barong prevents their *keris* from piercing their skin. The dancers are in trance, and they are not play-acting when they turn the blades upon themselves. If an injury does occur, it is said to be a sign of some form of divine displeasure. The priest *(pemangku)* must revive the trance dancers at the end of the performance by sprinkling them with holy water. He uses the beard of the Barong to do this, which is the sacred part of the mask and is made from human hair. ❑

LEFT: Barong performance. **RIGHT:** carving of Hanuman, the monkey general, protecting Sita in the *Ramayana* epic.

Ramayana

One of the two main Indian epics informing Indonesian theatre and dance, including that of Bali, is the *Ramayana*, or Story of Prince Rama. The other is the *Mahabharata*, War of the Bharatas. Whereas the *Ramayana* illuminates the ethics of human relationships, the *Mahabharata* sings of the glorious battle exploits of the Bharatas, an ancient, war-like people in the north of India.

The *Ramayana* is a moral tale, full of instructions and examples on how to lead the good life. It praises the rectitude, wisdom, and perseverance of the noble *satria* or warrior class, while stressing faithfulness, integrity, and filial devotion. The *Ramayana* acknowledges that the trek along the path of virtue demands humility, self-sacrifice, deprivation, and compassion. Too, it is a cautionary tale, less a battle between good and evil (in which evil must always lose) than a recognition of the perpetual ebb and flow of the spirits of darkness and light. Much of the world is in shadows, grey.

In its homeland, India, the *Ramayana* has been known for 3,000 years. With the spread of Indian religions and culture throughout Southeast Asia over the past many centuries, the *Ramayana* has become part of the mythology of Burma, Thailand, Laos, Cambodia, the Malay Peninsula, and of Java and Bali. The epic is long and quite complex; in India, the *Ramayana* consists of 24,000 verses divided into 500 songs.

The characters: In the *Ramayana*, the chief characters are Rama, his wife Sita, his brother Laksmana, the monkey-general Hanuman, the king of giants and antagonist Rawana, and Rawana's brother, Wibisana.

Rama is semi-divine (an incarnation of Wisnu), and a consummate archer. He is of noble birth, for he moves in a refined manner. Even in battle, he is graceful and delicate, using his mind as much as his muscles. Rawana, Rama's implacable foe, thrusts and struts upon the stage, every step filled with menace. His head turns sharply with each movement. His face is impassioned, furious red in keeping with his aggressive, hostile nature.

The story: Rama, Laksmana, and their half-brother Barata are the sons of the king of Ayodya. An accomplished bowman, Rama wins the hand of the beautiful Sita in an archery contest, but through the intervention of Barata's mother, Rama is prevented from succeeding his father as king. Instead, Barata is made king. Rama, Sita and Laksmana go into exile. In the forest they meet Rawana's sister, Surpanakha; she falls in love with Rama, is spurned, and then she turns to Laksmana, who promptly cuts off her nose and ears.

Rawana, determined to avenge this indignity, sends off a servant in the form of a golden deer. Rama stalks the animal and kills it. Its dying cries sound like Rama calling for help, and hearing it, Laksmana goes in search of his brother. Rawana appears, abducts Sita, and flies off with her.

Searching for Sita, the brothers meet Hanuman, a general in the kingdom of apes. Rama assists the apes in their own local struggle. In

appreciation, Hanuman places his army at Rama's disposal. Rama and Laksmana set off with Hanuman and the ape army to Langka, Rawana's homeland. Hanuman undertakes a daring reconnaissance of Langka and finds Sita in Rawana's palace. He gives her a token from Rama, and Sita gives Hanuman one of her rings. Hanuman is caught and sentenced to be burned at the stake but escapes back to Rama.

The ape army builds a giant causeway across the sea to Langka and attacks it. One of Rama's magic arrows eventually fells Rawana, and the victors return home with Sita. Rama receives a boisterous welcome, Barata cedes his regency, and Rama ascends the throne of the kingdom. ❏

WAYANG KULIT

Plato saw shadows as a philosophical tool. Balinese see within the shadows of wayang kulit *spiritual and moral truths in a tradition of storytelling*

The *wayang kulit,* or shadow play, is guaranteed to capture the attention of a Balinese audience whenever it is performed. The stories of *wayang kulit,* taken from the great Indian epics *Ramayana* and *Mahabharata,* which relate the exploits of heroes and maidens, have been acted out for centuries, yet they are still able to hold the rapt attention of audiences who go to see them over and over again. The *wayang kulit* is wonderful entertainment, but the Balinese are also keenly aware that within the stories repeatedly told there are important moral lessons that comment on the conditions of humanity.

The origins of the shadow play are not known for certain. However, much of the modern Balinese *wayang kulit* is derived from Javanese sources. The refugees from Java's Majapahit empire who came to Bali in the 14th century brought with them palm-leaf manuscripts – *lontar* – that were inscribed with the ancient stories. The Balinese *wayang kulit* as it exists today is very different from the Javanese original, however, adapted and modified over the centuries. Although today's *lontar* (recopied over the centuries) still contain the rules concerning the presentation of the shadow play, the way in which these rules are interpreted varies from village to village.

Sacred shadows

Most *wayang* performances are regarded as sacred performances. It is widely believed that the first *wayang* were shamanistic performances carried out to conjure ancestors into this world in order to communicate with their descendants. The figures flickering on the screen were the shadowy images of the ancestors, and the projecting light can be equated with the sun, which illuminates the world. The screen itself is sometimes described as representing the world, and the *dalang,* or puppeteer,

sits as a representative of the supreme deity, the greatest puppeteer of all.

All performances begin with a figure known as the *kayonan* (tree) or *babad* (story). It serves as a marker between scenes, and when it is placed still in the centre it denotes the beginning and end of the play. The *kayonan* has a

tree depicted on it, and it is generally argued that it represents the tree of life, a gate to the supernatural world, and a mountain or forest. Within each scene marked by the *kayonan,* the *dalang* puts together scenes of standard types, depending on the particular story being told.

Then the shadow puppets are introduced to the audience one by one – not that they will need an introduction to most Balinese, who will know them by heart. Each figure that will be featured in the performance is then stuck in a banana stem sitting to the side so that the audience may see its silhouette. Different figures will be placed on the right and left of the *dalang.* Characters that are considered good

LEFT: traditional *kulit* are made of carved buffalo hide, painted and mounted on split wood. **RIGHT:** shadows projected on a screen.

and noble – gods, kings, princes, princesses and their attendants, for example – will be on the right, while evil characters like ogres, demons, and witches will be placed on the left.

The accompanying *gamelan* music is also an integral aspect of the performance. The musicians have to be able to convey the moods of the scenes through the music, and they must anticipate changes in the scene and in the dramatic mood and the appearance of each puppet in performance. Signals from the *dalang* are conveyed

MAJAPAHIT INFLUENCE

The form of the headdresses and costumes of the Balinese *wayang kulit* hark back to the styles of the Javanese Majapahit court, from where they are derived.

and painted in colours and gold leaf. They are manipulated by three rods attached to the body and to each of the arms, which are jointed. Some of the traditional Balinese comic characters also have a lower jaw that can be moved.

The puppets that will be needed to tell the story are carefully taken out of their storage chest *(grobag)* and the buffalo-horn handles stuck into the trunk of a banana plant until their presence on screen is required. On either side of the *dalang* sits an assistant, while behind him sit the four musi-

by means of a wooden hammer he holds between his toes to rap the side of the puppet box. Verbal cues are concealed in the narrative.

Setting the stage

The stage upon which the performance takes place is a white cotton screen, or *gedebong*. Shadows of flat puppets cut from leather will be cast onto the *gedebong* by an oil lamp suspended above the centre of the screen. Flickering flames create a muted, ethereal effect upon the screen. The *dalang* or puppet master sits on the oil-lamp side of the screen and manipulates the puppets to tell the story. The puppets are made from buffalo hide that has been pierced

cians who accompany the performance. The audience sits on the other side of the screen. Usually there is also a small group of men and boys sitting on the *dalang*'s side of the screen, for there is a great deal of interest in the goings-on backstage.

The *wayang kulit* is performed mainly at religious functions, such as the temple *odalan*. On these occasions, the *wayang kulit* will be performed in the middle courtyard of the temple and is intended to entertain the gods. However, human audiences will also enjoy the show, and hundreds of people will squeeze themselves in to watch. Performances are also held at life-cycle ceremonies, such as for the newborn, tooth-filing ceremonies, weddings, and cremations. It is also possible to hire a *dalang* to give a performance to fulfil a vow made to one of the deities. *Wayang kulit* is also performed in schools as a teaching tool or for political purposes, and local governments have used the *wayang kulit* to educate village people about family planning.

Although the most common stories are derived from the two great Hindu epics, *Ramayana* and *Mahabharata*, there are also others that are found. The *wayang gambuh* takes stories from the epic Javanese romance of Prince Panji, while the *wayang arja* draws

tually becoming the witch Rangda. She is reputed to have tried using her witchcraft – without avail – to destroy her son's kingdom after he refused to support her against his father. When the story is performed, it is widely believed that if it is not properly executed, it can bring disastrous results for both the *dalang* and the audience.

This reflects an important aspect of the *dalang*'s abilities, for a powerful *dalang* can call up the village *leyak,* people who have used black magic to turn themselves into malevolent creatures. (In reality, however, Airlangga's mother appears to have been a greatly revered

upon court stories from Majapahit-era Java. Another type of shadow play concerns the exploits of a bawdy anti-hero, Cupak, and his more refined brother, Grantang.

Another *wayang*, considered to be magically dangerous, or *tenget*, is the *wayang calon arang*. It tells the story of an evil witch and is based on a story about the mother of the legendary king Airlangga. She was banished from the Balinese court for practicing black magic. She continued to practice her evil ways, even-

LEFT: illuminated profile of a puppet showing the detailed leatherwork. **ABOVE:** the *dalang* moves the puppets, narrates the story, and guides the *gamelan*.

WAYANG FOR THE GODS

An unusual form of the *wayang* performance, the *wayang lemah,* is performed at the religious ceremonies in which priests are called upon to make the holy water.

Wayang lemah differs from the more usual performance in that there is no screen or lamp. Instead, puppets are leaned against cotton thread that is stretched between two branches of the *dadap* tree. The *dadap* is regarded as a sacred tree and grows on the slopes of the volcano Gunung Agung. The performance is decidedly for the benefit of the divine rather than human audience.

queen. She is supposedly immortalised in a portrait statue as the goddess Durga at Kutri, hardly the way a wicked queen is expected to be remembered.)

Another ritual-based performance is the *wayang sapu leger*, which is performed to free a victim from illness or misfortune. There are certain inauspicious Balinese weeks, called *waku wayang*, that are ruled by Batara Kala, the deity of time who may devour certain people before they have reached their allotted life span. People born in these weeks are likely victims, and the *wayang* performance is given for their protection. The story features a play

within a play, for the gods are depicted descending to earth to perform the first shadow play and thereby charming the ravenous Kala from devouring his prey. The *dalang* who performs the *wayang sapu leger* must be spiritually pure, for part of the performance involves him creating holy water. Hence, he combines the role of both exorcist and priest.

Master storyteller

The *dalang* is a remarkable individual who possesses extraordinary stamina to be able to remain seated and speaking the narrative for up to six hours without a break. His other skills and knowledge are equally impressive. For example, he will have mastered the characters, plots and dialogue of well over a hundred stories, and he will tell these through the shadow play without the use of script.

Because of the wide variety of characters in the *wayang kulit*, the *dalang* has to have knowledge of Kawi – in which the plays were written – and of high, middle and low Balinese, all of which are used in a single performance. The deities that appear in the plays will be addressed in high Balinese, while royalty has to be addressed in middle Balinese and the common characters in low Balinese. The comic characters, known as the *panasar*, apart from providing humour, pungent critique and slapstick comedy, have the important task of translating for the benefit of the audience any Kawi that is used.

The *dalang*'s literary knowledge has to be supplemented by details of Balinese religious practice and philosophy, as well as having a familiarity with folk tales and proverbial knowledge. He will also be an adept comedian, for some of the key characters in the plot of any story are the clown servants who provide the translations, as well as comic interludes.

An important text, *Dharma Pawayanga,* which provides a legendary and spiritual source of the *dalang*'s art, states that the *dalang* is "one who is empowered to command speech" and that "his voice says all that can be spoken".

He is also a verbal artist who has to know how to use language to bring the story and the puppets to life. Each character will have a particular way of speaking, and the *dalang* must switch from the low pitch of a male character to the sweet high tones of a female and then to the gruff, deep voice of another.

The *dalang* must also have a good singing voice, for he will often be called upon to embellish dialogue with songs.

It takes many years for an individual to master this knowledge and skill. Often a young boy will follow his father and play the music to accompany him or act as his assistant to acquire a great deal of knowledge. Others may be following a calling and so attach themselves to a proficient *dalang* in order to learn, and there are yet others who take up the art following a profound mystical experience. ❏

LEFT: *wayang lemah* puppets sans screen. **RIGHT:** an early photograph of a Balinese *gamelan gong.*

Gamelan

No one will ever leave Bali without having heard the sound of the *gamelan.* The tones and melodies of these musical ensembles may be heard in every village throughout Bali, accompanying every theatrical, religious and social function. There is a deep belief among the Balinese that without music and dance, no gathering is complete. The music is played not just to accompany an event but also to entertain the gods and the people gathered, so that by hearing the music they are filled with a sense of well being.

There are a large number of gamelan, ranging from a group of four musicians *(gender wayang)* who accompany the *wayang kulit,* or shadow play, to a huge group that may comprise up to 40 players *(gamelan gong),* and which accompanies important ceremonies. Many of the ensembles – called *gamelan gambuh* or *gamelan legong* – as their names suggest are used to accompany a particular kind of performance. Up to 20 different genres and ensembles have to been recorded, but young musicians continue to experiment and develop new forms.

A range of instruments are to be found in the gamelan, most consisting of bronze keys suspended on bamboo resonators and beds of gongs, all of which sit in wooden frames and which may be beautifully carved and gilded. The different metallophones have different musical functions. The *gong gangsa,* for example, is pitched very high and is used to play rapid melodies, while the *gong calung* and *gong jublag,* which have lower tones, play the melody. Not all the metallophones will be played in one ensemble.

At the heart of the gamelan are two drums *(kendang),* one male and one slightly larger one, which is considered to be female. These control the tempo of the music, the drummers using either their hands or a stick. Small hand cymbals *(cengceng)* accent the music, while the steady beat of a single gong *(kempli)* keeps the orchestra together. Other instruments may include flutes *(suling)* and a two-stringed violin *(rebab).*

The gongs and metal keys are forged by hand using the same methods that have been used for centuries. Tuning to one of two scales – the five-toned or rarer seven-toned – is done by filing and hammering away at each piece. However, there does not exist a standard, and each ensemble will have its own unique sound. For the Balinese, this is as it should be, the individual voice of the instrument must be born out of the bronze. The idea of the instruments having their own voice is reflected in the belief that gamelan instruments also contain a spiritual power. No Balinese would ever step over an instrument and deeply offend the spirit. These spirits must also be accorded due respect through offerings made at appropriate times and on particular occasions.

One very unusual gamelan is the *gamelan jegog* from Jembrana regency. The instruments are made from bamboo, and the deep, pure tones produced by striking them with a padded mallet resonate through the body so that the listener feels part of

the sound. The largest instruments consist of bamboo tubes up to 3 metres (10 ft) long and 30 centimetres in diameter, and the musicians have to sit on top of them to play.

In Bali, the word *gamelan* refers not only to the instruments but also to the musicians of whom there are thousands in Bali. Nearly every village owns at least one set of instruments that are kept in a special pavilion *(bale gong).* Different wards *(banjar)* may have their own gamelan, and anyone may join the village music club *(seka),* which jointly owns and maintains the instruments.

There are children's gamelan clubs, perhaps as many as 2,000, where boys and girls as young as nine to twelve play. ❏

TRADITIONAL ARCHITECTURE

Nothing in the layout or construction of a Balinese village or home is left to chance.
The order of the universe defines how a building must be presented

All Balinese buildings, both sacred and secular, have for centuries been laid out according to ideas of sacred orientation. It is possible, though it's not known for certain, that even in prehistoric times some kind of orientation was used in architecture. Ancient megalithic stones, for example, are oriented towards one of the main volcanoes of Gunung Agung, Gunung Batur, or Gunung Batukau.

In order to understand the principles of Balinese architecture, one must first grasp certain religious and cosmological notions. Since early historic times, the key principles of sacred orientation have been the *kaja* and *kelod* axis. *Kaja* means "towards the mountains", while *kelod* means "towards the sea". The direction of *kaja* – the mountains – is regarded as the most sacred direction, being the direction in which the deities and ancestors live. Towards the ocean – *kelod* – is conversely regarded as being the direction of evil, demonic forces. The area of land on the island of Bali that lies between the mountains and sea is regarded as neutral.

Hindu influences

The above scheme adheres to the Hindu concept of *dharma*. This tells us essentially that everything in the universe has its allotted place and that any transgression of this natural order will lead to disharmony. Architectural structures and layout must adhere to *dharma* as much as human behaviour. This special layout and orientation of Balinese architecture, moreover, conforms to Hindu ideas about the division of the universe into three realms, the Tri Loka: the realm of the gods, the realm of humankind, and the realm of the demons and other negative forces.

This notion is reflected in the *kaja-kelod* layout and in the vertical structure of the classical Hindu temple. In this scheme, the temple is also conceived as representing the Tri Loka. The roof

of the temple represents the abode of the gods, the middle section where people enter to worship represents the abode of people, and the base or foot of the temple represents the underworld and the abode of demonic forces. In the Balinese context, this scheme is more apparent in the shrines found within the temple compounds.

These architectural ideas developed over the centuries, evolving with time as new ideas filtered onto the island of Bali. Before the advent of Hinduism, the Balinese already held the mountains in great reverence, for they were regarded as the abode of the ancestors and as the navel *(puseh)* of the world. For the Bali Aga people, this is still a relevant notion.

In the Hindu-Buddhist cosmological scheme, the sacred mountain, Semeru or Meru, forms the centre of the universe and is the abode of the gods. When Hinduism began to trickle into Bali, this idea was easily adopted, and Gunung Agung, Bali's highest mountain, became the Balinese Meru. It is on the slopes of this vol-

---

PRECEDING PAGES: multi-tiered temple *meru.* **LEFT:** ornamental temple gateway. **RIGHT:** domestic architectural elements: brick, bamboo, grass and wood.

cano that Pura Besakih, the great mother temple of the island, lies, with its architecture and layout following the orientational principles.

During the 11th century a new axis was added to the north-south, or *kaja-kelod*, one: the east-west, or *kangin-kuah* axis. It was at this point in Bali's history that the concept of the Tri Loka was introduced. It soon played an important role in architectural design and layout, so that house compounds, temples, villages, and the island itself as a whole could be divided up

BUILDING BLOCKS

No cement or mortar was used in construction with stone or mud brick. By rubbing two surfaces together using water, the joints could be made to fit perfectly.

This design of extreme sophistication was introduced to Bali from Java. The idea of placing a series of open or partially open pavilions *(bale)* within a walled-off area existed in Java from a very early period. The open pavilion is a common feature of Austronesian architecture and is found throughout the Indonesian archipelago.

The typical Balinese home *(kuren)* conforms to the compound layout, and most Balinese will tell you that they feel uncomfortable if they are not walled in. The walls surround-

into realms for the gods, humans, and demons.

Another important concept that came into play was the Tri Angga, whereby the human body could also be divided into three parts: the head, trunk and lower body. This in turn influenced the architectural layout of the family compound. It was also at this time that rules governing certain priestly rituals connected to the building trade were introduced.

The compound concept

The first thing that many visitors to Bali will notice is that the traditional Balinese house, palace, temple or other public buildings are all built within a courtyard or series of courtyards.

ing the *kuren* may be made from mud, brick or stone, and they may be carved with decorative motifs in the more well-to-do houses.

Entry is by way of a small, covered gate in the wall on the *kuah* (west) side of the compound. It may consist of two simple mud pillars with a thatch roof or a more elaborate affair of brick and carved stone with a tiled roof. Two small shrines *(apit lawang)* are placed on either side of the gate. Just inside the gate a wall is built obscuring the interior view of the courtyard from outside. This wall, called an *aling-aling*, is to prevent evil spirits from entering the compound. It is believed that demons and other negative beings cannot turn corners.

The family house compound is perceived as being an organic unit. Just as the human body is divided into a head, trunk and limbs, so too is the house. The head of the compound, which is the most sacred part, is the north-east corner where the family shrines are located. The sleeping quarters are the arms, the courtyard is the navel, the gate represents the sex organs, the kitchen and granary are the legs and feet, while the refuse tip is the anus.

The house compound is made up of several pavilions or *bale* that serve different purposes. The pavilions are built on platforms of mud, brick or stone, depending on the owner's

The measurements of a building are traditionally taken from the human body. An ideal house should be harmonious with the body of the family patriarch. The architect, or *undagi*, who usually has priestly duties, takes the measurements of the owner's body – or in the case of a temple, from the priest. For example, the main measurements for the ground layout are based on the foot, and for the outside wall, on the outstretched arms. All these measurements are inscribed on a rule that is then used throughout the construction. The building of a house and its occupation must be on an auspicious day specified by the religious calendar. ❑

means, and a few steps lead up to the top. Some are completely enclosed, such as the sleeping quarters *(uma meten)*, and there may or may not be windows. Whether the house compound is that of a wealthy or poor family, the essential layout is the same. Only the building materials and adornment may differ. Palaces, temples and public buildings traditionally were made from the soft sandstone *(paras)* found all over Bali. Ordinary dwellings were made from baked brick and mud, with bamboo and thatch roofs.

LEFT: village avenue and houses. **ABOVE:** elegantly carved wooden door, and portrait of traditional village life and architecture.

AN UPRIGHT BUILDING

The body symbolism is also reflected in the placing of the posts of all buildings. The timber columns have to be erected so that the posts stand the same way they did when they were growing as a tree. In this way the house will stand "upright". Knots in the wood are regarded as eyes and must be placed above the shoulder of the post.

If one looks closely at the joints of a *bale*'s posts and beams, they resemble a wooden jigsaw puzzle in that they fit ingeniously together without the use of nails. The pieces of wood all interlock, and where necessary wooden pegs are inserted to hold them in place.

THE TEMPLE

While Balinese temples sometimes look unused and neglected,
in fact they are an essential anchor for both community and individual

Some scholars believe that the basic form of the Balinese temple originated during the Balinese neolithic period, perhaps as early as 2500 BC. These early Balinese had already accepted a belief that their ancestors lived at the top of the volcanic mountains that lay to the north of Bali's population centres.

Temple layout

Balinese temples follow the same principles of spatial organisation followed by all other traditional architectural forms. They are aligned on the *kaja-kelod* axis, outlined in the last section. Balinese temples are constructed so that they are higher in the ocean or *kelod* side.

This alignment is a legacy from Bali's prehistoric past, when stepped terraces formed sacred sites where the ancestors were revered. Besakih, the mother temple of Bali, exemplifies this scheme very clearly. It is built on the site of ancient terraces, the northern and most sacred courtyard lying on the upper terrace. In lesser temples, this scheme generally prevails.

Even if the temple is built on flat ground, the central and innermost courtyards will be built on artificially raised land, so that one has to go a few steps higher to enter each successive one.

During the 16th century, a priest named Nirartha arrived in Bali from Majapahit on Java. He was to have a great influence on many Balinese religious ideas. One of the ideas he introduced was the Sad Kahyangan, a system whereby the lotus of the Hindu universe was laid over the island of Bali. The Sad Kahyangan temples – the seats of the gods – were placed on each of the eight petals, and Pura Besakih was placed in the centre. This system, more commonly known as the *nawa sanga*, incorporates the idea that a separate aspect of God inhabits each of the eight cardinal points. Originally, these aspects of the supreme deity were Indian gods, but over time different Balinese deities came to be identified with them.

Types of temples

There are literally thousands of temples throughout Bali. One estimate puts the number as high as 20,000, ranging from irrigation and village temples to Pura Besakih, the island's central temple. If chanced upon when things are quiet, many of these temples have an air of neglect and abandonment about them. This can be misleading. When a ceremony is about to take place, especially the temple's own anniversary ceremony – the *odalan*, which takes place every 210 days – they will suddenly come to energetic life.

The most common word for temple is *pura*, derived from the Sanskrit word for a town or palace. Most correctly, a *pura* is a temple built on public land. Other expressions used to refer to a temple are *sanggeh* and *marajan*, which refer to a private temple, usually within the family domain.

Much to the confusion of many visitors, there are various categories of temple. The three main categories are local temples, descent temples, and irrigation-association *(subak)* temples. The local temples may range from the village temples to temples that have regional or island-wide significance, such as Besakih or Tanah Lot. Descent temples belong to particular clans.

Within the village there are three temples *(kahayangan tiga)* that are arranged along the *kaja-kelod* axis.

The village's temple of origin *(pura puseh)* is always located at the *kaja* (mountain) end of the village and is dedicated to the god Brahma. In the centre of the village is the *pura bale agung*, or the temple of the great assembly hall, which is where village meetings are held. This temple is always dedicated to the god Wisnu.

Finally, there is the temple of death *(pura dalem)*, also sometimes called the "temple of the mighty one". Dedicated to Siwa and his consort Durga, it is always located at the *kelod* (ocean) end of the village, near the cemetery and cremation grounds.

In addition to these temples, each family has its own family temple located in the northeast *(kaja kangin)* corner of the family compound. Often this consists of little more than a walled-off area containing several shrines, mainly dedicated to deified ancestors.

Common characteristics

Although each temple will have individual characteristics, there are certain features that are common to all Balinese temples. Enclosed by walls, most will have three courtyards. In practice, many temples appear to have only two courtyards. This is because the outer courtyard is not walled off and rather is a recognised space. The inner courtyard *(jeroan)* is the most sacred and always lies nearest the mountains, to the north. The middle courtyard is the *jaba tengah,* while the outer one is the *jaba.*

This three-fold division is conceived as a reflection of the universe, with the innermost courtyard representing heaven, the outermost representing hell, and the middle one an intermediate area. In fact, the alignment and spacing mirrors the *kaja-kelod* divisions. As one moves through the first courtyard and passes through the middle one to the *jeroan,* one is perceived as passing from profane space or the earthly realm into increasingly sacred space.

LEFT: Pura Tanah Lot is one of Bali's most sacred temples, dedicated to the deity of the sea and protected by sea snakes. **RIGHT:** Pura Besakih is the so-called mother temple and Bali's most sacred.

Inside the temple

One enters the temple from the south through a split gate, or *candi bentar.* This architectural feature is a very important one in Bali, and many hotels and public buildings have incorporated it into their architectural design. The *candi bentar* looks like a tower that has been cut in half and the two sides separated. What the origin and meaning of this unusual feature are is uncertain.

One Balinese legend has it that they represent the two halves of the mythical Mount Meru, which was split by Siwa to become Gunung Agung and Gunung Batur, Bali's two

THE ODALAN

Balinese don't make regular visits to a temple except on its anniversary, a three-day celebration held at all of Bali's 20,000 temples every 210 days (a traditional calendar year) or maybe every 365 days.

This anniversary rite, or **odalan**, can be seen somewhere on Bali nearly every day, performed to invite the temple's deities to visit so that they can receive the people's devotion. Temple images are dressed, and women carry offerings *(banten)* to the temple to be placed within the inner sanctum. Gamelan ensembles perform, and sacred dances and *wayang kulit,* the shadow-puppet play, are staged.

primary volcanoes. One scholar links them firmly to the funeral temples of former kings, a suggestion that carries some weight, given the cult of deified kings, which in turn is linked to ancient ancestor worship. This *candi* form, moreover, repeatedly appears in Balinese rituals symbolising the universe. Other explanations see the *candi bentar* as symbolic of the splitting of the material world, allowing the physical body to enter the spirit world. It also has been said to represent the duality of male and female, and so forth.

Inner courtyards

The area inside the *jaba* is essentially a place of assembly where offerings will be prepared, meetings held, and where cockfights may take place. It contains several *bale*, or open-sided pavilions with *atap* roofs. These are used for various purposes, including as a place to rest or to prepare food. A pavilion for a large wooden drum called a *kulkul* is also found in the right-hand corner, used to summon people to meetings or as an alarm in times of danger. There may also be a small rice barn *(jineng)* to store the grain from the temple's own fields.

The entrance to the second courtyard is usually entered via a gateway called a *candi kurung*, which resembles the *candi bentar* except that it has a pair of wooden doors. This courtyard of the village temple is usually dominated by the *bale agung*, a village conference hall, and there will be other pavilions to house the instruments of the village gamelan, for example. This courtyard is essentially an antechamber to the inner courtyard, a place where everything is made ready for the gods.

The inner courtyard is entered through another gate called a *kori agung*. This is a more monumental structure, raised off the ground and accessed by a series of steps. Unlike the other gateways, it has a roof and a narrower entrance. Above the gate, the round face and bulging eyes of Boma, son of Siwa and Ibu Pertiwa, or Mother Earth, look down. Boma symbolises the middle world, along with this world's vegetation and fertility.

On either side of the stairs are two *raksasa* or guardians whose task it is to scare away demons. Some temples may also have a screen

in the form of a wall *(aling-aling)*, which prevents one from seeing into the temple. Its function is not to prevent prying human eyes from peering in, but to prevent evil spirits from gaining access. Evil spirits can only move in straight lines, and the wall effectively prevents them from entering – they cannot turn right or left when they come up against the wall.

The *jeroan* contains all the shrines and altars. The most sacred are ranged along the furthest wall in the direction of *kaja*. The most noticeable feature of these shrines is their towering tiered roofs, known as *meru,* which symbolise the cosmic Hindu-Buddhist Mount Meru. The tiers on the roofs of the *meru* are always uneven in number, between three and eleven. The more important gods have more tiers on their shrines; Siwa alone has an 11-tiered *meru*. Unlike shrines in Java, most Balinese shrines do not contain images of the deities, nor are the deities supposed to reside there permanently. Rather, they descend through a vertical open shaft to their seat when invited to attend ceremonies.

Unseen symbology

What the eye cannot see, however, are the little iron, gold and silver implements that are buried under the structure or the container of nine precious stones – *piripih* – inscribed with magic words concealed in the rafters of the uppermost roof. The *piripih* symbolise the material world; nine corresponds to the *nawa sanga*.

The most important element of the *jeroan* is the *padmasana,* a throne of stone for Surya, the sun god. It stands in the most sacred position of the courtyard, the uppermost right-hand corner, and with its back always oriented towards Gunung Agung. It is here that Siwa, in the form of the sun god, descends during the temple festivals. The *padmasana* is a representation of the universe. The stone base may be shaped like the mythical turtle Bedawang, with two coiled serpents resting upon his back, thus forming the foundation of the world. In some temples, Siwa is equated with Sanghyang Widi Wasa, the supreme deity. In such cases, his image is carved on the back of the throne. ❑

TEMPLE DRESS
The Balinese are very strict about appropriate dress in any temple. Visitors whose legs are exposed will be asked to don a sarong, and everyone must put a sash around the waist. Both sarong and sash are often available to rent at larger temples.

RIGHT: ornamental temple gateway.

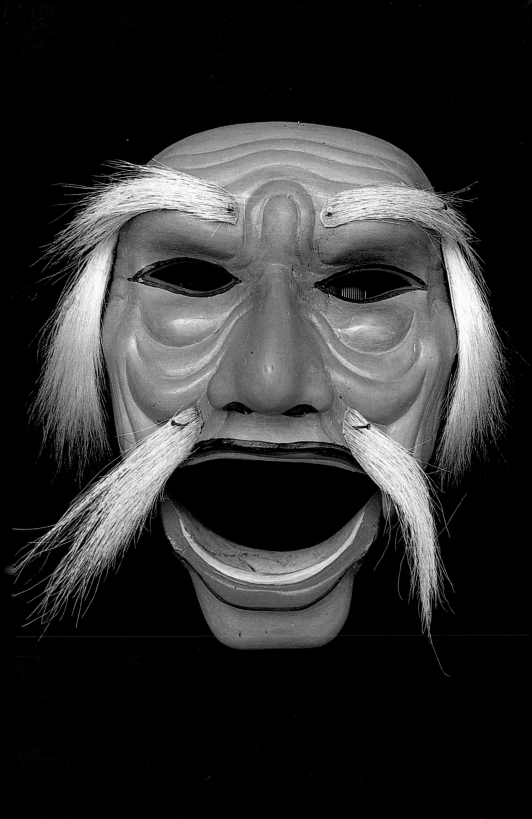

I Goesti Njoman Lëmpad
Oeboed. Bali.

THE BALINESE AESTHETIC

Originally, art on Bali was an obligation and testament to the deities.
It sometimes still is, but tourism has changed much of Bali's aesthetic purpose

Everywhere one turns in Bali, there seems to be art of some sort. It is almost a cliché now to describe Bali as an island of artists, but one would not be far wrong in describing every Balinese as an artist or a potential artist. Certainly the intrinsic beauty of the island must have something to do with it. Also, by the 16th century, the rice-farming system on Bali had become so efficient that even the lowliest farmer found ample time for creative pursuits. In the widest possible sense, art has been expressed on the island through music, dance, carving, and painting, and in more unusual creations such as the ephemeral offerings. *(See pages 126–27.)*

Modern Balinese art had its beginnings in ancient history. Beautifully decorated bronzes survive from the early centuries AD. Early artists undoubtedly also created a range of other arts, but the tropical climate is unkind to all but the hardiest of materials, and most objects have not survived. Soft volcanic stone quickly erodes, and carvers and stone masons had to replace temple carvings, copying the originals, then copying the copies. Cloth paintings rot in the humidity and had to be recreated, and woodcarvings on pillars were eaten by termites. Earthquakes and volcanoes have also destroyed numerous works of art.

Art found its primary expression in the honouring of the deities, and it never became a conscious production for its own sake. Rather, it was almost a religious obligation to make things beautiful to adorn temples with carvings or to paint cloth images to hang at ceremonies. Art was to serve the gods and the community.

Each village, moreover, owed its allegiance to a particular raja, and talented artists were constantly called upon to serve their lords. A great deal of rivalry existed between the rajas who tried to outdo each other, giving high status to their most talented artists.

Painting

One particular art form that survived from ancient times in Bali, but not in neighbouring Java, was painting. The oldest known works of Balinese painting to survive are executed on two wooden boards, kept in two of the temples at Besakih, the Balinese "mother" temple. They

are of a lotus flower and of the Hindu elephant-headed deity, Ganesa.

From the 14th century onwards in Bali we find episodes from the Hindu epics such as the *Ramayana* and other literary sources painted with natural pigments on cotton, which had been primed with a lime base. These paintings were religious in subject matter, and their style was derived from the two-dimensional figures of the *wayang kulit*. They remained unsigned, for the painter was a craftsman who was working for the glory of his gods, not for his own glorification and immortalisation.

These paintings were commissioned as decorations for the palace or temple, and they had

---

PRECEDING PAGES: *topeng* masks, and early 20th-century painting. **LEFT:** *Ramayana* illustration by I Gusti Nyoman Lempad. **RIGHT:** modern Balinese art.

three basic forms: *ider ider* (long scrolls), *tabing* (square paintings), and *langse* (hangings). Variously called *wayang* or *kamasan* painting, the technique is still practised in the village of Kamasan, whose craftsmen had been supported by the raja's court.

It has often been claimed that without the encouragement and interest of a group of European artists who settled in Bali in the 1920s and 1930s, Balinese art would never have become as important and popular as it subsequently did. Because there was a tendency for Balinese artists to create images to replace deteriorating existing ones, a great degree of repetition

existed. However, it would be unfair to say that Balinese art was static. By the end of the 19th century, Balinese artists had already begun experimenting with new media and styles. Paper became more plentiful during this period, and artists began to use crayons and gouache. One finds, for example, paintings of this period from Sanur and Singaraja, where instead of the flat stylised *wayang* forms, some concept of perspective was used. More naturalistic features in the figures and scenery are also noticeable. Many traditional subjects were treated in this way, but the artists were also beginning to paint scenes from everyday life.

LITERARY AESTHETICS

Another type of two-dimensional art, which is still practised, is the adornment of *lontar* (palm-leaf) manuscripts, a technique originally from India. The making of *lontar* may go back to the first century AD in Bali. These long, thin books, inscribed with histories, poetry, medical texts, epic stories, and religious mantras, are sometimes lavishly illustrated *(see page 220)*. The prepared leaves were inscribed with a stylus, and then soot mixed with a little oil was rubbed over the surface to leave a more permanent mark.

Traditional calendars *(wuku)* are another type of art with strange markings and astrological symbols.

Later, in the first few decades of the 20th century, there developed in the Gianyar area a naïve and naturalist style of painting that incorporated the more traditional *wayang* figures.

With the break-up of the old system of royal patronage, there was a very real danger that the arts might similarly fall into a decline. It was, ironically, tourism that played a large part in preventing this. The Balinese were also in need of hard cash to pay taxes, and tourist dollars helped change artistic patronage.

The name of Walter Spies crops up repeatedly in books on Balinese art. This rather shy German artist, who settled in Campuhan near Ubud in 1927, together with the Dutch artist

Rudolf Bonnet, did indeed have a profound effect on the development of Balinese painting. Spies gained fame for his particular style of landscapes with their double and even triple horizons, while Bonnet was widely noted as a more naturalistic, romantic painter.

It was Bonnet who claimed that he and Spies helped shape the future development of Balinese art. He was quick to draw on claims that Balinese art was a static and exhausted force when they arrived on the island. Spies did not deny this claim, which was repeated by numerous other influential Western visitors to the island, including Margaret Mead, Claire Holt,

was evolving during that period. The Europeans certainly had a hand in steering the Balinese in the direction of their own artistic aesthetics, but there are critics who claim that many talented artists were not promoted because they did not fit the criteria laid down by the Europeans.

There were artists, moreover, who were developing their own styles away from the influence of Spies and Bonnet. One such person was I Gusti Made Deblog, who was taught by a Chinese photographer to use charcoal and ink. He created peculiarly surreal landscapes inhabited by witches and demons and depicting struggles that reigned in the world.

and William Stutterheim, to name but a few. They supported claims that Western artists introduced the more naturalistic painting style and scenes of everyday life. There is no record of how the Balinese artists felt about this.

The Balinese artists during this period drew upon their traditional forms and techniques, elaborating on them and experimenting with new ideas and expressions. And because there was no local market for their creations, they were essentially creating for the blossoming tourist market, moulding images of the Bali that

LEFT: detail of Barong from Batuan-style painting.
ABOVE: classic painting by Walter Spies.

HIGH-PRICED WESTERN ART

The Europeans who painted in Bali during the 1920s and 1930s came to be known as the Indo-European artists. Today their paintings can fetch high prices at auction, and since the beginning of the 1990s, especially, some have achieved record bids for their work. Interest in the Indo-European paintings comes from both Western collectors and those in the region, including Indonesian collectors who have been some of the biggest buyers in recent years. Walter Spies, who probably produced fewer than 100 paintings in Bali, has been one of the most sought-after artists. One of his paintings fetched US$750,000 at Christie's in 1996.

Centres of art

The town of Ubud has become renowned as a centre for the arts. This came about when the *cokorda,* or prince, of Ubud played host to Walter Spies and showed him his first Balinese dance, a *sanghyang* trance dance. Spies settled in the area, and soon other Europeans followed suit. It was this expatriate circle that promoted the image of Ubud as the cultural centre of Bali, an image encouraged by the *cokorda.*

To this end, they were supported by a gifted Balinese artist and craftsman, I Gusti Nyoman Lempad, who had built some of the most beautiful palaces and temples in Bali. Lempad began

drawing when he was in his 60s, and in the 50 years that followed (he died at age 116), he produced some of the most innovative and imaginative pen-and-ink drawings imaginable *(see page 116).* He was influenced not by European ideas but by Balinese tradition, and in the 1920s he began producing a new variant of painting that greatly impressed Spies.

Other talented artists came from all over Bali to work under Lempad. A musician from a nearby village, Anak Agung Mandera, ensured that Ubud became known as a centre for music and dance. Artists in other media came also, including wood sculptors such as I Cokot and

THE ASCENDANCY OF THE FEMALE ARTIST IN BALI

The Seniwati Gallery of Art by Women, set up in Ubud in 1991, is the first gallery in Asia to concentrate on promoting and selling the work of female artists.

Mary Northmore, an English woman living in Bali and married to an Indonesian artist, came up with the idea when she realised that female artists received almost no recognition in Bali amongst Balinese or foreigners, even though they had demonstrated their talent. As a result, she established the Association of Women Artists in Bali. One of the most important things that the gallery and association do is to facilitate contact between female artists, establishing a sense of community amongst

them, and to allow them to discuss and develop their work. The gallery is managed by Balinese women and provides a showcase for the paintings of any female artist living in Bali, whether Balinese or from elsewhere. The Seniwati Gallery also provides a space for visiting female artists who wish to display their work. The first visiting artist to do so was Kartika Affandi, the famous artist-daughter of an equally famous father and artist.

The profits made by the gallery have enabled groups of women to travel to Jakarta to exhibit their work and to study art trends in other countries. In addition, the gallery supports an art school for young girls.

Ida Bagus Njanja. These artists were among the best in their fields, and what they achieved at Ubud was the nurturing of Balinese art and the creation of a new artistic identity.

As in the past, Klungkung remained the centre for traditional styles of painting, but irrespective of the influence of Spies and Bonnet, the Balinese began to cultivate their own styles within the traditional framework. Ubud became an important centre, characterised by refined polychrome figures in the *wayang* style. They are often set in a Spies-style landscape, depicting scenes from every aspect of Balinese life, from harvesting to making offerings in the temple.

Another centre of art developed at Sanur. The Sanur artists tended to work in ink on paper. One notable feature of their work is the depiction of marine subjects, themes rarely found elsewhere in Bali, given that the sea is the realm of the underworld. The most famous of the Sanur artists was Ida Bagus Rai.

The third centre that developed was at Batuan, where painting is characterised by half-*wayang*, half-naturalistic figures executed in black ink and crayon, with backgrounds and foregrounds dense in colour and detail.

Artistic associations and styles

The Pita Maha Artists group was formed in Ubud in 1936. This group, made up of painters, sculptors and silversmiths, was established to keep the standard of art high and to organise exhibitions and sales of work abroad. It was disbanded in 1942, but after World War II, the Ubud Painters Club was established.

A new style of painting developed in the 1950s under the guidance of Dutch-born artist Arie Smit, who subsequently took Indonesian citizenship. He taught art to a group of young Indonesian boys, who developed a distinctive "naive" style depicting different aspects of Balinese life in strong acrylic colours. This group, known as the Young Artists, quickly became popular. A third generation of this group has now emerged.

JAVA'S CONTRIBUTION

Many of Bali's internationally recognised artists – including Nyoman Erawan, Made Wianata and Nyoman Gunarsa – actually studied art in Yogyakarta, Java.

Contemporary Balinese art

Today, Balinese art has spread beyond Balinese artists. In the stretch between Ubud and Mas, one will find artists from Java and Sumatra who have decided to absorb some of Bali's creative energy. New expressions and techniques are developed all the time, but there are many people who argue that few, if any, of the modern artists have achieved the deeper search for aesthetic perfection personified by the best of the Pita Maha group. Most artists appear to be working to meet

the demands of tourists rather than exploring art for art's sake. Very few artists working in Bali have received a formal art training. Those who have been trained generally work in particular styles and produce subjects very different from those of the non-academic artists. These latter still tend to create paintings that are influenced by traditional themes, as well as scenes of everyday life. It is this group that produces mainly for the tourist market.

There are several places to see quality Balinese art: the Puri Lukisan Museum, Neka Museum, and Agung Rai Museum, all near Ubud. The Art Centre in Denpasar also has collections of traditional and contemporary art. ❑

LEFT: the Neka Museum in Ubud offers a collection of both traditional and contemporary Balinese art.
RIGHT: foreign interest has nurtured Balinese art, but tourism has perhaps lessened aesthetic standards.

CARVINGS, TEXTILES AND METAL

*The innate aesthetics of the Balinese are found in the traditional
and modern crafts of Bali – carvings in stone and wood, textiles and metalwork*

It has been estimated that there are over 90,000 producers of handicrafts in Bali. Crafts are wide ranging, from woodcarving to weaving, from metal and silver work to basketry. Small children will pick up a knife to whittle away at a piece of wood. A little girl plays with strips of palm leaf and produces a small container. From the cradle to the grave it seems that the Balinese are always creating something. A master carver will, as likely as not, also be a gifted dancer or musician or painter. Particular villages – Mas, Batuan, Gelgel, Ubud, Badung – are famous for having families of craftsmen and artists who have, over the years, consistently produced high-quality workmanship. Writers and scholars have long debated as to why there should be this innate creativity among the Balinese. Explanations are as hypothetical as the art is expressive.

Wood and stone carving

Balinese woodcarving is famous the world over. The skill goes back many centuries to the time when the courts began demanding that the finest adornment be used to embellish their palaces. The opulence and splendour can now only be imagined. The craftsmanship remains, however, and visitors to Bali need only look at the beautifully carved windows, doors and supporting posts in many of today's buildings to appreciate how the old palaces must have looked. The dazzling effect of these former royal residences, with their painted and gilded woodwork, must have been breathtaking.

The stonework of the temples has always been carved. The stone used is the soft sandstone called *paras* or tuff. Definite rules govern the carving in temples. A figure known as *karang cewiri* with fangs and bulging eyes should always be placed over the gateway, for example, and free-standing guardian figures or *raksasa* should be placed on either side of an entrance. However, there is some degree of imagination allowed, and relief carvings on the temples of northern Bali can be a source of great entertainment – a bandit holding up a car,

two fat Dutchmen drinking beer, and a Dutchman riding a bicycle may all be seen.

Carved wood figures consist mainly of figures of demons, heroes and deities. Pavilions are frequently decorated with figures of the *garuda*, the mount of Wisnu. These kinds of carvings are widely available, though the qual-

ity differs widely. Increasingly one finds woodcarvings aimed specifically at the tourists, such as cartoon characters, and carved and painted fruit and plants have been developed as part of Bali's cheap souvenir range. Some carvers have gone on to make carved mirror frames, carved stools and any number of items that they think will attract the tourist. Cheaper crafts are also aimed at the export market.

There is, however, a more artistic end of the woodcarving market. During the 1930s, carvers as well as painters were encouraged to begin experimenting with new ideas. They began to move away from the more stylised painted figures and produced forms from everyday life.

They often left the wood unpainted and found that the natural beauty of the grain was more appealing to many foreign buyers.

Today, talented woodcarvers are making some highly imaginative and beautiful sculptures of figures that have been elongated and distorted. One of the earliest proponents of this style of carving was Ida Bagus Njanja. His son, Ida Bagus Tilem, would also become a famous woodcarver, using good-quality wood to make graceful figures of humans, deities and animals. He

RICE-GODDESS MOTIF

One commonly recurring motif is the *cili*, the stylised representation of the rice goddess Dewi Sri, adorned with a fan-shaped headdress and huge ear-plugs.

Textiles

One of the first kinds of textile that the visitor to Bali will find is *batik*. Every imaginable style and quality of the material is found throughout the island, but newcomers to the region may be surprised to learn that almost no *batik* is actually made on Bali. It is nearly all produced in central Java and shipped to Bali, where it as popular with the Balinese as with the tourists.

Bali's home-produced cloth is a weft *ikat* called *endek*. *Ikat*, which means "to tie", is pro-

was recognised internationally as a master carver, and many of his pieces were sold for thousands of dollars. Today, his style of wood sculpting is widely copied.

Other styles of carving have developed. The so-called driftwood carvings reflect the imagination of the artist who has allowed the natural shape of the wood to suggest the finished form. Nyoman Cokok, from the village of Jati near Sebatu, originated yet another type of carving using hollow logs that were carved with hoards of overlapping demons and other figures.

LEFT: exquisitely carved mask. **ABOVE:** souvenir carvings, and souvenir vendor.

duced by tying the weft threads of a cloth before it is woven and dying them so that the tied areas do not take up the dye. The cloth is then woven, and the pattern produced by the tying of the threads emerges. Although unpopular with visitors, the Balinese use it a lot. Authentic *endek* is made from silk, but cotton and synthetic yarns are also widely used. Traditionally it was woven on a backstrap loom, but today semi-mechanised looms produce the cloth in greater quantities, especially in Denpasar and Gianyar. Most good *endek* is manufactured in Gianyar, Sideman and Bubunan on Bali, as well as in Cakrenegara on the neighbouring island of Lombok.

One of the masterpieces of Balinese crafts-manship is the double-*ikat* cloth known as *geringsing*, woven only in the eastern village of Tenganan Pegeringsing. A double *ikat* means that both the warp and weft threads are tied and dyed before being woven. The weaving requires a special skill. It is difficult to maintain the tension in the threads while they are on the loom so that they become properly aligned and the correct pattern emerges. There are only two other places in the world – Japan and India – where double *ikat* is woven.

The beautiful muted colours of these cloths, with groups of geometrical or floral patterns,

are produced by dyeing them with indigo and morinda, which produces a reddish-brown colour. It has been claimed, and refuted, that formerly the blood of a human sacrifice was used to produce the red colour.

The *geringsing* are of particular interest and importance because they are considered sacred. The word *geringsing* means "without sickness". It is widely believed that they have the power to protect the wearer against both earthly and supernatural enemies. They are used throughout Bali at religious ceremonies such as cremations and tooth filings.

Songket, a brocade cloth with threads of gold or silver forming the floating weft, is popular for ceremonial and special occasions. In the past, *songket* could only be woven by women of the brahman caste and by aristocrats. Although this rule no longer applies, the main centres of *songket* production today are to be found in the areas around the old courts.

Another decorative cloth, *prada*, is also widely used in Bali. Traditionally used by members of the royal family, they are cloths that have been decorated with gold leaf. Designs of flowers, birds and other motifs are first drawn on the cloth, and the outlined area coated with glue before the gold leaf is applied. Today, gold-coloured paint is more likely to be used to produce the design.

Silver and gold

Like so many Balinese crafts, working with silver and gold had its origins in the royal courts. Members of the royal family wore gold and silver headdresses, belts, bracelets, earrings, anklets, and necklaces to indicate their high status. Even the handles of daggers (*keris*) and umbrella finials would be made from gold. Lost-wax casting, repoussé, chasing and engraving were all used.

There are numerous workshops found in several places on Bali selling jewellery of different qualities. The village of Celuk, for example, is noted for its rings, bracelets, necklaces, pins and utilitarian objects of silver. The village of Kamasan (*mas* means gold) remains the centre for the traditional production of gold and silver. It produces silver ritual vessels, amulets, and *keris* handles of gold or silver studded with semi-precious stones, as well as silver and gold figures of deities. Some workshops employ up to 300 workers to produce the huge quantities of gold- and silverwork for the tourist and international markets.

The Balinese are very quick to pick up on introduced ideas and copy things that they know will sell. More imaginative smiths are beginning to copy designs from magazines or from international jewellery designers who have now settled in Bali to work. It is also possible to find quality copies and designs derived from Western and Art Deco jewellery, as well as Art Nouveau styles. ❑

LEFT: eastern Balinese court wear of *songket*.
RIGHT: the difficult-to-produce *geringsing* cloth is made in only three places in the world, including Bali.

THE EPHEMERAL ARTS OF FESTIVALS

Consecrated offerings made of food, flowers and palm-leaf figures are essential to the numerous religious rituals that are performed in Bali.

Hindu Dharma, the religion of Bali, is a fusion of Hinduism, animism and ancestor worship. Deified ancestors, deities of fertility and the natural world are worshiped along with the Hindu trinity of Wisnu, Brahma and Siwa. The divine, however, is Sanghyang Widi Wasa, and all other gods are considered to be mere manifestations of him.

Hindu Dharma is founded on the Balinese system of cosmology that strives to maintain a balance, or harmony, between the cosmos, its divine principles and human existence. In consequence, gods and demons are worshiped equally and countless daily rituals are performed to maintain the cosmic balance. Religious life on the island thus revolves around sacrifices, offerings and purification ceremonies.

The most common daily ritual is Sajen, in which a small tray containing offerings of cooked rice, flowers and salt left outside every house and sprinkled with holy water three times a day. Offerings presented to the gods are made from the abundance of the land. They are left to decay naturally or are sometimes taken home and eaten by the family who made them. While offerings made to demons or evil spirits are left on the ground, those to gods are put on high altars and incense is used to carry the offering upwards to the heavens.

◁ **EPHEMERAL ART**
Offerings are made from natural materials. After they have served their ceremonial purpose they are left to decay.

△ **BABANGKIT**
*Babangkit,*made from dye rice dough supported by bamboo-and-cloth framework, symbolise the Balinese mythic world.

◁ CEREMONIAL OFFERINGS
Offerings are an essential part of religious ceremonies and festivals. In this cremation procession, *lamark* are held high among decorated parasols.

△ WEDDING *LAMARK*
Lamark (decorated mats) are woven from banana leaves. The geometric design of a woman in the centre is representative of the rice goddess Dewi Sri.

DEATH RITES
e base of a cremation
wer is shaped like a turtle
twined with two *nagas*
nakes) – symbolic of the
undation of the world.

▷ **GENDER DIVIDE**
Most offerings are made by women using plant materials. Offerings made by men use meat and represent the animal kingdom.

▷ *GEBOGAN*
Gebogan – fruit, flowers and rice cakes on a banana tree trunk frame – are presented to deities at *odalan* festivals.

BALINESE GODS AND GODDESSES

BRAHMA, Saraswati's husband, is ruler of five southern rivers. His symbolic colour is red.

DEWI SRI is Wisnu's consort. She is the Goddess of Agriculture, ruler of plants and trees, and the revered rice goddess who brings the rain and appears in dreams to give advice.

KALI is the wife of Siwa and the Goddess of Time. She is a manifestation of the Goddess of Death and is also the Goddess of Magic and Love Potions and of Wealth.

SARASWATI is the Goddess of books, knowledge and learning, her domain is *bayu* (action and learning)

SIWA is God of the Mountains of the East. Working with him is Dewi Uma, the Goddess of Meditation and Modesty.

WARUNA is the God of Wind. He rules the west and is associated with the colour yellow.

WISNU is the God of the North. He flies on Garuda. His colour is black or indigo.

YAMA-RAJA is the God of Judgement who is often depicted as a hideous monster.

THE FOOD OF BALI

*The fertility of Bali's soil assures that one's taste buds are never lacking
in challenges or surprises, whether of fish, fruit, meat, or vegetable*

Paradoxically, it is not easy for the visitor to find genuine Balinese cuisine, for the restaurants, food stalls and mobile food vendors generally offer pan-Indonesian or Indonesian-Chinese food. And then there are the countless restaurants in the main tourism areas featuring an astonishing array of international cuisine, from East-West fusion to Japanese to authentic American fast-food. But it's well worth tracking down the true tastes of Bali, found in some of the market stalls (especially on the big market day) and roadside *warung*, and even in a handful of chic restaurants that have begun to realise that adventurous visitors actually want to try authentic Balinese cuisine.

The balmy tropical climate and occasional layering of volcanic ash that enriches the soil give Bali a superb range of fruits and vegetables, not to mention several varieties of rice. And it's not just tropical produce. Up in the cool hills, temperate-climate vegetables such as carrots and cabbage are grown. Everything from coffee to cloves, cardamom to corn, and grapes to guavas can be found in this fertile land, while fiery hot chillies and vegetables are frequently planted between the paddy fields.

As with the rest of Indonesia, Balinese food has been influenced by centuries of foreign trade and by Dutch colonialism. Many of the spices and seasonings used to flavour Balinese cuisine were introduced, including the now ubiquitous chilli (brought to Asia by the Portuguese and Spanish in the 16th century). The Chinese, who traded and eventually settled in Bali as elsewhere in Indonesia, have also influenced the food, with noodles, soy sauce, bean sprouts, and beancurd prominent contributions.

Seasonings

Spices, herbs and a range of other seasonings give excitingly different flavours to meat, poultry, fish and vegetable dishes. A heady citrus fragrance is provided by fresh lime juice

(especially from the distinctive *lemo Bali*), kaffir lime leaf and lemon grass. Ginger and its relatives – the bright yellow turmeric, laos and camphor-scented rhizome known as *kencur* – go hand in hand with purplish shallots and garlic, pounded to a paste with chillies that range from the plump little fiery *tabia bun* to long, slender chillies. A distinctive tang is provided by dried shrimp paste, while the sweetness of palm sugar is often offset by the sour fragrance of tamarind juice.

Popular herbs include fresh basil, the fragrant screwpine, and *daun salam*, a long leaf that looks like a bay leaf but has a taste all its own. When it comes to dried spices, the Balinese have a limited range compared, for example, to the West Sumatrans.

Apart from black and white peppercorns, the Balinese cook makes use of coriander, cinnamon and the occasional cardamom pod or grating of nutmeg. Candlenuts *(kemiri)* are often ground to give a rich flavour and texture to the

LEFT: fruit at the Bedugul market. **RIGHT:** highland produce for sale at Kintamani market.

spice paste or *basa genip*, which is the basis of so many dishes.

Although almost all these seasonings are found elsewhere in Indonesia, the way the Balinese combine them, and their cooking methods, make a distinctive difference. Like other Indonesian cooks, the Balinese use coconut milk squeezed from the grated flesh of a ripe nut to provide a sauce for many dishes. But by first roasting the chunks of coconut directly on hot coals, the Balinese add a wonderful, faintly smoky tang to their coconut milk.

The Balinese are sometimes said to be a bit like the Chinese, in that they'll eat anything

that flies except a plane and anything with legs except a table. And it is true that eels, snails and frogs from the paddy fields, along with dragonflies and various other exotica, sometimes appear on the Balinese table.

And because the poultry – especially the ducks, which have been marched off to the paddy fields each day to feed and fertilise the growing rice with nature's recycling system – is not usually tender, it is often minced with a cleaver before cooking, as are eels and even fish and prawns. One very popular way of cooking is to wrap minced and often highly seasoned meat, fish or poultry in banana leaf and steam it, or else set the packages directly onto hot coals to roast. Known as *tum*, these wonderful packages are served at most home-cooked Balinese meals.

Balinese food at home

Balinese meals are always based on rice, except for breakfast, which is generally a very simple affair in most homes. The housewife may come back from the market with a few sticky cakes, which will probably be eaten with fresh bananas and washed down with coffee or plain tea. Before the midday meal is enjoyed, offerings of a few grains of cooked rice, incense and flowers must be made to all the resident gods in the family compound. Once the gods have been fed, it's time for ordinary mortals to tuck in.

The rice will be accompanied by a range of vegetable dishes, with protein in the form of meat (pork is considerably more popular than beef), seafood or poultry. *Tempe,* a nutty slab made from fermented soy beans, is a delicious and inexpensive source of protein. Although these dishes will all be seasoned, additional heat is available for those who want in a chilli-based sambal or condiment.

There may also be diced mango or crunchy cucumber to provide a refreshing contrast, as well as something crisp such as deep-fried *krupuk* (wafers made from tapioca flour with fish, prawns, vegetables or even *melinjo* nuts) or *rempeyek* (deep-fried rice-flour batter seasoned with tiny dried anchovies or peanuts). One dish will probably contain the thick, sweet soy sauce found everywhere in Indonesia, so that taken overall, the meal will have a fantastic range of flavours (sweet, sour, hot, spicy, fragrant) as well as textures.

Evening meals are usually composed of

BABI GULING

The best-known Balinese dish is spit-roasted suckling pig, known as *guling celeng,* or by its Indonesian name, *babi guling.* The inside is stuffed with a mixture of chopped herbs and spices, and the skin is anointed with diluted turmeric juice before the piglet is roasted over charcoal. A full meal will include tender flesh and portions of crisp skin; a few slices of spicy sausage made from the intestines stuffed with seasoned meat; some spicy coconut milk gravy; and *lawar,* an intricate mixture of pounded raw pork, a touch of pig's blood, steamed vegetable and seasonings. Add steamed rice and a vegetable dish of young jackfruit *(nangka).*

whatever was left over from midday, served with rice and another dish or two – perhaps an omelette or some fried noodles. Dishes that Westerners might regard as dessert, such as black rice pudding and rice-flour dumplings in a sweet coconut sauce, are eaten as a between-meal snack by the Balinese.

What to look for

Probably the best-known Balinese dish is *babi guling*, or suckling pig. *(See box on opposite page.)* Also very popular with visitors but generally reserved for festivals by the Balinese themselves, *bebek betutu* is duck rubbed inside and out with a mixture of fragrant herbs, spices and chillies before being wrapped in banana leaf and steamed. Once the duck is tender, the package is put over charcoal to impart a faint barbecue flavour. Many restaurants will prepare this dish given advance notice.

Saté elsewhere in Indonesia consists of morsels of meat or poultry threaded on skewers and cooked over charcoal, served with sweet soy-sauce *sambal* enlivened with sliced chilli. A Balinese version, *saté lilit*, is more sophisticated and infinitely more delicious, consisting of finely minced fish and prawns mixed with pounded herbs and spices, and with plenty of freshly grated coconut. If this pounded mixture is wrapped around sticks of fresh lemon grass rather than the normal skewers, the result is positively ambrosial.

Too sensible to waste anything that nature provides, the Balinese use the tender heart of the banana stem as a vegetable, generally cooking it in a spicy chicken stock to make *jukut ares*. Unripe papaya is also used to make a spicy soup, although in Bali the soups are not drunk as a separate course but are enjoyed together with rice and other dishes, the liquid helping to "wash down the rice".

One of the most common fish found in Balinese waters is tuna, which is often transformed into a spicy salad. Steaks of tuna covered with a cooked sambal of chilli, garlic, shallots, turmeric, ginger and other seasonings are fried. The fish is then flaked and mixed with a fresh sambal fragrant with lemon grass and kaffir lime leaves. The result, *sambal be tongkol*, will put you off tinned tuna for the rest of your life.

LEFT: hotels offer variations on local foods.
RIGHT: delicious *saté* on skewers.

Even simple grilled fish takes on a new flavour in Bali. Whole fish is seasoned with lime juice, salt and a tangy sambal before being roasted over charcoal and served with fresh tomato sambal. The most interesting vegetable dishes include young fern tips *(pakis)* with a dressing of garlic and *kencur*; young jackfruit simmered in spicy coconut milk and the tender leaves of the starfruit tree blanched and mixed with coconut milk and steamed minced beef. All types of leaves, from starfruit to young papaya, young tapioca to spinach, can be used for *jukut urab*; the leaves are blanched and mixed with beansprouts before being combined

with freshly grated coconut, chilli, garlic and a touch of dried shrimp paste.

One of the most refreshing dishes found in Bali is eaten as a snack rather than as part of a meal. Many simple roadside stalls or *warung* selling everything from cigarettes to soap powder signify that *rujak* is on the menu by the presence of a granite grinding slab and pestle, with a basket of unripe mangoes, papaya, pineapple, plus cucumber and perhaps some fresh yam bean nearby. Ask for a bowl of *rujak* and the *warung ibu* will start peeling and slicing the basic ingredients. Then a few hot bird's-eye chillies, a chunk of palm sugar and touch of roasted dried shrimp paste will be put onto the mortar and ground to a paste, with a little sour tamarind and salt added. If you don't want it too hot, ask the *ibu* to go easy on the chilli *(tidak mahu pedis)*. The result is mouth-puckeringly sour and sweet at the same time, as well as salty and spicy. Be forewarned the *rujak* is can be habit forming.

Sweet and sticky

Like other Indonesians, the Balinese have a sweet tooth and love to snack on cakes and dumplings, or on tiny finger bananas drenched in syrup or wallowing in sweetened coconut cream. Many visitors have discovered the

delights of black-rice pudding or *bubur injin*, in which a richly flavoured, purplish-black gluti-nous rice is simmered with white glutinous rice and fragrant screwpine leaves until it reaches the consistency of a porridge. It is then sweet-ened with palm sugar and served with thick coconut milk to make what is arguably the archipelago's most delicious breakfast or snack or dessert or midnight feast.

Since bananas are so abundant, it's not sur-prising to find them dipped in batter and deep fried, boiled and rolled in freshly grated coconut or simmered in coconut milk sweet-ened with palm sugar. Little dumplings of glutinous rice flour combined with tapioca

flour are cooked in a similar coconut milk sauce to make *jaja batun bedil*. Yet another variation on the glutinous rice theme is *wajik*, a substantial cake made by cooking the rice with water and fragrant screwpine before steaming it with palm sugar and coconut milk. The resulting sticky mixture is spread and cooled before being cut into chewy chunks.

Balinese drinks

You'll find plenty to quench your thirst in Bali, where it's a good idea to skip the usual carbonated drinks in favour of such local favourites as young coconut water *(kopyor)*, served with slivers of the tender coconut flesh and perhaps a few ice cubes. Another excellent option is *air jeruk*, which is juice squeezed from the local green-skinned oranges that have a completely different flavour to the navel oranges more common in the West. This is usually served with a liberal amount of sugar and can be enjoyed either hot *(panas)* or with ice *(es jeruk)*.

If you see a blender outside a stall or restau-rant, you'll know they're serving blended fruit drinks. These are much like the smoothies found in the West, and they generally consist of fresh fruit, ice and evaporated milk. How-ever, when you add palm sugar rather than bor-ing white sugar and use such fruits as soursop *(sirsak)*, avocado *(apokat)*, mango *(mangga)*, papaya *(pepaya)* and banana *(pisang)*, the resulting *es* will be incomparable in flavour.

Tea and coffee are normally served without milk but are laden with sugar unless you spec-ify that you want it *pahit*. Drinking the local coffee, which is made by stirring the grounds, sugar and boiling water in a tall glass, is an acquired art. You have to wait until the grounds of this *kopi tobruk* settle and then sip it cau-tiously, using your teeth as a strainer just in case any strange grounds are floating about. But the richly roasted flavour of the coffee makes it well worth the effort.

Should you want to relax over a drink at the end of the day, Balinese-style, you could try the sweet rice-wine or *brem*, or perhaps the fermented palm wine called *tuak*. You could, of course, have an Indonesian beer, but when in Bali, why not do as the Balinese do? ❑

LEFT: drinking the milk of a coconut. **RIGHT:** Bali's offerings of fruit are tropical and varied.

Fruits of Paradise

The colour and beauty of Bali are not confined to its landscapes, people and ceremonies. Even the fruits delight the eye and certainly the palate. The fruit can be mysterious, such as the crisp, cream-coloured *salak* fruit hiding within a snakeskin-like covering. Or it can be like the notorious *durian*, assailing the nostrils with such a powerful stench that they're banned from most hotels.

The better-known tropical fruits are found in Bali throughout the year. Of course, bananas come in an astonishing range of sizes, colours and flavours.

describe as discreet, the jackfruit has seeds covered by a firm yellow flesh with a delicious flavour that almost defies description. Pomelo, an excellent large citrus fruit with a very thick rind, is known here as *jeruk Bali*. Roughly heart-shaped and covered with a thin green bumpy skin, the soursop or *sirsak* has a perfect balance of sweetness and acidity and is often made into a juice. Also popular as a juice is the local passionfruit, or *markisa*, its greyish seeds covered with perfumed, translucent flesh.

Three popular seasonal fruits roughly the size of a golf ball include the *rambutan*, its furry red skin hiding a lychee-like white interior; the beige

Other year-round fruits include juicy pineapples and bright, orange-fleshed papayas, their flavour heightened with a squeeze of fresh lime juice. Mangoes drop from the trees during their season, and although you'll find them ripe in the markets, they, like both the papaya and pineapple, are often enjoyed unripe in the tart, spicy salad *rujak*.

Some of Bali's fruits are surprisingly large. The durian hides seeds covered with a creamy, ambrosial flesh inside a thick shell the size and shape of a spiky green football. Although the skin gives off an odour that newcomers generally find highly offensive, the flavour and texture of the flesh sends connoisseurs into ecstasy. Even larger in size and possessing a smell which no-one could

langsat with a delicious flavour hinting of grapefruit, and the mangosteen, with juicy white flesh inside hard purplish-black skin. The brownish, egg-shaped *sapodilla* or *sawo* has flesh that tastes of pears drenched in maple syrup, while the large green-skinned guavas (*jambu biji*) combine a mild flavour with a satisfyingly crunchy texture. Also favoured for their juiciness and crisp texture, several types of water apple or *jambu air* are eaten plain, dipped into soy sauce or mixed into a *rujak*. The five-edged starfruit simply drips with slightly astringent juice, while the creamy avocado, treated in Bali as a fruit rather than a vegetable, is frequently transformed into *es apokat*, one of the most delicious creamy fruit shakes imaginable. ❑

BALI

*A detailed guide to the island's destinations, with numbered
cross-references to detailed and comprehensive maps*

Bali is a magnet for the most consistently overused cliches to be
found in any bibliography of travel writing. Exquisite, seduc-
tive, mesmerising, enchanting, magical – these normally
expressive adjectives lose their power to convince after a while. It's
a writer's dilemma, this island of Bali, for these words are accurate
and to the point. Anything less seems inadequate.

The thinker who first said that great things come in small packages
must have been to Bali. A comparatively small parcel of an island –
one of over 17,000 in the world's largest archipelago – Bali reveals
an astonishing diversity in land and culture. Not only can you retreat
into a truly idyllic setting, but you can seek out centres of exquisite
arts, all of them with a solid tradition of quality and uniqueness.

Bali's social cohesion is derived from deities and history, and from
rice. The cultivation of rice defines the distinct community and the
collection of communities that make up Bali. More important,
maybe, has been the communal sharing of irrigation water – and the
social cooperation necessary to do so – for the growing of rice.

Bali's terraces of rice are not the visitor's first impression, however. The international airport is in the extreme south, and southern
Bali – the regency of Badung, one of eight – is urban, commercial
Bali. This is where ritual tanning, playing and partying amongst
visitors are to be found, most often in Sanur or Kuta. This is not to
imply the area is not without redemption, for beneath the blatant
commercialisation are some of Bali's most ancient and traditional
undercurrents.

Inland to the north in the regencies of Tabanan, Gianyar and
Bangli, the contours become softer, the villages smaller, and the culture more unfettered. Eastward, in the regencies of Klungkung and
Karangasem, was much of Bali's traditional power. Together, central
and eastern Bali are centres of art and performing art. A modern traveller must intentionally go out of the way not to encounter dance-
drama, *gamelan,* painting and woodcarving.

Anchoring the island spiritually, culturally and geographically are
three volcanic peaks in the north: Agung, Batur and Batukau. The
mountains are holy and the source of all water. The northern coast of
Bali, the regency of Buleleng, is dry and agricultural, growing everything from cinnamon to wine grapes. Western Bali – the regency of
Jembrana and part of Buleleng – is sometimes dry, sometimes lush,
but it is typically ignored by travellers, unfortunately. A national park,
the last refuge of several endangered species, graces the west. ❏

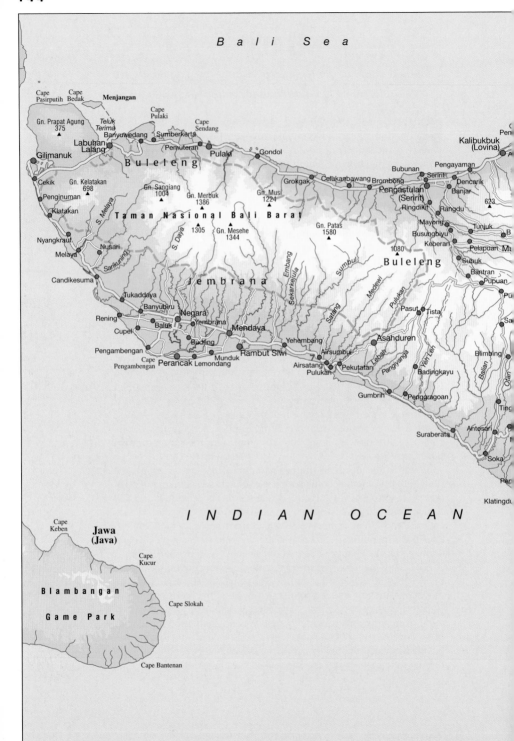

B a l i   S e a

Cape Pasirputih
Cape Bedak
Menjangan
Cape Pulaki
Cape Sendang

Gn. Prapat Agung
375
Teluk Terima
Banyuwedang
Sumberkerta
Pemuteran
Pulaki
Gondol
Kalibukbuk
(Lovina)
Pen

Labuhan Lalang

Gilimanuk

B u l e l e n g

Bubunan
Pengayaman

Celukanbawang
Brombong
Seririt
Dencarik

Cekik
Gn. Kelatakan
698
Gn. Sangiang
1004
Grokgak
Pengastulan
(Seririt)
Banjar

Penginuman
Gn. Merbuk
1386
Gn. Musi
1224
Ringdikit
Rangdu
623

Klatakan

S. Melaya
T a m a n   N a s i o n a l   B a l i   B a r a t
Mayong
Tunjuk
B

1305
Gn. Mesehe
1344
Gn. Patas
1580
Busungbiyu

Nyangkraut
S. Daya
Keberan

Nusari
Pelapuan
Mt

Melaya
Sankuning
1080
B u l e l e n g
Subuk

Candikesuma
J e m b r a n a
Embang
Sumbul
Bantran

Pupuan
Pu

Tukaddaya
Sekarkejula
Medewi
Pulukan
Pasut
Tista
Sa

Banyubiru
Negara
Satang
Asahduren
Blimbing

Rening
Baluk
Yembrana
Mendaya
Yehembang
Lebah
Yeh Leh
Ballan

Cupel
Budeng
Airsumbul
Pangiyanga
Badingkayu
Otan
Tin

Pengambengan
Munduk
Rambut Slwi
Airsatang
Pulukan
Pekutatan

Cape Pengambengan
Perancak
Lemondang
Gumbrih
Penggragoan

Suraberata
Antosari

Soka
Per

Klatingdu

I N D I A N   O C E A N

Cape Keben
Jawa (Java)
Cape Kucur

B l a m b a n g a n
Cape Slokah

G a m e   P a r k

Cape Bantenan

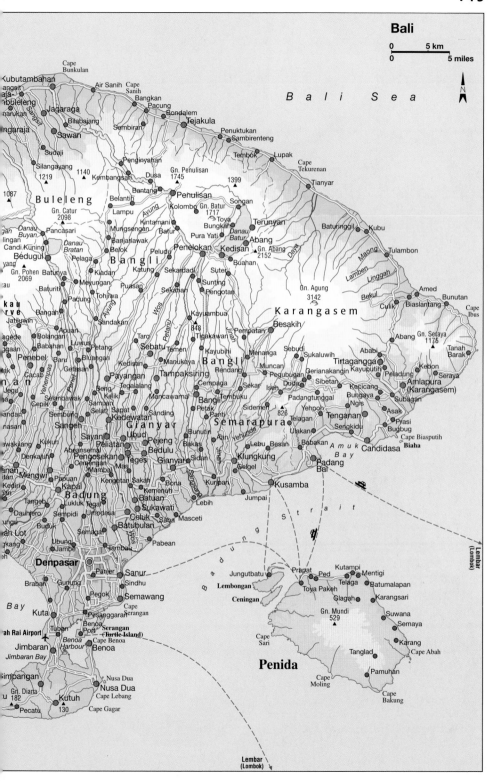

Bali

0   5 km
0   5 miles

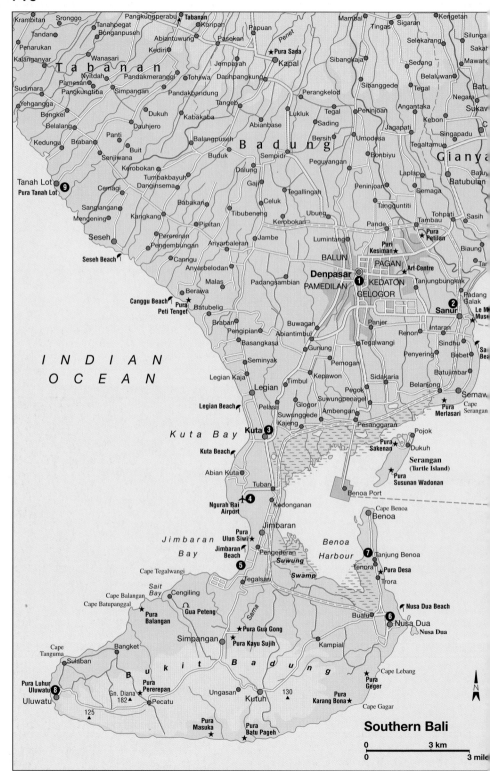

Krambitan Sronggo Pangkungperabu **Tabanan** Mambal Sigaran Kengetan
Tanahpegat Koripan Papuan Tingas Selekarang Silunga
Tandan Bonganpuseh Abiantuwung Pasekan Penet Sakah
Penarukan Kediri ★ Pura Sada Sibangkaja Sedang Mawang
Kalanganyar Wanasari Jempayah **Kapal** Belaluwan
T a b a n a n Nyitdah Tohjiwa Dauhpangkung Sibanggede Tegal Bat
Pamesan Pandakmeranggi Perangkelod Negara
Sudimara Pangkungtiba Simpangan Pandakbandung Tangeb Tegal Peninjoan Angantaka Sukav
Yehgangga Lukluk Kebon
Bengkel Dukuh Kabakaba Sading Jagapati Singapadu
Belalang Dauhjero Abianbase Bersih Umodesa Tegaltamu
Kedungu Braban Panti Buit Balangpuseh **B a d u n g** Bonbiyu **G i a n y a**
Senjiwana Buduk Sempidi Peguyangan Laplap Bajuy
Kerobokan Dalung Peninjoan Semaga Batubulan
Tanah Lot **9** Tumbakbayuh Gaji Tegallingah Tangguntiti Tohpati Sasih
Pura Tanah Lot Danginsema Celuk Ubung Pande Tambau ★ Pura
Cemagi Babakan Tibeneng Kerobokan Petilan
Sanglangan Pipitan Jambe Lumintang Biaung
Mendening Kangkang **Pura** Tar
Seseh Pererenan Anyarbaleran **Kesiman** ★
Pengembungan **BALUN** **PAGAN** Art Centre
Seseh Beach Canngu Anyarbelodan **Denpasar** **KEDATON** Tanjungbungkak
Malas Padangsambian **1** Padang
Berawa **PAMEDILAN** **GELOGOR** **2** Galak
Canggu Beach Pura Batubelig Buwagan Panjer **Sanur** Le M
Peti Tenget Braban Abiantimbul Renon Intaran Muse
Pengipian Basangkasa Gunung Tegalwangi Sindhu
Seminyak Pemogan Penyering Bebet Sa
Legian Kaja Kepawon Sidakaria Batujimbar Bea

I N D I A N Timbul
O C E A N **Legian** Pegok Belanjong Semaw
Pelasa Glogor Suwungpenagel **Pura** Cape
Legian Beach Ambengan **Merlasari** Serangan
Kajeng Suwunggede Pesanggaran
K u t a   B a y **Kuta 3** Pojok
Kuta Beach **Pura** Dukuh
Sakenan ★
Abian Kuta **Serangan**
Tuban (Turtle Island)
Benoa Port **Pura**
Ngurah Rai **4** Kedonganan **Susunan Wadonan**
Airport Cape Benoa
Jimbaran Benoa
J i m b a r a n Pura **B e n o a**
B a y Ulun Siwi ★ **Harbour** **7** Tanjung Benoa
Jimbaran Pengederan Tenora Pura Desa
Beach **5** **Suwung** Trora
Tegalsari **Swamp**
Sait Cengiling **Sama** Bualu ★ Nusa Dua Beach
Cape Balangan **Bay** Gua Peteng **6**
Cape Batupanggal Pura ★ Pura Gua Gong Nusa Dua
Balangan Simpangan ★ Pura Kayu Sujih Nusa Dua
Cape Bangket Kampial
Tanguma Sulaban **B u k i t   B a d u n g** Cape Lebang
Pura Luhur B Pura Pura
Uluwatu **8** Gn. Diana Pererepan Ungasan 130 Geger
Uluwatu 182▲ Pecatu **Kutuh** Pura Cape Gagar
125 Karang Bona ★
Pura Pura **Southern Bali**
Masuka Batu Pageh
★ ★ 0   3 km
0   3 mile

BADUNG: THE SOUTH

Maps on pages 148, 151

alinese cosmology considers south to be the most impure direction.
Yet it is the southern part of Bali where most travellers end up, and
where the infrastructure and commercialism are most developed

While the ambiance of Denpasar is that of a small city, the mood changes at the approach to Bali's tourist centres of Sanur, Nusa Dua and Kuta. Routine office-block facades give way to signs advertising hotels and ur operators, while droves of batik-clad tourists buzz by on motorbikes.

The development of southern Bali has generated endless squabbles and pos-ring, both amongst Balinese and foreigners, but the burgeoning development f the past 10 years now caters to every imaginable persuasion, whether it's eing pampered in a five-star spa or hurtling through the air on the end of a ungee. While the area's *leitmotif* – bustling beaches by day and non-stop bar-opping and dancing after hours – can prove frenetic, this part of Bali is with-ut doubt an intoxicating chameleon.

Throughout the island's history, southern Bali (together with the northern aports in Buleleng) has always been the first to welcome, or repel, outsiders. t Belanjong, at the corner of the turn-off to the Parkroyal Hotel, an inscription ngraved on a short pillar commemorates the victories of Sri Kesari War-adewa, Bali's first king, over his enemies in AD 913. In later times, famous riests from Java trod these shores. Empu Kuturan came to Bali in the 10th ntury and introduced the *meru,* or roofed shrine.

he three best-known temples of the area – Pura Sak-an, Pura Luhur Uluwatu, and Pura Petitenget at erobokan – are associated with the itinerant 16th-entury priest Danghyang Nirartha, also known as edanda Sakti Wawu Rauh. This eminent teacher rought the concept of the lotus throne, or *pad-asana,* for the worship of Sanghyang Widi Wasa, e Balinese supreme deity.

And it was at about this time that Bali's exposure to e West began. Many sailors from the fleet of the utch explorer Cornelis de Houtman were so ntranced by the island that they jumped ship to stay rever, starting a trend that has continued more or ss to this day.

enpasar

growing metropolis approaching half a million peo-e, **Denpasar ❶** (originally called Badung) is a busy ty of winding alleys, illogical one-way streets, pun-ent smells, and home to more cars per capita than akarta, Indonesia's capital. If your mind has been nwinding on the beach, it may well be rolled back up gain on an excursion into Denpasar. Yet there are ore than a few jewels to be found in this capital city. arking is easy, and most of the city's main sights are ithin a short hop of each other. Central to the city is **aman Puputan Ⓐ** (**Puputan Square,** and some-

PRECEDING PAGES: the fun life in Kuta. **BELOW:** statue at Puputan Square.

times called Alun-Alun Puputan), a large, grassy open space commemorating th
battle between the raja of the Badung regency and the Dutch militia in 1906
when thousands of Balinese warriors, dressed in their finest traditional regalia an
armed only with *keris* and spears hurled themselves against the line of Dutch so
diers in a tragically heroic sacrifice, dying either by their own hands or by Dutc
bullets in a Balinese ritual known as *puputan* (literally, "end"). Today, the slaugh
ter of the estimated 600 to 2,000 who died is remembered with the large bronz
statue of an adult and two children going to battle armed with bamboo stave:
spears and *keris*. West of the square is the bureaucratically styled national mili
tary complex. On the northern side is the former residence of the island's gov
ernor, used today as his guest house. The raja's palace once stood on this site

On the east side of the square is the attractive **Bali Museum** Ⓑ (open dail
except Monday, 8am–5pm; admission fee). Built in the early 1930s by th
Dutch government, it presents a comprehensive history of Bali's social and cu
tural development from prehistoric times to the early 20th century. Items are we
presented, although no specific dates of origin are given, but knowledgeabl
English-speaking guides are on hand. The museum is spread throughout tw
buildings. Begin with the Gedung Timur (Timur Pavilion) rooms, which consi
of prehistoric implements such as Neolithic stone implements, Bronze Age sa
cophagi, and Buddhist and Hindu bronzes. The display continues with a fin
variety of implements for hunting, gathering, and farming. Look out for th
charmingly ornate carrying cases for fighting cocks and crickets. There are als
beautifully carved antique doors, pillars, and gargoyles.

The Gedung Buleleng building is adorned with some beautiful examples c
wedding costumes, along with items used in Bali's religious rituals, such a

BELOW: exterior image at the Bali Museum.

oth-filing ceremonies, as well as ceremonial masks and *ukur,* which are human figies made from silver and Chinese coins and used in death rituals. (Cheap iitations are sometimes offered to tourists as antiques.) The museum is also otable for its fine architecture, which combines the two principal edifices in ali: the temple and the palace. The split gate, the outer and inner courtyards, id *kulkul* (signal drum) tower are characteristic of Bali's temples. Opposite the useum stands a raised pavilion, once used by a prince as a lookout for viewg his lands.

The main building, with its wide-pillared veranda, resembles the Karangasem laces of eastern Bali, where the porch would have been used by ministers id officials who had an audience with the raja. The windowless building on the ght reflects the Tabanan palace style of western Bali, while the brick building the left belongs to the northern palace style of Singaraja, making the museum presentative of the entire island.

Pura Jagatnata.

Next to the museum is **Pura Jagatnata G**, a state temple where young peoe go to worship every full and new moon. This modern temple is dedicated to anghyang Widi Wasa, the supreme god (in contrast to Bali's numerous local eities or to ancestral spirits). The tall padmasana, constructed of white coral, mbolises universal order. The turtle Bedawangnala and two *naga* serpents present the foundation of the world while the towering throne signifies the ceding heavens. *(See page 24.)* This design, so prevalent on the island, relates the Hindu myth of the churning sea of milk, when the gods and the demons irred the cosmic ocean to create the nectar of immortality. Festivals held here e usually boisterous affairs, with hordes of worshippers, announcements blarg from loudspeakers, and the atmosphere of a day's holiday celebration.

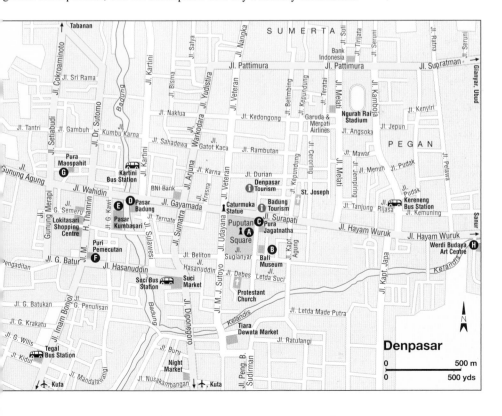

Catur Mukha, the great statue with four faces and eight arms in the middl of Denpasar's main intersection (at the northwestern corner of Taman Puputan represents Siwa manifesting himself as the lords of the four directions. It wa erected in 1972 as a secular monument to commemorate the puputan, althoug its imagery symbolises Hindu concepts. Don't be tempted into joining one of th hovering "guides" on their broken-English tours; their fee is better spent in th temple donation box.

Western Denpasar

At the centre of town is Pasar Badung **Ⓓ** (*den pasar* means market). While th four-storey building is under repair after a fire in 2000, Bali's largest tradition: market is scattered around inside. Locals shop here for fruit and vegetable: meat and seafood, clothing, spices, ritual paraphernalia, bamboo cooking uter sils, and pretty much everything else. Persistent women offer tours through th maze of wares for a negotiable fee, stopping off at shops where they earn commission from your purchases.

Across the small canal known as Tukad Badung is **Pasar Kumbasari Ⓔ**, market with kiosks jammed with clothes, woodcarvings and handicrafts, sma eateries, and cinemas on the fourth floor showing movies with alluring title such as *Sex Slave*.

Denpasar does not sport any grand hotels, but there are numerous small hote here. A hotel of historical note, on Jalan Thamrin, is **Puri Pemecutan Ⓕ**, renovated palace. At the turn of the century, much of it was destroyed in battle with the Dutch, during which the Balinese royalty here committed puputan, th ritualistic mass suicide. The hotel of losmen-style rooms follows the design c

BELOW: downtown Denpasar.

oyal residences of the old Badung kingdom, and this unique – but uninspiring
- accommodation comes with gratis mosquitoes and several noisy caged birds.
However, its central location is convenient, and it does offer some peace and
quiet from the commotion beyond its high walls.

Nightlife in Denpasar revolves around the three markets at the Kumbasari
shopping centre, the Kereneng bus station cum market, and the Pasar Malam
Pekambinan, just off Jalan Diponegoro and in front of the Kertawijaya shopping
centre. Here one can find all sorts of cooked foods for sale next to hawkers
pushing snake oil and charms, as well as the ubiquitous T-shirts and sandals. For
those craving modern conveniences, there are modern shopping centres.

An interesting temple is **Pura Maospahit G** on Jalan Sutomo, notable for
being the oldest temple in the city. It dates from the 14th century, when emis-
aries from the Majapahit empire arrived from Java. Extensive earthquake damage in the early part of the 20th century resulted in much of the temple since
being rebuilt; the section at the back is the only part that has remained unaltered
for 600 years.

Map
on page
151

*Exhibit in the Werdi
Budaya Art Centre.*

Eastern Denpasar

A permanent exhibition of modern traditional and contemporary Balinese visual
arts can be seen at the **Werdi Budaya Art Centre H** (open Tuesday–Sunday,
8am–5pm; admission fee), to the east of downtown and on Jalan Nusa Indah.
Each of Bali's numerous visual arts disciplines are represented at this large
complex, including painting, woodcarving, shadow puppetry, silverwork, weaving, Barong and Rangda dance costumes, and even some remarkable ivory
carving. There is an excellent portrait of Bali's most famous painter, I Gusti

BELOW: Werdi
Budaya Art Centre.

BELOW: lobby of the Bali Hyatt, Sanur.

Nyoman Lempad, done by I Gusti Bagus Wijaya and which wonderfully com bines the artists' two styles, as well as some examples of works by Bali's for eign artists. The art centre was established in 1973 to showcase Balinese culture and it includes teaching facilities, a restaurant, craft shop and a superb outdoo performance facility where *kecak* dances are staged daily at 6.30pm. Th grounds are also home to the Pesta Seni, or Bali Art Festival, every year i June for a month, when traditional music, dance, art exhibitions, cultural com petitions and sales of foodstuffs, hand-loomed fabrics and local handicraft highlight the best of Bali's talents.

At the northern end of the same road is the **Sekolah Tinggi Seni Indonesi** (STSI), the College of Indonesian Arts. Since 1967, students here have bee studying traditional dance, music and puppetry, and choreographing both clas sical and contemporary performing arts. Visitors are welcome to watch classe with prior approval from the school's secretary (tel: 273-160). For the seriou student of Balinese culture, the nearby Pusat Dokumentasi (Documentatio Centre) offers a collection of works in all languages on Balinese life and cul ture. Documents may not be taken out, but they can be photocopied on th premises. Adjacent is the Pusat Budaya (Culture Centre). Both centres ar located at Jalan Ir. Juanda.

Sanur

In l906, a Chinese schooner wrecked off the shores of **Sanur ❷**. Local traditio maintained that shipwrecks were bounty from Baruna, god of the sea, and thu anyone had rights to it. This was, in fact, a breach of a previous treaty betwee the Balinese and the Dutch, and pillaging shipwrecks was the excuse the Dutc

Maps
on pages
148, 155

...eeded to wage war against the raja of Badung. Rather than continue fighting against the better-equipped Dutch forces, the king and his entire entourage, dressed in white and carrying daggers, walked straight into the gunfire of the Dutch in the ritual suicide of puputan. Only one child survived the massacre.

Sanur was little more than a tucked-away beach in the 1930s, with barely a hotel to its name, that attracted modest interest from artists around the world. By the 1950s, the first cluster of bungalows in Sanur had been built, attracting international travellers. The Grand Bali Beach Hotel, a Soekarno-era project and something of an eyesore, was opened in 1966, built with Japanese reparation money for World War II. When the nine-storey hotel first opened, it was a source of wonder to the Balinese, with its running water, electricity and elevators. Bali's only high-rise structure at the time, it burned to the ground in 1992 but was rebuilt and reopened less than two years later.

Meanwhile, other hotels have followed in its wake, so that today the beach front is lined by accommodation, with access roads lined by kiosks selling tourist schlock. A wise government regulation forbidding buildings taller than a coconut palm (15 metres/50 ft) has allowed Sanur to retain its modest character. But while the rule remains on the books, new construction seems to have found creative ways around the law.

Sanur's waters are calm and shallow, disappearing altogether at low tide and leaving little more than great swathes of sandy mud and coral stretch for hundreds of metres out into the reef. When the tides are high, however, Sanur offers windsurfing and sailing, along with the numbing drone of Jetskis. The sybaritic if not romantic traveller can soak up the high seas on board a catamaran or Bugis schooner while enjoying a sumptuous seafood buffet.

BELOW: kite hawker on the beach.

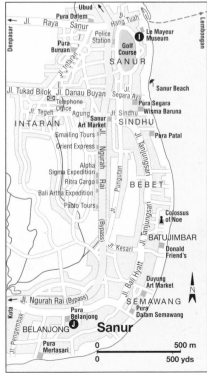

BELOW: busy street of downtown Kuta.

Amidst this development and tourism frenzy, Sanur has remarkably managed to retain much of its heritage as a Brahman-dominated village *(brahman kuasa)*, where trance performances are still staged during local temple festivals.

There are only a few historical sights in Sanur. The one surviving home from the aesthetic exploratory years of the 1930s is that of the Belgian painter Jean Le Mayeur de Mepres, who moved to Bali in 1932 and lived here for 26 years. He died in 1958. The **Museum Le Mayeur ❶** (open Tuesday–Friday, 8–11am; weekends 8am–2pm; admission fee), just north of the Bali Beach Hotel, offers gardens full of statues, luxuriant gold and crimson carvings, and Le Mayeur's own paintings, many of his late wife, Ni Polok, a renowned *legong* dancer.

Sanur has several temples to search out. At the southern end of Sanur is the **Pura Belanjong ❷**, notable as home to the island's oldest example of writing, the Prasasti Belanjong, an inscribed pillar dating from AD 913 and found in the early 1930s. The 177-cm-tall (70-inch) stone pillar is not much to look at, but close inspection reveals two forms of writing, an ancient Balinese language and a Sanskreta language. **Pura Segara** is the most unusual temple with its mounds of black rock and coral, and its brightly painted statues also made of coral. The restaurant at the front serves good Chinese-style seafood, along with Indonesian and international dishes in an idyllic beachside setting. Profits from the restaurant go back to the community.

For shopping, Sanur's beach-side shops offer the standard fare, while the Kita Bookshop in Batujimbar sells magazines and newspapers from around the world and has a good collection of books on Indonesian culture at decent market prices. Next door is Bali's most famous ceramics store, Bari Sumi; its ceramics are used at numerous hotels around the island.

Kuta and surroundings

Very few visitors to **Kuta** ❸ nowadays pause to consider that in former times it was both a leper colony and slaving station with poor soil, though cynics might suggest that there are parallels to be drawn in the hordes who flock to this tourism enclave for the heady combination of sun, sand, sea and various other -words. For many, Bali is at its best here, a veritable Saturnalia of pleasures, while others decry its plunge into rampant commercialism. But as long as the pleasure seekers are happy, and the ladies who work on **Kuta Beach** ❻ continue to leave *canang* – tiny banana-leaf tray offerings – at the high-tide mark each day to pacify the spirits, Kuta seems to embrace the best of both worlds.

Both Balinese and foreigners can be found along its gray sand day after day, surfing and sunbathing and strutting. Thatched beach bars quench thirsty throats, parched from saying no to the countless touts. Older women offering nail painting, hair braiding and massages huddle beneath umbrellas and trees. The waters off Kuta are among the best places to learn surfing. However, it is said the goddess of the sea claims at least one victim each year here. Still, if one stares out to sea and forgets the commercial swirl behind, the sunset is just as fine as it was a century ago.

The original villagers of Kuta were farmers, fishermen and metalsmiths. At the genesis of mass tourism, they looked askance at nearly naked foreigners romping on the beach, which traditionally fronted the ocean and the Balinese idea of the underworld. But they saw profits to be made and so invited travellers into their homes for clean, simple and cheap accommodation.

Inland from the beach, Kuta now is packed with a dazzling jumble of pubs, bars, souvenir shops, tattoo parlours, travel offices, accommodation, and fast-

Maps on pages 148, 158

BELOW: Kuta Beach.

food joints. Unregulated street-hawkers are an increasing annoyance in Kuta. The commercialism is stunning and annoying at the same time, but someone's buying this flotsam. Besides, the prices are pretty incredible and some of the shops have definitely gone up-market with their goods. Handmade Balinese lace, incense, soaps, antiques, artefacts (and their fakes), woven bags and dubious fashion items are all enticingly cheap. Australian surf culture has also taken a firm grip, as evidenced by the proliferation of surf shops. And nestled amidst all of this are a number of superb restaurants and bungalows, somehow retaining their dignity. Crime has escalated in Kuta, too, and this once peaceful village is now punctuated by drugs, prostitution and muggings. Don't get too starry-eyed and romantic on the dark beach at night.

Along Jalan Melasti and Jalan Legian, the shops continue unabated for more than a kilometre. At the bottom of Jalan Legian is the Gapinsia Trade Centre, an orderly stretch lined with palms, designer shops and American fast-food places busy with tourists and Balinese alike. It also sports the Matahari department store, a great attraction for the local youth. At the back is the "art market", undeniably a generous moniker for two long stretches of stalls selling all the usual tie-dye and batik fabrics, surf gear, and T-shirts, as well as other things of interest only to tourists. Prepare your bargaining skills. Down Jalan Kartika is **Waterbom Park ❶** (open daily 9am–6pm; admission fee) with water slides, restaurant and decent spa treatments. For demented sophisticated travellers there is Le Speed Karts, with go-karts.

Heading back into town, seek out **Pasar Senggol ❷**, the night market. This courtyard of hawker stalls is a favourite with budget travellers who come for the satay, noodles, soup and the chance to select a fish and have it cooked to

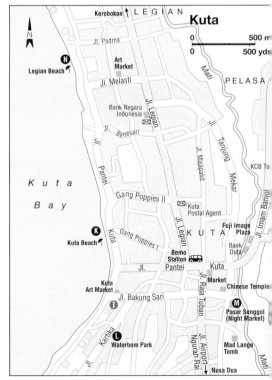

Map
on page
158

rder, at perhaps the best prices in town. Kuta's **Tourist Office** is at Jalan Benasari and is open until 8pm. Down the hall is the **Bali Hotel Reservation Service** for those without accommodation, but it is rarely staffed. The Legian Medical Clinic is next door, as is an *apotik* (chemist).

Head north up Jalan Legian to experience the loud obnoxious chaos of Kuta dropping off, replaced by a more cultivated beach scene with strong leanings towards new-age holistics. Even the surf culture seems more refined here. Lovely **Legian Beach**  is a centre of activity, preferably performed in a tie-dye G-string. Although Legian Beach is undoubtedly more sedate than Kuta, don't expect to be completely free of hawkers. This is also the preferred beach for Bali's enormous expatriate population, with more than a few ageing characters from the long-lost Summer of Love in Legian. Their admirable influence can be seen throughout Legian in boutiques specialising in the use of sustainable resources and the number of excellent restaurants, cafes and bars.

Further north is the upcoming area of **Seminyak**. This once distant Kuta suburb is slowly merging with Legian, and exclusive hotels are increasingly appearing, such as the Legian and the Oberoi. If interested in buying some Balinese furniture to ship back home, this area is home to a dozen furniture manufacturers. Continue along Jalan Raya Seminyak to two right-hand turns, both of which lead to Denpasar. The second turn, at **Kerobokan**, is the faster and more direct route, at least until the proposed road further south is finished.

Outrigger prahu *for hire, southern Bali.*

Bukit Badung

Connected to the mainland by a low, narrow isthmus, the limestone tableland of **Bukit Badung**, a peninsula rising to just 200 metres (660 ft) above sea level, is

BELOW: Kuta *saté* vendor.

in striking contrast to the lusher Bali mainland. Cacti grow upon this arid land, with some parts of the peninsula used for grazing cattle. Good surfaced roads meander across Bukit Badung. Vantage spots along the peninsula's road afford breathtaking northern vistas of Bali rising to the peaks of distant volcanoes. This is also a beautiful spot to watch the sunset. (Plan ahead: it's one hour or more, depending upon traffic and distractions, from Sanur.)

Aircraft from all parts of the world swoop low over the sea here, bound for **Ngurah Rai International Airport** ❹, which is attractively laid out and designed along Balinese lines, although the queues at the immigration counter can be tiresomely long. Fixed-price taxis are plentiful and their drivers obliging, and you will soon be heading out past twin icons of late 20th-century Balinese tourism – a gigantic mythological statue and a sign advertising McDonalds. is about 10 km (6 miles) to Denpasar and 3 km (2 miles) to Kuta.

Bali's latest exclusive resort area is along the coast south of **Jimbaran** ❺, housing the Ritz-Carlton, Four Seasons and Inter-Continental, all in their own immaculately landscaped compounds but within easy reach of Jimbaran village and its justly celebrated seafood restaurants.

Nusa Dua ❻, on the northeast coast of Bukit Badung, is a slightly clinical paradise in a ribbon-wrapped package. A purpose-built luxury hotel complex sprawling in the middle of a coconut grove and alongside a white-sand beach, it caters decidedly to the upscale traveller, especially those seeking refuge from the pushy hawkers found elsewhere – they are banned from Nusa Dua, although they continue to importune at its edges. In many ways, Nusa Dua is thin on local ambiance, as it was built on unused land in a concerted effort by the government to separate the tourists from the locals' lifestyle.

Bali has three world-class and internationally acclaimed golf courses: in a volcanic caldera, along the sea and in the shadow of a sacred temple.

BELOW: Nusa Dua is known for golf and luxury hotels – and no hawkers.

Today a dozen luxury hotels wrap around the white-sand beaches, including the Grand Hyatt, Hilton, Sheraton Laguna, Sheraton Nusa Indah, Melia Bali, Club Med, Amanusa, Putri Bali, Nusa Dua Beach and Nikko Bali. As far as architecture is concerned, the best choice is Nusa Dua Beach Hotel, which has incorporated traditional Balinese elements into its basic design. Nusa Dua has a fabulous beach front of clear and calm water. A number of water sports are available here as well, including spectacular parasailing and, frustratingly and increasingly throughout Bali, noisy Jetskis.

For many years, the fishing village of **Tanjung Benoa** ❼, on a long peninsula off the northeast of Bukit Badung, was overlooked by hotel developers blinded by the obvious potential of Sanur, Kuta and Nusa Dua. This oversight has actually worked to the area's benefit. A new type of developer is now attracted to the area and is keen to retain its traditional and authentic Balinese village atmosphere. Led by properties such as Novotel's Coralia Benoa Beach, smaller hotels are being built with an emphasis on incorporating local building styles and materials. For its part, Tanjung Benoa offers an attractive stretch of white-sand beach, which, like Sanur, is susceptible to the tides. Although the village doesn't boast any grand sights, a walk north up the peninsula will satisfy exploratory urges as well as reveal a multicultural community from its decades as a trading centre, reflected in the Chinese and Muslim cemeteries and the Chinese, Muslim and Hindu temples. The morning market and giant tuna hauled off the docks opens a window into local daily life.

At the western tip of Bukit Badung, where rocky precipices drop almost 100 metres (330 ft) to the ocean, is **Pura Luhur Uluwatu** ❽, balancing 70 metres (230 ft) up on a dramatic promontory's edge. Originally dating from the 10th

Map on page 148

Cliffs near the temple of Uluwatu.

BELOW: tourists along ocean-cliff wall, Uluwatu.

Map
on page
148

century or before, it is one of the Sad Kahyangan, or Six Temples of the World revered by all Balinese. The ancient priests Empu Kuturan and Danghyang Nirartha helped to establish this temple, and it is said that Danghyang Nirartha achieved *moksa* – enlightenment – here. The temple's *candi bentar*, or split gate, is unusual in that the carvings are in the shape of wings. The entrance to the second courtyard (*jaba tengah*) is flanked by a statue of Ganesha, the elephant god revered as the remover of obstacles. The innermost sanctuary, or *jeroan*, is off limits to those who are not praying here. However, one can still watch from off to the side. South of the temple and parking area, a short path leads along the cliff tops with views of ocean and temple.

*One of many lures
for a fine sunset.*

Tanah Lot

While not in the Badung district (it's in Tabanan, just across the regency boundary), one of Bali's most noted sites is easily reached from Bali's southern tourist centres. From Denpasar, head west towards Canggu and Bali's most famous – and photographed – temple: **Pura Tanah Lot** ❾, on a huge rock just offshore.

Set apart from the land by a stone basin, the rock has been carved by incoming tides. Tanah Lot, with its solitary black towers and tufts of foliage spilling over the cliffs, recalls the delicacy of a Chinese painting, although the gauntlet of souvenir stalls and hawkers on the approach to the temple can diminish the image and mood somewhat. In caves surrounding the temple dwell striped sacred snakes, discreetly left undisturbed by Balinese. Erosion along the base of the temple forced the government to build concrete reinforcements, which have marred the beauty of this much-photographed holy spot. Only worshippers are allowed into the temple, but visitors can get a dramatic view from the adjacent hill, especially at sunset.

OPPOSITE: sunset
over Pura Tanah
Lot. **BELOW:** Tanah
Lot at high tide.

Although a small sanctuary, Pura Tanah Lot is linked to a series of sea temples along Bali's southern coast: Pura Sakenan, Pura Uluwatu, Pura Rambut Siwi and Pura Petitenget. These temples are related to the principal mountain sanctuaries: Besakih at Gunung Agung, Pura Batur at Gunung Batur, and Pura Luhur at Gunung Batukau. These upland temples are for the veneration of the deities associated with mountains and mountain lakes, while rituals at the sea temples include homage to the guardian spirits of the sea.

The chronicles attribute the temple at Tanah Lot to the 16th-century priest Danghyang Nirartha. During his travels, he saw a light emanating from a point on the west coast. When he came to this spot, he stopped and meditated. A local spiritual leader's followers became entranced with Nirartha and began studying with him. This so angered the local priest that he challenged Nirartha. Not to be bothered, Nirartha simply moved the spot upon which he was meditating to the middle of the ocean, and it became known as Tanah Lot, or Land in the Middle of the Sea.

Returning back to Kediri, stop in at the village of **Pejaten**, famous for its pottery. Unfortunately, the ceramics industry here is in decline. Or else detour off to expansive and embracing **Canggu Beach**, a black-sand beach lacking both tourists and hawkers but blessed with spectacular ambiance.

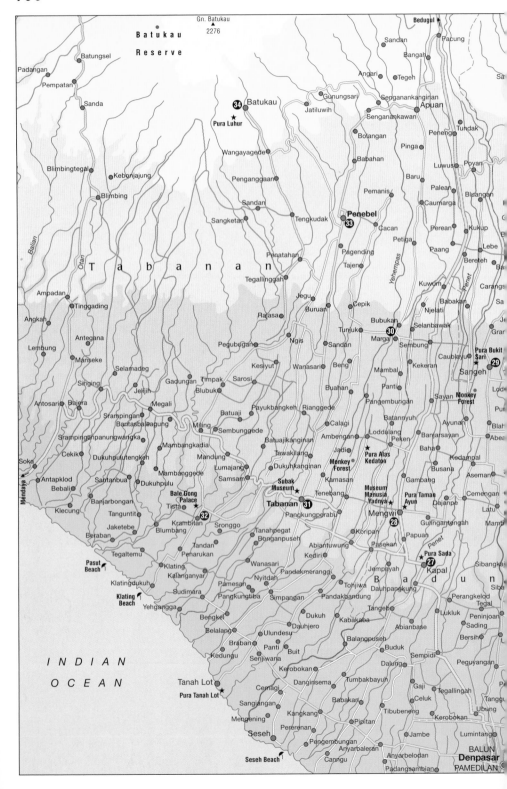

Gn. Batukau
▲
2276

B a t u k a u

R e s e r v e

Bedugul

Sandan   Pacung

Bangah

Padangan

Batungsel

Angari   Tegeh   Sa

Pempatan

Gunungsari   Senganankanginan   Apuan

Sanda   (34) Batukau   Jatiluwin

Senganankawan

★
Pura Luhur   Peneng   Tundak

Bolangan   Pinga

Wangayagede   Babahan

Blimbingtegal   Baru   Luwus Poyan

Kebonjajung   Penganggaan   Pemanis   Palean

Blimbing   Caumarga Blpangan

Sandan   Penebel

Sangketan   Tengkudak (33)   Perean   Kukup

Cacan

Petiga   Paang Lebe

Penatahan   Pagending   Bereteh   Ba

Tegallinggah   Tajen   Paang

Kuwum   Carangs

Ampadan   Jegu   Cepik   Babakan   Sa

Tinggading   Buruan   Njelati

Angkah   Rajasa   Bubukan

Antegana   Tunjuk Marga (30)   Grar

Lembung   Pegubugan Ngis   Sandan   Sembung

Manseke   Caublayu Pura Bukit
                                                                  Sari (29)

Selamadeg   Kesiyut Wanasari Beng   Kekeran   Sangeh

Singing   Gadungan Timpak Sarosi   Mambal   Lod

Antosari Bajera   Jeljih Blubuk   Buahan   Panti   Sayan Monkey
                                                                        Forest

Megali   Payukbangkeh Rianggede Pangembungan   Pur

Srampingan Bantasbalaagung Batuaji   Batannyuh   Ayunan   Blah

Srampinganpanungwangka Miling Sembunggede Calagi   Loddalang Peken Banjarsayan Abea

Mambangkadia   Batuajikanginan Ambengan   Baha   Kedampal

Cekik Dukuhpulutengkeh   Tawakllang Jadi ★   Busana

Mandung   Monkey Pura Alas
Soka   Forest Kedaton   Aseman

Antapklod Santanbua Mambanggede Lumajang Dukuhkanginan   Gambang Cemengan

Bebali   Dukuhpulu Samsam   Kamasan   Latu

Banjarbongan   Subak   Tenebang Museum Pura Taman

Klecung   Bale Gong   Museum ★   Manusia Ayun Dajanpe

Tanguntit   Palace Tabanan (31)   Yadnya ★   Mengwi   Mamt

Jaketebe   Tista ★ (32)   Pangkungperabu   (28)

Beraban Krambitan Sronggo   Koripan Papuan Gulingantengah

Tandan   Blumbang   Tanahpegat   Pasekan

Tegaltemu Penarukan Bonganpuseh Abiantuwung   Pura Sada

Pasut   Klating   Wanasari   Kediri   Jempayah (27) Sibangkal

Beach   Pandakmeranggi   B   Kapal   a   d   u   n

Klatingdukuh Kalanganyar Nyitdah   Tohjiwa Dauhpangkung   Siba

Klating   Sudimara Pamesan   Perangkelod

Beach Yehgangga Pangkungtiba Simpangan Pandakbandung   Tangeb Tegal

Bengkel   Dukuh Kabakaba   Lukluk Peninjoan

Belalang   Dauhjero   Abianbase Sading

Braban Ulundesu   Balangpuseh   Bersih

Kedungu Panti Buit   Buduk

Senjiwana   Dalung   Sempidi Peguyangan

Kerobokan   Gaji Tegallingah

Tanah Lot   Dangfinsema   Celuk   Tangg

★   Cemagi   Tumbakbayuh   Ubung

Pura Tanah Lot   Babakan   Kerobokan Lumintang

Sangfiangan Kangkang   Tibubeneng

Mengening   Pererenan Pipitan   Jambe Lumintang

Seseh   Pengembungan   BALUN

Anyarbalaeran   Anyarbelodan   **Denpasar**

Seseh Beach   Canggu   PAMEDILAN

Padangsambian

I N D I A N

O C E A N

Baliar

Otan

T a b a n a n

Yehempas

Penet

Penet

Mendaya

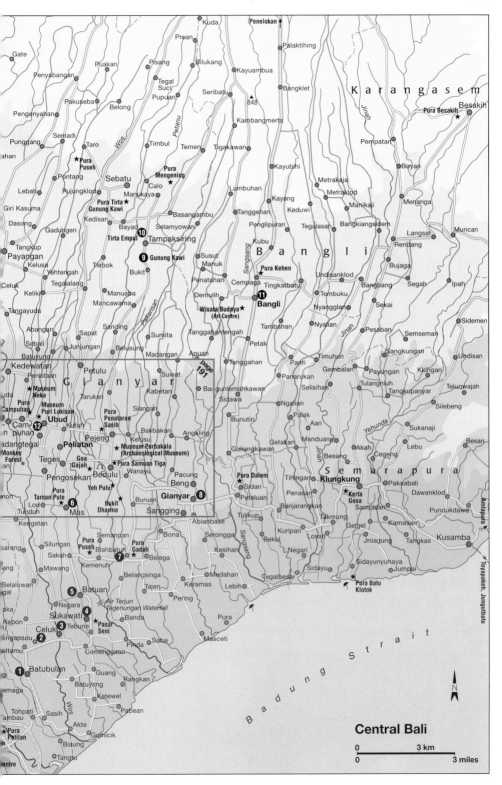

Central Bali

GIANYAR

Map on pages 166-7

Once one of Bali's more powerful kingdoms, the regency of Gianyar is today a centre of incredible aesthetic and creative talent. Much of this has been funnelled towards the dollars of foreign travellers

Driving northward from Denpasar, the cacophony of the city recedes a little, depending upon exactly where one is headed, and landscapes of verdant rice paddies soothe one back to sanity. Palm-leaf images of Dewi ri, the rice goddess who guards the crops, wave from the fields, while small uts provide shelter to those who work them. Shrines and temples stand sennel at every water source. To the north, high above all, Gunung Batur rises to ver 1,700 metres (5,600 ft).

The road from Denpasar to Ubud is dotted with countless villages, originally solated hamlets but nowadays nearly indistinguishable from one another in he continual roadside sprawl. Non-stop driving should take just over an hour, ut doing so would be a great pity as just about every village specialises in ome kind of art form. The drive can at times be stressful, given the free-form riving of many Balinese and the exceedingly narrow roads.

This richly cultural region is part of the old Gianyar kingdom, extending from he centre of Bali down south to Denpasar like a long, winding snake. And it is his region in particular that has given Bali much of its reputation as a focus of reativity – born literally from the incredible fertility of the spring-fed, lava-nriched soil. With such bountiful fields and harvests, ae people had ample time to cultivate artistic talents, pplying these to their daily tasks and religious duties. he result is an island where aesthetic excellence is a iven, even in the commercial stuff sold to tourists.)ne rarely sees any craft done badly in Bali.

OPPOSITE: Barong, a mythical creature. **BELOW:** plastic strips scare away birds from fields.

₄orth from Denpasar

he first "village" outside Denpasar is **Batubulan ❶**, tretching for about 2 km (1¼ miles) and distinguishble from urban Denpasar only by the stone-carving hops lining the roadside. The soft tuft or soapstone)aras) used for temple carvings and ornaments is so orous that the harsh weather of the tropics wears it)wn, so that every couple of centuries temple carvıgs must be renewed. Paras is found in nearby ıvines, and it is used to create protective deities and emons for temples and households and now for)urists. Men and boys carve in groups at roadside factories", copying in stone what their ancestors arved before them and increasingly what appeals to isitors. Contrary to popular belief, many of the montrous-looking statues are not at all diabolical; when laced in front of a temple or home, they scare away ubious visitors such as demons and evil spirits.

Aside from stone carving, Batubulan is noted for ne daily performances of the Barong dance on a urpose-built stage near Pura Puseh. More a drama,

Javan kingfisher, found only on Bali and Java.

the story depicts the age-old struggle between good and righteousness – th path of *dharma*, or right-doing – and the forces that seek to destroy them Barong is a mystical lion-dragon creature played in the dance-drama by tw men. He is a benevolent fellow, and the hairs of his beard are said to hold hea ing powers. His adversary is Rangda, queen of the underworld, who is equall feared and respected by the Balinese. In the dance-drama, Rangda is neve destroyed, for the Balinese believe that the balance between positive and neg ative must be maintained. Therefore, to kill Rangda on stage would be destroy ing one half of the life-force. Even though, to an outsider, this may seem like ju a play, to the Balinese it is a serious portrayal of the struggle of life.

(As an aside, it is interesting to note that even the most serious of Balines staged dramas are imbued with humour. When watching the Barong, don't b surprised to see bawdy portrayals of life-threatening situations. The Balines love to laugh at themselves.)

Near the Barong dance site is a turn-off for **Sekolah Menengah Karawita Indonesia** (SMKI), or High School of Indonesian Performing Arts, and **Sekola Seni Rupa Indonesia** (SESRI), or High School of Indonesian Fine Art. From th road, the schools appear to be a huge temple complex, with grand carvings an coloured banners waving in the wind amidst the rice fields. Visitors are welcom to watch the classes held in the mornings. To enroll in SMKI, a potential stude must first audition, as this is essentially a teacher's training school. After gra uation, students are expected to return to their villages to teach the tradition dances and music that they have learned here. Many continue at Sekolah Ting Seni Indonesia (STSI), the College of Indonesian Arts, in Denpasar, the colleg level school for the performing arts. *(See page 154.)*

BELOW: Barong dance costumes, Batubulan.

Performances of a winged sort are at the **Taman Burung Bali Bird Park** pen daily 9am–6pm; admission fee). Over 1,000 specimens of 250 exotic rd species live in this well-designed aviary, dedicated to the preservation and onservation of rare and endangered birds from Indonesia and elsewhere. ndangered Bali starlings, the first ever born in captivity in Bali, are among xamples of the programme's success. Paved paths lead through 2 hectares (5 cres) of gardens and aviaries representing deserts, rain forests and marshlands. he park also has an attractive open-air restaurant and gift shop.

Singapadu ❷ is comparatively small. From the roadside, it appears as a row f woodcarving shops and a few more stone carvers, but it is actually home to ome superbly skilled mask carvers. Instead of turning right at the bend in the oad bordering Batubulan and Celuk, continue straight for about 1 km to a junc- on with a huge banyan tree on the left and the *pura desa* (village temple) on ie right. (Follow signs to the Taman Burung Bali Bird Park; the *pura desa* lies ist beyond it.) Next to the temple is the main *puri* or palace of Singapadu, and ie of the places where Barong are made. Further down the road is the home and orkshop of I Wayan Tangguh, one of Bali's most prominent mask makers. he main prototypes of *topeng* dance masks are in his collection, some of Bali's nest specimens. To see a mask evolve from a hunk of wood into an intricately irved and painted piece of art is fascinating.

Singapadu, by the way, also stages a Barong-dance performance, and some of ie finest Barong "legs" (men who play the front legs of Barong) hail from ere. Yet, not only does this tiny village produce Barong dancers of high cali- re but also the best *arja* singers and dancers on the island as well. *Arja* is a nre of dance-drama that is closest to Western operetta. But it is losing popu-

Map on pages 166-7

Singapadu means "twin lions", referring to the two princes and heirs to the throne of a local king near the village centuries ago.

BELOW: family on a motorbike.

larity in Bali, and is not performed as frequently as the *topeng* dance-drama

Just behind the *pura dalem*, down in the river gorge, is an amphitheatre where *kecak* and fire-dance performances are conducted on Monday nights. While the performance is good, it really is enhanced by the setting, with a rock grotto as backdrop and the area lit by torches. The theatre is a cooperative project between the village and the Taman Burung Bali Bird Park.

Celuk and Sukawati

Synonymous with silver and goldsmiths and 4 km (2½ miles) from Batubalan, **Celuk ❸** has the second-highest per-capita village income on Bali. Art shops beckon visitors to buy sterling silver and gold butterfly brooches, garnet-studded bracelets, earrings and ear-clips of all kinds. The intricacy and detail they obtain with simple hand tools can be amazing. Craftsmen use a tree stump with a protruding metal spike for an anvil, a bamboo stem to catch the filings, and a manually operated gas pump for heat. As with most Balinese crafts, smithing is largely an art passed down in a family. It's usually possible for visitors passing through to observe the workshops, which are often small rooms or work areas in the back containing five to 20 workers, some not even in their teens. Be sure not to miss the shops on the road just north and parallel to the main road, as many fine jewellers dwell here off the beaten track. Beyond the bulk of the art shops, on the left, is an asphalt road flanked by two small stone statues and which leads travellers to the back roads of Celuk and Batuan.

Across the Wos River lies **Sukawati ❹**, once the anchor of an extremely powerful kingdom prior to the 20th century and a place where many of the Peliatan and Ubud aristocracy have their roots. Sukawati now sports a modern

TIP

Simply because Celuk is famous for its silver work doesn't mean that what's offered to travellers is of any exceptional quality. Indeed, a lot of it is of mediocre quality. But there is, of course, some excellent work in Celuk.

BELOW: shadow puppet, and silver from Celuk.

rt market and is home to some of the best *dalang* (shadow puppeteers) on Bali. Many Balinese feel that *wayang kulit* – shadow puppetry – is the most difficult f the island's arts. Aside from having to learn how to manipulate different uppet characters, memorise hundreds of stories, sing, cue the musicians, and e able to create a variety of voices, a *dalang* must be clean in mind, body and oul. He is akin to a priest in many respects and can even make the holy water o necessary for Balinese ritual (usually reserved for the domain of Brahman riests). The stories of the *wayang kulit* are imbedded with innuendo and impart ne values of daily life to the audience.

Often, these *dalang* make their own puppets, which are delicately carved out f buffalo hide and then painted. A number of *dalang* live in the *banjar* (neigh- ourhood association) behind the food market. To see how the buffalo hide is arved into puppets, stop by the homes of puppeteers I Wayan Wija (the first treet to the left behind the food market) and I Wayan Nartha (just south of the rt market, on the other side of the street and inwards about 50 metres). Cowhide , also made into dance accoutrements in the village of Puaya, north of Sukawati.

It is here that the production of traditional *legong* dance costumes – orna- nented filigree leather headdresses, gilded clothes and beaded epaulets – can e seen. Even if not a dancer, it is rivetting to watch the process of cloth paint- ng. If in the market for dance costumes, test the quality by rubbing the painted urfaces together; if it flakes, don't buy. It is said that I Dewa Agung Made Karna, a ruling prince of Sukawati, ascended to heaven while meditating and aw celestial nymphs dancing to the accompaniment of divine musicians. Awakening from his meditative state, he created the *legong* dance, an exquis- e dance for two pre-adolescent girls.

Map on pages 166-7

BELOW: *legong* dancer, and rooster for cockfighting.

The *pasar seni* or art market is a two-storey building filled with woodcarvings clothing and knick-knacks, although an assortment of items such as ink drawings, gilded umbrellas, stone statues and bamboo flutes can also be found here in varying degrees of quality, but all are much less expensive than at the large art shops. Should you pass by Sukawati early in the day, take a look at the *pasar pagi* or morning market, about a block behind the pasar seni. In this steaming, packed, warehouse-like barn is – in bulk – every trinket that is on sale in Kuta but for half the price. The market closes around mid-morning.

Batuan to Gianyar

Most famous for its dense painting style, **Batuan ❺** is also the site of some exquisite temple carvings and superb dancers. At any time during a temple festival, it might be possible to see one of the three *gambuh* troupes, of which there are less than a dozen on the entire island. Moreover, some of the fine exponents of the *topeng*, or masked, dance-drama are from Batuan. Banjar Den Tiis, just up the main road, claims a club of *wayang wong* dancers.

Gambuh is considered by many scholars to be the precursor of classical Balinese dance. Currently, it is not a popular form among the Balinese, as the language used is archaic and not understood by many, and the jokes are few and far between. Nevertheless, it is in a period of revival. A stately form, it is unique in its movement style and for the accompanying gamelan orchestra, best known for its metre-long flutes. A more modern dance genre with its roots here is the so-called frog dance. The instruments are unique: *suling* (flute) and *genggong* (Balinese-style jew's harp). This dance is often performed in the major hotels.

The dance most popular in Batuan is the *topeng* dance-drama, which chron

Notable aspects of the Batuan style of painting are the "otherworldliness" of light and shadow and the fine detail of the brush strokes.

BELOW: temple festival in Mas.

les the lives of Balinese kings and their subjects, as opposed to the tales of dian heroes and heroines of the *Ramayana* epic. Studded with educational ecdotes, bawdy jokes and beautiful dancing, a good *topeng* troupe commands ite a crowd. Two of Bali's best topeng dancers and teachers reside in Batuan: Ketut Kantor (son of the late I Nyoman Kakul, one of Bali's finest masters of nce) and I Made Jimat. Both have schools in their homes and will gladly ach foreigners who are serious – and are willing to spend the time – about arning the art. Batuan is also home to some of Bali's most talented artists, ith I Wayan Bendi an international favourite. His studio is along the main ad, showing work by him and also his brother, uncle and father. Each of them actices the traditional Batuan style, adding a humourous modern element to ch – long-nosed tourists armed with cameras and surfboards, for example. nother well-known Batuan painter is Ida Bagus Ketut Togog.

Map on pages 166-7

The *pura puseh* (village temple) in Batuan dates back to the 11th century, ith fine examples of temple carvings. Head straight at the bend in the road and the little hill. It is directly across from the *wantilan*, or open-air pavilion.

Detail of traditional Balinese door.

Best known to the outside world for its intricate woodcarvings and masks, retched-out **Mas ⑥**, 20 km (12 miles) from Denpasar, was the home of the late la Bagus Nyana, who passed on his talent to his son, the late Ida Bagus Tilem d who opened the Tilem Art Gallery. It's on the main road and is a fine place view highest-quality woodcarvings (and at some of the highest prices). Many Ida Bagus Nyana's innovative pieces are on display, along with those of his n. A third generation of the family manages the shop.

Carvings and masks can be found up and down the street and in side alleys. ring along a photograph or design of something you'd like carved and place

BELOW: Mas village woodcarvers.

a special order. One of the best-known artists for new designs in masks here is Ida Bagus Anom. He has carved masks for pantomimes and many *commedia dell'arte* performers, as well as performance artists from all over the world. His yawning masks have been widely copied throughout the island.

Despite the creative background, the historical importance of Mas should not be overlooked. Its inhabitants are primarily Brahmans, the priestly caste, and they trace their roots back to Danghyang Nirartha, the founder of Pura Taman Pule, which is just behind the soccer field. This great Brahman sage created the system of the traditional village, or *desa adat*, whereby the village becomes a microcosm of the larger order of the cosmos. He also conceived the *padmasana*, an open-roofed shrine found in every household and village temple and dedicated to the omnipotent supreme god, Sanghyang Widi Wasa. At the Pura Taman Pule, performances of *wayang wong* are held all day and night on Kuningan (the Saturday after Galungan, every 210 days). One of the largest cockfights in Bali takes place here in the early morning hours.

Travelling north from Mas, and just before the junction with a statue of a female dancer, is Tjokot and Sons, a home workshop of "primitive" wood carvings. Natural tree roots are sculpted into grotesque figures that allude to the demonic. For more woodcarvings, head north past the *bale banjar* (community hall) and stop at Wayan Pasti's house. Aside from being an amazing carver, he is also a traditional Balinese architect and one of the finest makers of bull sarcophagi used for cremations. His speciality is life-size horses and dogs, and the realism often makes one do a double-take.

In the market village of **Blahbatuh** ➐, Pura Puseh Gaduh is associated with Kebo Iwa, the legendary giant from Bedulu. He is honoured in temples all over

BELOW: bamboo furniture in Bona.

ali, and here is no exception. Enshrined in a small pavilion is a massive stone ead over a metre high, said to be a portrait of Kebo Iwa. Gajah Mada, the eat minister of the Majapahit kingdom, realised he could never conquer Bali hile Kebo Iwa lived. So he enticed him to Java with the promise of a beauti-l princess as a wife, and then Gajah Mada had him killed, thereby leaving Bali en to his conquest.

A visit to I Made Gableran's gamelan factory in Banjar Babakan, Blahbatuh, a treat. Here, barefoot men blow bellows to stir up the heat for forging. They uat with large hammers, bending the bronze alloys into the desired shape for e metallophones used in Balinese gamelan. After they are cooled, the mas-r himself, Gableran, tests the tuning by striking the key with a tuding, a bam-o tuning fork. Gamelan casings are assembled and painted here, and entire chestras (worth well over US$10,000) may be purchased. Orders must be aced far in advance, of course.

On the road from Blahbatuh to Gianyar is the village of **Bona**, which spe-alises in quality bamboo furniture. Plain or fantastically carved, virgin or var-shed, chairs, beds, and tables are available here. At night, Bona offers a trance ow for tourists. Three forms of trance dancing – *sanghyang dedari*, *sanghyang ran* and *kecak* – are performed practically every day.

Map on pages 166-7

Bamboo is a member of the grass family, with nearly 500 species worldwide, but mostly in Asia. "Bamboo" come from the Malay word bambu.

ianyar and beyond

nce the capital of a powerful kingdom of the same name, **Gianyar** ❽ is now sleepy and overgrown, but contemporary, village. During the confrontations ith the Dutch, the regency of Gianyar was sympathetic to the Dutch and thus ffered considerably less violence than other southern regencies.

The former palace, Puri Agung Gianyar, is not open the public. Gianyar's open-air cafe-market, one ock west of the *puri*, specialises in a Balinese light: *babi guling*, or roast suckling pig.

The speciality of this area is the *ikat* weaving the alinese use in traditional wear. There are a number of ctories that hold informal tours, and it's intriguing to atch the process of turning white threads through a mplex dyeing process into patterns of colour. But ding superb examples of ikat nowadays is hard.

Following the road south of the *puri*, you'll come to ebih, a fishing village. Men gather tiny tadpoles ener), which are then sold to merchants, who in turn ise them in ponds in Java and sell them when ey're mature. A view of **Nusa Penida**, or Bandit land, is a delight, but don't go swimming: the under-w is treacherous. *(For more information about Nusa enida, see page 233.)*

On the road to the west of Gianyar is the village of emenuh, the source of Bali's woodcarvings for gen-ations. Prices are much lower here than in Mas.

orth of Gianyar and on a curve in the road near the llage of **Sidan** stands a small, elegantly carved tem-e – a particularly fine example of *pura dalem*, the mple of the dead. The *kulkul* drum tower is decked ith reliefs showing tormented wrongdoers being nished by devilish giants. The gates are flanked by ities of death and transformation. ❑

BELOW: harvested rice stalks.

Map
on pages
166-7

NORTH TO BATUR

Ascending one of Bali's great volcanoes from the central lowlands
takes the traveller into another realm of this surprising island.
Up here are the veiling mists, healing waters, and the Bali Aga

Cloaked in mystery and legend, the Batur region is another face of Ba altogether, one that seems at odds with the more gentle and convention image of the island. At **Gunung Kawi ❾**, a complex of rock-hewn *cand* and monks' cells overlooks the Pakrisan River in a valley near Tampaksirin There are 10 *candi* in all, grouped in three locations.

Legend has it that Kebo Iwa, the powerful prime minister for the king c Bedulu, used magic to carve out all the monuments with his fingernails. Datin back to the 11th century, the *candi* are remarkably preserved. People mistakenl say that the *candi* at Gunung Kawi are tombs, but in fact the latest researc indicates they are monuments commemorating the royal family of the Udayan dynasty. (In Bali, the development of royal funeral cults – in which king queens and consorts were deified after death – began around the 11th century

One theory says that the main group of five *candi* honoured Udayana, h queen Mahendradatta, his concubine, and his two sons, Marakata and An Wungsu. Another theory suggests they honoured Anak Wungsu (king of Bali i the 11th century) and his royal wives, with the next group of four *candi* enshri ing his concubines. The 10th *candi*, which stands alone, honours a high offici

BELOW: overview of
Gunung Kawi, and
one of 10 *candi.*

The sacred spring of **Tirta Empul** , in **Tampaksiring**, is revered by all Bali-
ese. They say that it was created by the god Indra when he pierced the earth to
create a spring of *amerta*, the elixir of immortality (with which he revived his sol-
iers poisoned by the evil king Mayadanawa). The bathing place was built under
the rule of Sri Candrabhaya Singha Warmadewa in the 10th century. The waters
re said to have magical curative powers and, every year, people journey from all
ver Bali to purify themselves *(melukat)* in the clear pools, especially pregnant
omen and those who have survived a long illness. After leaving a small offer-
ig of thanks to the spring's deity, men and women go to opposite sides to bathe.
  On the full moon of the fourth month (October), the villagers from nearby
Manukaya bring a sacred stone, which is housed in the Pura Sakenan, in Manuk
ya, to be cleansed at Tirta Empul. Early this century, the old inscriptions on this
tone were deciphered for the first time by a Dutch archaeologist. The inscriptions
ead that on the anniversary of the construction of Tirta Empul, falling on the full
moon of Kartika (the fourth month, or October), the stone would be purified at the
ells. It was dated AD 962. The villagers had been performing this ritual for over
,000 years without having been aware of the meaning on the inscriptions.

ura Mengening

North of Tirta Empul, on a line that joins it with Gunung Kawi, is **Pura Men-
ening**. There is a definite connection between Tirta Empul, Gunung Kawi,
nd Pura Mengening. At the latter temple there is a free-standing *candi* similar
to those hewn from the rock at Gunung Kawi. And as with Tirta Empul, this tem-
le has a spring of pure water, also a source of the Pakrisan River. Pura
Mengening might well be the commemorative temple of King Udayana.

BELOW: Tirta Empul.

Further inland the weather is cooler. Plots abound with sweet potatoes, peanu corn, and spices. A *kulkul*-drum tower marks the entrance to **Bangli** ⓫, capita of a kingdom whose rulers were descended from the early Gelgel dynasty. Th largest and most sacred temple of the district is Pura Kehen, a terraced mour tain sanctuary and state temple of Bangli. An ancient document tells of th slaughter of a black bull during a feast held at this temple in 1204.

Down below the foot of the stairway there is an old temple that contains collection of records inscribed on bronze plates. Statues, in *wayang kulit* styl line the first terrace, from which steps lead to a magnificent closed gate that th people of Bangli call "the great exit". Above the gate looms the hideous fac and splayed hands of Kala Makara, the demonic one who catches harmful spi its to prevent them from entering. On either side are statues of villagers ges turing a welcome. An enormous banyan tree shades the first courtyard, wher the walls are inlaid with Chinese porcelain. An 11-tiered *meru* dominates th inner sanctuary. Here, on the right, is the three-throned shrine of the Hind trinity: Brahma, Siwa and Wisnu.

By turning west at Bangli, the route bypasses the volcano and takes a shor cut to Tampaksiring. Just 3 km (2 miles) out of Bangli on this road is the hill o Demulih. It is well worth the climb up, for the view of central Bali from on to is superb, and the hilly setting is conducive to peace and relaxation. To reach th volcanoes of Batur and Agung, continue straight north.

Bali's first mental hospital is in Bangli. The island's other mental hospital is in Denpasar. They say that those who can't be cured by a local balian, *or shaman, are sent here.*

Gunung Batur

Less than an hour north of Bangli lies the tranquil crater lake of **Gunung Batu** and the impressive temple gates of Pura Ulun Danu Batur, one of the two majo *subak* (irrigation society) temples on the island. Thes waters, rich with volcanic minerals from the Batu highlands, lead from one terrace to another in step down to the sea. Instead of rice, crops grown here ar peanuts, yams, coffee, cloves, vanilla and citrus.

Gunung Batur is 1,717 metres (5,635 ft) above se level, and it is significantly cooler than beach an foothill areas. The crater itself is 11 km (7 miles) i diameter and 180 metres (115 ft) deep. The volcan appears dormant, but it is still active . Legend tells o Pasupati (Siwa) dividing the sacred Hindu mountai Mahameru and placing the halves in Bali as the vo canoes Agung and Batur. Next to Agung, Batur is th most revered of Bali's mountains and symbolises th female element next to Agung's male.

Just to the east, one can glimpse the cone o **Gunung Abang**, a towering giant at the height o 2,153 metres (7,064 ft). It is best to get here in th early morning, before mist descends.

Ribbons of black lava ripple down the valley fro the peak of Gunung Batur. **Penelokan** ⒶⒶ literal means "the place to look", and at 1,450 metre (4,800 ft) above sea level, it is where the worl changes colours. The still lake can resemble blu glass or a sheet of platinum. Penelokan is a goo place to make a lunch stop; the Lakeview Resta rant is literally on the edge of the crater. However, seeking to breathe in the beauty of Batur, it's be

BELOW: profile of temple carving.

to do it from Kintamani, further west, as the hawkers in Penelokan can be boringly and uninspiringly persistent.

Batur's last volcanic activity was in 1994, but nothing major has occurred since 1926. In 1917, Batur violently erupted, destroying 65,000 homes and 2,500 temples and taking more than a thousand lives. Lava engulfed the village of **Batur ❸** but miraculously stopped at the foot of the village temple itself. The people took this as a good omen and continued to live there. In 1926, a new eruption buried the entire temple except the highest shrine, dedicated to the goddess of the lake. The villagers were then forced to resettle on the high cliffs overlooking Batur. They brought the surviving shrine with them and began rebuilding what is Bali's second-most important temple after Besakih – **Pura Ulun Danu Batur ❻**. An ambitious project, the majority of the 285 planned shrines of the temple are yet to be completed. Two august gateways, severe in contrast to the elaborate split gates of southern Bali, open onto spacious courtyards laid with black gravel. Rows of *meru* towers silhouette against the sky, in full view of the smoking volcano. The *bale gedong*, a storehouse of precious relics, contains a bell of solid gold. As the story goes, the bell was presented to the treasury of the temple by a king of Singaraja in atonement for his having insulted the deities. There is also a *gamelan gong gede* here, which accompanies the sacred dances of the *baris gede* and the *rejang* during the festival here.

The ritual in this temple is closely linked with the veneration of Bali's largest lake, **Danau Batur** (Lake Batur), and supplication for the blessing of irrigation water. Here, once a year, heads of all the local *subak* gather to discuss the distribution of water to their rice lands and to pay homage to Dewi Danu, goddess of the lake, and her consort Wisnu, who rules over water. The mountain lakes

Map on pages 166-7, 181

TIP

There are a number of starting points for climbing Batur. The journey takes less than three hours round-trip. (From Purajati, two hours.) There are plenty of guides waiting to take visitors up.

BELOW: temple atop Gunung Batur.

Map on page 181

Danau Batur.

help regulate the flow of water to the extensive fields and villages by way of th numerous natural springs to be found lower down the mountain's slope.

Inscriptions from the 10th century indicate that **Kintamani** ❶ – a high mour tainous area that takes its name from the wind-blown town at 1,500 metre (4,920 ft) – was one of the earliest known kingdoms in Bali. It is a rather scruff township nowadays, but every third morning, on *pasah* of the Balinese caler dar, the main street becomes a bazaar for all the surrounding villages. (There ar several mediocre losmen for an overnight stay.)

The main road continues its ascent to a hillside in the clouds. On a clear day the view from **Penulisan** ❷ encompasses half the island, from the crest c Gunung Bratan in the west to the Java Sea. A paved road at Sukawana leads t **Pinggan** on the north side of the crater, where the symbol of modern civilisa tion, Bali's television aerial, claims its place beside a flight of some 300 step rising to the mountain sanctuary of Pura Tegeh Koripan. The highest temple i Bali at 1,745 metres (5,725 ft), Pura Tegeh Koripan is actually a complex of ten ples at which a circle of surrounding villages worship. The sparsely adorned bal shelter sculptures of kings, queens and divinities, and *lingga*. Several statue date from the 11th century and another from the 15th century.

Bali Aga

A steep, corkscrew road leads down to **Kedisan** ❻, on the lakeside, wher boats can be hired. The road does not go all along the lake, although it is pos sible to hike it. On the flank of the volcano, opposite Trunyan at Toya Bungka are hot springs, which the locals use for bathing. The bubbling mineral water reputedly have medicinal qualities and are said to be the personal fount of Dev Danu. Few people bathe in the lake itself, although it is not forbidden.

The mountain areas are known as the home of the Bali Aga villages – place relatively untouched by Hinduism and where ancestral rites take precedenc Here, the arts are not as developed and ceremonies tend to be simpler. In th Batur area, **Trunyan** ❼, across the lake, is perhaps the most well-known Ba Aga village, named after a *taru menyan* (fragrant tree) that grows in the cem tery outside the village. There is no cremation here, and the cemetery is wher the dead are left for vultures to feast upon. According to Trunyanese, the bor ies do not decompose normally and there is no odour of rotting flesh, due to th fact that they are placed under this sacred tree.

TIP

Many domestic and foreign tourists avoid going to Trunyan, as it is not what one would call a pleasant excursion. However, it is a rare example of Bali's pre-Hindu past.

To get to Trunyan, take a boat from Kedisan (set the round-trip price befor hand) or Toya Bungkah, or else make the lengthy trek around the lake. Trunya is also one of the few villages in Bali where begging is condoned; as soon as vi itors step off the boat, villagers who have traditionally had to beg from oth Balinese for food beg rather aggressively for money. Expect to have to pay a "entrance fee" at the minimum, and some tourists have reported being charge to be allowed to leave.

If you venture here, however, don't expect to see piles of rotting cadavers, a they are covered by bamboo coverings. Still, there will certainly be some skul and bones lying about. The Trunyanese have been isolated for centuries fro mainstream Balinese, and they are quite reticent about sharing their cultur Secretive and protective about the customs exclusive to their community, th people keep Bali's largest traditional statue – the 4-metre-high (13-ft) image the patron guardian of the village – hidden in a pagoda, as they believe he is th "God who is the Centre of the World". Once a year, the Berutuk ritual is pe formed for him by dancers, dressed in coconut masks and shredded palm ar banana leaves, who cavort around Trunyan's main temple, Pura Gede Pancerir Jagat, the Temple of the Navel of the World.

OPPOSITE: Balinese girls.

THE PERFORMING ARTS OF BALI

The performing arts of Bali reflect an integration of environment, religion and community, in which every individual is a part of the experience

Wayang kulit (shadow-puppet theatre) is perhaps the most popular of all Balinese performing arts. The two-dimensional puppets are carved from leather and jointed from the elbows and the knees. Most of the puppets are based on characters from epic Indian tales such as the *Ramayana* or the *Mahbharata*. Suspended at the centre of a white screen is the *damar*, a coconut-oil lamp that illuminates and casts a shadow on the screen, though today electric light bulbs are also common. The audience usually sits on the other side of the screen and is entertained by the shadows; the *dalang* – the storyteller and puppeteer – remains behind the screen with his assistants (right and left) and musicians. On the *dalang*'s left is his puppet chest *(grobag)*, while a quartet of musicians, playing the accompaniment on the ten-keyed *gangsa* instruments, sit behind him. A performance can last for up to nine hours.

DANCE-DRAMA

The exuberance of Balinese dance gives it an air of spontaneity, yet beneath lies a learned set of motions presented in a highly stylised form. Each gesture has a name that describes its action; for example a sidestep may be named after the way a raven jumps. No play is complete without music, no dance without a story or meaning.

△ **DANCE SCHOOL**
Dance pupils learn one dance only. After teaching the basic moves, the teacher adjusts the pupil's body into position.

△ **PUPPET MASTER**
The *dalang,* or puppet master, is a consecrated priest. He moves the puppets while narrating the story.

▷ **GAMELAN GONGS**
Gamelan gongs are made from bronze and are still crafted in Bali. Most villages have clubs *(sekaa)* that own and cooperatively maintain the village *gamelan.*

◁ **LEGONG DANCE**
The classical Balinese *legong* dance is performed by young girls wearing elaborate costumes and headdresses.

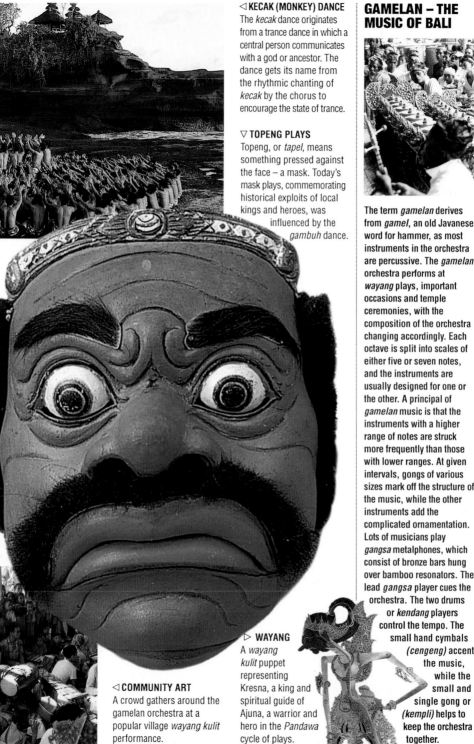

◁ **KECAK (MONKEY) DANCE**
The *kecak* dance originates from a trance dance in which a central person communicates with a god or ancestor. The dance gets its name from the rhythmic chanting of *kecak* by the chorus to encourage the state of trance.

▽ **TOPENG PLAYS**
Topeng, or *tapel*, means something pressed against the face – a mask. Today's mask plays, commemorating historical exploits of local kings and heroes, was influenced by the *gambuh* dance.

GAMELAN – THE MUSIC OF BALI

The term *gamelan* derives from *gamel*, an old Javanese word for hammer, as most instruments in the orchestra are percussive. The *gamelan* orchestra performs at *wayang* plays, important occasions and temple ceremonies, with the composition of the orchestra changing accordingly. Each octave is split into scales of either five or seven notes, and the instruments are usually designed for one or the other. A principal of *gamelan* music is that the instruments with a higher range of notes are struck more frequently than those with lower ranges. At given intervals, gongs of various sizes mark off the structure of the music, while the other instruments add the complicated ornamentation. Lots of musicians play *gangsa* metalphones, which consist of bronze bars hung over bamboo resonators. The lead *gangsa* player cues the orchestra. The two drums or *kendang* players control the tempo. The small hand cymbals *(cengeng)* accent the music, while the small and single gong or *(kempli)* helps to keep the orchestra together.

◁ **COMMUNITY ART**
A crowd gathers around the gamelan orchestra at a popular village *wayang kulit* performance.

▷ **WAYANG**
A *wayang kulit* puppet representing Kresna, a king and spiritual guide of Ajuna, a warrior and hero in the *Pandawa* cycle of plays.

UBUD AND ENVIRONS

*The highland town of Ubud is always on the traveller's itinerary.
Although increasingly taking on a rather kitschy and trendy veneer,
Ubud is still a focus of aesthetic pursuits and inspiration*

Map on page 191

Imbued with a poetically beautiful locale and a natural inclination to the arts, it was inevitable that **Ubud ⑫** and its 6,000 inhabitants should be subjected to foreign invasion. The first few foreigners to settle here, from Europe in the 1920s, were artists seeking inspiration within their surroundings. The masses that followed in the decades to come brought the sort of commercialisation only to be expected. This is not to be lamented, for the money that tourism brings has benefited the arts here. And although parts of Ubud might be "funky" if not contrived, at its core Ubud is still a centre for artists.

A few minutes away from the "cool" souvenir outlets, "cafes" with stereos turned up a notch too loud, and loquacious dance-ticket salesmen lies a gentler, calmer Ubud unaltered one iota by the tie-dyes on their rental scooters or the fact that Mick Jagger decided this was the cosmic spot to get married. Yet, still, like Denpasar and Sanur and Kuta to the south, as Ubud has increased its wealth and international appeal, neighbouring villages such as Peliatan and Campuhan have lost some of their geographical distinctiveness beneath Ubud's sprawl.

The name of Ubud comes from the word *ubad*, Balinese for medicine and stemming from the healing properties of a certain herb growing near the Campuhan River. Many of Ubud's aristocrats were (and some still are) renowned for their healing powers, and even into the 20th century and long after the Dutch invasion and conquest of Bali and Indonesia's independence, Ubud's royalty commanded great respect.

Almost alone among Balinese communities, Ubud has set up a tourism foundation known as the Yayasan Bina Wisata, with the aim of preserving the area's natural and cultural beauty. Instead of simply encouraging tourism on a grand scale, the foundation strives to unify the needs of both visitors and locals. Visitors are asked, for example, to respect the local ceremonies, wear traditional clothing when appropriate, and in general learn more about Ubud's people. The office is about 500 metres east of the main market; the staff is helpful in answering questions and plotting journeys, and a message board carries details of festivals, ceremonies and cremations in the area.

Central Ubud

Like markets in all Balinese towns, **Ubud Market** is a decent enough place to begin one's walkabout of the town. The market, at the junction of Jalan Raya Ubud and Jalan Wanara Wana (also known as Monkey Forest Road), is open daily, but on *pasah*, which takes place every three days, it is packed to the seams. Even travelling medicine men appear here. The market is for early birds; after two in the afternoon, it is quiet.

PRECEDING PAGES: dance-drama performance. **LEFT:** Ubud's streets are full of colour. **BELOW:** no shortage of places to stay.

Across the road from the market, on the northeast corner of the intersection is **Puri Saren Agung**, from where Ubud was ruled from the late 1800s until World War II. The buildings standing today were erected following a devastating 1917 earthquake. Evenings here bring on traditional dance performances.

Bali's most legendary figure in artistic circles at home and abroad is I Gusti Nyoman Lempad (1862–1978). His fame derives from his broad range of talents in many media, including painting, sculpture and architecture. Lempad was involved in creating the buildings of Museum Puri Lukisan and the Kemuda Taman Saraswati temple in Ubud. However, it was with his fluid, concise linework that he created formal, classical scenes that gained him the most recognition. *(See example on page 116.)* The **Lempad House** (open daily 8am–6pm; free) is just to the east of Puri Saren, on Jalan Raya.

Around the corner from the Lempad house, on Jalan Sriwedari, is the **Seniwati Gallery of Art by Women** (open daily 10am–5pm; tel: 975-485; free). In 1991, British expatriate Mary Northmore decided that too much of Balinese art was dominated by men, and with the help of her Balinese husband, himself a painter, she found four female artists and established the Seniwati. The gallery represents female artists from all over Bali, including several resident foreigners. With an outlet for their work, the artists have gained a source of income, developed self-esteem and self-respect, and have travelled to Jakarta, Singapore, Hong Kong and Europe for exhibitions.

To the east of the market and Puri Saren on Jalan Raya Ubud is **Museum Puri Lukisan ⓭** (open daily 8am–4pm; tel: 975-136; admission fee). This is one of Ubud's most attractive museums, considerably restored in the mid-1990s. Opened in 1956 to preserve and exhibit the rich heritage of traditional and mod

BELOW: Ubud street commercialism.

Map below

rn Balinese art, works have been carefully selected to show a representative cross-section in the development of the visual arts. Although this collection is somewhat smaller and not nearly as well documented or displayed as that of the formidable Neka Museum, it is worth seeing. The museum's main building exhibits its permanent collection from the *wayang* style, with paintings by I Gusti Nyoman Lempad and works from the Pita Maha period. The second building displays works of the Young Artists style and modern traditional Balinese style, while the third building only houses temporary exhibitions.

A gallery that has its focus firmly on the future is Komaneka Fine Art Gallery, on Jalan Wanara Wana (Monkey Forest Road). Operated by Koman Wahyu Neka, this stylish gallery specialises in the second generation of Indonesian artists, who, it is hoped, will become masters of the next generation. These works, and those of several established foreign artists from Singapore and the Philippines, are uniquely contemporary and reveal new visions and ideas.

Ubud is a walking town. If with sturdy feet and shoes, one could walk to nearly anywhere in this chapter. One of the most popular excursions for first-time visitors – more out of tradition, perhaps, than for intrinsic value – was once considered to be way out of town. But the popularity of the so-called **Monkey Forest** ⑭ (open daylight hours; admission fee) with tourists has led to the 2-km (1¼-mile) road properly called Jalan Wanara Wana but commonly referred to as Monkey Forest Road, becoming lined if not overdeveloped with tourist-related establishments. (Indeed, the whole neighbourhood of Jalan Wanara Wana and Jalan Dewi Sita, south of Ubud's main boulevard Jalan Raya Ubud, has been enlivened in recent years by the arrival of galleries, cafés ranging from excellent to atrocious, and a deluge of designer shops – many dubious,

In the 1930s, fearful of tourism's effect on the quality of art, Balinese and foreign arts established Pita Maha, an artists' association, in Ubud. Painters, sculptors and others joined, seeking to make all artists aware of the need to maintain aesthetic quality and to set up exhibitions outside of Bali.

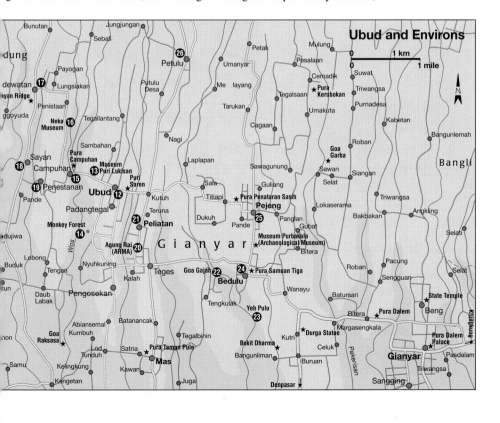

Ubud and Environs

One of Bali's ubiquitous monkeys, more correctly known as macaques.

some delightful – that specialise in jewellery, handmade silk batik, baskets, and other domestic goods. But back to the monkeys.)

Once at the forest, walk along a rough path through some beautiful and dense tropical jungle. Like all "monkey forests" throughout Bali, the experience is punctuated by roving gangs of mischievous, annoying, and fearless macaques, who ostensibly protect the temple inside. They're adorable up to a point, usually the point when one of them pinches your film, keys, sunglasses or any other shiny object, no matter where perched, and runs off with it. Forget about retrieving anything. Monkeys or not, this walk is best done early morning or late afternoon when the sun isn't so scorching. If you continue until the end, you'll come across a hidden oasis, Lake Leki, which serves great international cuisine amongst its idyllic surrounds. A temple in the forest, **Pura Dalem Agung Padangtegal**, is dedicated to Durga, the goddess of death who often takes the form of Rangda, the witch.

Painting is just one of Ubud's mainstream arts, and woodcarving is also something that residents seem to do with a natural intuition equalled by skill. Seek out **Museum Patung**, either by walking to the end of Jalan Wanara Wana beyond the monkey forest, or by heading down Jalan Handman, then turn right at Nyuh Kuning, then right again. The museum is up a dirt path and is distinguishable by a huge, sashed banyan tree. In this one-room museum are 35 wood carvings executed in extensive styles. The oldest dates from 1959 and is by the late sculptor Mangku Tama.

From wood to bamboo, the **Yayasan Bambu Lingkungan Lestari (Environmental Bamboo Foundation**; open by appointment; tel: 974-027) was established by designer Linda Garland in 1993 to protect tropical forests by promoting

BELOW: Ubud lotus pond, and Ubud sculpture.

nd demonstrating the conservation and development opportunities of bamboo. As a remarkably strong and versatile wood with a rapid growth rate, bamboo has enormous potential, whether for buildings or furniture. In less than 10 years, the foundation has helped put bamboo on the conservation and development agenda of Indonesia, while at the same time stirring up a fair amount of international interest. Visitors to the 10-hectare (25-acre) foundation can see its nursery, which nurtures 67 varieties of Indonesian, Japanese, Chinese, Thai and Colombian bamboo, grown here before being transplanted to villages elsewhere. Bamboo furniture is for sale, and there are huts for accommodation.

West of downtown Ubud

Jalan Raya Ubud heads west from downtown Ubud towards **Campuhan ⑮**. Along the way, artist Antonio Blanco's fabulous mansion is at the top of a steep driveway, just after Campuhan Bridge and before the road bends right. This ornately decorated home still harbours the self-professed "maestro", who roams around his manor in various coloured berets and espouses his worldly views to anyone with patience. To be fair, this modern artist does produce some very beautiful, erotic paintings and illustrations of his attractive wife and daughter, his favourite models. He is also a keen poet, and there are dozens of examples where he combines his two creative talents.

Further along on Jalan Campuhan (what Jalan Raya Ubud turns into after making a sharp northward bend west of town) stands what is undoubtedly the finest collection of Balinese artwork on the island, the **Neka Museum ⑯** (open daily 9am–5pm; tel: 975 074; admission fee). This wonderful display of assorted art is the private collection of former school teacher Suteja Neka, today regarded

Map on page 191

TIP

When in Campuhan, drop by the Hotel Tjampuhan for a quick dip in its swimming pool. This hotel was once Ubud's top place to stay, and its rustic charms linger. In the 1930s, artist Walter Spies lived here.

BELOW:
Neka Museum.

as one of Bali's best art dealers. Opened in 1976, the museum's works are chronologically displayed and well documented, providing an excellent background to the history of Balinese art.

Galleries reveal the classical narrative *wayang* style, the first signs of Western artistic influences from the likes of Spies and Bonnet, and the highly individual and stylistic drawings of I Gusti Nyoman Lempad. A special photography archive features black-and-white photographs of Bali during the 1930s, taken by an American, Robert Koke. Another separate pavilion is devoted to the work of Arie Smit and his students of the Young Artists style, which blossomed in the 1960s. The museum's display is rounded off with works by Bali's foreign-born artists and modern works by Indonesian artists. There is also an excellent gallery with contemporary works of art for sale. Nothing's cheap here, but the quality is superb and the art diverse in coverage. (In downtown Ubud, Neka Gallery, on Jalan Raya Ubud, is Suteja Neka's commercial venture.)

North leads to **Kedewatan** ⓲, a village blessed with an outstanding view. More upscale accommodation is available along the ridge here in all ranges from the Kedewatan intersection further north toward Payangan.

South from Kedewatan is **Sayan** ⓳, a small Ubud "suburb" that teeters on the edge of the devastatingly beautiful Sayan Gorge, with the Agung River tumbling through at the bottom. The scenery here is undoubtedly some of Bali's most dramatic, and spending some time amongst its dense and earthy smells and sounds is invigorating. The Agung is increasingly a popular rafting trip for visitors, although the nagging hawkers along the trail from the road to the river can get in the way. The two-hour rafting journey floats through 25 class-2 rapids, meaning an adrenaline rush without too much danger.

The so-called Young Artists style came about when Dutch-born Arie Smit (now an Indonesian citizen) arrived in Bali in the 1950s and taught painting to young boys. They developed a use of bright colours and a naive style in their images of Balinese daily life and environment.

BELOW: Amandari pool, and rafting on the Ayung River.

This area might be called Bali's Beverly Hills because of its exclusive retreats, such as the Chedi and the venerable Amandari, which were joined recently by the Four Seasons.

Penestanan ⑲ grew from obscurity when Arie Smit, a naturalised Indonesian citizen who lived and worked in the area as a respected artist, established a small art school here for locals during the early 1960s. With Smit's generous encouragement and enormous freedom on subject matter and style of expression, the young painters produced imaginative, naive-style scenes of village life and rituals. From these experimental beginnings emerged a lively art known as the Young Artists style.

This genre, still relatively unique to Penestanan village, is distinguished by the oils thinned to create matte effects, used in flat, bright areas of colour and surrounded by dark outlines. Lighting and shadow are absent, there is little perspective and sometimes no facial features, and decorative multicoloured foliage dominated the scenes. The area is still dedicated to producing this style of art, and although there is no one main Young Artists studio per se, the pretty streets of this tiny village are dotted with art galleries selling original works.

Down by the Campuhan River is a small temple built by Mpu Narada. A bamboo spout pours out pure spring water, and some Balinese come here to bathe in the evening.

East of downtown Ubud

From central Ubud, head down Jalan Handman or Jalan Wanara Wana (a.k.a. Monkey Forest Road), past the Monkey Forest, towards **Pengosekan** and the **Agung Rai Museum of Art** (ARMA) ⑳ (open daily 8am–6pm; admission fee).

Map on page 191

BELOW: bungalows outside of Ubud.

Opened in 1996, the museum (not to be confused with the Agung Rai Fine Art Gallery, in Peliatan) has an extensive collection of permanent works by Balinese, Indonesian and foreign artists in classic Balinese and contemporary styles. This superb collection is remarkable because the majority of the pieces are on loan from the personal collection of Mr and Mrs Agung Rai. Works are titled in English, Indonesian and Japanese. This museum is widely acknowledged as the only other important gallery in Ubud besides Neka.

The top floor of the museum is dedicated to traditional painting by Balinese masters such as I Gusti Nyoman Lempad, Ida Bagus Made, Anak Agung Gde Sobrat and I Gusti Made Deblog. The lower floor features classical Kamasan style paintings on tree bark and boards dating from the 1900s; antique *ikat* textiles; a stunning Barong and Rangda mask display; and the only collection of works on Bali by the 19th-century Javanese artist Raden Saleh Syarif Bustaman. Walter Spies is also represented, although in this hall they are reproductions. There is one original Spies painting, however, in the contemporary hall, along with work by other foreign artists who lived and worked in the area: Willem Gerard Hofker, Rudolf Bonnet, Adrien Jean Le Mayeur de Merpres, Miguel Covarrubias, Hans Snel, Arie Smit, Antonio Blanco and many others, as well as Indonesians I Nyoman Gunarsa, Soedarso and Hendra Gunawan. Some of these artists' old homes in Ubud are now open to the public.

Apart from offering works of art, ARMA also aims to promote the visual and performing arts, produce workshops, and act as a bookshop and library. The grand Balinese-style buildings are set in lush grounds next door to the Kokokan Hotel, in Peliatan. (The museum's commercial venture is the Agung Rai Fine Art Gallery, around the corner on Jalan Peliatan.)

BELOW: furnishings in the Ubud palace.

From here, continue south on the main Denpasar road to **Museum Rudana** (open daily 8am–5pm; tel: 975-779; admission fee), a three-storey museum opened in 1995 to commemorate the 50th anniversary of Indonesia's independence. The top floor consists of mostly anonymous works in the classical Kamasan style and in the Ubud and Batuan styles seen in the half-dozen works by I Gusti Nyoman Lempad, I Gusti Ketut Kobot and Wayan Bendi. A room to the side features photos from the opening celebration, as well as a rare, original Walter Spies. The first and the lower floors of the museum display works by well-known contemporaries Affandi, Srihadi Sudarsono and Gunarsa. There is also an extensive display of fine wooden sculptures by artists such as I Wayan Jumu and I Wayan Pasti. The museum's extensive grounds also house two galleries, a small one at the front and an enormous gallery at the back with half a dozen rooms lined with originals.

Peliatan ㉑ was famous in the 1950s for its *legong* dancers, who took New York by storm while on tour. Today, the daughters of these one-time performers, along with their cousins and friends, continue the tradition. Every Friday night at the hamlet square in Banjar Teruna, some of Peliatan's finest exponents of music and dance take to the stage performing the *tirta sari gamelan*. Originally, these artists were all trained under the discerning and critical eyes and ears of the late Anak Agung Gede Mandera.

For decades, Gung Kak, as he was affectionately called, groomed both dancers and musicians alike, and his legacy lives on today in Peliatan. One of the few all-women performing *gamelan (gamelan ibu-ibu)* rehearses here; many of the women are relatives of Gung Kak. They perform every Sunday night with a dance troupe of children.

Map on page 191

BELOW: overview of Goa Gajah.

Beyond Ubud

The "elephant cave" off the Ubud–Gianyar road, west of Peliatan near Bedulu, **Goa Gajah** ② (open during daylight hours; admission fee) is immediately apparent from the many stalls flogging cheap souvenirs to tourists. Some think it is one of Bali's more overrated attractions, though it's an important site. There are certainly no elephants here, and no one knows for sure why it was accorded this appellation, except that some say an early European mistook the carvings at the cave's entrance for that of an elephant. There is also a reference in the 1365 *lontar* (palm-leaf manuscript) *Nagarakertagama* to a Balinese place called Lwa Gajah (Elephant Water, or River), which was a dwelling place of a Buddhist priest. Elephant Water may refer to the Petanu River, near to the cave.

Goa Gajah, which dates back to at least the 11th century, was excavated in 1922. The cave's entrance is a monstrous head with a gaping mouth, with hands that appear to be pushing apart the entrance. All around are fantastically carved leaves, animals, waves and humans running from the mouth in fear. Some say that these represent humanity's helplessness in the face of natural danger. Inside is a 13-metre-long (43 ft) passage stopping at a T-junction 15 metres (50 ft) wide. This decidedly unimpressive inner sanctum contains several niches, which could have served as sleeping compartments for ascetics.

At one end of the passage is a four-armed statue of Ganesha. At the opposite end is a set of three *lingga*, or phalluses. Since Ganesha, the elephant-headed deity, is the son of Siwa, and *lingga* are generally attributed to Siwa worship, one might conclude that Goa Gajah is a temple. But the sleeping niches and Buddhist ruins just outside the cave suggest otherwise. The sculpted face of the cave wears large earplugs and is therefore a woman; many interpret her as a Rangda-

There are elements of both Hinduism and Buddhism found at Goa Gajah, derived from the 8th to 14th centuries. The cave may be an early precursor to the Hindu-Buddhist character that to a large degree defines Bali today.

BELOW: niche at Goa Gajah, and the cave's entrance.

type witch figure, which could be linked to Tantric Buddhism or Bhairavite Shivaism. Another theory is that this cave is being pushed apart and split into two, just as Siwa pushed apart the great cosmic mountain and created Gunung Agung, the male, and Gunung Batur, the female. (Ceremonies propitiating the deities in the temple of one mountain must often be held in the other as well to complete the ritual.)

To the side of the cave's entrance is a 1,000-year-old statue of Hariti, a Buddhist demoness-cum-goddess. At one time she devoured children, but she then forswore her cannibalistic diet, became a good Buddhist, and took on the role of the protector of children. The Balinese have adapted her as their own Men Brayut, a poor woman who, along with her husband Pan Brayut, had so many children she just didn't know what to do. Large gargoyle nymphs spout water from their stomachs in a bathing place in front of the cave. Water is the source of life to the Balinese, and sacred wells like this are often found near temples.

Continue down the road and turn right at the white statue of the lady if you want to see unique and rarely visited 14th-century reliefs at **Yeh Puluh ㉓** (open daily during daylight hours; admission fee). Good walking shoes are needed to reach the site.

This 25-metre-long (80-ft), 2-metre-high (7-ft) rock wall is carved in high relief, which is unusual in that, aside from a statue of Ganesha, there are no depictions of religious themes. Instead, carved into the wall are scenes from daily life. The sequence begins with a *kayon*, the first puppet used in the *wayang kulit*, which represents the creation of the world. The first figure is a man with his hand raised in what looks like a salute. Scholars say this is a representation of the incarnation of Wisnu, or Krishna as a young boy.

Map on page 191

BELOW: At Yeh Puluh.

*The Javanese
Majapahit empire
arose after the
Javanese repelled
Kublai Kahn's
attempt to subjugate
Java in 1293.
Majapahit general
Gajah Mada invaded
Bali in 1343. The
empire lasted until
the early 1500s,
replaced by ascend-
ing Islamic power,
causing Hindu-
Javanese aristocracy
to flee to Bali. This
had a profound
influence on today's
Balinese culture.*

BELOW:
artefacts at Pura
Penataran Sasih.

The village of **Bedulu** ㉔, which stands at the crossroads between Pejeng and Yeh Puluh, was once a centre of the early Hindu dynasties. In the 11th century, when the rulers of the Majapahit empire on Java were attempting to unify the Indonesian archipelago, all but one king on Bali had agreed to submit to this outside power. King Beda Ulu was reputed to be a man of supernatural strength made invincible by his powerful brand of magic.

To show off his amazing prowess, Beda Ulu order a servant to decapitate him and then replace his head on his torso, with no apparent ill effects. One day the king's head accidentally rolled into the river after being sliced off and was carried away by strong currents. The servant looked around for another head to put back on the king's shoulders, and failing to find it, hastily chopped off a pig's head. After that, Beda Ulu (from *beda hulu*, or changing heads) forbade anyone to look up at him. When Gajah Mada, a government minister, came to talk strategy with Beda Ulu, he requested to eat boiled ferns and drink from a spouted pot. But in order to eat and drink, he had to tilt his head back, and so his eyes fell on the bestial visage of the king. Beda Ulu was enraged by this act of defiance and wanted to kill Gajah Mada. Yet according to Balinese custom, one cannot disturb even one's enemy during a meal.

One version of the story has it that the king literally burned up in a flaming rage at Gajah Mada's impudence. Another version, based more on historical evidence than embellished narrative, says that the king died of sadness after Gajah Mada's troops killed his beloved son. The Pejeng dynasty finally fell to Majapahit forces in 1343.

Centuries prior to this, Bedulu was the centre of another meeting at the **Pura Samuan Tiga**, which means the temple "of a meeting of three parties" – it is

tuated at the junction of three roads. In the late 10th century, Balinese religion lacked cohesion; a number of separate sects, each with their own codifications of religious law, were coming into conflict with each other. So six holy men gathered at Pura Samuan Tiga to simplify the existing religion. Out of this exceptional meeting emerged the key tenets of Balinese Hinduism today: the three elements of manifestation of Sanghyang Widi Wasa, or the Absolute God, being Siwa, Brahma and Wisnu.

Map on page 191

Moon of Pejeng

To see the area's richest temples, it's just a short drive to **Pejeng** ㉕, where there are literally hundreds of old shrines and sacred springs. One of the most impressive antiquities in this area – in all of Indonesia, for that matter – is the Moon of Pejeng at **Pura Penataran Sasih**, to the east off the main road from Bedulu. Actually a large 190-cm (75-inch) bronze kettle drum, the Moon of Pejeng dates back to Indonesia's Bronze Age, which began in 300 BC. It is the largest drum in the world to be cast as a single piece. Shaped like an hour glass, the drum is a rare type decorated with eight stylised heads. Ornamentation on both the heads and body suggest that this drum had its origins in northern Vietnam during Vietnam's Dong Son era. The Chinese rulers of northern Vietnam, or Tonkin, as it was then known, attempted to take over the whole country, which sparked several indigenous revolts. One theory has it that Tonkinese aristocrats fled to Southeast Asia, bringing with them, among other things, the metal drums. Why does this artifact carry the name Moon of Pejeng? Legend says that the drum used to be a wheel of the chariot that drives the moon on its nocturnal journey through the sky. This illuminated wheel fell from the heav-

Detail from the Moon of Pejeng drum.

BELOW: temple relief, Pejeng.

Map on page 191

Temple detail.

OPPOSITE: rural *penjor*, placed in front of homes for Galungan, a holy day. **BELOW:** white heron at Petulu.

ens and landed in a tree near the Penataran Sasih temple, where it has bee housed ever since. Another story relates of the night that a thief broke into th temple and was annoyed at the drum's brilliant light, which revealed his deed So he climbed a tree and urinated on the wheel, whereby the wheel lost i shine and the thief his life. Since then, no one has dared touch the drum. Th temple was the main religious centre of the old Pejeng kingdom, and therefor Balinese from all over the island still make pilgrimages here.

Pura Arjuna Metapa (Temple Where Arjuna Meditated) is just south c **Pura Pusering Jagat** (Temple of the World's Navel). Arjuna is an epic her throughout South and Southeast Asia, and a warrior supreme. In the stor depicted here, Arjuna is meditating on a mountain top, gathering his energies fe a battle with the evil ogre-demon Niwata Kawaca. Pictured with this divir hero are his two attendants, Tualen and Merdah, trusted servants who neve leave his side. The gods test Arjuna's powers of concentration by sending dow two celestial *bidedari*, or angels, to rouse him out of his ascetic state. But Arjur is not disturbed by the celestial beauties and passes the gods' test, marrying th bidedari much later in heaven after he defeats the ogre king.

Pura Pusering Jagat is decorated with dancing figures called *catuhkaya*, sta ues carved with a figure on all four sides. Like the Pejeng giant, these ar demonic with large, open eyes and sneering mouths. The Pejeng Vessel, als called Naragiri or Mountain of Man, is a remarkable cylindrical vessel that rep resents the "churning of the ocean" when the gods produced the elixir of immo tality from the bottom of the sea. **Pura Kebo Edan** (Temple of the Mad Bul is in the rice fields south of **Intaran**. Take the first left west off the main roa after arriving in Pejeng. The site is remarkable for a statue over 3 metres (11 f high, locally called the Pejeng Giant. Restored i 1952, this giant is a male figure in a dance postur standing on a wide-eyed human, perhaps a corps His face is covered by a stone mask, which curious has no face of its own, only abstract designs, horr and fangs. Scholars say that this giant symbolise Bhairava, a Tantric Buddhist manifestation of th Hindu god Siwa. A visit to the archaeology museur **Museum Purbakala** (open daily 8am–12pm; admi sion fee), is possibly worthwhile. Four houses in th first courtyard contain dimly lit and poorly explaine displays of megalithic and Bronze Age remains four in this area, including huge stone sarcophagi.

Ghostly herons?

A little way north of Ubud, **Petulu** ❷⑥ is known for i art works, but most spectacular are the *kokokan*, white herons. Every morning at dawn and then aga right around sundown, they circle the trees in flock In the morning, they head off to neighbouring ric paddies in search of worms, fish and tadpoles befo coming back to Petulu to roost.

Some say the herons are, in fact, manifestations restive spirits. Once there were no herons here. I 1966, the civil war that tore apart Indonesia also de astated Bali. Many of those killed in Bali during th anti-Communist slaughter were buried near where th herons began to nest – just weeks later.

TABANAN

Along with neighbouring Mengwi, Tabanan was once a forceful island regency. Today, its rich agricultural lands make it one of Bali's most prosperous areas and a centre of traditional music

Map on pages 166–7

abanan and Mengwi were once powerful and warring regencies, but the bellicose days of absolute rule ended with the Dutch conquest of southern Bali in 1908. Unlike the raja of Karangasem to the east, however, the raja f Tabanan had no agreement with the Dutch and so lost the rights to his lands, hich were then distributed amongst the councils of individual villages. With eir own land, the communities thrived, and Tabanan is today a prosperous rea, due almost entirely to its fertile rice fields.

Despite being deprived by the Dutch of political power, the rajas remained aders among their people. Palaces continued to serve as centres of the arts, and oyal families retained their pivotal role of presiding over devotions at temples. Residents throughout Mengwi, for example, still participate in the *odalan* t Pura Taman Ayun, the old kingdom's state temple. In the jungle near the eak of the volcano Batukau lies the mountain sanctuary of Pura Luhur, also a oyal temple. The gigantic forests that surround the sanctuary are uninhabited ilderness, yet thousands have journeyed there to pay homage.

The central mountains of northern Tabanan eventually extend to the western p of Bali, rising through the darkest and most mysterious regions of the island, ow a protected national park. *(See chapter on West-rn Bali, page 245.)* Deer, crocodile and wild hogs)am these dense bushlands. Some even say the last ger of Bali stalks here, although no one has sighted for some years. To the north is Gunung Bratan, and eyond, the northern coast of Buleleng regency. *(See hapter on Northern Bali, page 217.)* At the southern xtent of Tabanan regency, on the coast and nearly on 'abanan's border with Badung, is what is perhaps 'ali's most photographed image, Pura Tanah Lot.)ne may reach Tanah Lot from Tabanan and 'Iengwi, but often it is part of a traveller's excursions within southern Bali, from Denpasar or Kuta. 'or this reason, this guide's coverage of Tanah Lot is n the Southern Bali chapter *(page 162)*.

PRECEDING PAGES: *gebogan* offerings enroute to temple. **LEFT:** *gamelan* leader, Tabanan. **BELOW:** sculpture at Pura Sada.

Mengwi

)n the road north from Denpasar and about 6 km 4 miles) south of Mengwi, **Kapal ㉗** shelters the 1ost important temple in the area, **Pura Sada**, an ncestral sanctuary honouring the deified spirit of Ratu Sakti Jayengrat, whose identity remains uncertain. The temple's original foundations may be as old s the 12th century, but the temple itself was rebuilt luring Majapahit times by one of the early rajas of 'Iengwi, perhaps in the 16th century. The oldest of he Mengwi state shrines and predating Pura Taman Ayun in Mengwi, Pura Sada was destroyed in the

great earthquake of 1917 and restored in 1950. A large brick *prasada*, ornamented with modern statues, dominates the complex. Seven saints adorn the
body of this structure, and at the top are the nine gods, the lords of the eight
directions and of the centre. The temple's 54 stone seats represent either the
raja's wives and concubines or else the servants of three royal leaders.

A turn-off toward the mountain leads to the principality of **Mengwi ㉓**,
which until 1891 was the centre of a powerful kingdom dating back to the Gelgel dynasty, whose kings continue to be venerated in temples of Mengwi, in particular, at **Pura Taman Ayun**.

Taman Ayun was founded by a raja of Mengwi, I Gusti Agung Anom, in the
17th century. The small doors of the shrines here are beautifully carved, and the
surrounding moat gives the impression of a garden sanctuary in the middle of
a pond, explaining the name *taman*, or garden. This temple is a *penyawangan*,
or a place to worship other sacred sites or temples. Here are shrines to Bali's
mountain peaks of Agung, Batukau, Batur and Pengelengan, as well as to Pura
Sada. There are three main courtyards that represent the three realms of the
earthly spirits, humans and the gods. The entire complex symbolises the Hindu
holy mountain of Mahameru floating in a sea of milk. Across from the temple
is the somewhat mediocre Manusa Yadnya Museum (open during daylight
hours; donation), where ritual artifacts used in life-cycle rites are on display. The
most interesting are the cremation tower and wooden bull sarcophagus.

Monkeys from the sky

Rawana, the villainous giant of the classical *Ramayana* epic, could perish neither on earth nor in the air. To effect his demise, the monkey general Hanuman

cided to suffocate the giant by crushing him between two halves of the Hindu ly mountain, Mahameru, a destruction effected between earth and air. When anuman took Mahameru, part of the mountain fell to the earth in **Sangeh** ㉙, ong with a group of monkeys from his army and whose descendants remain the island to this day to pester travellers. Such is the legendary origin of the onkey forest of Bukit Sari, a cluster of towering nutmeg trees and home to undreds of rude monkeys. The forest is sacred, and for many years no one as permitted to chop wood there.

A moss-covered 17th-century temple, **Pura Bukit Sari**, lies in the heart of the oods, a familiar hideout for its nimble simian inhabitants. Vendors sell peanuts feed the monkeys, but be sure to keep sunglasses, dangling earrings, satchels d cameras out of temptation's way. Like most of their cousins elsewhere on ali, at least in the areas frequented by people, these monkeys are tourist-savvy d rather intelligent, and they expect considerable remuneration, if not pro-ction money, for their antics.

Pura Bukit Sari was originally built as a meditation temple, then converted an agricultural temple. It has been restored several times, most recently in 973. In the central courtyard, a large statue of a *garuda*, an old carving of ncertain date, symbolises freedom from suffering and the attainment of *merta,* the elixir of life. The surrounding nutmeg trees were presumably anted deliberately a long time ago; it is a unique grove in Bali.

A separate route linking Sangeh directly with Denpasar begins at Jalan artini. A side road joins Blahkiuh, just south of Sangeh, with Mengwi, hich can also be reached by returning to Denpasar and heading west. An sphalt road links Sangeh with Ubud.

Map on pages 166–7

BELOW:
temple statue.

Marga memorial.

North from Taman Ayun is the village of **Marga** ③⓪, important historically an[d] socially to the Balinese. In 1946, the commander of Indonesian troops in Bal[i] Lt. Col. I Gusti Ngurah Rai, and his company of guerrilla fighters were kille[d] in a battle at Marga. Surrounded and outnumbered by Dutch forces and und[er] bombardment from the air, Ngurah Rai's 94 men refused to surrender. Instea[d] they attacked the Dutch positions and died to the last man – a suicidal assau[lt] reminiscent of the royal *puputan* carried out 40 years earlier, also in defiance [of] the Dutch. A monument in Marga – Margarana – honours these valiant so[l]diers, inscribed with a courageous letter written by Ngurah Rai refusing su[r]render until their cause was won. Nearby are 94 stone markers, each with th[e] name and home village of the Balinese killed here. The anniversary of Ngura[h] Rai's death, 20 November, is a Balinese holiday and a time when many of Bali['s] finest musicians and dancers perform to pay tribute to him. Bali's internation[al] airport and a university are named in his honour.

Tabanan

The town of **Tabanan** ③⓵, like the capitals of the other regencies on Bali, [is] dwarfed by Denpasar. However, Tabanan is a spirited town, its shops in th[e] hands of industrious Chinese merchants. Together with the other souther[n] regencies of Badung and Gianyar, Tabanan forms the island's most prosperou[s] region, an extension of the rice belt of the southern plains. Kept in impeccab[le] order by the *subak* associations, the fertile fields stretch from the foothills [of] Batukau volcano to the southern coast. Farmers adhere to no special season f[or] planting and harvesting; cycles of growth vary with individual plots, and plan[t]ing continues throughout the year.

BELOW: martyr memorial at Marga.

Tabanan became a separate and powerful kingdom during the shake-up of political domains in the 17th century. It has long been the home of some of the most admired *gamelan* orchestras and dancers, among them the great male dancer I Ketut Mario. Born at the end of the 19th century, he was already dancing at the age of six. Somewhat later, he developed and perfected the spectacular solo dances of *kebyar duduk* and *kebyar trompong*, which began in northern Bali during World War I. Mario's grace and movement enraptured European audiences who saw him dance in the 1930s. When Mario was shown his photograph in a book by the Mexican Miguel Covarrubias, one of many foreigners drawn to Bali by its exotic arts, he exclaimed, "That man is a good dancer. How is it that I have never seen him?" – then he laughed with amazed delight to discover it was himself.

From Tabanan, it is an easy journey southward to Pura Tanah Lot, on the coast. *(See Southern Bali chapter, page 162.)* Tabanan's coast is being developed with tourist resorts, even though the coastal waters are quite rough and dangerous, as there is little reef to protect the southwestern beaches. At the end of every side road to the coast lies a long and deserted black-sand beach, with surf that sometimes breaks over 3 metres (10 ft) high. The undertow and currents here can be quite treacherous, and drownings are not uncommon.

If it's more of the village ambience that one is seeking, then stay at the *puri* **Krambitan ③**. Belonging to the royal family of Tabanan, two palaces – **Puri Anyar** and **Puri Agung Wisata** – have showcased their *tektekan gamelan* ensemble, with bell-like wooden split-drums with clappers, here for several decades, along with the local cuisine. For a fair amount of money, anybody can participate in one of these chartered evenings, which include either a *joged*

Map on pages 166–7

Famed dancer I Ketut Mario, of Tabanan.

BELOW: Tabanan *gamelan* orchestra.

Map on pages 166–7

(flirtation dance accompanied by a bamboo *gamelan*) or a *calon arang* tranc performance, complete with a buffet dinner. If it's just the surroundings one i after, then rent a small, elegant room in Puri Anyar.

Northward towards Bedugul and Bratan

North of Tabanan, on the road that eventually leads to Bedugul and Dana Bratan *(see chapter on Northern Bali, page 217)*, is **Penebel ㉝**. This mountai village has a *pura puseh* with a *lingga-yoni*, an ancient fertility symbol of bot a penis and vagina, representing Siwa and his consort Uma.

More popular with travellers is one of Bali's most venerated, but still modes temples – **Pura Luhur Batukau**, near **Batukau ㉞** on the slopes of Gunun Batukau, 2,278 metres (7,474 ft) high. The western highlands of Batukau a famed for magnificent landscapes. The view from the mountain village c **Jatiluwih** takes in the whole of southern Bali. Perched on a high terraced slop Jatiluwih deserves its name – Truly Marvellous.

Temple offerings at Batukau.

Pura Luhur Batukau is an important temple, and every other temple in wes ern Bali has a shrine dedicated to Pura Luhur Batukau, which is located withi solitary grounds far above the farmlands. The forest and the green moss ever where are Pura Luhur's modest decorations, and there are no ornate carvings c gilded shrines to be found in this mountain sanctuary.

A single seven-tiered *meru* exalts Mahadewa, the deity associated wit

OPPOSITE: market in central Bali.
BELOW: temple at Batukau.

Gunung Batukau. As this was the state ancestral temple of the royal family c Tabanan, each of the shrines also represents one of the deified ancestors. Th seven-tiered *meru* is also the home of Di Made, a ruler of the Gelgel court in t late 17th century. The three-tiered shrine is dedicated to a former king c Tabanan. The adjacent stone shrines, called *prasad* are similar to those at Kapal and Serangan.

Not far from the temple itself, a square lake recal the moat of Pura Taman Ayun to the south in Mengw In fact, both temples are classed as *pura taman* – tem ples with a garden pond and maintained by a raj Lakes are also related to mountain sanctuaries, ar the rituals here include veneration of the lakes and blessing for irrigation water. At Pura Luhur star shrines for the three mountain lakes *(danau)* within i catchment: Bratan, Buyan and Tambelingan.

Near Pura Luhur is the spring **Yeh Panas**, whe hot water surges from the river bank. Natural ph nomena that are unusual or not quite so common a believed to be frequented by spirits, and so Yeh Pan is graced by a small temple where people mak prayers with offerings. During World War II, t Japanese made the first artificial improvements of t springs when they tried to create a Japanese-style ou door *onsen*. Fortunately or not, depending upon one inclinations, the springs are now part of a modest ho spring resort complete with spa and hotel. Non-gues can utilise the spa for a fee.

On the road south a few kilometres from Batukau an intersection with a winding road that skirts eas ward across the mountain to the main road headi from Denpasar to Bedugul and Lake Bratan and eve tually to the north coast at Singaraja.

NORTHERN BALI

Few travellers end up along the northern coast. A pity, since the architecture can be more flamboyant, the beaches less claustrophobic, and life's rhythms less driven by tourism

Map on page 219

I n contrast to the south, northern Bali – the regency of Buleleng – presents an altered landscape and a different history. On the other side of Bali's central volcanic peaks from the populous south, northern orchards of citrus fruits, vanilla, coffee and cocoa, not to mention fields of strawberries, replace the familiar rice paddy. Red grapes, too, thrive in the dry heat here. The countryside is more golden in the north due to the lower rainfall.

The feudal rule of local rajas here ended in 1848, when the Dutch gained control a full 60 years before they conquered the south. In fact, many descendants of the rajas joined the Dutch administration, and the resulting European influence gave the way of life in northern Bali a more Westernised hue than in most of the communities in the south. The art of northern Bali is also distinctive. The intricate sandstone carvings found in the southern temples are more restrained than those of the northern temples, where tall gates have a dynamic, flaming ascendancy and are covered with luxurious designs and images. The pink sandstone of the north, quarried near Singaraja, is extremely soft, in turn inspiring northern carvers to give full vent to their creative imaginations, an advantage that often leads to humourous and Rabelaisian scenes. Temple offerings here differ, not as elaborate as elsewhere in Bali.

PRECEDING PAGES: a harvest of grapes going to Lovina. **OPPOSITE:** Rangda image at a village *pura dalem*. **BELOW:** boats for hire, Danau Bratan.

Danau Bratan

From the southern plains of Tabanan and Gianyar, heading northward to the central mountains, the landscape changes from flowing tiers of rice to motley patches of onion, cabbage and papaya growing in the cooler highlands. The clusters of farmhouses along the way are no longer the familiar thatched huts of the south but instead are sturdy cottages made of wood and roofed with tiles. The road climbs and winds its way around steep cliffs covered with ferns, wild flowers and elephant grass. Up into the mountains, the air becomes clearer, crisper and cooler.

Bedugul ❶ lies 1,300 metres (4,300 ft) above sea level and is the name of both a small town and a mountain-lake resort area, which the Balinese have long used as a weekend retreat.

At the mountain crest dividing northern and southern Bali lies serene **Danau Bratan**, a lake filling the long-extinct crater of Gunung Catur and often veiled with mist veiling the ancient crater. Because the lake is an essential water source for surrounding farmlands, the people of Bedugul honour Dewi Danau, goddess of the lake, in **Pura Ulun Danu Bratan**, a temple on a small lake-shore promontory. Apart from the peak tour-bus hours, it is usually peaceful and cool here, although on weekends the drone of motorboats and

Parasailing on Danau Bratan, near Bedugul.

Jetskis is decidedly incongruous with the surroundings. Built in the early 1600 by a raja of Mengis, this temple, along with Pura Ulun Danu Batur, is the mos important irrigation temple in Bali. Slender *meru* rise along the lake's edge the three-tiered *meru* for Siwa, the seven-tiered for Brahma, and the 11-tiered *meru* for Wisnu and Dewi Danau.

Just north of Bedugul proper is the market of Bukit Munggu, popularly called **Candi Kuning ❷** and where wild orchids and brilliant lilies are sold alongside temperate and tropical vegetables grown in the region's fertile soil. Adjacent to the market is **Kebun Raya Eka Karya Bali (Bali Botanical Gardens**; open daily, 8am-5pm; admission fee). This is a refreshing 130-hectare (320 acre) stop. Hiking trails slice through towering forests – there are over 650 species of trees in the gardens – and sprawling grounds. For those with their noses close to the ground, gardens nurture more than 400 species of orchids.

Nestled just before the highway starts its descent to the north is **Danau Buyan**, a quieter and lower-profile lake than Bratan and embraced by cozy hill sides of coffee.

To the north coast

From the highest point on the road, 1,220 metres (4,000 ft) above sea level, spectacular and twisting descent leads into Buleleng regency proper and th northern coast. Buleleng is open to the sheltered waters of the Java Sea, and throughout history, Buleleng has been more accessible to the world than th rest of Bali. Buleleng rose to prominence at the beginning of the 17th century under Raja Panji Sakti, who conquered the eastern tip of Java. In 1604, he buil a palace called Singaraja on fields where the grain *buleleng* was grown.

BELOW: Pura Ulun Danu Bratan.

In 1814, a British military expedition stayed several months in Singaraja. The British left, only to be promptly replaced by the Dutch, who came first with demands and later with military force, accusing the rajas of raiding wrecked ships along the coast, actually a time-honoured and justified practice to the Balinese. Initial attempts by the Dutch to subdue the north ended in defeat. After a long, fierce battle in 1849, a reinforced expedition captured the Buleleng stronghold of Jagaraga, to the east of Singaraja. The Dutch imposed direct colonial rule upon Buleleng and Jembrana, to the west, in 1882. Singaraja became the capital and chief port, and it was the colonial government seat for the old Lesser Sunda province, now called Nusa Tenggara, until 1953.

About 10 km (6 miles) before the descent from Danau Bratan ends in Singaraja, the waterfalls at **Air Terjun Gitgit** ❸ have long lured travellers. The falls are fine enough, especially at the peak of the rainy season, but the commercialisation at the end of the severely rutted approach road can tax anyone after a long journey. Even the 500-metre-long (1,600 ft) footpath to the cascading falls is peppered with kiosks selling non-essential junk.

An important shipping and trading centre for the export of coffee and rice, **Singaraja** ❹ has a cosmopolitan flavour about it, derived from several centuries as an important trading port. Bali's second-largest city after Denpasar, Singaraja's population of 150,000 comprises many ethnic and religious groups – Muslim, Christian, Buddhist, Arabic, Indian – and it is not unusual to see an Islamic procession pass before a Chinese temple flanked by office buildings of European design. Arriving in the city from the lofty heights of the central mountains, one is embraced by a pleasant and comfortable urban centre with textures unlike elsewhere in Bali.

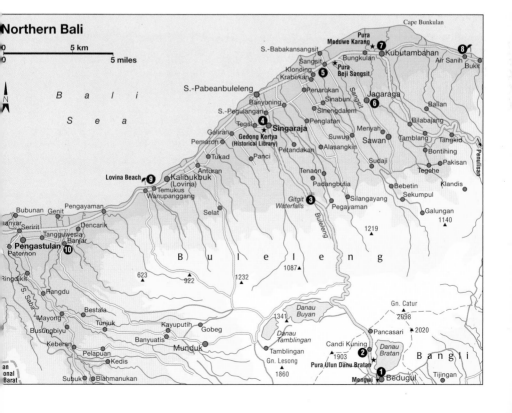

Northern Bali

Feeling guilty after their bloody conquest of Bali in the early 20th century, the Dutch began a systematic preservation of Balinese culture. On Jalan Veteran, Singaraja houses a historical library, **Gedong Kirtya**, a repository of some 3,000 Balinese manuscripts established by the Dutch in the late 1920s. In addition to books and manuscripts, Gedong Kirtya has what is perhaps the world's finest collection of *lontar* – a traditional Southeast Asian style of book made from inscribed leaves of the *lontar* palm, cut into strips and preserved between two pieces of precious wood, or even bamboo. Subjects covered in these ancient works include literature, mythology, historical chronicles and religious treatises. Some works are relatively new, while others are almost a millennium old, although they have been constantly recopied. Miniature pictures, incised on the leaves with an iron stylus, are masterpieces in the art of illustration. Many of Gedong Kirtya's *lontar* were acquired in Lombok; some of these were earlier retrieved from Java during the collapse of the Majapahit empire. The library also holds *prasasti*, metal plates inscribed with royal edicts of the early Pejeng-Bedulu dynasty that are among the earliest written documents found in Bali

In Southeast Asia, the technique of inscribing lontar probably came by way of India. Indian manuscripts were "illuminated" in palm-leaf books from 1100 to 1350. Eventually, paper replaced palm-leaf in the making of books in India.

East of Singaraja

Eastward from Singaraja are some of the finest examples of northern Balinese temples. Instead of the small shrines and *meru* towers of southern temples, a single pedestal built on a terraced stone base furnishes the inner courtyard of most northern temples. Often, the pedestal supports a *padmasana* – a throne of the sun god. Compared with the classical lines of southern decoration, northern Balinese carving is forcefully baroque. Every crevice of the temple is carved in curves flames, arabesques and spirals.

BELOW: traditional Balinese books, known as *lontar.*

In **Sangsit** ❺, a *subak* (irrigation association) temple, **Pura Beji**, is dedicated to Dewi Sri as Ratu Manik Galih, the goddess of rice. Built in the 15th century, this temple sports many *naga*, serpents that are symbols of earth and
fertility. Naga snakes form the balustrade of the fine gateway, and fantastic but
imaginary beasts and devilish guardians peer from the entangled flora, their
heads deliberately cocked at an angle to throw the façade slightly off balance.
Lawless birds, fierce tigers and sunflowers project from every part of the
pedestal. Rows of stone towers jut up from the terraces, forming a labyrinth of
pink sandstone. To counterbalance the overpowering decor, the courtyard is
spacious and decorated with frangipani trees.

About 15 km (10 miles) southeast of Singaraja, **Jagaraga** ❻ is famous for a
bloody 1849 battle between the Balinese and the Dutch that killed much of the
village's population and ended several years of fighting between the two. However, Jagaraga's main attraction today is **Pura Dalem**, the temple of the dead
where Siwa, in his manifestation as destroyer, presides. Here, reliefs portray life
before and after the Dutch arrival, including two smug Europeans in a Ford
Model T being taken unaware by armed bandits, flying aces in aircraft plunging into the sea, and a Dutch steamer, under attack by a crocodilian sea monster,
signaling an SOS. Even the wicked Rangda and fertility statues – a dazed mother
buried under a pile of children – are skilfully hewn with a sense of humour.
Southward is **Sawan**, a village with a *gamelan* gong-casting industry, a talented bamboo *gamelan angklung* orchestra, and a nice night market.

The main road descending to the north coast from Danau Batur and the mountain town of Kintamani meets the coastal road in **Kubutambahan** ❼. Along the
main coastal road further east is **Pura Meduwe Karang**, a temple dedicated to

Map on page 219

*Model-T image, Pura
Dalem, Jagaraga.*

BELOW: Pura Beji,
Sangsit.

Map on page 219

In the north, water is relatively scarce. Less than 150 centimetres (60 in) of rain fall during the rainy season along the northern coast, compared to 300 centimetres (120 in) in the mountains. Bali's longest dry season is also along the northern coast, lasting 8 months.

TIP

While watching dolphins is a popular activity with travellers in Lovina, increasingly it is controversial. Bobbing convoys of early-morning boats carrying tourists in search of dolphins can take on comedic if not pathetic appearances. The chase may also disturb the morning activities of the dolphins.

OPPOSITE: black sands of Lovina.

dry-land agriculture. It was built in 1890 and has many fertility themes, including numerous portrayals of erotic acts. Temple carvings also show ghouls, domestics, lovers and noblemen, and even include a rendition of a bicycle-riding Westerner, believed to be Dutchman W.O.J. Nieuwenkamp, who travelled everywhere on Bali by bicycle at the beginning of the 20th century.

Pura Meduwe Karang literally means "Temple of the Owner of the Land", and it honours the earth and the sun that nurture the crops of dry agriculture. Just as subak temples ensure harvests on irrigated rice fields, this temple assures a "blessing" for plants grown on unirrigated land, including fruits, coconut, maize and coffee. On the temple's festival day, farmers from the surrounding villages come to ask for remnants of the offerings, which are then buried in the fields. This is a ritual intended to transmit divine benevolence to the soil.

Further eastward along the coast are the ice-cold springs at **Air Sanih** ❸, also known as Yeh Sanih and 17 km (11 miles) from Singaraja. For a small fee, travellers can take a dip in this natural, spring-fed swimming pool. Accommodation and restaurants are available. Sunrise from the beach at Sanih is beautiful, providing a precursor for an early departure.

If continuing eastward, the road becomes simpler, as do the villages, and less travelled. The land grows drier and less lush, and few tourists will be encountered along this road, at least until Tulambon and Amed *(See Eastern Bali chapter, page 238.)*

Westward from Singaraja

Six km (4 miles) west of Singaraja is an 8-km-long (5-mile) stretch of black sand beach comprising the villages of Anturan, Tukad Mungga, Kalibukbuk, Kalisasem and Temukus, collectively and commonly called **Lovina** ❾. The term *lovina* refers to "love", and was given by the last raja of Buleleng in the 1960s. Caressed by gentle waves and anchored by the main village of Kalibukbuk, Lovina is a decent but not exceptional area in which to snorkel, dive and watch dolphins. Accommodation ranges from simple *losmen* to more upmarket resorts. The pace is slower than at other beach resorts, but tourist interest is picking up.

One of the more intriguing features of this area is the Brahma Arama Vihara, a Buddhist *ashram* founded in 1958 in the village of **Banjar** ❿. To get there, go 3 km (2 miles) west of Temukus to Dencarik, then take an *ojek* (motorcycle taxi) up the hill. Classes in Buddhist meditation are available only twice a year – in April and September – but visitors are allowed to come year-round, as long as they are dressed properly and speak and walk quietly. This village is also home to the **Air Panas**, hot springs that are now a public bathing area with changing rooms and a restaurant, along with the obligatory gauntlet of souvenir vendors between the parking lot and the springs. On 17 August – Independence Day – have a look at the buffalo races *(sapi gerumbugnan)*, an exciting and colourful event greatly enjoyed by the locals.

Much further west near the village of **Banyupoh** is **Pantai Gondol**, a lovely beach with good snorkelling. Just down the road is the temple of Pulaki, sacred space guarded by a band of monkeys. The temple is hewn out of the mountain rock and overlooks the ocean. It is said that the itinerant priest Danghyang Nirartha came here with one of his wives and daughter in the 16th century. Residents asked him to render them invisible. Today, it is still believed that an entire village of people – and a jungle full of tigers – exist unseen here.

One can continue westward along the coast to Teluk Terima, a departure point to the island of Menjangan, or to Gilimanuk, from where the ferry to Java departs. *(See Western Bali chapter, page 248.)*

EASTERN BALI

East is the most auspicious of compass points in the Balinese world-view, and today an excursion amongst the temples, palace ruins and unfettered black-sand beaches reveals why

Map on page 229

Neither as developed nor as rich as the southern part of the island, the eastern side of Bali has a different ambience that is defined by its archaic rituals, lava-strewn landscapes, and high, bare hills ribbed with ancient terracing. The coastal strip along the eastern shore consists primarily of coconut and banana groves, although it has become a tourist destination in its own right. (Unfortunately, however, the gathering of coral – which is ground into lime and used in the local construction of *losmen* and restaurants – has eroded some of the reefs irreparably.)

Partly hidden by the eastern coastal ranges is the colossal cone of Gunung Agung, which on clear days soars high above the countryside.

From Gianyar, follow the main road to Klungkung, which is the capital of the Klungkung regency. East of Klungkung, the landscapes are still blackened by the lava streams of the 1963 eruption of Agung, which isolated this area for several years. To see the east, it's better to plan a night or two in Manggis or Candidasa and then explore the area in two or three days – the first to Klungkung and Besakih and the second to Tenganan and the seacoast.

Klungkung

As the seat of the Dewa Agung, nominally the highest of the old Balinese rajas, **Klungkung ❶** holds a special place in the island's history and culture. As artistic centres, the palaces of Klungkung's rajas and noblemen supported and developed the styles of music, drama and the arts that flourish today in Bali.

The regency capital was shifted to Klungkung from nearby Gelgel in 1710 and a new palace built. Today, the remains of the palace, razed in 1908, are within the grounds of **Taman Gili** (open daily 7am–6pm; admission fee). Probably toward the end of the 18th century, the original **Kerta Gosa**, or Hall of Justice, was erected. The present justice hall, actually an open *bale* and located at the town's main intersection within Taman Gili, is beautifully laid out within a moat and provides an exquisite example of the Klungkung style of painting and architecture. Disputes were heard here only if they could not be settled among families or individual villages, as the Kerta Gosa was the island's highest court of justice, and by far the strictest.

Ceiling paintings here include the story of Bima Swarga (Bima in Heaven). One of the great *Mahabharata* heroes, Bima went looking for his parents in heaven and in hell. As the Balinese believe in reincarnation, they strongly believe in *karma phala*, whereby one is punished or rewarded for one's actions, either in this lifetime or a subsequent one.

PRECEDING PAGES: Eka Dasa Rudra ceremony. **OPPOSITE:** Kerta Gosa, Klungkung. **BELOW:** detail of souvenir kites.

Thus a miserly king, for example, might be reincarnated a pauper, so that he would learn about the true value of material wealth. Such paintings, styled *kamasan* and dating back to the 18th century, show the good and bad consequences of our deeds, and are named after the village where artists still paint in the same fashion. The **Bale Kambang**, or the Floating Pavilion, is similarly decorated and used by the attending royal family as a place to rest. Pan Semaris and Mangku Mura, both from Kamasan, directed the restoration of the paintings in 1945. This structure is all that is left of the old palace, which was destroyed by the Dutch during a battle in 1908.

Most techniques of painting found in Bali today have their roots in the Kamasan style that is reminiscent of shadow puppets.

The actual village of **Kamasan** lies 2 km (1¼ miles) to the south and draws its main themes from Old Javanese classics, and the figures look like wayang puppets. In 1973, Nyoman Mandra started a painting school here so that young artists could imitate the master's stroke. Kamasan is also a thriving centre of gold and silver work. In the shops of Klungkung itself, one can buy modern and antique Klungkung-style paintings, carvings and silks.

About 5 km (3 miles) west of Klungkung, near Takmung, is the modern **Museum Seni Lukis Klasik Bali** (open Tuesday–Sunday, 9am–5pm; admission fee). Housing both traditional Balinese art and historical artefacts, it also includes the works of Nyoman Gunarsa, founder of the museum.

Gunung Agung and Pura Besakih

According to mythology, when the deities made mountains for their thrones they set the highest peak in the east, a compass point that is a place of honour to the Balinese. In every temple in Bali, a shrine is dedicated to the spirit of **Gunung Agung**. The tapering form of cremation towers, *meru*, and even tem-

BELOW: vendors at Klungkung temple.

ple offerings bear the shape of a mountain, mirroring the people's reverence for this holy volcano. Here, on the slopes of Gunung (Mount) Agung, lies Pura Besakih, the Mother Temple, so called as it houses ancestral shrines for all Hindu Balinese. Pura Besakih, actually a cluster of temples, is the acme of the sacred to the Balinese. *(See full description of Pura Besakih on page 230.)*

Map below

Besakih can be reached from both the south and the east. Usually visitors come through Klungkung and then continue north. This route is probably the best way to travel, then turning east through Selat. One can then head on to the coast through Bebandem or turn right after Selat and return to Klungkung. Either road offers spectacular views of terraced rice fields.

From Klungkung turn north, passing through the astonishing landscapes of Bukit Jambul. In **Sideman**, every household is engaged in some aspect of textile weaving. This is one of the centres of *ikat* weaving, and from the road, one can hear the click-click-click of looms. *Songket* cloth (cotton and silk with an overweft of silver or gold threads) also is produced here.

There are four homestays here, each owned by one of the four wives of the local prince. If looking for an isolated place to stay, to stroll through the rice fields and drink in the view, then this is it. Another unique aspect about this village is a school of cultural arts. Here, adolescent students can study traditional literature, painting, dance, music, and Balinese language, in addition to the regular school work.

Iseh ❷, a mountain village where people grow rice and onions, was chosen in 1932 by the German artist Walter Spies as a site for a country house, which has an uninterrupted view of Gunung Agung. The massive slope is cut by deep ravines, forming serpentine shadows descending to a wide valley of rice fields.

In the 1920s, Western artists began arriving in Bali, including Walter Spies. Their introduction of earthly themes and new artists' media influenced modern Balinese art.

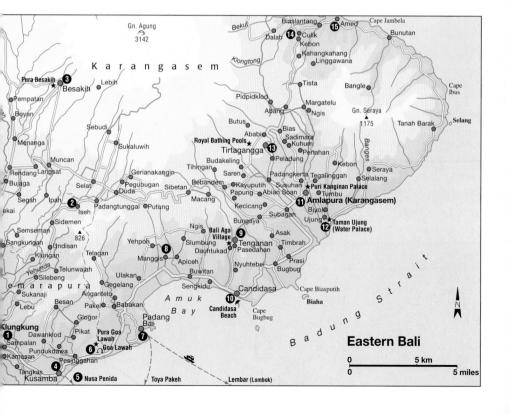
Eastern Bali

Temple meru *at Pura Besakih, on the slopes of Agung.*

BELOW: taking offerings to Pura Besakih.

Hues vary from luminous yellow to the opulent light green of mature rice to red-stemmed stalks before harvest.

In **Muncan**, a unique ritual occurs the day before Nyepi (mid-March), the Day of Silence. Here, Jero Ding and Jero Dong – represented by two tree trunks, one with a natural hole in it, the other with a protruding stick attached to it – are used to re-enact an old fertility ritual. After they have been mated, the figures are taken to the river, where they are discarded; it is believed that the surrounding rice fields are fertilised by this river water after the ritual. Beyond Selat, make a right turn southward.

Once in the village of **Besakih** ❸, climb up to **Pura Besakih** (open daily, 8am–6pm; admission fee), actually a complex of nearly two dozen temples. Non-worshippers are not allowed into the temple, but one can see the layout quite easily from the open gates. Do not enter the temple grounds.

In 1963, devotees of this temple were busily engaged with last preparations for the Eka Dasa Rudra, the greatest of Balinese sacrifices that occurs once every 100 years. Suddenly, a glow of fire shone from the crater and Gunung Agung began to rumble. A priestess interpreted the ashes of the volcano as a sacred portent sent to purify Besakih, and the people continued with their festival arrangements. By the time the great sacrifice was held in March, thick columns of dark smoke were surging from the summit. Shortly after, Gunung Agung exploded, killing over a thousand people.

Westerners might say it was a remarkable coincidence, for the volcano had been dormant for centuries. To most Balinese, of course, the eruption did not occur by chance, but was chastisement for having offended the gods. The volcanic ash destroyed most of the crops on the island. The ceremony was held

again in 1979, after priests decided they had been wrong in their calculations.

Besakih originated most probably as a terraced sanctuary in the eighth century, where worship and offerings were made to the god of Gunung Agung. Over a period of a thousand years or more, it was enlarged until it grew into the present complex of over 80 temples, with 22 main temple complexes. Many of the structures were added between the 14th and the 18th centuries. According to inscriptions kept here, an important event of some sort took place here in 1007. It can only be guessed that this was associated with death rituals for Queen Mahendradatta, Udayana's co-ruler who died the previous year.

In the 15th century, it was the state temple of the Gelgel-Klungkung dynasty, which built a series of small temples in honour of its deified rulers. Nowadays, it is the state temple for the provincial and national governments, which cover all the temple's expenses.

Within the Besakih complex, the paramount sanctuary is **Pura Penataran Agung**, with its lofty *meru* on a high bank of terraces. Steps ascend in a long perspective to the austere split gate. Inside the main courtyard are the three shrines enthroning the three aspects of god: Siwa, god as creation; Pramashiva, god without form; and Sadashiva, god as half male and half female. Many interpret this trinity to be Wisnu, Brahma and Siwa. Three sacred colours are associated with this shrine: red, black and white. Red symbolises the earth as lava and is associated with Brahma; white is light and is associated with Siwa; black is both water and heaven and is associated with Wisnu. During festivals, the shrines are wrapped in coloured cloth. Often one will see yellow used as well, which symbolises compassion. Besakih's main temple festival is held in the fourth lunar month of the Balinese calendar (March or April), in a ritual called Bhatar Turun

Map on page 229

BELOW: Pura Besakih visitors.

Kabeh (The Gods All Descend Together). Balinese from all over the island come to pay homage to their gods and deified ancestors during this month-long festival. Don't expect serenity and solitude outside of the temple, of course. Like other sacred places, there is commercialism directed at travellers.

Along the coast

For those seeking history, a 4-km-long (2½-mile) side trip south from Klungkung to **Gelgel**, the former capital, is essential. In the 1400s and 1500s, the Dewa Agung (a title given to the current king of the time and meaning, literally, Great God) of Gelgel held immense power. However, in the 17th century, with the decline of his power, he lost both battles and allegiances. It was said that a curse had befallen the palace during the rule of Gusti Sideman. As a consequence, the palace was moved to Klungkung. However, small conflicts and jealousies broke out among the kings, resulting in the emergence of numerous minor rajadoms. The eight regencies of today in Bali are based upon the last eight kingdoms. Pura Jero Agung, or Great Palace Temple, is the ancestral shrine of the local palace. Just to the east is another temple, Pura Dasar. Families of the royal caste from all over Bali come here for the temple festival.

Colourful outrigger *prahu* line the black-sand shores of **Kusamba** ❹, a fishing village that also engages in salt-making. Where the road nears the sea, rows of brown, thatched huts emerge from the sands. These huts are small factories for making salt. To make salt, the Balinese gather wet sand from the sea and spread it along sand banks on the beach. After drying, the sand is dumped into a large bin inside the hut. Slowly, water with a high salt content drains through the sands, and the residue is then poured in bamboo troughs to evaporate in the

BELOW: Kusamba black-sand beach, and boatman to Nusa Penida.

un, leaving salt crystals. The entire process takes two days, and if the weather s good, the salt panner can make 5 kilograms (11 lbs) of salt.

Nusa Penida, Nusa Lembongan and Nusa Ceningan

Kusamba lies directly across from Nusa Penida ❺, an island of around 40,000 people. The strait between Bali and Nusa Penida is prime fishing ground. Twice a day, fishermen set out for Nusa Penida with cargoes of peanuts, fruit and rice, as Nusa Penida is only sparsely cultivated. Islanders subsist largely on fishing and trading.

Originally a penal colony for the Klungkung kingdom, Nusa Penida remains dry and austere, and to the Balinese it is an island of mystery and magic. Inhabitants are considered to be expert in black magic, and are treated with great kindness by the Balinese. The legendary sorcerer Jero Gede Macalang came from here, sending invisible henchmen to Bali to claim victims. His temple, Pura Peed (pronounced *pehd*) is 3 km (2 miles) west of Toya Pakeh. Balinese come from the mainland to pay homage on its *odalan*.

Northwest of Nusa Penida are two islands, Nusa Lembongan and Nusa Ceningan. Lembongan is growing as an offshore destination, with several bungalow resorts, beach huts and homestays. There are numerous opportunities for watersports in the bay: a stationary activities platform is used for snorkelling, diving and swimming, boating and coral viewing. The islanders farm and export seaweed, and visitors can bicycle, trek, motorcycle or sail around the island to seaweed farms and mangrove swamps.

The sea around the two islands is particularly noted for fine diving, and the area is frequented by migratory gigantic sun fish in October. Numerous diving,

Map on page 229

TIP

To reach Nusa Penida, take a boat from Kusamba or Padang Bai. The cheapest option is one of the regular boats taking locals out, especially in the morning. There are no scheduled departures.

BELOW: ducks practising for a parade.

day sailing and cruising operators offer access to the islands, departing from Bali's Benoa Harbour.

Kusamba to Manggis

The road continuing east from Kusamba runs parallel to lovely seascapes with a full view of Nusa Penida. It passes close to **Goa Lawah** ❻ (open daily 7am–6pm; admission fee), whose walls vibrate with thousands of bats – their bodies packed so close together that the upper surface of the cave resembles undulating mud. An extraordinary phenomenon, Goa Lawah is considered holy and a temple and surrounding shrines protect the entrance. The cave is said to extend all the way back to Pura Besakih and may continue to an underground river that comes up, it is said, at Pura Goa within the Besakih complex. (Besakih is a temple associated with the mythological naga or serpent Basuki, also honoured at Pura Goa Lawah, where a snake is said to live, feeding on the bats.)

To the east, a perfectly shaped bay is cradled in the hills. The harbour of **Padang Bai** ❼ is the main port of transit to the neighbouring island of Lombok, with passenger and cargo vessels departing each morning. International shipping lines making stopovers in Padang Bai anchor to the left of the bay; visitors and cargo are ferried to the pier. Enclosed by white-sand coves and turquoise sea, the small harbour makes a good port of call for yachts sailing to Bali. There are few bed-and-breakfast places here, and the beach is ideal for playing the sybarite. The history of this coastal village is connected with those eventful years that saw the deaths of Mahendradatta and Udayana at the beginning of the 11th century. At that time, a priest of great stature, Kuturan, lived here. He is now remembered for his reforms of Padang Bai's organisation. Pura Silayukti

BELOW: bats at Goa Lawah cave.

Padang Bai, was built on the site of his former hermitage in the 11th century. Named after the delectable mangosteen fruit, **Manggis** ❽ is primarily a fishing village. Some of the best *prahu* are made here. Down the road, Balina Beach has a few high-class hotels, along with lower budget *losmen*. Take the turn-off to the right for Puri Buitan. The sparkling white-sand beach is inviting and relatively untouched by art shops and beach vendors.

For a quiet, relaxing spell at the beach, stop in **Sengkidu**. Here, there are a couple of *losmen* on the beach, along with a fancy but sterile hotel. Erosion has not been as bad here, and at low tide, one can stroll the beach.

Map on page 229

Tenganan

Further east is the turn-off for **Tenganan** ❾, a Bali Aga ("original Balinese") village. Even though there are numerous Bali Aga villages scattered around the northern part of Bali, the most famous is here in Tenganan, near Candidasa. Within its bastions, all living compounds are identically laid out and arranged in rows on either side of the wide, stone-paved lanes running the village's length.

There is some evidence that the people of Tenganan originally came from the village of Bedulu. The legend of how they acquired their land dates from the 14th century: the mighty King Beda Ulu lost his favourite horse and so sent the villagers of his kingdom in all directions to search for it. The men of Tenganan travelled east and found the corpse of the horse. When the king offered to reward them, they requested the land where the horse was found, that is, all the area in which the carcass of the dead horse could be smelled. The king sent an official with a keen sense of smell to partition the land. For days, the chief of Tenganan led the official through the hills, yet still the air was pungent with the odour of

BELOW: village girls preparing for temple dance.

the dead horse. At last, the tired official decided this was enough land and departed. After he had left, the Bali Aga chief pulled a smelly remnant of the horse's flesh from inside his clothes.

Tenganan still owns, communally, these larger tracts of well cultivated land and is one of the richest villages on the island. Traditionally, the men of the *krama desa*, or the elders' association, were not permitted to work in the field with their own hands. So they hired out their land to men of neighbouring villages. The aristocratic Tenganese went to the fields chiefly to collect *tuak*, popular palm wine. The women of this village weave the famous "flaming cloth, *kamben geringsing*, which supposedly has the power to immunise the wearer against evil. Through double *ikat*, an intricate process of weaving and dyeing known on Bali only in Tenganan, a single cloth can take up to five years to complete. Only the finest *geringsing* pieces are worn by Tenganan people, for ceremonial dress. The imperfect ones are sold, since they are much in demand throughout Bali. A large piece can cost well over a thousand dollars.

During ceremonies here – the most spectacular occurring in January and June – girls from the age of two wrap their bodies in silk and don multi-coloured scarves and flowered crowns of beaten gold. The *geringsing* cloth tends to shimmer in the sunlight. Men play the *gamelan selunding*, an archaic orchestra of iron-keyed metallophones, which are only allowed to be played at specific ceremonies. The National Arts College has made a replica, and young composers have adapted the traditional melodies to make up their own "fusion" music. *Gamelan selunding* accompanies the *rejang* dance, a ritual-offering dance composed of slow, elegant and simple movements. The Fight of the Pandanus Leaves, at Tenganan, takes place only once a year during a festival called

BELOW: Candidasa guest houses.

Jsaba Sambah. To the accompaniment of the sacred *gamelan* selunding, two men – each with a round, plaited shield – attack each other with bunches of round pandanus leaves with thorns down either side of the leaf. The favourite tactics are to rush and clench the opponent. The clench has one disadvantage, however. While one man rubs this thorny weapon across his opponent's back, he is rather open to the same treatment. After battles, wounds are treated with a mixture of tumeric and vinegar, which leaves no scars. During this festival, creaky ferris wheels are set up on the rising terraces of the village. The unmarried girls of the village are spun in these as part of ancient rites, the turning representing the unification of the earth with the sun.

Map on page 229

Candidasa

Just past Tenganan is **Candidasa** ❿, a resort area that has seen drastic development in the past decade. Most of the accommodation here is at the low end of the scale, although there are a few decidedly upscale hotels and more are being built. Further east is less densely packed.

The beach at Candidasa has been blighted by jetties protruding into the water, intended to stop the erosion from years of coral blasting. These structures make it impossible to walk more than 50 metres on the beach, once a truly lovely landscape. In any case, now the beach is only visible at low tide.

Serious students of culture should visit Ibu Gedong's **Gandhian Ashram**. Started in the 1970s as a self-sufficient community based on Gandhian principles, the *ashram* was once the only structure along this isolated beach. The founder, Gedong Bagoes Oka, has worked courageously in support of the environment and to help young people learn useful trades. There are now bungalows

Candidasa is at the eastern end of Amuk Bay. While the area is fine for snorkelling and diving, much of the offshore coral was extracted for use in cement. Without the reef's protection, the beach is exposed to erosion.

BELOW: palace at Taman Ujung in the 1930s.

Map on page 229

TIP

Take some time and visit the small and traditional villages outside of Amlapura, including Asak, Timbrah, Bungaya and Jasi. Ask about any village festivals.

OPPOSITE: tourists crowd out temple worshippers, Pura Besakih. **BELOW:** extracting salt.

for rent, and it's possible to stay in simpler accommodation while volunteering here. (Note that there are strict rules on behaviour.)

Just east of Candidasa lies the village of **Bugbug**, more like a Bali Aga village in structure. Here, once every two years on the full moon of the fourth month (October), Perang Dewa (War of the Gods) takes place on top of a hill. Villagers from four surrounding villages gather here, carrying offerings of suckling pig, which they hang in the trees. They also bring their gods (as *pratima*) which then battle each other. Many of the men go into trance during the ritual.

Crossing a wide, solidified lava flow that is slowly being returned to cultivation (this area was ravaged by the volcanic eruption in 1963), the road enters **Amlapura** ⓫, the main town of Karangasem regency. The former kingdom, founded during the weakening of the Gelgel dynasty late in the 17th century, became, in the late 18th and early 19th centuries, the most powerful state in Bali. Puri Agung Karangasem long served as the residence of these kings, who extended their domain across the eastern straits to Lombok. During the Dutch conflict at the turn of the century, the raja of Karangasem cooperated with the European army and was allowed to retain his title and autocratic powers. Puri Kanginan, the palace where the last raja was born, is a 20th-century creation of designs from Europe, China and Bali. The main building, with a large veranda, is called Bale London – its furniture bears the royal crest of Britain. The wooden paneling appears to be Chinese, while *Ramayana* reliefs, on the adjacent tooth filing pavilion, retain a Balinese flavour. The photograph over the entrance to Bale London portrays the late king, Anak Agung Anglurah Ketut, who delighted in making fantastic moats and pools. Eight km (5 miles) south, near the beach at **Ujung** ⓬, he helped design a palace with a moat, opened in 1921. Unfortunately, two earthquakes in 1963 and 1978 destroyed most of the standing structures. Still, it is an interesting sight. In the late 1940s, the late king built **Tirtagangga** ⓭ (open daily, 7am–6pm; admission fee) – 6 km (4 miles) north on the road to Culik – as a retreat, with a series of pools decorated by unusual statuary. Tirtagangga, with its commanding hilltop view of the surrounding rice fields and its isolation, is a wonderful place to spend a few days. Lodging and fare are simple, the air and pools refreshing.

Remote excursions

One can continue up north through **Culik** ⓮ and on to **Tulamben**, with the scenery drastically changing to dry hills covered with scrub. Diving or snorkelling is good at the site of an old shipwreck.

One can drive completely around the eastern coast to Singaraja, although the road deteriorates into a pot-holed track. Villages and life are simple and rustic along here, and while the views of the ocean are few, experiencing this part of unfettered Bali is worthwhile for those with an adventurous bent. After a long and tortuous drive is **Amed** ⓯. Compact black-sand beaches are lined with colourful fishing vessels that take to the sea before dawn, returning in late morning with their catch. Every sail has a different pattern, turning the horizon into a colourful forest. There are also some excellent bungalows here.

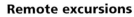

BALINESE PLACES OF WORSHIP

Temples (pura) play an integral role in the life of the Balinese community. Each village has at least three temples and there are 20,000 island-wide

Within the boundaries of each village and looking towards the interior mountains is the *pura puseh*, dedicated to Brahma the Creator and used for ancestor worship. In the centre of the village is the *pura bale agung,* dedicated to Vishnu the Preserver, and used for meetings. The *pura dalem*, the temple of the dead dedicated to Shiva and his consort, is found outside the village near the sea. The basic design of a Balinese temple complex consists of three courts (or two in northern Bali) each separated by walls: the *jaba* (front court); the *jaba tengah* (central court) and the *jeroan* (inner court). The jeroan is the most sacred and represents heaven; the jaba, the underworld, and the jaba tengah, an intermediate place. In one corner of the jaba is the bale kulkul, containing a large wooden gong or drum. The entrance to the jaba tengah is through *candi kurung,* similar to the *candi bantar* (split temple gates) but with a large wooden doorway, usually flanked by *raksaka* (guardian figures) to ward off evil spirits. Also in this area is the *bale agung* (conference hall). The *paduraksa* is the final candi kurung leading to the jeroan containing shrines, *tugu* (stone pillars for offerings) and *meru,* pagoda-like shrines symbolising Mount Mahameru (the home of the gods). The number of roofs a meru has is determined by the importance of the shrine's god. The *padmasana* (throne for the gods) can be found here, along with two *sanggahs,* helpers of the various gods.

▷ **STONE LOTUS THRONE**
A *padmasana* (throne for the gods) in Pura Jaganata and dedicated to the Supreme God Sanghyang Widi Wasa.

△ **THE** *CANDI BANTAR*
The *candi bantar* (split temple) gate of Pura Meduwe Karang representing the splitting of the material world, so that the body can enter the spirit realm.

▽ **THE** *JEROAN*
The *jeroan* (inner court) of temple has a *padmasana* (throne of the gods) and *meru* (pagodas). Merus hav odd-numbered roofs made from wood and thatch.

TEMPLE ETIQUETTE

IF YOU WANT TO COME IN PLEASE BE PROPERLY DRESSED
bila anda hendak masuk berpakaianlah YG SOPAN

Most rules of temple etiquette are common-sense but some of them may be less apparent to visitors. Before setting out on a temple visit, dress modestly: women should not wear shorts or have bare shoulders. Before going into the temple, take off your shoes and put on a traditional *adat* (sash) around your waist. Some temples also require visitors to wear a sarong, but these can usually be hired. Menstruating women or anyone with a bleeding cut should not enter a temple because of a general sanction against blood on holy soil. If you want to take pictures during temple festivals do not use flash photography or stand directly in front of the priest or walk in front of the kneeling congregation. Your head should not be higher than that of the priest – so don't climb on temple walls to get a better view of proceedings. Also, do not remain standing when people kneel to pray. Move to the back until the ceremony has finished.

PILGRIMS

il spirits are rendered rmless in temples but the ds must be appeased h offerings at the temple hey are to continue to e their protection.

△ STONE CARVINGS
Reliefs and sculptures are made from the local soft sandstone or volcanic tuff. They weather quickly as a result of the high humidity and need replacing frequently.

▷ TEMPLE FESTIVALS
Temples are not used for everyday prayer but come to life during festivals, when they are decorated with flowers and offerings.

WESTERN BALI

Map on page 247

An invisible village, a rare ghost-white starling, and Bali's finest underworld diving make the western part of the island an engaging journey. It also has bullracing and Bali's only national park

Any traveller fed up with the claustrophobic roads of southern Bali may greet the seemingly empty roads of western Bali with euphoria. Not only are there fewer vehicles in the west, there are fewer people, Balinese and foreigners alike. West of Tabanan, the southern road through the old regency of Jembrana parallels the southwestern coast through groves of coconut palms and rice fields before terminating at Gilimanuk, on Bali's western tip. Of black sand and often unprotected by offshore reefs, beaches along the way are usually empty, although the waves may be graced by surfers. Between Tabanan and Negara, there is little accommodation.

This is Bali's outback and its wild west, a place settled by people migrating here over the many decades from more populated areas – Java, Madura, Sulawesi, even Bali's Badung. Half of Jembrana, the old regency making up this part of Bali, is forested – thus Jimbar Wana, the Great Forest. A national park takes up much of this regency, extended by a nature reserve running up Bali's central mountain spine – long ago the home of tigers.

A civil war broke out here in the 1400s, a consequence of sibling rivalry between two royal brothers. One brother finally ended up near Negara, while the other settled near Gilimanuk. As a result, court culture in Jembrana regency was never quite as developed as in the neighbouring regencies of Buleleng, on the northern coast, and Tabanan, to the east.

PREVIOUS PAGES: one of Bali's black-sand beaches. **OPPOSITE:** harvesting the rice. **BELOW:** market sandals.

hole in a bunut

About 50 km (30 miles) west of Tabanan on the road to Gilimanuk is **Pekutatan ❶**, where a spur road leads north up the mountain slopes. In fact, it climbs over the mountain and descends to the northern coast at Pengastulan. This narrow, paved road is one of the most beautiful drives on Bali, and even driving just 10 km (6 miles) or so up the road through rain forest and old plantations of coffee and cloves is an exquisite experience. Two villages clinging to both road and mountain slopes, **Asahduren ❷** and **Manggisari**, permit a look at contemporary Balinese life unfettered by the demands of tourism.

The road passes directly through an old *bunut* tree, which, with its aerial roots wrapped around both sides of the road, looks something like a banyan. At one time, the road went around this old tree, but as the tree grew larger, the only choice was to go through it. Cutting it down would have left its soul without a place to exist. To locals, the tree is known as **Bunut Bolong** – *bolong* means "hole". On the left, just before passing through the tree, is a small shrine with two brightly painted tigers, places for wayward spirits to take up

abode and usually veiled with offerings. Immediately beyond the tree, also on the left, is an overlook onto the expansive and forested mountains of western Bali.

Medewi to Negara

Medewi is an undistinguished village, but the beach nearby is a popular surfing hangout. Not far away is a tranquil temple, **Pura Rambut Siwi**, on a spectacular length of beach. It's said that the temple was founded by the priest Danghyang Nirartha in the 16th century. Story has it that during his wanderings he stopped at the nearby village of Yeh Embang and put an end to an epidemic that was ravishing the region. Before moving on, he presented them with a gift of his hair, thus the name of the temple, Worship of the Hair *(rambut)*. Nirartha's hair and some of his personal belongings are enshrined within the central three-tiered *meru*. Perched on a hill overlooking the ocean, this is a wonderful place to stop and rest, if not indulge in a picnic lunch on the superb black-sand beach.

To the west 25 km (15 miles) is **Perancak** ❸, at the mouth of the Perancak River south of Negara. This is said to be the spot where Danghyang Nirartha first landed in Bali. Commemorating the spot is the simple **Pura Gede Perancak**. Carved out of white stone, this shrine overlooks the Perancak River. It is not that easy to find: at Tegalcangkring, turn left off the main road to an intersection with a monument in the middle of it, then turn right. The temple is 9 km (6 miles) down the road.

Perancak was the primary entry point for migrants and traders from Java and elsewhere until the 1930s, when the ferry service at Gilimanuk started. Also located in Perancak is a Worldwide Fund for Animals (WWF) **sea turtle conservation centre**.

BELOW: bullracing in Negara.

Following their arrival in Perancak a century ago, boats from Java would sail up the river to **Negara** , where the raja of Jembrana kept his palace. Downtown Negara has little to offer the traveller, but the exceptionally wide boulevards are something of a Balinese marvel and suitable for jumbo-jet landings. The most exciting event today in Negara – the largest town in Jembrana and the regency's administrative centre – are the *mekepung*, or traditional water-buffalo races, a secular entertainment first introduced by immigrants from Madura, an island off Java's northeastern coast, about a century ago. Possibly it developed from the custom of carrying home harvested rice by bullock cart. Dressed up in silk banners with painted horns and enormous wooden bells, the bulls are paraded before the crowd of spectators.

The course is a 4-km-long (2½-mile) stretch of road; the teams are judged for speed and style. It is remarkable to see such ordinarily docile creatures thunder across the finish line at speeds up to 50 kilometres an hour (30 mph). The agile charioteers often drive while standing up, twisting the bulls' tails to give them extra motivation.

A kilometre south of Negara is **Loloan Timor**, a small village with an ambiance found nowhere else in Bali. Residents are Muslim Buginese, originally from Sulawesi several generations back, and many of their homes retain a unique traditional Buginese style.

One of the most unique aspects of this area is the music, which is quite different from the standard *gamelan* music heard elsewhere on the island. *Gamelan jegog* is a musical ensemble entirely of bamboo instruments, and giant bamboo at that. Some have likened its resonant sound to roaring thunder; it can be heard – and felt – from quite a distance. *Jegog* accompanies the standard tra-

Map
below

TIP

Bullracing season, not to be confused with the year-round exhibitions for tourists, is between July and October. There are two main races in Negara: the Regent's Cup, on the Sunday before Independence Day (17 August), and the Governor's Cup, in September or October.

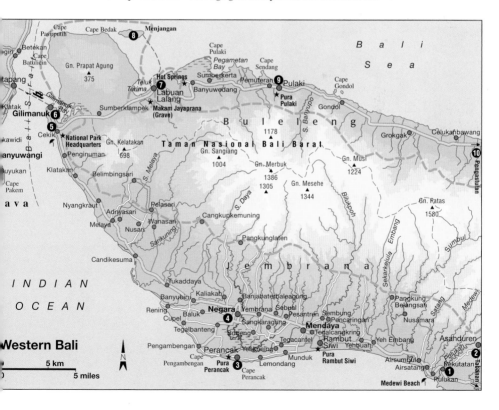

Western Bali

5 km

5 miles

ditional dances and has some of its own repertoire as well. The instrument may be seen up close at a privately run museum, Sangkar Agung, 3 km (2 miles east of Negara and just off the main road near Pangintukadaya.

Negara to Gilimanuk

Thirty km (20 miles) east of Negara, at **Cekik ❺**, the highway splits: one par branches to the northeast to follow the northern coast eastward towards Sin garaja, while a short spur road heads on straight a few kilometres into **Gilimanuk ❻**, perhaps the most nondescript town anywhere in Bali and announced by one of the most distinctive town monuments on the island: towering arch comprised of four serpents over the road. An unforgettable entrance into a forgettable town.

A captive chicken.

But Gilimanuk is not there for aesthetic reasons, but rather for the half-hour long ferry ride – operating 24 hours a day – across the Bali Strait to the island of Java. Literally at the end of the road, beyond Gilimanuk's commercial stretch is a modern and efficient ferry terminal for passengers, buses and cars. Accom modation in Gilimanuk is mainly in homestays.

The strait between Bali and Java is not wide – just 3 km (2 miles) – but th waters are treacherous. Legend has it that the strait, and Bali itself, was create when a high priest on Java banished his misbehaving son to the eastern tip c Java. The priest drew his finger across the land, literally cutting his son off by creating the island of Bali and distancing it with the strait. In fact, geologica records confirm that Java and Bali were once connected.

BELOW: a captive Bali starling, and jungle greens.

Back at Cekik is the rather expansive headquarters (open weekdays 9am–3pm) for **Taman Nasional Bali Barat (West Bali National Park)**. It's no

known exactly what goes on inside all of these buildings, but while printed information for travellers is limited, the staff are quite helpful. Permits for hiking in the park are obtained here. One must also engage the services of an official guide for hiking within the park, much of which is actually off-limits.

Established in the mid-1980s, the park has limited facilities. The 760-sq.-km (300 sq.-mile) national park is one of Bali's few remaining pristine areas. It is the home of deer, civets, monkeys and the wild Javan buffalo, a rare species with just a few dozens remaining in the park. The park is also home to the Bali starling *(Leucopsar rothschildi)*, a small white bird with brilliant blue streaks around its eyes and black-tipped wings; it is also known as Rothschild's mynah. Nearly extinct, with less than a dozen of the birds remaining in the wild, zoos around the world maintain about 3,000 specimens. Previous local breeding programmes have been fraught with corruption, but renewed efforts are under way.

The birds once populated the gentle slopes of **Gunung Prapat Agung**, which anchors the western tip of Bali and the national park. A 24-km (15-mile) trail encircles Prapat Agung.

Up along the northern coast

The road that splits off at Cekik and heads north passes Prapat Agung on its eastern flank. The scenery then shifts from canopied jungle to a more varied and spectacular coastal corridor with dynamic mountain scenery buttressing the inland side. Jembrana regency is left behind for Buleleng, which extends all along the northern coast to Gunung Batur.

In **Labuan Lalang** ❼, the first village after Cekik and on the shores of **Teluk Terima** (Terima Bay), are some outfitters. Besides arranging guided hikes into

Map on page 247

TIP

Hiking permits for Taman Nasional Bali Barat can be obtained at park headquarters in Cekik or from the Department of Forestry in Denpasar. The mandatory guides, hired in Cekik, usually speak English.

BELOW: gambling.

Map
on page
247

Cocoa beans.

OPPOSITE: cloves
from Bali's north.
BELOW: net fishing.

the national park, they can arrange scuba diving at **Pulau Menjangan** ❽ (Deer Island), part of the national park. Menjangan, an uninhabited island less than 10 km (6 miles) offshore with coral reefs extending deep to the ocean floor, is part of Taman Nasional Bali Barat and is considered to offer Bali's best diving. Above water, the deer for which the island is named, including the rare Java deer, are rarely seen, but the island is a protected sanctuary for the Bali starling.

Not far from Labuan Lalang and still within the national park is the burial site – **Makam Jayaprana** – of local hero Jayaprana. An orphan raised by royalty in the 17th century, Jayaprana was married to a beautiful woman who was also coveted by the local ruler. Claiming that pirates had landed in northwestern Bali, the ruler had Jayaprana lead a group of warriors to confront the marauders, which were in fact imaginary. Waiting for Jayaprana on the shores of Teluk Terima was one of the ruler's trusted ministers, who killed Jayaprana. Rather than submitting to the advances of the ruler, Jayaprana's widow, Layonsari, killed herself. Now a temple, the tomb is a hike to reach but with worthwhile views.

Further west are **Pemuteran** and **Pulaki** ❾, which offer some nice bungalow accommodation, several of which cater to divers. Boat arrangements for Pulau Menjangan can easily be made here. For some, Pulaki might be a place to avoid. Long ago, a village here with 5,000 to 10,000 people was visited by Danghyang Nirartha, the wandering 16th-century priest. The villagers requested the knowledge, which Nirartha gave, to move beyond the material world. These invisible villagers, known as *gamang*, are believed by Balinese to live today, occasionally making an appearance (noted by the lack of an upper lip and carrying a satchel over the shoulder) or setting hound dogs to barking for no (apparent) reason. It is also said that a number of tigers, too, were made invisible.

Dry land of spices and wine

Continuing eastward, the land takes on a drier texture, and the northern coast's agricultural diversity becomes apparent, especially in the growing of cocoa and spices on the northern slopes of the mountains. Northern Bali is a good place to purchase fresh spices and most visitor sites have stands offering variously packaged spice collections, both ground and whole. Clove and vanilla grown in the north are well regarded. Even more interesting is that this is a good environment for raising wine grapes.

At **Pengastulan** ❿, a road heads south, climbing the mountains through a potpourri of rice fields and clove plantations before descending back down towards the southern coast in what is one of Bali's most beautiful drives, through Asahduren and Mangisari. *(See page 245.)*

Twenty km (12 miles) east, beyond Lovina, is Singaraja. The main road to Denpasar begins here, climbing to Danau Bratan and Bedugul before descending the southern slopes. *(See chapter on Northern Bali, page 217.)* One can also continue eastward along the northern coast beyond Singaraja to Kubutambahan and the road to Danau Batur. Beyond Kubutambahan, the northern coastal road arcs around Bali's eastern tip and back down to Denpasar. *(See chapter on Eastern Bali, page 227.)*

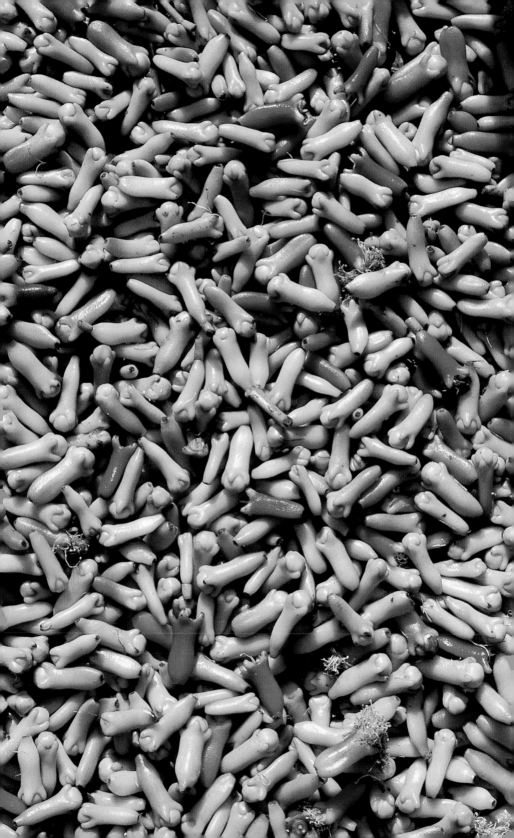

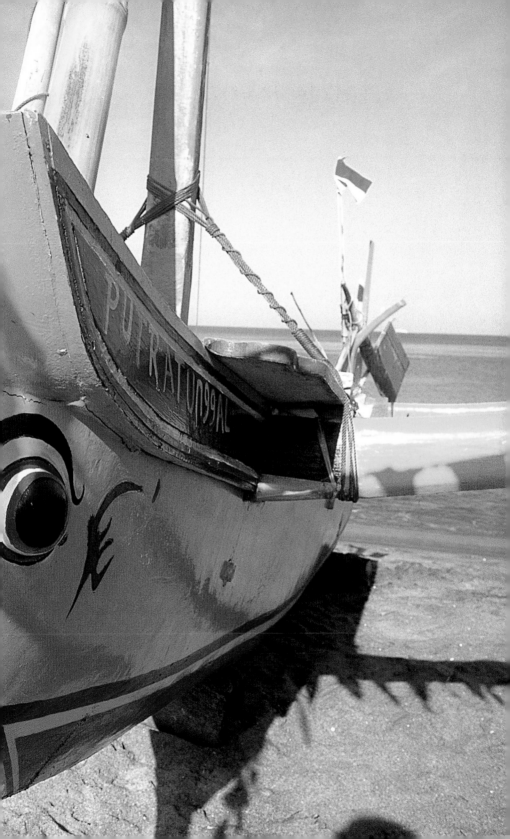

LOMBOK

Bali's neighbour across the strait to the east is a conservative, uncommercial and unhurried island

Lombok often is called Indonesia's island of 1,000 mosques. Of all Indonesian Muslims undertaking the *haj* to Mecca, the greatest percentage in the nation – and Indonesia has the world's largest Islamic population – is in Lombok. Yet it is a culturally diverse island. Buginese dominate the coasts and there is a Javanese-style aristocracy, while Arabs and Chinese are the merchants. The Sasak, the majority ethnic group, comprise about 95 percent of Lombok's population of more than 2½ million. The remaining people consist of Balinese, Buginese, Chinese, Javanese and Arabs.

Lombok, which means "chilli peppers" in Javanese, is an island of roughly 4,700 sq. km (1,800 sq. miles) immediately to the east of Bali. Dominating the landscape is a mountain range of 13 peaks anchored by the volcanic Gunung Rinjani, at 3,726 metres (12,224 ft) the third-highest peak in Indonesia. The so-called Wallace Line, named after naturalist Sir Alfred R. Wallace, runs between Bali and Lombok, demarcating climatic, zoological and botanical distinctions within the region. The Bali side is more like Asia, the Lombok side is more like Australia.

Most of western Lombok is green and looks like Bali, but to the east and south, the island becomes progressively drier, until wet-rice agriculture turns to dry-rice cultivation. Mataram, Lombok's main city, is the provincial seat of Nusa Tenggara, which includes Lombok and its eastern neighbour, Sumbawa.

The so-called dark-time, when religious leaders banned all traditional arts and cultural activities not considered Islamic, is over. Today, artists and young people are rediscovering a variety of cultural influences – Javanese, Balinese, Malaysian, and Islamic. The local government supports preservation of traditional arts, maintaining Sasak cultural identity and history. These arts, even those associated with religious practice, often are considered traditional rather than religious. Efforts to retain traditional arts are paying off. Tourism is rising in Lombok, now adding substantially to the economy of rice, coffee, tobacco, fisheries, livestock, mining, and textiles.

While there are several world-class hotels on the island, visitors to Lombok should not expect the overwhelming cultural experience – and commercialism – of Bali, but they can expect a great sense of adventure. ❑

PRECEDING PAGES: anchored by its mosque, a village on Lombok is surrounded by paddies of rice; boat on Senggigi Beach.
LEFT: Lombok aristocrat in traditional clothing.

LOMBOK

Part of the Nusa Tenggara island group to the east and of a distinctly different culture than Bali, Lombok's proximity to Bali makes it a worthy excursion for the traveller

Map on page 260

The Sasak, a Malay race inhabiting Lombok for at least 2,000 years, probably settled on coastal areas as long as 4,000 years ago. For much of the last 1,000 years, Lombok was a feudal state with many small kingdoms, some of which followed animistic beliefs, while others combined animism with Hinduism or Buddhism. Over the centuries, Java influenced Lombok in varying degrees. Java conquered Lombok in the 14th century, incorporating it into the Majapahit empire. Several small kingdoms on Lombok were ruled by Javanese nobles who had been exiled to Lombok, and today's Sasak aristocracy still claims Javanese ancestry. Java introduced both Hinduism and Islam to Lombok, but religious and political influence waned by the 17th century. Islam gradually spread through eastern and central Lombok, while Balinese – and thus Hindu – influence began dominating western Lombok.

The Balinese entered Lombok from Karangasem, ruling the island for 150 years until 1894. Balinese influence always centred in the west, where today Balinese constitute 10 per cent of the population. They cleared forests and engineered irrigation systems and terraces, creating extensive wet-rice agriculture under the Balinese system of *subak,* a water-use cooperative.

The last king of Karangasem, Anak Agung Ngurah Gede Karangasem, managed to gain extensive influence over eastern Bali as well during the mid-1800s. Overseeing development of the arts and the construction of an impressive number of temples, he also restricted the land rights of the Sasak aristocracy on Lombok, introduced an inflexible taxation system, and demanded forced labour of Sasak peasantry. Revolts erupted several times in the 19th century, with Islam the rallying cry among the Sasak.

In the early 1890s, Sasak leaders approached the Dutch for help in overthrowing Balinese rule. The Dutch, mistakenly believing Lombok was rich in gems, assisted the Sasak. War broke out in 1894. The Balinese were eventually, and soundly, defeated, and a number of temples and palaces on Lombok were destroyed. Many of the final confrontations ended in *puputan,* the mass suicides of palace nobles, their families and followers.

The Sasak leaders believed they would have the right to rule with the defeat of the Balinese. Instead, the Dutch colonised the island, banishing the king and his remaining family and offering only minor government positions to Sasak and Balinese leaders. Colonisation intensified land use and taxation until the Japanese took control of the island in 1942. When the Japanese left in 1945, the Dutch returned briefly but were repelled by guerrillas.

LEFT: planting rice is back-breaking work. **BELOW:** shopping at the morning market.

Kecodak dance.

Today, Lombok retains many traits and customs similar to those of Java and Bali, and the Sasak language is closely related to Javanese and Balinese. How ever, Sasak culture still contrasts sharply with that of Java and Bali.

There are two main groups among the Sasak: Wetu Lima and Wetu Telu. The Wetu Lima are orthodox Sunni Muslims, while the Wetu Telu are nominal Muslims, who combine the first tenet of Islam – belief in Allah with Muhammad a Prophet – and some Islamic observances with a mosaic of ancestor worship, Hinduism and Buddhism.

While Wetu Lima (meaning "five times") indicates the Wetu Lima should carry out the five daily prayers and fulfil the five tenets of Islam, Wetu Telu ("three times") suggests that the Wetu Telu should pray at three different periods and acknowledge three types of ceremonies: life-cycle rites (birth, marriage, death), Islamic ceremonies (Maulid, Lebhran), and cyclical rites associated with agriculture.

The Wetu Lima have adopted the emerging Islamic identity of Muslims throughout Indonesia, while the Wetu Telu are generally uninterested in the world at large, focusing instead on their strong ties to ancestral lands. Many fought beside the Balinese against the Dutch and Wetu Lima, in 1894, to retain their way of life.

Wetu Telu rituals have diminished to a point that few people on Lombok identify themselves as Wetu Telu. Most of the remaining Wetu Telu festivals are at the start of the October–December rainy season or else the April–May harvest Wetu Lima religious leaders *(tuan guru)*, on the other hand, are very active with thousands of followers, demanding that all Sasak Muslims observe Islamic religious practices, especially the end of Ramadan.

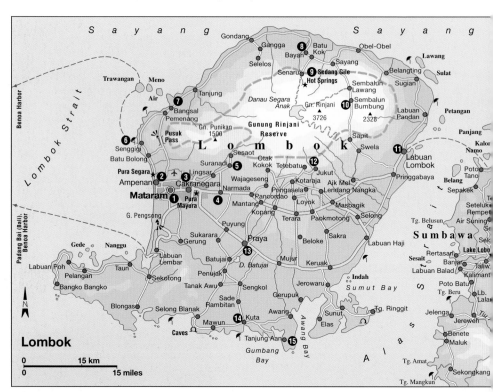

Lombok

0   15 km
0   15 miles

Western Lombok

Three main towns in western Lombok – Ampenan, Mataram, and Cakranegara
– meld together to create what is, for Lombok, an urban sprawl. **Mataram ❶**
is the administrative centre of the political and cultural life of Lombok, with
provincial government offices, banks, mosques, bookstores, the main post office,
and Mataram University downtown.

In Mataram, the **Nusa Tenggara Barat Museum** (open Tuesday–Sunday,
8am–4pm; admission fee) houses historical and cultural artifacts from Lombok and Sumbawa, and it occasionally hosts special exhibits. Displays include
exhibits on geology, history and culture. The cultural centre, **Pusat Budaya**, on
Jalan Pariwisata, presents traditional music and dance nightly. The provincial
tourist office is on Jalan Langko.

Just west of Mataram is **Ampenan ❷**. With its numerous shops, cheap hotels,
dusty roads, plentiful horse-drawn *dokar*, Islamic bookstores, and its Arab quarter, Ampenan is easily the most colourful town of Lombok. Early Arab traders
were drawn to Ampenan when it was the only harbour for incoming and out-
going ships. Nowadays, Ampenan is used only for fishing and shipping cattle.
The beach at Ampenan occasionally is a venue for performances of the dance
gandrung or for the shadow play known as *wayang sasak* on special holidays.
Sometimes both go on simultaneously, while young people flirt or create a little mischief on the beach.

Most of Lombok's shipping today arrives at **Gerung**, near **Lembar**. Gerung
is the village of the famous *cepung*, a men's social dance in which they read and
sing from the *Lontar Monyet* (*Monkey Manuscript*), drink *tuak* (palm wine),
dance, and vocally imitate *gamelan* instruments. The road southward continues

Map
on page
260

*In the late 1980s,
New Zealand
initiated a program
with local craftsmen
to improve the
quality of locally
produced pottery.
This effort has been a
tremendous success,
and Lombok is now
internationally noted
for its pottery.*

BELOW: gate and
meru of western
Lombok temple.

A festival, held during the November or December full moon, brings together sacred Balinese performing arts with sacred Sasak arts. This is the only event that ties together the Balinese and Sasak, and it is the second-biggest event in Lombok.

BELOW: *odalan* at Pura Meru, and Pura Narmada priest.

to the easternmost point of Lombok – a sheer cliff and **Bangko Bangko** beach This is a good surfing spot but dreadful for snorkelling.

Cakranegara ❸, to the east of Mataram, is Lombok's main market centre It also is home to many Chinese and Balinese, who make up more than 50 per cent of the town's population. Many of Lombok's weaving and basketry indus tries are located in Cakranegara. The baskets, in particular, are sold in Bali a many times the Lombok price.

Several important Balinese temples are in Cakranegara and the surrounding area. **Pura Meru**, built in Cakranegara in 1720 by Balinese prince Anak Agung Made Karang, is the largest temple on Lombok. Its giant *meru* for the Hindu trinity – Shiva (Siwa in Bahasa Indonesia), Vishnu (Wisnu), and Brahma – is the "centre of the universe" temple for most of the Balinese here, and its annua Pujawali festival, held over five days during the September or October ful moon, is the biggest Balinese Hindu event on Lombok. The outer courtyard hall has drums that call the devout to ceremonies and festivals. Two building with raised offering platforms are in the centre courtyard, while the interio enclosure has 33 shrines and the three multi-tiered *meru*.

Across the street stands **Pura Mayura**, built in 1744 as the court temple o the last Balinese kingdom in Lombok. A large artificial lake holds an open ha or *bale kembang* (floating pavilion). It was used as a justice hall and meeting place. Today the palace gardens are a playground for children and grazing live stock. The temple sits behind the sedate water gardens.

The temple of **Gunung Pengsong**, south of Mataram, sits on a hilltop wit vistas of rice fields, the sea and Gunung Rinjani. Populated with monkeys, thi is the hill the Balinese aimed for in the mythic account of their initial arrival i

western Lombok. In March or April, a buffalo is sacrificed here to ensure a rich harvest. The Bersih Desa, or "clean village" festival, at harvest time finds the area spruced up annually to honour the rice goddess Dewi Sri.

Map on page 260

The structures and pool at **Pura Narmada**, 10 km (6 miles) east of Cakranegara in **Narmada** ❹, were reportedly built in 1805 as a replica of Gunung Rinjani and Segara Anak, the lake within Gunung Rinjani's caldera. (Segara Anak takes its name from a sacred river in India.) Elderly king Anak Gede Karangasem of Mataram did not like the long and mandatory annual trek to Segara Anak, where he was to throw crafted gold pieces into the lake as offerings. When he could no longer climb Rinjani, he built Pura Narmada. The annual pilgrimage and offering at Segara Anak remains today, however, and the festival at Pura Narmada coincides with this pilgrimage during the full moon of either October or November. The gardens at Narmada are splendid, with special performances of *gandrung, kendang belek* and other traditional dances on special occasions. Some of the other pools at Narmada are available for swimming (modest attire, please) and are popular with local kids.

Pura Suranadi, a complex of three temples located a few kilometres north of Narmada in **Suranadi** ❺, is the oldest and holiest of the Balinese temples in Lombok, founded by a priest, Pedanda Wawu Rauh, to obtain the proper holy water for cremations. Chilly spring water bubbles up into restored baths, open to modestly dressed swimmers. Nearby **Pura Lingsar**, with two shrines, is the mother temple of Lombok, not only for the Hindu but also for the Wetu Telu. This is the temple where even local Buddhists, Christians and occasionally Wetu Lima come to pray for prosperity, rain, fertility, health, and general success. The temple is associated with irrigation and rice, and the annual festival

BELOW: royal pool, Pura Narmada.

features a ritualised war, *perang topat*, which acts as an offering. While the main courtyards of Pura Suranadi and Pura Lingsar symbolically unite the deities of Bali and Lombok, the second courtyards, called *kemaliq*, contain sacred pools and unique altars of rocks reminiscent of ancient megalithic worship. Both temples have sacred spring-fed pools within the temple grounds, home of large freshwater eels. Visitors are welcome to feed the eels hard-boiled eggs, which can be purchased at nearby stands.

Beyond Suranadi is **Hutan Wisata Suranadi**, literally the Suranadi Tourist Forest. Stroll through the botanical garden with labelled specimens and observe birds, monkeys and butterflies. The little market town of **Sesaot**, 5 km (3 miles) beyond Suranadi, and **Air Nyet** village, another 3 km (2 miles) up the road, are good spots for river swimming and picnicking.

Northern Lombok

North of Ampenan is **Pura Segara**, a Balinese sea-temple. The Chinese and Muslim cemetery is nearby, providing an interesting look at the sea-facing graves that appear as seats marked in bright colours.

Outrigger boat.

About 10 km (6 miles) north of Ampenan, **Senggigi** ❻ has become the main tourist area of Lombok. With its beautiful beaches, picturesque views of Bali's Gunung Agung to the west, good coral for snorkelling and diving, and millions of dollars invested for tourism, Senggigi is an attractive place to stay, with several deluxe hotels as well as budget accommodation.

BELOW: vendor at Senggigi Beach.

Batulayar, near Senggigi, has an important ancestral grave *(makam)* where nominal Muslims come to picnic and to pray for health and success. There are many *makam* all over Lombok, as the graves of all important religious leaders become shrines. The *makam* at Batulayar is near **Pura Batu Bolong**, an interesting Hindu temple on a cliff facing Bali. It sits beside the large rock with a hole from which the temple takes its name. This is a great sunset point with fantastic vistas across to Bali.

North of Senggigi, toward Bayan along the hilly coastal road, are a variety of terrain and villages. First is **Pemenang**, then further west is **Bangsal** ❼, which has a beautiful beach. Boats depart here for the three islands with the best diving and snorkelling in Lombok: **Gili Air**, **Gili Meno**, and **Gili Trawangan**. There are many bed and breakfasts amongst these islands, the best of which are on Gili Trawangan, the furthest island from Pemenang and the most difficult to reach.

Gili Trawangan's charm lies in what it isn't rather than what it is. The largest and most distant of three islands off Lombok's northwest coast, Trawangan isn't highly developed, overrun with visitors, or particularly beautiful. This former penal colony is a virtual clone of Bali's Kuta Beach three decades ago. For those hungry for what Bali was, this is it. A mediocre white-sand beach rings the island and rustic accommodation lies just along the beach fringe.

But forget surface matters here: The beauty of Trawangan lies below the water. Whether one snorkels or dives, this island is famed for its vast gardens of blue coral. This is among the best dive spots in Lombok. Strong currents are a bother, especially

in the strait with neighbouring Gili Meno. There is no fresh water on the Gili islands. Problems with cholera during the dry season (May–October) and malaria and dengue fever during the wet season (November–March) have been recorded. Drink only bottled water, eat only cooked food, and choose accommodation with mosquito nets, or bring your own.

The south-facing beach at **Sira**, along the peninsula north of Bangsal, is beautiful, pristine and, for the moment, unblemished. A golf course is planned on this point of land, however, so things are due to change. The white-sand beach is a good launch spot for snorkelling on the offshore coral reef. Around the point, in Medana Bay, is a luxury Oberoi resort.

Tanjung, north of Bangsal, is another interesting village; Sasak Muslims, Balinese Hindus and Sasak Buddhists, known as Boda, live here. Tanjung has an interesting Sunday market, Pasar Minggu.

West of **Gondang**, up the coast, is Tiu Pupus waterfall, a 20-minute walk beyond the end of a poorly marked, rocky road. While the spring-fed falls are disappointing during the dry season, they still flow into a deep and swimmable pool. The trek through a traditional Sasak village, Kerurak, makes the effort worthwhile. The dusty, traditional village of **Segenter**, about 35 km (20 miles) north of Bangsal on the road to Anyer, provides a glimpse into the harsh reality of life on the island's dry side. The 300 villagers in this northern interior village eke out a living raising corn and beans, yet they welcome visitors with a smile and proudly share their simple life.

Bayan ❽, a source of early Islam, maintains old dance and poetic traditions, as well as *kemidi rudat*, a theatre based on the *Thousand-and-One Nights* fables. One of the most important Wetu Telu mosques is in Bayan. In **Sedang Gile** ❾

Map on page 260

BELOW: lake in the caldera of Gunung Rinjani.

BELOW: weavers in
central Lombok.

nearby, the waterfalls are among the island's most spectacular, even after climbing the 200 vertical steps down to see them.

Eastern and central Lombok

Southward and inland further along the road, **Sembalun Bumbung** ❿ is located in a high, cool valley on the slopes of Gunung Rinjani, along with a neighbouring village, **Sembalun Lawang**. There are many *haji* (Muslims who have gone to Mecca) in both villages, but Sembalun Bumbung has retained the older traditions, such as *tandang mendet*, a men's martial dance, and a unique version of *wayang wong* theatre. In contrast, Sembalun Lawang has become an orthodox village banning most arts. Sembalun Bumbung has an old tomb that holds the remains of a Majapahit ancestor. It is also the site of the phenomenal *alip* festival held about every three years.

Well-known as a source of traditional Sasak music and dance, **Lenek** also offers *tari pakon*, a medicinal trance dance. A local cultural patron of the arts has established an organisation to reinvigorate the performing arts in Lenek. Visitors are welcomed for a rustic, although healthy, stay at the facilities.

Other villages in eastern Lombok are strongly Islamic. Although transportation and lodging are difficult, worth visiting are **Labuan Haji**, with its beautiful beach on the southeastern coast, and **Labuan Lombok** ⓫, a friendly harbour north along the coast and with ferries running to Sumbawa.

Tetebatu, at the southern foot of Gunung Rinjani, is a cool mountain retreat with beautiful rice terraces. It is wet and misty during rainy season. The waterfall at **Jukut** ⓬, to the northwest of Tetebatu, is a good, monkey-filled trekking forest. **Bonjeruk**, in central Lombok, is a village of numerous *dalang*, or pup-

peteers, for the shadow play *wayang sasak*; many of the puppets are made here. Near **Lendang Nangka** is Jojang spring with great vistas and a forest inhabited by black monkeys. In August, Sasak boxing takes place in the village.

To the south

Southeast of Cakranegara, **Praya** ⓭ is a crossroads and the hub of the south. Home of the Saturday market, it is central to many of the area's handicraft villages. The Thursday market is further south at Sengkol. Beleka, due east of Praya, is the site of a Wednesday market. The main crop in this dry region is tobacco, which requires little water.

    Rambitan and **Sade**, on the road leading south from Praya to the coast, are traditional Sasak villages sandwiched between the main road and the riced fields. On the east side of the road is Rambitan, a village that caters to tourists. Nonetheless, it has authentic clusters of thatched *lumbug*, or rice barns. On the west side of the road is Sade, a more authentic hilltop village with the oldest mosque in Lombok, **Mesjid Kuno**. This thatched-roof house of worship can only be entered by Muslims. An interesting walk through the village is encouraged by residents, who act as guides for a small fee.

    The beach at **Kuta** ⓮ is behind Senggigi Beach in development. Still, Kuta is fronted by an expansively beautiful white-sand beach, about 45 km (30 miles) from Cakranegara. The Novotel Coralia on Mandalika Beach is moderately priced; the Kuta hotels and homestays are cheap. Kuta market is a lively cacophony of chickens and friendly locals and is brightened by an array of colourful fruits and woven baskets. It's open early on Wednesday and Sunday mornings.

    A few minutes east of Kuta village, on Mandalika Beach, is the site of the

Map on page 260

Rare today, traditional Sasak rites occasionally occur in Bayan, Lenek, and Sembalun Bumbung. These villages are known for their Wetu Telu traditions and customs. Bayan is also is the site for traditional Hindu dances.

BELOW: sorting basketry at market.

Map on page 260

TIP

Visiting villages where arts are produced and buying direct from the artist assures that the artisan benefits directly. The craft villages are mostly in the south.

OPPOSITE: beach near Malimbu.
BELOW: net fishing on beach at Kuta.

annual Putri Nayale festival. (Just in front of and to the east of the Novotel Coralia Hotel.) This festival commemorates the legend of the beautiful Putri Mandalika princess, who was sought as the bride of every Lombok raja. Local legend says that when she could not choose between the suitors, she threw herself into the sea from a headland, saying, "Kuta", or "Wait for me here", in the local Sasak language. When she jumped, hundreds of *nayale* – sea worms – floated to the surface.

Thus, every year on the February anniversary of her fateful demise, the nayale worms return to the site. People come from all around to Kuta village to collect the ugly sea worms and to fry and eat them, rather like a love potion. This event, which is primarily a secular gathering, attracts over 100,000 (yes – 100,000) young people, who flirt and strut while watching the sea worms spawn. They may also find time to sing improvised *pantun* poetry and to watch a dance-drama based on the myth. Associated with fertility, the sea worms are ground up, then the resulting mixture is placed in irrigation channels to help assure farmers' crops.

Astonishing landscape

A dirty little fishing village lies on the fringe of **Selong Blanak** beach, east of Kuta. Instead of detracting from the wide, sweeping beach's beauty, the village adds to it. Colourful, small fishing prahu rock in the gentle waves on the bay's east end. The livelihood of these shy but hospitable and industrious people, who originate from eastern Lombok, is fishing, especially for squid. White, sugary sand rings the gorgeous bay. But what sets this site apart is the scale of the surrounding landscape, which is of continental, not islandic, proportions. The sand, sea and distant hills are painted in an astonishing palate of colours. Rather than a haunt for sunbathers, this is a place to bathe in the beauty.

West of Kuta village, the beach at **Mawun** rings a perfect half-moon bay, flanked by massive headlands. This deserted, off-the-beaten-track beach is barren of trees, which accentuates the spectacular scenery and sound of the sea. Apart from the occasional fisherman, it is likely that you'll have this fine beach all to yourself. It also can be reached by bicycle from Kuta, although the road is a bit steep.

East of Kuta lie a series of beautiful, untouched beaches. **Tanjung Aan** ⓑ has spectacular scenery off the peninsula, just a few vendor shacks, and a virtually undisturbed, sugary-white beach. Another 3 km (2 miles) east is the beach and fishing village of **Gerupuk**, where there is a market every Thursday. Local fishermen harvest seaweed in this bay. It is also an ideal spot for wind- or body-surfing.

Further east, beyond **Batu Nampar** village, is the infrequently visited village of **Batu Rintang**. With traditional thatched-rice barns and huts, it offers an honest look at local life. Outside Batu Nampar are salt works and floating seaweed frames, farmed by migrants from South Sulawesi and Madura. Continuing around the bay, north and east of Batu Nampar is **Jerowaru**, site of a Thursday market. South and east, respectively, are the coastal settlements **Ekas** and **Tanjung Luar**, inhabited by Bugis fishermen from Sulawesi, arriving here during the early 1600s. ❑

INSIGHT GUIDES
Travel Tips

New Insight Maps

Maps in Insight Guides are tailored to complement the text. But when you're on the road you sometimes need the big picture that only a large-scale map can provide. This new range of durable Insight Fleximaps has been designed to meet just that need.

Detailed, clear cartography
makes the comprehensive route and city maps easy to follow, highlights all the major tourist sites and provides valuable motoring information plus a full index.

Informative and easy to use
with additional text and photographs covering a destination's top 10 essential sites, plus useful addresses, facts about the destination and handy tips on getting around.

Laminated finish
allows you to mark your route on the map using a non-permanent marker pen, and wipe it off. It makes the maps more durable and easier to fold than traditional maps.

The first titles
cover many popular destinations. They include Algarve, Amsterdam, Bangkok, California, Cyprus, Dominican Republic, Florence, Hong Kong, Ireland, London, Mallorca, Paris, Prague, Rome, San Francisco, Sydney, Thailand, Tuscany, USA Southwest, Venice, and Vienna.

👁 INSIGHT GUIDES
The world's largest collection of visual travel guides

CONTENTS

Getting Acquainted

The Place

Area: 5,620 square kilometres (2,170 sq mi), about twice the size of Luxembourg, or about the size of the American state of Delaware.
Situation: Nearly in the middle of the Indonesian archipelago. Java lies to the west, and Lombok, part of Nusa Tenggara Province, is to the east. Borneo is due north, western Australia due south.
Population: Over 3 million.
Language: Over 350 languages and dialects are spoken in Indonesia, but Bahasa Indonesian is the one national tongue.
Religion: Hinduism, Buddhism, Islam, Protestantism, Catholicism. Every Indonesian must declare one of these five official religions.
Time zones: There are three time zones in Indonesia. Bali follows Central Indonesian Standard Time, which is eight hours ahead of Greenwich Mean Time. Bali is on the same time zone as Singapore and Hong Kong.
Currency: Indonesian Rupiah (Rp). Exchange rates have been unstable since 1997.
Weights & Measures: Indonesia employs the metric system. One kilometre is equal to 0.6 miles; one metre is equal to 3.3 feet; one kilogram is equal to 2.2 pounds; one litre is equal to 0.3 US gallons or 0.2 imperial gallons. To convert Celsius to Fahrenheit, multiply by 1.8 and add 32; to convert Fahrenheit to Celsius, subtract 32 and multiply by 0.56.
Electricity: In most places, 220 volts, 50 cycles – but check first, as 110 volts is still used in a few areas. Be warned that power failures are common except in the

large hotels, which have their own backup generators. The plug is two-pronged round. Converters should be bought abroad, as they are difficult to find in Bali, although one can buy voltage regulators with a 110-volt outlet.
International Dialling Code: 62-361

Climate

As Bali is quite close to the equator, its temperatures vary between 21°C and 32°C (70–90°F), with an average temperature of 26°C (78°F) and only two seasons: dry and rainy.

The dry season lasts from May to November, with July being the coolest month of the year. The rainy season lasts from November to April, with January being the wettest month of the year. Humidity is 75 percent year-round.

Government

Bali is one of 32 provincial regions of the Republic of Indonesia, each of which is ruled by a governor. The governor of Bali lives in Denpasar. The province is divided into eight *kabupaten* (counties or regencies), each headed by a *bupati* (regent) under the governor. There is further division into 51 *kecamatan* (subdistricts) under a *camat*. There are 564 incorporated villages, each ruled by a *perbekel* or village head. There are another 1,456 *desa adat* (traditional villages) subdivided into 3,627 *banjars* (hamlets or wards), each administered by a *klian* (*banjar* head).

The *banjar* system is unique to Bali. Essentially, every married male is a member of a *banjar* and must attend meetings held every 35 days, when issues pertinent to the well-being of the village are discussed.

If someone is having a ceremony, then all the members (both male and female) are obliged to help; conversely when they have a ritual, they have the right to ask their neighbours to assist them.

It is said that the family planning programme in Indonesia is highly

successful because of this system of *gotong royong* (mutual assistance) and the way news spreads through these monthly meetings. Each *banjar* also has a youth club, the *seka teruna-teruni*, which often holds fund-raising events and helps in keeping the village grounds clean.

Economy

Agriculture was once the main economic activity of the people in Bali, who grow rice for personal consumption, but tourism is now the largest income source per capita. Their main sources of agricultural income are coconuts (for copra) and the sale of cattle and pigs. Coffee and tobacco are also sold to wholesalers for export.

Business Hours

Indonesians like to get their work done in the morning to avoid working in the heat of the day, so if you need to visit a government office, try to get there between 8am and 11.30am. This also applies to banks and private businesses. Government offices close early on Friday and Saturday. Generally, offices are open 7am–3pm Monday–Thursday, 7.30am–noon on Friday, closed Saturday and Sunday.

Public Holidays

Religion is a way of life in Indonesia, and throughout the entire archipelago people enjoy and celebrate Buddhist, Hindu, Muslim and Christian holidays.

New Year's Day (1 January) is observed throughout the country. Although celebrations vary from area to area, it is often celebrated with street carnivals, fireworks, special entertainment and shows.
Chinese New Year is timed according to the lunar calendar, usually in February or March.

The Balinese New Year, **Nyepi** (Day of Silence), is also a national holiday and usually falls in March. It is a Hindu holiday of retreat and spiritual purification; no lighting of

Culture & Customs

To the Balinese, the world is their home and its travellers their guests. Decades of tourism have somewhat dimmed this positive attitude, but the Balinese remain remarkably friendly and courteous. They also remain staunchly conservative, for tradition is the backbone of their highly civilised culture. Please try to respect their traditions and attitudes. The Balinese are a very polite people and smiles are an island-wide characteristic. Shaking hands on introduction is the usual thing nowadays for both men and women. The use of the left hand to give or to receive something, however, is considered taboo (the left hand is used for hygienic purposes), as is pointing with the left hand. Crooking a finger to call someone is impolite.

When buying something, settle all prices in advance. Don't ask the price or make an offer unless you intend to buy. When bargaining, generally start at half the asking price and then work out a compromise. Remember that Rp 500 can mean the difference of a day's meals to them; to you it is nothing. It is silly to quibble over small sums because of principle.

Don't display large sums of money – in a place where the average annual income is under US$500, all tourists are considered wealthy. The Balinese have a strong sense of pride and consider temptation an affront, suspicion an insult.

Wear a shirt when not on the beach and don't walk around outside the beach or pool area in a swimsuit. What may seem like a quaint beachside alley may be the courtyard of a house or holy temple. Nude bathing is illegal and impolite. Before entering a private house, leave your shoes outside on the steps. Shoes and a collared shirt or modest skirt and blouse must be worn when visiting government offices.

It is compulsory for anyone visiting temples to wear a waist sash. Any material will do, although the Balinese admire colourful brocades or woven cloths. By an ancient law, menstruating women and anyone with a bleeding cut are asked not to enter temples. This is based on a general sanction against the presence of blood on holy soil.

Begging is not a tradition in Bali and most of the annoying beggars in Kuta are not Balinese. If you freely hand out money, you will only be encouraging people to ask again. The only exception is a small contribution at the entrance to a temple. This is used to offset the cost of maintenance, so give what you can afford, as you would for a church or house of worship in your own country. At temple festivals or dance performances, the Balinese are relaxed around a camera, providing the photographer does not interfere by standing directly in front of the priest or the kneeling congregation. According to custom, one's head should not be higher than that of a priest or village headman. Therefore, it is rude to climb on the walls of a temple. Likewise, do not remain standing when the people kneel to pray. Move to the back and wait quietly until the blessing has been completed. The same applies to a procession. If local bystanders kneel in veneration, you should always move to the side. The Balinese are not performing for the benefit of tourist cameras, but are performing a sacred ritual.

fires (including electricity), no work and no travel may occur on this day: the airport is closed for 24 hours and only designated hotel buses are allowed on the roads. You are confined to your hotel or *losmen* on this day. (It is best to choose a hotel which has dispensation from the government to use electricity after dark.)

The most important Muslim celebration is **Idul Fitri** (Grebeg Sjawal), on the first day of the 10th month (Sjawal) of the Islamic calendar, symbolising the end of the fasting month of Ramadan. All over the country, mass prayers are held in mosques and town squares, and everyone wears new clothes and visits relatives seeking forgiveness for past transgressions. It is a two-day public holiday, and in Bali is

secular, as few Muslims live on the island. Other Islamic public holidays occur throughout the year, including **Mohammad's birthday** and the day of sacrifice, **Idul Adha**, but as they are based on a lunar calendar the exact dates vary.

The Buddhist day of enlightenment, **Wisak**, is a public holiday. **Good Friday**, which usually falls in April, is a national holiday, as is the Ascension of Christ, the 14th day after the resurrection. 21 April is **Kartini Day**, a national holiday commemorating the birthday of the late Raden Ajeng Kartini, the pioneer for the emancipation of Indonesian women at the beginning of the 20th century. Everywhere, women appear in national dress.

The Indonesian national **Independence Day**, 17 August, is

celebrated throughout the country with organised sports events, puppet and shadow plays, traditional cultural performances and carnivals.

Armed Forces Day, 5 October, is the anniversary of the founding of the Indonesian armed forces, and is celebrated with military parades and demonstrations of the army's latest achievements.

A national holiday, **Christmas** is celebrated with candlelight gatherings and religious ceremonies; most Christian holidays are overlooked by Hindu Balinese.

Consult a Balinese calendar (any day marked in red is a holiday) or your local Indonesian consulate for holidays falling during your visit.

Planning the Trip

Visas & Passports

Under current regulations visitors from EU member states and the following countries will automatically be issued a two-month tourist visa: Argentina, Australia, Brazil, Brunei, Canada, Chile, Egypt, Hungary, Iceland, Japan, Kuwait, Liechtenstein, Malaysia, Maldives, Malta, Mexico, Monaco, Morocco, New Zealand, Norway, Philippines, Saudi Arabia, Singapore, South Korea, Switzerland, Taiwan, Thailand, Turkey, United Arab Emirates, United States, Venezuela and Vietnam. But do check with your local Indonesian embassy or consulate, as requirements may change.

Visitors from all other countries must obtain a tourist visa from their local Indonesian consulate or embassy. Make sure your passport is valid for six months upon entry into Indonesia, otherwise you'll find yourself on the next plane out. You also must have proof of onward passage, that is a ticket out of Indonesia. Tourist, social and business visas can be obtained from any Indonesian embassy or consulate abroad. To obtain a visa, submit two application forms with two passport photographs, the appropriate fee and proof of onward passage. Employment is strictly forbidden on a tourist visa, visa-free entry, social visa or business visa.

You will fill out a white, disembarkation/embarkation document, half of which should be retained and returned upon departure. Don't lose this card. **Immigration offices** are near Ngurah Rai Airport, tel: 751-038, and at Jl. Panjaitan, tel: 227-828.

Animal Quarantine

Bali, unlike its neighbours, is rabies-free. Importing a dog or cat (or monkey) is close to impossible. You will need an official letter from your veterinarian stating that the animal is disease-free, although this won't guarantee exemption from quarantine. Contact your local Indonesian consulate/embassy for details.

Extending a tourist visa is impossible; you must leave the country and come back in again. But this is a simple matter of going to Singapore and coming back the same day. Extending business and social cultural visas involves more paperwork, but can easily be done once per visa. See your local Indonesian consulate/embassy for details, or Immigration once in Bali.

In Singapore, the Indonesian Embassy (Kedutaan Besar Republik Indonesia) is at 7 Chatsworth Road, tel: (65) 737-7422.

Tourist Information

For tourist information enquiries before departure, consult your local Indonesian embassy or consulate. The following websites all provide comprehensive hotel and travel information on Bali:
www.balinetwork.com
www.bali-paradise.com
www.baliweb.net
www.baliwww.com
www.indo.com

Customs

Regulations prohibit the entry of weapons, narcotics and pornography as well as radio-cassette players (yes, an odd thing to prohibit, but rarely enforced) and anything written in Chinese characters. Fresh fruits, plants, animals and exposed films and videos may be checked.

A maximum of 1 litre of alcohol, 200 cigarettes, 50 cigars or 100 grams of tobacco, and a reasonable amount of perfume may be brought into the country. Photographic equipment, typewriters and radios are admitted provided they are taken out on departure. A customs declaration form must be completed before arrival. There is no restriction on the import or export of foreign currencies and traveller's cheques. However, the import and export of Indonesian currency exceeding Rp 5 million is prohibited. Upon leaving, limited quantities of duty-free purchases and souvenirs are exempt from taxes, but the export of "national treasures" is frowned upon. Ivory, tortoise shell and crocodile skin are not allowed to be taken out. **Airport Customs**, tel: 751-037.

Lost Luggage

File a claim at the airline's office. In theory, they will bring your luggage to your hotel when it has arrived, but it may be quicker for you to check at the airport after the next scheduled flight has landed.

On Departure

Leaving Bali by the airport, you must first make sure that your reservation is reconfirmed – do this three days in advance of leaving. Many airlines, particularly Garuda, overbook. To make your confirmations, go to the airline office in person, as a phone confirmation is not a "real" confirmation. Make sure you get the computer printout that says you have a reserved seat. Some international airlines, such as Cathay Pacific, do not require reconfirmation. Seats cannot be assigned beforehand; arrive at the airport two hours prior to departure. There is an international departure tax of Rp 50,000.

Health

International health certificates of vaccination against cholera and yellow fever are required only from travellers coming from infected areas. Typhoid and paratyphoid vaccinations are optional, but still advisable. If you intend to stay in Bali for a long time, gamma-globulin injections are recommended by some doctors; they won't stop hepatitis, but may reduce the risk of infection. For Hepatitis B, you can get the series of three shots (manufactured from yeast, not blood products) in Denpasar. It is less than half the price it costs abroad, but shots are administered over a six-month period.

Most people travelling through Bali get the infamous **"Bali Belly"**. Taking Lomotil and Imodium will stop the symptoms, but it keeps the infection inside. At the first sign of discomfort (diarrhoea and cramping), drink strong, hot tea and avoid all fruits and spicy foods. Taking charcoal tablets (Norit is the brand name) will help alleviate the cramping. If you get a fever along with the above symptoms, then get to a doctor who will prescribe antibiotics. Oralite (mineral replacement salts) for dehydration is available at every local pharmacy. Drink as much liquid as possible.

Malaria is not a significant problem in Bali; however, **dengue fever** is. Dengue-carrying *Ades egypti* mosquitoes are distinguished by their black-and-white banded legs and by biting in the daytime. They hide out in dark and dank places like bathrooms, closets and curtains. Protect yourself with long sleeves and trousers or use insect repellent *(obat anti nyamuk)*.

Minor ailments: Treat cuts or abrasions immediately. Betadine, a powerful non-stinging, non-staining, broad spectrum antiseptic, is available in solution or ointment at any drugstore. You could bring along antihistamine cream for relief of itches, a triple antibiotic cream (such as Neosporin), an ointment for fungoid skin infections, a good prickly-heat powder (Purol, available in Indonesia, works well), some insect repellent (Off! and local brands available), and aspirin.

Protect yourself against the **sun.** Use a protective sunblock and protect your head, perhaps with a Balinese-style straw hat.

Promiscuity is not a cultural trait of Indonesians. However, **sexually transmitted diseases** (especially gonorrhoea and herpes) are on the increase in Indonesia, and Aids and HIV infection, although still rare, are a harsh reality. Please act responsibly and use condoms. If you have not brought your own, they are available over the counter at pharmacies *(apotik)*. Indonesian and imported brands are for sale. Popular brands include the government-approved brand used in the Indonesian Family Planning programme, Simplex, and Durex.

Prostitutes are not checked for STDs (sexually transmitted diseases) and the Bali Cowboys or local gigolos have multiple female, mostly foreign, partners from all over the world. For those hoping for a little tropical romance, remember that some of the men (gay and straight) and women you may find yourself involved with are at least semi-professional and may ask for money "after the fact". Be warned.

Money Matters

CURRENCY & EXCHANGE

The **rupiah** is the basic unit of money, normally abbreviated to Rp followed by the value. Often travellers call rupiah "rupees" or "roops", which makes little sense to Indonesians. Smaller denomination Rp 25 are quite rare; Rp 50, 100, 500 and 1,000 are in the form of coins, and larger ones – Rp 100, 500, 1,000 – in coins or bills. Bills are available for Rp 5,000, 10,000, 20,000, 50,000 and 100,000. Values below Rp 50 are rarely seen except in the supermarket, where they are used as change. Don't be surprised when totals are rounded up in the seller's favour and small change (under Rp 100) is given in sweets instead of coinage. Change or *uang kembali* for high-value notes is often unavailable in smaller shops, stalls or from taxis. In view of this, carry a handful of coins or Rp 100 notes, especially when travelling in outlying areas. Don't exchange large sums of money if you plan to be in Indonesia for a long time.

The postal service offers **cek pos**, a kind of postal traveller's cheque. You can exchange your cash for these cheques from a main post office and use them throughout Indonesia as traveller's cheques, or cash them at any post office; they cannot be accepted by individuals. When you sign them at money-changers, you must put your passport number and a second signature on the reverse.

CHANGING MONEY

Foreign currency, in banknotes and traveller's cheques, is best exchanged at major banks or authorised money-changers. Hotels generally give rates far below what a money-changer will offer.Wherever you change currency, calculate and verify the amount according to the given exchange rate. Money-changers in Kuta and at the airport have been known to use quick fingers or rigged calculators to short-change travellers. Make sure you get a receipt for your transaction, and hang on to it.

Avoiding Stomach Upsets

All water, including well-water, municipal water and water used for making ice, MUST be made safe before consumption. Bringing water to a rolling boil for 10 minutes is an effective method. Iodine (Globolien) and chlorine (Halazone) may also be used to make water potable.

All **fruits** should be carefully peeled before eating, and no raw **vegetables** should be eaten, except at the fancier eating establishments.

Ice in all eateries is safe, as it is manufactured at a government factory, but often it is dumped in front of the restaurant on the dirty pavement and then only perfunctorily washed.

Watch what and where you eat, and wash your hands with soap.

Traveller's cheques are accepted at all major hotels and at some shops. Money-changers are much quicker than banks when it comes to changing traveller's cheques and the rates are often better. The best rates are to be found in Kuta; Ubud rates are generally 3–4 points below market rates. Rupiah may be converted back into foreign currency when leaving the country.

CREDIT CARDS

Many shops, large and small, accept plastic; an additional 3–5 percent may be added to the bill.

Cash advances can be obtained in all the major tourist resorts – Denpasar, Kuta, Sanur, Ubud. Automatic teller machines (ATM) are popping up all over the place, especially at shopping centres and bank branches. Many are connected to international banking networks, so you can look for those affiliated with your own ATM network. Bank Bali handles Cirrus cards and has ATMS located at: Jl. Legian 188 (Hotel Sol Legian) in Legian, Matahari Department Store at Kuta Centre; Tiara Dewata Shopping Centre on Jl. Sudirman; and at bank offices on Jl. Gunung Agung, Jl. Gatot Subroto, Jl. Teuku Umar, Jl. Ngurah Rai Airport and in Ubud.

American Express offices are at: Hotel Grand Bali Beach, Sanur (tel: 286-060, 288-449, fax: 282-447) and in Kuta, Kuta Centre, Jl. Kartika Plaza Blok E2-19 (tel: 758-842, 758-843).

Diners Club is at Hotel Natour Bali, Jalan Veteran, Denpasar (tel/fax: 227-138).

Visa/MasterCard office is at Bank Duta, Jl. Hayam Waruk 165, Denpasar (tel: 226-578).

RECEIVING MONEY TRANSFERS

Trying to have money sent quickly to you from home can be a real headache. If you can't bring it all with you in traveller's cheques, then there are two options: have

someone send you a **telex transfer** (money wire) to one of the banks listed below, or an **international money order** from a major bank (those from Bank of America and Chase Manhattan are readily accepted). The bank at home should send you money via a telex transfer to a specific bank, with your name, address and passport number on the telex. Make sure that the bank also sends approval of the money transfer at the same time as they send the money; otherwise you'll be waiting – sometimes for months – for your money to be cleared. There are no foreign banks in Bali yet, although a number of them operate out of Jakarta. What sometimes happens is that if you ask your home bank to send money to Bank A in Bali and they don't have a direct line to that bank, then your home bank will use whatever bank they do have relations with in Bali. Tracing your money can then be a bit difficult.

There are branches of major banks at the leading hotels and in Ubud and Kuta. If you have an account in one of the branches, you can have the money sent directly.

What to Bring

Travel as lightly as possible, as there are many great things to buy in Bali, and never enough luggage space. Essentials are insect repellent, a flashlight (roads and even paths to your hotel room can be dark), sunscreen, prescription medicines and an extra pair of glasses (or the prescription, which can be refilled here quickly for less than in the West).

What to Wear

Indonesians are concerned with how they present themselves. The nonchalant hippie look is not well accepted by locals; in fact, wearing ragged clothing can hamper your chances of getting good service, particularly in government offices. Singlets, halter tops, shorts and miniskirts are frowned upon. Government offices may post dress

Banks

ABN AMBRO, Jl. Diponegoro 150, Pertokoan Genteng Biru Blok A 1/3, Denpasar (tel: 244-277)
Bank Danamon, Jl. Gunung Agung 1A, Denpasar (tel: 436-490, fax: 425-782); Jl. Diponegoro 151, Denpasar (tel: 262-538, fax: 262-859)
Bank Lippo, Jl. Tamrin 59 (tel 436-048, fax: 427-461); and Jl. Bypass Ngurah Rai, Simpang Siur (tel: 761-788)
Bank Negara Indonesia (BNI), Jl. Raya Puputan 27, Renon, Denpasar (tel: 263-304, fax: 227-874)
Bank Panin, Jl. Legian 80X, Kuta (tel: 751-076, fax: 752-815)
OUB, Jl. Niti Mandala 17, Renon, Denpasar (tel: 245-204, fax: 245-978)

codes: trousers and shirt with sleeves for men, and dress or skirt with blouse, again with sleeves, for women. As the climate is quite humid, it is best to bring all-cotton sundresses, short-sleeved shirts, etc. Bali has a thriving garment industry and clothes made out of fabulously hand-dyed and hand-woven fabrics are readily available everywhere. Sandals or footwear that can be slipped off easily are a good idea, especially if planning to visit locals' homes, as shoes are always taken off before going into a house. However, avoid rubber thongs or slippers. Suits and party dresses are rarely worn. For formal occasions, men wear *batik* or *ikat* (dyed off the loom) shirts and trousers; women modest dresses. A light jacket or sweater is necessary for visits to mountain spots – and if spending a lot of time in air-conditioned lounges.

Entering a temple: *pakaian adat*, or customary clothing, requires that women wear a *kain* (sarong), *kebaya* (blouse) and sash, while men are dressed in *kain*, with a *saput* (overskirt) and shirt, sash and *udeng* (head-cloth). Throwing on a sash over shorts just won't do; make sure you have a sarong handy as well. It's best to wait outside the temple if there is a festival going on. Temple ceremonies and other rituals are sacred to the Balinese and appropriate clothing should be worn.

Getting There

Unless otherwise stated, telephone numbers are preceded by the **area code 0361** and prices are in US$.

BY AIR

Bali's **Ngurah Rai International Airport**, which straddles the narrow Tuban Isthmus in the south of the island, is served by many daily flights from Jakarta, Yogyakarta, Surabaya and various other cities in Indonesia, as well as a growing number of international flights from around the world. Some airlines fly only to Jakarta, where you must transfer to a domestic flight to Bali.

Flights to Bali from Jakarta's Soekarno-Hatta International Airport are frequent, and you can generally make an on-going connection if you arrive in Jakarta before 5pm. The flight takes only 80 minutes, and includes an incredible view of several volcanoes from the starboard (right) windows.

There is a taxi service from the airport in Bali; fixed rates for air-conditioned cars are posted at the counter. Pay the cashier at the desk and receive a coupon that is to be surrendered to your driver. These fixed rates range from $4 for a ride to Kuta to $20 to Ubud. Refuse offers from informal "guides" who may be loitering in the airport.

Rather than taking a taxi from the airport, you can walk about a kilometre out to the main road (if travelling light) and catch a local *bemo* to Kuta or Denpasar. There are also "wild taxis" in the parking lot that will take you to your destination for a bit less than the taxis (but you have to bargain).

Airline Offices
Indonesian Carriers:
AirMark, Ngurah Rai Airport Domestic Terminal, tel: 759-769

AWAir, Jl. Veteran 3, tel: 225-681
Garuda Indonesia, Natour Kuta Beach Hotel, Kuta, tel: 751-179; Sanur Beach Hotel, Sanur, tel: 289-135; Jl. Melati 61, Denpasar, tel: 254-745. Ticketing hours: Monday– Saturday, 8am–5pm. Airport: 751-177; reservations until 11pm, tel: 770-595.
Merpati Nusantara, Jl. Melati 51, Denpasar, tel: 235-358. Ticketing hours: 7am–8pm daily, reservations 7am–9pm.
Bouraq, Jl. Sudirman Mal, Blok A 47–48, Denpasar, tel: 241-397. Reservation hours: 8am–9pm.
Others:
Air France, tel: 287-734
Ansett Australia, tel: 289-632
Cathay Pacific, tel: 753-942
China, tel: 754-856
Continental Micronesia, tel: 287-775
Eva, tel: 759-733
Japan, tel: 287-460
Kuta, tel: 758-686
Lauda, Jl. Bypass Ngurah Rai 12, LTU, Jl. Kuta Raya 88R, Kuta, tel: 757-552
Malaysian, tel: 764-995
Qantas, tel: 287-331
Royal Brunei, tel: 757-292
Singapore Airlines, Bank Bali Building, Jl. Dewi Sartika, Denpasar, tel: 261-666
Thai, tel: 288-063

International airlines with offices at Grand Bali Beach Hotel, Sanur, can be reached through the hotel operator, tel: 288-511.

Airlines with offices at Wisti Sabha Building at Ngurah Rai International Airport can be reached through the airport operator, tel: 751-011.

BY RAIL

From Jakarta, Bandung or Yogyakarta, travel first to Surabaya's Gubeng Station: a first-class night train, *Mutiara Utara*, connects Jakarta with Surabaya every day. It departs from Jakarta's Kota Station in the late afternoon and arrives in Surabaya early the next morning. In Surabaya, choose from two daily departures from Gubeng Station, at 11am and 9.30pm, for the eight-hour trip on the *Mutiara Timur*, a non-airconditioned train bound for Banyuwangi, at Java's eastern tip. In Banyuwangi, catch the ferry to Bali. A bus takes you across the straits on the ferry and over to Denpasar, an extra four hours (although sometimes you have to wait quite a while for the ferry).

BY BUS

With improved roads, the *bis malam* (night bus) from Java to Bali is now faster than the train, although some say more dangerous as well (drivers like to go fast). There are air-conditioned buses from Surabaya (a 10- to 12-hour trip) to Denpasar and from Yogya (15–16 hours) to Denpasar. This is the way most Indonesians travel – one's tolerance for cigarette smoke and noise must be high, as there are no non-smoking buses and videos are loud. Avoid the first row, which is dangerous in case of an accident. Be sure to specify A/C (air-conditioned) to avoid inhaling the noxious fumes spewed out by trucks and buses. Meals are included.

One of the best Jakarta–Bali buses is the **Lorena**, which for a little more money includes deluxe services and a toilet. Contact any travel agent or their office in Jakarta: Jl. K.H. Hasyim Ashhari 15 C2-C3, tel: (021) 634-1166, fax: 350-0066. In Bali: Jl. Hasanudin 6 or Jl. Diponegoro 100/A12, tel: 237-660, 235-010.

The buses leave Jakarta at 9am, 1.30pm or 2pm and arrive in Denpasar 24 hours later. (Bali departures: 6.30am, 3 and 4pm.) The complete route is Bogor–Jakarta–Semarang–Surabaya–Malang–Denpasar. Non-somnambulists will want to stop over along the way to Bali. If anywhere, you should stop in Yogyakarta, the cultural centre of Java. The bus from Yogya to Bali is 15–16 hours; from Surabaya, 11 hours. The same buses leave Denpasar from the Ubung terminal for Yogyakarta, Surabaya, or Jakarta. Companies have an agent around Jl. Hasanudin and Jl. Diponegoro; tickets are available at the **Ubung bus terminal**.

Those with a lot of luggage will need to charter a **minibus** on arrival; these are readily available. You should refuse to pay over $3 to go to the beach areas (Kuta-Legian) from Denpasar.

Minibuses

Families or small groups can hire a private minibus *(colt)*, with driver, between Bali and all cities in Java, at about $30–$40 per day plus fuel. Going to and from Java this way costs about the same as flying, but you get to see more. Some minibuses are air-conditioned. Stopovers and side-trips can be planned, so this is a good way to see Java.

BY CAR

You can rent your own car in Java and drive to Bali, but the cost will be about the same as that of hiring both a driver and car, and then there is the added hassle of returning the car. If using your own transport, you need to get to **Banyuwangi** in East Java and take the ferry over to Bali.

You can now drive your own car across from Asia or Australia, travel cross-country and re-export it. Restrictions apply, so check with an Indonesian embassy or consulate if you are considering this route.

BY FERRY

There are both private and state-run ferry services that operate between Java and Bali. Visitors who have travelled overland from Java will have to take this 25-minute trip that runs at intervals of 15–25 minutes to get to Bali. This is a pleasant trip, but be warned that you might have to wait several hours before boarding, especially if it is a public or religious holiday.

Language and Culture Programs

Learning the language is the best way to learn about a culture. It makes communication possible and enhances human relationships. Balinese have their own language, but the national language (Bahasa Indonesian) is what is used in commerce, schools and in the media. Balinese is a very complex language and one that, if spoken incorrectly, can deeply offend. Indonesian, on the other hand, is an easy language to learn. There are no schools for learning Indonesian; you must find private tutors. At Udayana University in Denpasar, tutors are available for a hefty price; out in the villages, it's much cheaper. Be wary of those too willing to teach; trained language teachers are few and far between. Those who do teach and have been trained are: I Wayan Sidakarya, c/o Mudita Inn, Peliatan, Ubud or Pondok Pekak, Ubud Jl. Monkey Forest, tel: 975-179; Cok. Gd. Mudita Peliatan, Ubud, tel: 975-179.

A cultural course is a novel way to immerse oneself in Bali.
Agung Rai Museum of Art (ARMA), Jl. Pengasekan, Ubud, tel: 976-659, fax: 974-229, offers lessons in music, painting, art, and dance with masters. Accommodation is available.
Pusat Saraswati, Centre for Studies in Balinese Art & Culture; Jl. Goa Gajah, Teges, Peliatan, Ubud, PO Box 60 Ubud, tel: 96-303. Courses in Balinese dance, gamelan music, woodcarving, shadow-puppet making, palm-leaf decorations. Guesthouse lodging available.
Sua Bali, Language in Culture Centre, Desa Kemenuh, Gianyar, PO Box 155, Denpasar, tel: 941-050, fax: 941-035. An international award-winning facility, offering courses in Indonesian language covering politics, economy, socio-geographical development, herbal medicine, arts and handicraft. Strives to bring Bali to visitors and integrate visitors into Balinese ways. Accommodation is available.

Practical Tips

Media

NEWSPAPERS & MAGAZINES

There are two English-language papers published in Jakarta: the *Jakarta Post* and the *Indonesian Observer*. These are available at all major hotels, most bookstores and the magazine kiosks in Sanur, Kuta and Denpasar. *Time, Newsweek* and the *International Herald Tribune* are also available at these places. The deluge of Indonesian magazines includes many devoted to the private lives of film stars and pop culture heroes. *Bali News* is a bimonthly newspaper dedicated to culture and the arts. *Bali Advertiser* lists items for sale, properties for rent and "job wanted" ads. *Bali & Beyond, Bali Echo* and *Hello Bali* are among the local tourism-oriented publications.

RADIO & TELEVISION

Radio is a vital force in the dissemination of Bahasa Indonesia and a vehicle for the aural aspects of Indonesia's diverse cultural traditions. Besides the government radio, Radio Republik Indonesia, (RRI 93.5 FM), which plays a lot of traditional Indonesian music and also has morning and evening programs in English, many other FM stations play Western pop and rock music. For those who must keep up with the world they left behind, the BBC and the Voice of America both broadcast in Indonesia on shortwave. Check the times and frequencies in newspapers.

Indonesian television has a good portion of the broadcasting time devoted to news. There are two stations run by the government: TVRI and TPI, which is educational. The four private channels are SCTV, Indosiar, ANTV and RCTI. "Bali Vision", a locally produced English news broadcast, appears daily at 6pm.

Postal Services

There are post offices in every major town and village; Monday–Thursday 8am–2pm, Friday 8am–noon, Saturday 8am–1pm, and in some places (such as Ubud) Sunday 8am–noon. The **central post office** in Denpasar, Jl. Raya Niti Mandala, Renon, tel: 223-565, is open daily 8am–8pm. Other main post offices: in Sanur, Jl. Danau Buyan; in Kuta between Jl. Raya Kuta and Jl. Tanjung Sari; and in Ubud, Jl. Jembawan, just off the main road. Letters and parcels take two to three weeks to arrive from abroad.

Poste restante is available in Denpasar 80000, Kuta 80361, Singaraja 81100 and Ubud 80500. When picking up letters, take identification. Letters should be clearly addressed: Recipient's Name, c/o Post Restante, City, Post Code, Indonesia. If mailing anything crucial, use international couriers: **DHL**, Jl. Hayam Waruk 146, tel: 262-713, fax: 234-489.

ELTHEHA, Dipenogoro, Kompleks Dipenogoro Megah, tel: 222-889, fax: 235-261.

Federal Express, Jl. Bypass Ngurah Rai 100X, Jimbaran, tel: 701-727, fax: 701-725.

TNT Express Worldwide, Jl. Bypass Ngurah Rai 56, Jimbaran, tel: 730-520, fax: 703-521.

Local Tourist Information

Ngurah Rai International Airport, tel: 751-011
Denpasar Government Tourism Office, Jl. Surapati 7, Denpasar, tel: 223-602
Hours: Mon–Fri 7am–3.30pm
Bali Government Tourism Office, Jl. S. Parman, Renon, tel: 222-387, fax: 226-313
Hours: Mon–Fri 7.30am–3.15pm

VIP, Jl. Dipenogoro 218, tel: 240-033, fax: 231-329.

Use DHL for receiving/sending express mail in Ubud – the agent is Ary's Jasa Wisata, tel: 96-130. Also Federal Express, Jl. Sanggingan 100X, Ubud, tel/fax: 977-575.

Telecommunications

More and more individuals and businesses now have telephones. However, not everyone is used to "telephone culture", so you must exercise great patience.

Numerous government and private **Telkom Wartel** *(warung telekomunikasi)* offices dot the streets, from where you can place local and international calls, send and receive faxes, purchase telephone cards, etc. A list of 142 Telkom Wartels appears in the front of the Denpasar telephone directory. The **main office** (including IDD, fax, telex and telegram services) in Denpasar (Jl. Teuku Umar 6, tel: 232-112, fax: 236-021) is open 24 hours a day. The Ubud branch in Andong is open from 7am–7pm every day (fax: 95-120). You can receive faxes, which you must collect. There is a service charge per page.

Ary's Tourist Services, Jl. Ubud Raya, Ubud, also has an incoming fax service, tel: 961-30, 963-51, fax: 975-162. The cost is much higher than the telecoms office. You must collect your own fax.

Pay phones are few and far between, and most of them are not in working order. But those that do work cost Rp 100 for a two-minute call; this is much cheaper than

Bali Tourism Board, Jl. Raya Puputan, Niti Mandala, Denpasar, tel: 237-272, fax: 237-373
Tourist Information Office, Jl. Benisari 7, tel: 753-530, fax: 754-146
Ubud Tourist Information Service, Jl. Raya Ubud, tel: 973-285
Hours: 8am–8.30pm

making a local call from a phone office. Pay phones that operate with a phone card, which can be bought from post offices, Wartels, airports, and supermarkets are abundant and are a handy way to make international calls, especially if you are staying in one of the larger hotels, which slap hefty surcharges on calls made from the room.

Internet: For internet addicts and business people who travel with laptops, there are numerous local internet service providers. America Online has a Bali node, Compu-Serve has access through Infonet and Sprintnet, via Jakarta. Lines do not always hold well; you may have trouble getting hotel staff to understand that you are trying to bypass the PBX, even when there are modem outlets in larger hotel rooms. Many cybercafés are available.

International access codes: AT&T: 001 801 10; MCI: 001 801 11; Sprint: 001 801 15

Consulates

Australia: Jl. Prof. Moch. Yamin 4, Renon, Denpasar, tel: 235-092, fax: 231-990.
France: Jl. Bypass Ngurah Rai 155, Sanur, tel/fax: 285-485. After hours: 288-224.
Germany: Jl. Pantai Karang 17A, Sanur, tel: 288-535, fax: 288-826.
Italy: Lotus Entp. Bldg., Jl. Bypass Ngurah Rai 126G, Jimbaran, tel/fax: 701-005.
Japan: Jl. Raya Puputan 170, Renon, Denpasar, tel: 227-628, fax: 265-066.
Netherlands: KCB Travel, Jl. Raya Kuta 127, Kuta, tel: 751-517, fax: 752-777.
Norway & Denmark: Mimpi Resort, Jl. Kawasan Bukit Permai, Jimbaran, tel: 701-070, fax: 701-073.
Sweden & Finland: Segara Village Hotel, Jl. Segara Ayu, tel: 288-407, fax: 287-242.
Switzerland & Austria: Swiss Restaurant, Jl. Pura Bagus Teruna (Jl. Rum Jungle), Legian Kelod, tel: 751-735, fax: 754-457.

Tipping

- At most of the larger **hotels and restaurants**, a government tax and service charge of up to 21 percent is added to the bill automatically. Tipping is not usual, so do not feel compelled to tip at restaurants.
- If you've hired a **taxi** and liked the driver, then a tip of 10–15 percent would be appreciated. Always carry small change with you, as taxi drivers are often short of change – or so they claim. Rounding up the fare to the nearest Rp 500 is standard.
- If travelling in a group, a tip to **drivers and guides** is a good idea.
- An **airport or hotel porter** expects about Rp 1,000 per bag depending on the size and weight of the bag.

United Kingdom: Jl. Mertasari 2, Sanur, tel: 270-601, fax: 270-527.
United States: Jl. Hayam Wuruk 188, Renon, Denpasar, tel: 233-605, fax: 222-426.

Travelling with Kids

Children are so loved in Bali that it would be a shame not to bring any along with you. Babysitters are available at all major hotels, and even the owners of the smallest inn would be happy to look after kids for a day. Disposable nappies are not widely available here. Bring your own or else use cloth ones (the disposables get dumped in the river). Baby food is available at the supermarkets for exorbitant prices. Remember to bring sunhats and sunscreen. Soybean-based formula is only available at Tiara Dewata supermarket, and is expensive. Many larger hotels now offer kids' clubs and children's activities; ask when booking.

Matahari Department Store, Jl. Legian, Legian; Jl. Dewi Sartika, Tuban, and Taman Festival, Sanur have amusement centres packed with interactive and video games guaranteed to amuse the young and young at heart for a couple of hours, for a sum.

Gay Travellers

Male homosexuality is tolerated to a certain degree in traditional Balinese society, but the people involved are expected eventually to marry and have children.

Due to Aids, gay men are regarded in a different light these days – flagrant displays of romance are considered distasteful. (This also applies to heterosexuals.) There are no real gay hang-outs, although there are a few pubs in Kuta where gay behaviour is more accepted. Note that the Campuhan Hotel in Ubud is no longer a gay haven.

Disabled Travellers

Balinese tend to believe that all physical and mental disabilities are due to behaviour in a past life; that imperfections of any kind are punishment for how we acted in the past. Because of this, any blemish we have may be remarked upon in front of us. Although people with disabilities are often treated with compassion, there is very little consciousness in Indonesia about the special needs of the disabled. It would be very difficult to negotiate the island in a wheelchair, for example.

Religious Services

There are a number of churches and mosques in Bali, mainly in Denpasar, Sanur and Nusa Dua. Kompleks Puja Mandala, Denpasar, has a mosque, Catholic and Protestant churches, and a Hindu temple. Andong Ubud has a church.

CHURCHES

Catholic Masses
Grand Bali Beach Hotel: tel: 288-511. Saturday 5.30pm.
Bali Hyatt Hotel: Saturday 7pm.

Greja Puja Mandala: tel: 774-811 for times of services.

Interdenominational Services
Grand Bali Beach, Sanur, tel: 288-511. Protestant, Sunday 6.30pm.
Catholic Church, Jl. Kepundung 2, Denpasar, tel: 222-729. Sunday 7am, 9am, 5.30pm.
Church of St Francis Xavier, Jl. Kartika Plaza, Kuta/Tuban, every other day, 6am and 6pm; Sunday 8am.
Mary Mother of All Nations Church, Nusa Dua. Monday, Wednesday and Thursday 6am; Sunday 8am.
Protestant Maranatha, Jl. Surapati, Denpasar, tel: 222-591. Sunday 9am and 6pm.
Protestant Bali, Jl. Patimura, 7.30am; off Jl. Legian Kelod, Sunday 10am.
Seventh Day Adventist, Jl. Surapati, Gg IV no 6, Denpasar, tel: 233-677. Wednesday 7pm; Saturday 8.45am, 5pm.
Pentecostal, Jl. Kresna 19, tel: 234-352. Sunday 8am; Wednesday, Saturday, Thursday 7pm; Tuesday 6pm.
Evangelical, Jl. Melati 3, Denpasar, tel: 227-180. Saturday 7pm; Sunday 9am–6pm.

Mosques
Raya Mosque, Jl. Hasanudin, Denpasar, tel: 243-569.
Al-Hisaan Mosque, Grand Bali Beach, tel: 288-079.
Taqwa Mosque, Jl. Supratman, 9 Denpasar, tel: 237-152.

Medical Services

Ambulance: tel: **118** (it is often quicker to hire a taxi).

Every major village has a small government clinic called **puskesmas** (open 8am–2pm), but for major problems visit one of the hotel clinics or one of the public hospitals in Denpasar. The major hotels have on-call doctors and well stocked clinics. For parasite, hepatitis, pregnancy or a myriad of other **tests**, the reliable **Prodia Laborotorium**, Jl. Diponegoro No 192, tel: 227-194, fax: 236-133, is open daily 6.30am–10pm.

Hospitals

Rumah sakit means hospital. If you have a real life-threatening emergency, get thee to Singapore. If your insurance policy covers SOS or medical evacuations, you're in luck (but you have to have proof of this). If not, you need to pay $30,000 for the special jet to Singapore in cash or by credit card. Your consulate should be able to help you.

Bali International Medical Centre, Jl. Bypass Ngurah Rai 100X, Simpang Siur, Kuta, tel: 761-263.
SOS Medika Clinic, Jl. Bypass Ngurah Rai 24X, Simpang Siur, Kuta, tel: 755-768.

If you intend to seek medical treatment locally, the major hospitals' emergency rooms have English-speaking staff, but the quality of service is not up to Western standards. Pregnant women can go to the **maternity hospital** *(Rumah Sakit Kasih Ibu)*, Jl. Teuku Umar 120, tel: 223-036.
Rumah Sakit Umum Sanglah (public hospital), Jl. Kesehatan Selatan, Sanglah, Denpasar, tel: 227-911.
Rumah Sakit Dharma Usada (private), Jl. Sudirman No 50, Denpasar, tel: 227-560, 234-824.
Psychiatric clinic: Dr I Gusti Putu Panteri, Rumah Sakit Bina Atma, Jl. Hos Cokroaminoto km 5, No 30, tel: 425-744.

Specialists

The following specialists in Denpasar all have open clinics 4–7pm daily, except Sundays and holidays. No appointment is needed, although some will take your name over the phone or in person and put you on a list.

Paediatricians
Dr Hammid, Jl. Diponegoro 126, tel: 227-605. Open 6pm.
Dr Widia, Jl. Nangka Gang Murai 1, tel: 436-035.

Internists
Dr Tuti Parwati, Jl. Diponegoro 115A, Denpasar (no phone). Open 5–6pm.
Dr Moerdowo, Jl. Melati No 24 (no phone).

Surgeons
Dr Otong Wirawan, Jl. Danau Poso, 47 Sanur, tel: 287-482.
Dr Ketut Budha, Jl. Hasanudin, tel: 421-345. Open Mon–Fri till 7pm.

Ophthalmologists
Dr I Ketut Rai Tista, Jl. Sutoyo 50, tel: 223-941. Open 8–10am, 5–7pm.

Obstetricians/Gynaecologists
Dr Suanda Duarsa, Rumah Sakit Kasih Ibu, tel: 223-036.
Dr Gede Surya, Jl. Diponegoro 204, tel: 223-736. Open 5pm.

Dentists
Dr Retno Agung, Jl. Bypass Ngurah Rai, Sanur, tel: 288-501. Also has an open clinic every weekday morning at Rumah Sakit Kasih Ibu.
Dr Indra Guizot, Jl. Patimura 17, tel: 222-445.

Psychiatrists
Dr I Gusti Putu Panteri, Jl. Hos Cokrominoto, tel: 425-744.
Dr Robert Reverger, Jl. Patimura 15, Bangli, tel: (0366) 91-074.

Dermatologists
I Gusti Ayu Sumeda Pinda, Jl. Diponegoro 115A (no phone).

Security & Crime

Be warned! Bali, once blissfully free of theft and petty crime, is now a bit of a haven for petty thieves. Carelessness by foreign visitors has a lot to do with this.
● Don't leave **valuables** unattended. Lock up your room securely and make sure that your windows are locked at night – no matter how hot it is. Put all valuables in the hotel's safe or lock them up in a cupboard in your room. Straight off the plane and the first night in a new place are times to be wary. Be extra careful with purses, wallets and backpacks at festivals or in the back of a *bemo (see page 283)*. It's often when you are hot and flustered that the pickpocket strikes.
● There are two **scams** frequently used on public transport. First, you will be flanked by two friendly, usually English-speaking young men – one will engage you in conversation and distract you while the other picks your pocket. The second is to get you distracted and take your wallet and put it under a large package on the pickpocket's lap. This is usually just a piece of plywood wrapped in brown paper, but looks like a painting. Or they might ask you to change a large bill to see how much money you're carrying.
● Don't fall asleep on a *bemo*, and don't get on an empty one leaving a bus station (they never leave until full and you might be taken for a ride, literally).
● Don't lend **money** unless you don't mind not getting it back.
● It is unsafe to walk alone along **Kuta Beach** at night and along the Kuta–Legian road. Tourist Police patrol the main road from Tuban to Seminyak. They speak English and are helpful. Sanur Beach is fairly quiet, and its hotels are patrolled.
● All **thefts** should be reported immediately to the police, even though there is little chance of recovering stolen belongings. This applies especially to passports and other official documents. Without a police report, you will have difficulty obtaining new documents and leaving the country. It's a good idea to keep photocopies of your passport, ticket and driver's licence in a separate place from the originals. If you have an old or expired passport, throw it in the bottom of your suitcase when travelling. This will be handy for identification if your passport is lost or stolen.
● All **narcotics** are illegal in Indonesia. The use, sale or purchase of narcotics results in long prison terms – even death – and/or huge fines. This is one area in Indonesia where bribery can't help. Be aware that a lot of planting goes on in the Kuta area. Don't keep or carry packages for people that you don't know.

General Practitioners

Dr Conny Pangkahila, Jl. Bypass Ngurah Rai 84, Sanur, tel: 288-128; Jl. Bypass Ngurah Rai 35. Padang Galak, Sanur.

Pharmacies

Most pharmacies or *apotik* are open daily 8am–6pm. Late at night on Sundays and holidays, there is a rotation system in Denpasar. Check the *Bali Post* newspaper or ask your hotel.

Kimia Farma, Jl. Diponegoro 123-125, Denpasar, tel: 227-811.

Ria Farma, Jl. Veteran 59, Denpasar, tel: 222-635.

Bali Farma, Jl. Melati 9, Denpasar, tel: 225-152.

Dirga Yusa, Jl. Surapati 18, Denpasar, tel: 222-267.

Farmasari, Jl. Danau Buyan 74, Sanur, tel: 288-062.

Apotik Maha Sandhi, Jl. Raya Kuta 38, Kuta, tel: 751-830.

Smaller "drugstores" are also found on many streets, selling film, toiletries, etc.

Getting Around

Although one can circumnavigate Bali in a single day, some claim that you will see more by standing still, thus allowing the island and its life to come to you.

While in principle this is true, not all of us have the time to wait, and the opportunity for serendipitous encounters certainly increases when on the move. Don't try to go everywhere, however. The real Bali is all around, not in a remote village on the other side of the island.

The main tourist hub is in the southern triangle formed by Sanur, Kuta and Nusa Dua. Half-day outings are best, leaving the other half of the day to relax on the beach, stroll through a nearby village or sit in a cafe. If you're a sun-lover and prefer the comforts of home and the relaxation of the beach, then stay at Kuta (a wild and crazy kind of place).

If you prefer something quieter, there are the sister beaches of Legian and Seminyak up the road to the north, Candidasa on the east coast, Canggu and Yeh Gangga in the west, Sanur in the south or Lovina in the north.

Culture-lovers are advised to stay in Ubud, where outlying villages offer everything from basket-making to woodcarving and dance-drama. Denpasar has little of interest for the traveller, save for a museum and palace. (If you're on business, stay in Sanur and commute the 7 km/4 mi to town.)

Balinese roads are a parade ground, used for escorting village deities to the sea, funeral cremation processions, filing to the local temple, or the performances of a trans-island *barong* dance. They are also becoming ever more crowded, and the increase in traffic has been dramatic over the past two decades.

Domestic Travel

If travelling from Kuta to:

Denpasar: Hop on a *bemo* at "*bemo* corner" going to Tegal Station. Either walk into Denpasar or jump on an *ojek* motorcycle taxi to get into town.

Ubud: Go to Tegal, transfer to Kereneng station, get on a *bemo* to Batubulan station and then another one to Ubud.

Sanur: Go to Tegal, transfer to Kereneng, then get a Sanur *bemo*. Sometimes you'll be able to get a Sanur *bemo* at Tegal.

Singaraja: Go to Tegal, to Kereneng, then to Ubung station. From there you can get buses and vans to all points north and west.

Lovina: From Singaraja bus station.

Teluk Terima: From Singaraja.

Tanah Lot: Go to Ubung first, then get a van going to Kediri. At Kediri, get a *bemo* to Tanah Lot.

Candidasa: Go to Tegal, Kereneng, Batubulan, get on a van going to Klungkung, transfer to an Amlapura van. Sometimes vans go direct from Batubulan station.

From Ubud to:

Denpasar: *Bemo* to Batubulan station, transfer to Kereneng. Walk into town or get an *ojek* motorcycle taxi to Gajah Mada.

Kintamani/Gunung Batur: Go to Sakah, hop on a *bemo* to Bangli, then on one to Kintamani.

Candi Dasa: Go to Sakah, then to Gianyar town where you can pick up a van to Klungkung. There get on a bus/van going to Amlapura (which passes through Candi Dasa).

Besakih: Get to Klungkung, then transfer to Besakih.

Points west: Batubulan, then Ubung.

Public Transport

The Balinese travel by *bemo*, which is a minivan with two benches facing one another in the back. *Bemos* are hot, dusty and full of diesel exhaust, but are a great way to meet the local people. Buses travel on longer routes and are not as common. Minibuses (called *colt*) are very popular now and go all over the island. You don't need to go to a "*bemo* stop" to get on a *bemo*; just flag them down and yell "stop" when you want to get out.

The **major bus terminals** are at Tegal (in Denpasar going to Kuta, Sanur airport and Nusa Dua); Kereneng (in Denpasar going to Batubulan, Sanur and in the city); Ubung (going to all points north and west, including Java); Batubulan (going north and east) and in Singaraja (going to Java and Denpasar).

Intercity buses leave for Java from Ubung Terminal, and the bus companies have their offices in town on Jl. Hasanudin, near Jl. Sumatra, as well as at the Ubung Terminal. Within Denpasar, you have to travel a distance to cross town, as the city is full of one-way streets. It may be quicker to walk.

TAXIS

Taxis are metred. Private cars can be hired by the half- or full-day, not the hour.

Private Transport

CHARTERING A VEHICLE

Walking down the street, inevitably you will be approached by young men waving their arms in front of them as if turning a wheel and yelling, "Transpor? transpor?" It is easy to charter a minivan with a driver (and a guide if through a tour agency or hotel) for an hour, day or month. There are also shuttles from Kuta and Ubud, and from major resorts and Lombok. For quick, fixed-price transport without the hassles of a *bemo*, check with:

Ganda Sari Transport, Jl. Raya Ubud 33X, Ubud, tel: 975-520.
Perama Tourist Service, Jl. Legian 39, Kuta, tel: 751-551.

Chartering a car or minivan and driver can be done by the half-day or full-day. It is only courteous to give your driver money for a meal if you pause for lunch or dinner. If you are pleased with the driver, a tip of around Rp 10,000 is appropriate.

CAR RENTAL

Driving in Bali is dangerous. Other drivers are not defensive, the roads are narrow and poorly maintained, and stray dogs and chickens frequently dart into the road. If you collide with anything, you are responsible for all costs. If you feel comfortable driving among unexpected processions – of both the human and animal variety – on potholed and narrow roads in a land where defensive driving means nothing, by all means put yourself behind the driver's seat. Otherwise, hire a driver, relax and enjoy.

Self-drive cars are available in Sanur, Kuta and Ubud. You must have a valid Indonesian or inter-national driving license. Petrol is not included in the price. It's advisable to buy the extra insurance. You can book a car through your hotel or from any of the companies listed below. They will deliver the car and pick it up. Test drive the car before paying in advance.

Rental companies:
Avis, Jl. Uluwatu 84, Jimbaran, tel: 701-770.
Bali Car Rental, Jl. Bypass Ngurah Rai 17, Sanur, tel: 288-550, fax: 282-384.
Bali Baru Wisata, Jl. Legian, Kuta, tel: 761-153.
CV Agung Rent Car, Jl. Pratama, Nusa Dua, tel: 771-275.
Norman's Rent a Car, Holiday's Art Shop, Jl. Danau Tamblingan, Sanur, tel: 288-328, 288-830.
Nusa Dua Rent a Car, Jl. Pantai Mengiat 23, (100 metres from Hotel Bualu), Nusa Dua, tel: 771-905, fax: 772-432.

Taman Sari Rent a Car, Jl. Danau Buyan 21, Sanur, tel: 288-187, 281-868.
Toyota Rent Car & Leasing, provides Ngurah Rai Airport, tel: 753-744, Jl. Bypass Ngurah Rai, Jimbaran, tel: 701-747.

In Kuta, Candidasa and Ubud, you will see numerous "Rent Car" signs, which are fine to use.

MOTORCYCLES

Each year, several tourists are killed in motorbike accidents, and many others spend time in hospital. If you do rent a bike, drive slowly and very defensively. This is a convenient and inexpensive way to get around the island, but the traffic is heavy. Helmets are required by law and the ones provided by rental agencies offer little protection. If you know you'll be using a motorcycle while in Bali, bring your own helmet.

The cost of hiring a motorbike in Bali is negotiable, and varies according to the condition of the machine, length of rental and time of year. There are 90cc, 100cc and 125cc models available for rent. You buy the petrol. It's a good idea to buy insurance so that you are not responsible for damages. Be sure to test drive it and see that everything is in good working order.

You should have an international driving permit valid for motorcycles, or else spend a morning at the Denpasar Police Office to obtain a temporary permit, valid for three months on Bali only. This entails passing a driving test and paying a fee. Bring along passport, visa and three passport-sized photos, plus your driving licence from your home country. Normally the person who rents you the bicycle will accompany you to the police station. Getting an international driving permit in your own country will avoid this hassle.

BICYCLES

The only bicycles available used to be one-speed clunkers. Now, mountain bikes are everywhere. Make sure the wheels align properly, the brakes work well, and that your bicycle has a light.

On Foot

This is probably the most pleasant way to see Bali. As it is a small island, it is quite possible to traverse the entire island by foot. Most people do day hikes in and around Danau Batur, Danau Bratan in Bedugul, West Bali National Park, and around Ubud.

The **Travel Treasure**, a map and guidebook available in Ubud, outlines a number of interesting walks throughout the island.

Water Transport

Most large ships sail out of Surabaya Bay, but a few go out of Bali (Padangbai and Benoa). You can sometimes find a yacht which will take on an extra person or two – just ask down at the ports.

Indonesia's national shipping line, PELNI (tel: 721-377), offers travel to many islands in the archipelago. There are five classes of rooms to choose from in its modern fleet of passenger ships. Boats go to Lombok twice a month as well; check with the PELNI office Jl. Pelabuhan Benoa, PO Box 3386; Monday–Friday 8am–4pm for days and costs. Tickets until noon only.

Hitchhiking

Hitchhiking just isn't done and people probably wouldn't understand what you were doing. But this doesn't mean that you can't ask someone to take you somewhere. There are *ojek* or motorcycle taxis that will take you wherever you want to go for a fee; trying to get free rides from someone is not culturally appropriate, but you'll often find people offering to take you places.

A warning to women: beware "fast boys on fast bikes" as they may want more than just to give you a ride.

Where to Stay

There is a huge range of accommodation types to choose from in Bali, from five-star luxury hotels to concrete slabs for just a few dollars a night. Recently, the basic comforts we take for granted (tiled bathrooms, hot-water showers, towels) have made their way even to the most remote regions. If staying in budget places, bring towel, soap, toilet paper and mosquito coils, as these are not provided. Most budget and intermediate range *losmen* (a small inn, usually family-run) and hotels include a simple breakfast in their rates; most luxury places charge extra.

Reservations are recommended for the larger hotels during July–August and around Christmas–New Year. Deluxe and luxury properties will include hot water, air-conditioning, usually IDD telephone and other facilities, along with up to 21 percent government tax and service charge.

Hotel Listings

All **telephone codes are 0361** unless otherwise indicated.

DENPASAR

There's no real reason to stay in Denpasar unless you have business that can't wait until after a commute in from Kuta or Sanur. If you really must stay here, the old Natour Bali Hotel or the Pemecutan Palace Hotel are the nicest places. The Bali Hotel was built in the early 1930s and was once the colonial oasis in Bali – the *rijstaffel* is still good and the swimming pool courtyard delightful. The Pemecutan Palace is actually located in the

Badung palace and one has the feeling, at least, of hobnobbing with Balinese royalty here in the extensive courtyards. There are scores of other hotels in the $3–$20 category, most of them catering to domestic Indonesian tourists. Many are located on Jl. Diponegoro. There are also cheap but clean inns on Jl. Suli and Jl. Trijata, by the Lila Buana Stadium.

Adi Yasa, Jl. Nakula 23B, Denpasar, tel: 222-679. 40 rooms; price includes breakfast. *Losmen*-style rooms arranged around a central garden.

Natour Bali, Jl. Veteran 3, Denpasar, tel: 225-681, fax: 235-347; www.asiatravel.com/indonesia/natourbali/. 76 rooms. Centrally located in Denpasar, just a block from the main intersection and town square. Good restaurant and bar. Hot water and a/c. Swimming pool, tour service. **$$**

Pemecutan Palace, Jl. Thamrin 2, Denpasar, tel: 423-491. 30 rooms. This hotel takes one side of the extensive Badung palace, where day-to-day palace life continues all around. Rooms have a/c. Laundry service available.

Wisma Taruna, Jl. Gadung 31, tel: 226-913. 10 rooms. A youth hostel run by a friendly family. To get there, walk east on Jl. Hayam Wuruk from the centre of town, then turn left at the Arya Hotel and go about 100 metres. It's on the right side.

SANUR

Sanur is for gracious living, peace and quiet; it's more "international" but somehow far less cosmopolitan than frantic Kuta. Foreigners have been staying in Sanur since the 1920s, and they know how to take care of guests here, in both first-class and budget hotels. The main choice is between the convenience and luxury of the large five-star establishments (such as Grand Bali Beach, Sanur Beach and Bali Hyatt) or the quietude and personality of a private bungalow by the sea. Reservations are advisable during the peak tourist seasons. During

Holiday villas beyond indulgence.

BALEARICS ~ CARIBBEAN ~ FRANCE ~ GREECE ~ ITALY ~ MAURITIUS
MOROCCO ~ PORTUGAL ~ SCOTLAND ~ SPAIN

If you enjoy the really good things in life, we offer the highest quality holiday villas with the utmost privacy, style and true luxury. You'll find each with maid service and most have swimming pools.

For 18 years, we've gone to great lengths to select the very best villas at all of our locations around the world.

Contact us for a brochure on the destination of your choice and experience what most only dream of.

INTERNATIONAL
CHAPTERS

Toll Free: 1 866 493 8340
International Chapters, 47-51 St. John's Wood High Street, London NW8 7NJ. Telephone: +44(0)20 7722 0722
email: info@villa-rentals.com www.villa-rentals.com

the low seasons (15 January to 15 July and 1 September to 20 December) a 10–20 percent discount from the published rates is available at many hotels just for the asking.
Abian Srama Inn, Jl. Ngurah Rai Bypass 23, Sanur, tel: 288-792, fax: 288-415. 53 rooms. Ten minutes from the beach. Pleasant rooms with a/c and hot water, all with laundry service. Free airport transfers and swimming pool.
Alit's Beach Bungalows, Jl. Hang Tuah 41, PO Box 3102, Denpasar, tel: 288-560, 288-567, fax: 288-766. 84 rooms. At the north end and two minutes from the beach. Cottages in a garden that borders a small road, and a beachfront packed with brightly painted sailing craft. A/c and hot water. Pool. **$$**
Bali Hyatt, Jl. Danau Tamblingan 89, Sanur, tel: 281-234, 288-271, fax: 287-693; www.balihyatt.com. 390 rooms with television and suites overlooking the sea. A remarkably breezy, spacious feeling with public areas, clay tennis courts and fabulous gardens. Several restaurants, swimming pool, badminton, luxury spa, boutiques, convention facilities. **$$$$**
Baruna Beach Inn, Jl. Sindhu 17, Sanur, tel: 288-546, fax: 289-629. Nine rooms. Oldest hotel on the beach. Traditional thatched rooms furnished with Balinese antiques open onto a wide courtyard bordering the sea. Small and personal. A/c and hot water. **$$**
Belcont, Jl. Hangtuah, tel: 288-250. 15 rooms. Seven minutes from the beach. All rooms have a/c and hot water.
Besakih, Jl. Danau Tamblingan 45, Sanur, tel: 288-423, fax: 288-426. 79 rooms. Each room is set in a meandering garden that winds its way gracefully to the sea. All bungalows have a/c, baths and hot water. There's a pool and two restaurants. **$$$**
Diwangkara Hotel, Jl. Hangtuah 54, Sanur, PO Box 3120, Denpasar, tel: 288-577, fax: 288-894. 40 rooms. Private double bungalows in a secluded compound just behind Museum Le Mayeur, at the north end of the beach strip. All with a/c

and hot water. Swimming pool, one minute from beach. **$$$**
Grand Bali Beach, Jl. Hangtuah 58, Sanur, tel: 288-511, fax: 287-917. 523 rooms; www.asia123.com/balibeach/home.htm. 10 stories, private beach, three swimming pools, four restaurants, bowling alleys, tennis courts, golf course, water sports, convention facilities, airline offices, banks. **$$$ +**
Hotel Griya Santrian I, Jl. Danau Tamblingan 47, Sanur, PO Box 3055, Denpasar, tel: 288-181, fax: 288-497. 90 rooms. Private seaside bungalows in a spacious garden, some of which open into a garden; others have a view of the ocean. All rooms a/c with a private terrace. Two pools, two restaurants. **$$$ +**

Price Guide

Price categories for standard rooms (or suites in larger hotels), usually without breakfast, are:

No $: very cheap
$: under $30
$$: $30–$60
$$$: $60–$100
$$$$: $100–$150
$$$$$: above $150, often hundreds of dollars

La Taverna Bali, Jl. Danau Tamblingan 29, Sanur, tel: 288-387, 288-497, fax: 287-126. 34 rooms. Delightful thatched bungalows with Italian stucco walls and elegantly styled rooms set in a Balinese garden. Private beach, pool and pizzeria. **$$$ +**
Laghawa Beach Inn, Jl. Danau Tamblingan 51, tel: 288-494, fax: 289-353. 30 rooms. Simple cottages with a/c or fan-cooled rooms in a garden; hot water. Five minutes from the beach. Excellent restaurant on premises. **$$**
Peneeda View, Jl. Danau Tamblingan 89, Sanur, tel: 288-425, fax: 286-224. 56 rooms. A bungalow-style hotel right on Sanur beach. A pool and two restaurants. All the bungalows have a/c, western baths and hot water. **$$ +**

Puri Dalem, Jl. Hangtuah 23, Sanur, PO Box 3224, Denpasar, tel: 288-421/2, fax: 289-009. 41 rooms. All rooms surround a central garden with two pools, seven minutes from the beach. A/c and hot water. **$$ +**
Puri Kelapa Garden Cottages, Jl. Segara Ayu No 1, Sanur, PO Box 3436, Denpasar, tel: 286-135, fax: 287-417. 47 cottages. Each cottage hsd a/c, hot-water shower and bathtub. Two minutes' walk to the beach. **$$ +**
Raddin Sanur Bali, Jl. Mertasari 6, Sanur; PO Box 3476, Denpasar, tel: 288-833, fax: 287-303. 196 rooms. Down past the Sanur Beach Hotel at the very southern end of the strip. Rooms with tub, in-house video, IDD, restaurants, swimming pool and wet bar, tennis court, sauna and massage. Quiet and secluded. **$$$$ +**
Ramayana, Jl. Danau Tamblingan 130, Sanur, Denpasar, tel: 288-429. 20 rooms. Clean, a/c rooms with hot water, five minutes from the beach. Takes pride in catering to the individual traveller's needs. **$**
Rani, Jl. Danau Buyan 33, Sanur, tel: 288-578, fax: 288-674. 30 rooms. Opposite the Post Office, 10 minutes from the beach. These losmen-style rooms are clean and quiet. The 17 rooms have a/c, cold-water showers and western toilets.
Respati, Jl. Danau Tamblingan 33, tel: 288-427, fax: 288-046. 25 rooms. Duplex bungalows with white-tiled floors, twin beds, a/c, fan, bathtub and shower. Comfortable but basic. Narrow beach, restaurant and pool. **$$ +**
Sanur Beach, Jl. Danau Tamblingan, PO Box 3279, Sanur, tel: 288-011, fax: 287-566; www.aerowisata.co.id. 425 rooms, all with balcony. This four-storey international hotel with attached bungalows is known for its friendly staff and excellent service. Restaurants, swimming pool, ocean sports facility, tennis courts, mini-golf. **$$$$$**
Sanur Indah, Jl. Danau Buyan 29, Sanur, tel: 288-568. 20 rooms. Several losmen-style rooms with a fan, 10 minutes from the beach. Laundry.

Sativa Sanur Cottages, Jl. Danau Tamblingan 45, Sanur, PO Box 3163, Denpasar, tel/fax: 287-881. 50 rooms. Well managed hotel, which is very cosy and the food is excellent. $$$

Segara Village, Jl. Segara Ayu, Sanur, PO Box 3091, Denpasar, tel: 288-407, fax: 287-242; www. baliwww.com/segara-village. 144 rooms. A variety of lovely, private bungalows, some patterned after traditional rice granaries, arranged in tiny gardened "villages" bordering the sea. Three swimming pools, watersports facilities, classes in traditional Balinese dance, music, painting, woodcarving, batik, plus a children's recreation room, tennis courts and lots of personal attention from the staff. $$$ +

Sindhu Beach, Jl. Pantai Sindhu 1, Sanur, PO Box 3181, Denpasar, tel: 288-351, fax: 289-268. 59 rooms. Bungalow hotel right on the beach, with a swimming pool. All with a/c and hot water. $$$ +

Swastika, Jl. Danau Tamblingan 128, tel: 288-693, fax: 287-526. 80 rooms; all have hot water and most have a/c. Two pools and restaurant. Breakfast. $ +

Taman Agung Beach Inn, Jl. Danau Tamblingan 146, tel: 288-549, fax: 289-161. 33 rooms. Very pleasant, *losmen*-style rooms with a/c or fan. All have hot water and face a well kept garden. Minutes from the beach. Laundry, restaurant. $$

Tanjung Sari, Jl. Danau Tamblingan 41, Sanur, tel: 288-441, fax: 287-930. 28 bungalows, 16 villas. the name means "Cape of Flowers". Serene and stylish, with private bungalows by the sea and lovely gardens. Excellent service and food. Swimming pool. $$$$$

KUTA

Kuta nowadays resembles a malignant seaside Carnaby Street of the 1960s; chaotic, noisy, lots of hype, but a great playground. Originally what drew visitors to Kuta was the wide beach and the surf. It

still has the best seafront on the island, though now it is cluttered with hundreds of homestays, restaurants, bars, boutiques, travel agencies, artshops, car and bike rentals, banks and loads of tourists, both domestic and foreign. Though there are now many first-class hotels, the 5-km (3-mi) strip still caters best to the economy traveller who likes to be in the thick of things.

The Legian-Seminyak end of the beach is the best place to stay for any period of time – much quieter and more relaxed. Stay in Sanur or Jimbaran if you want solitude.

There are so many bungalows, hotels and homestays (called *losmen*, essentially a bed-and-breakfast) that no list could ever be complete, nor is a list really needed. Drop in and shop around. The difference between Kuta and Sanur is that there are far more choices in the lower price range in Kuta. The best way to find a budget room is just to walk around in any area that you fancy. From the airport, the areas headed northward are: Tuban, Kuta, Legian, Seminyak, Petitenget, Canggu.

Tuban & Kuta

Barong Cottages, Jl. Legian, Gang Poppies II, Gang Batu Bolong, Kuta, tel: 751-804, fax: 761-520. 98 rooms. Two-storey hotel with two pools, near the beach. $ +

Bali Dynasty, Jl. Kartika Plaza, Tuban, tel: 752-403, fax: 752-402. 267 rooms. Conference facilities, beachfront restaurant. $$$$ +

Bali Padma, Jl. Padma 1, Legian, PO Box 1107 TBB, Tuban, tel: 752-111, fax: 752-140; www.hotelpadma.com. 417 rooms. Big beachfront hotel with attractive wooden cottage-style rooms. Pool and lounge. $$$$

Bintang Bali Resort, Jl. Kartika Plaza, Tuban, tel: 753-292, fax: 753-288. 401 rooms. Pool and jacuzzi near beach, gym, spa, tennis court, restaurants, and conference facilities available. $$$$

Hard Rock Beach Hotel, Jl. Kuta Beach, Kuta, tel: 761-869, fax: 761-868. 421 rooms and suites on the site of the very first hotel in Kuta, along the beach. High energy fun, incorporating Hard Rock Café and seven other food and bar outlets, live entertainment daily, Bali's largest free-form pool, health club, kids' club, laundromat, spa, games, recording studio and karaoke, a radio station and, of course, retail outlets. Not the place for quiet relaxation but great for families and fun. $$$ +

Maharani Hotel, Jl. Pantai Kuta, tel: 751-863, fax: 752-589. Right next to the beach, this is a very friendly mid-sized hotel. Some rooms have hot water and a/c. $$

Melasti Beach Bungalows, Jl. Kartika Plaza, Tuban, tel: 751-860, fax: 751-563. 140 rooms close to the beach. Swimming pool. $$ +

Natour Kuta Beach Hotel, Jl. Pantai Kuta, Kuta, tel: 751-361, fax: 751-362. 137 rooms. A bungalow-style hotel 150 metres from the beach. Refrigerator, television, private balcony or garden veranda. Restaurant, bar and swimming pool. $$$$

Patra Jasa Beach Resort, Jl. Juanda, PO Box 3121, Tuban, tel: 751-161, fax: 752-030. 206 rooms. Located five minutes from the airport. This hotel was first built as a convention centre by the state oil monopoly, Pertamina, and then opened to the general public in 1975. Restaurants, conference facilities, tennis courts, badminton, canoeing, windsurfing, and a pool. Refrigerator, telephone, and in-house movies. $$$ +

Poppies Cottages I, Gang Poppies I, Kuta (near Jl. Pantai Kuta and Jl. Legian), tel: 751-059, fax: 752-364; www.poppies.net. 20 rooms. Well designed cottages in a beautiful garden, with hot water and refrigerator, only 300 metres from the beach. Often filled to capacity, so reservations essential. Pool, restaurant. **$$$**

Poppies Cottages II, Poppies Lane II, Kuta (north of Poppies I between beach and Jl. Legian), tel: 751-059, fax: 752-364. Smaller than Poppies I – four rooms with fans only – but still quite popular, so necessary to make reservations in advance. **$**

Ramayana Seaside Cottages, Jl. Bakung Sari, Kuta, tel: 751-864, fax: 751-866. 54 rooms. Located 100 metres from the beach. All rooms with a/c, hot showers. Swimming pool, restaurant, laundry. **$$$**

Ravi Segara, Jl. Singa Sari, Kuta, tel: 751-261, fax: 752-896. 100 rooms. In the middle of Kuta, quiet bungalows and rooms surround a patio garden. All rooms with a/c and hot water. Swimming pool and restaurant. **$$ +**

Sahid Bali, Jl. Pantai Kuta, Kuta, PO Box 1102, Denpasar, tel: 753-855, fax: 752-019. 407 rooms. Just across from the beach, part of a large domestic chain. **$$$ +**

Santika Beach Hotel, Jl. Kartika Plaza, PO Box 1008, Tuban, tel: 751-267, fax: 751-260. 171 rooms. An exquisite hotel with three swimming pools, coffee shop, restaurant, bar, tennis courts, and in-house video. All rooms are a/c and have refrigerators and taped-in music. **$$$$**

Yulia Beach Inn, Jl. Pantai Kuta 43, tel: 751-893, fax: 751-056. 46 rooms. Variety of rooms from which to choose. **$**

Legian, Semiyak, Petitenget, Canggu

The villages of Legian and Seminyak lie at the north end of the Kuta Beach strip. As the beach continues northward, it becomes Petitenget and Canggu. These are the places to stay for the best of both worlds. Conveniently located 15–20 minutes from the centre of Kuta, yet safely removed from the nerve-wracking intensity and hype, the villages are perfect for extended vacations. There are several first-class hotels, a great number of intermediate-range bungalows, and a plethora of inexpensive *losmen*. As is true in Kuta, you will find what suits you best by shopping around.

Bali Intan Cottages, Jl. Melasti 1, Legian, tel: 751-770, fax: 751-891. 146 rooms. Nice grounds and facilities but rooms need renovation. Tennis court, coffee shop, snack bar, and seafood restaurant. Wall-to-wall carpeting, colour television, and private balcony. **$$$ +**

Bali Mandira Cottages, Jl. Yucistira, Legian, tel: 751-381, fax: 752-377. 117 rooms. Built in 1982, this friendly and immaculate hotel provides tennis courts, tours for snorkelling and an open view of the ocean. **$$$$ +**

Blue Ocean, Jl. Arjuna, Legian, tel: 730-289, fax: 730-590. 28 rooms. Right on the beach; very popular with locals and surfers. A/c and hot water, restaurant, tour service. **$**

Dhyana Pura Beach, Jl. Abimanyu Pura, Seminyak, tel: 730-442, fax: 730-463. 125 rooms. Close to the beach, this more isolated hotel has pool, restaurant, a/c rooms with hot water and bathtubs. Continental breakfast. **$$**

Jayakarta Bali, Jl. Werkudara, Legian, PO Box 324, Denpasar, tel: 751-433, fax: 752-074. 180 rooms. A pleasant atmosphere which caters to the young, complete with three swimming pools, garden, weekly barbecue with performances of Balinese dance. **$$$$ +**

The Legian, Jl. Laksamana, Petitenget, tel: 730-622, fax: 731-291. 71 suites on the beach, satellite television, sound system, pool and bar, restaurant, library, meeting room, shuttle to Kuta, airport transfers. **$$$$$ +**

Legian Beach Hotel, Jl. Melasti, Legian, tel: 751-711, fax: 752-652. 215 rooms. Large complex wrapped in a relaxed atmosphere near the beach, the hotel offers free airport transport and tour service. **$$$ +**

Oberoi Bali, Jl. Laksamana, Petitenget, PO Box 3351, Denpasar, tel: 730-361, fax: 730-791; www.oberoihotels.com. 73 rooms. Luxury sea- and garden-view rooms and villas with satellite television, sound systems, some with private pools. The hotel's coral-rock *lanai* and villas are adaptations of classic Balinese *puri*, or palace, designs. Secluded beach, shuttle to and from airport, pool. This is the place to stay – pamper yourself. Massage and sauna in health centre. **$$$$$ +**

Pelasa Cottage, Jl. Tunjung Mekar, Legian, tel: 753-423, fax: 753-424. 14 rooms. Very clean and well maintained. All rooms with a/c, hot water and kitchen. **$**

Rama Garden Cottages, Jl. Padma, Legian, PO Box 3334, tel: 751-971/2, fax: 755-909. 30 rooms. Modern in style and comfort, offers refrigerators and a/c in every room, tiled bathrooms with hot water. Pool and restaurant. Breakfast and tax included. **$$**

Resort Seminyal, Jl. Leksmana, Petitenget, tel: 730-814, fax: 730-815. 69 rooms. Near the beach and far from the crowds. **$$$ +**

JIMBARAN

This is the latest area to emerge as a hidden, luxury destination. The calibre of its hotels has begun to attract some of the jet-set for a hideaway holiday.

Hotels are situated around a clean, white-sand bay facing toward Ngurah Rai airport. Beachside seafood grill restaurants provide popular dining alternatives to hotel food. Jimbaran is tranquil, with a delightful fishing village. Continuing south on the dry Bukit peninsula, a new enclave of hotels is being constructed.

Bali Cliff, Ungasan, PO Box 90, Nusa Dua, at the extreme south of Bukit peninsula, tel: 771-992, fax: 771-993; www.balicliff.com. 174 rooms above a cliff overlooking the sea. Cliff drops down to beach and seafood restaurant. **$$$$$ +**

Bali Inter-Continental, Jl. Uluwatu, Jimbaran, PO Box 35, Nusa Dua, tel: 701-888, fax: 701-777; www.bali.interconti.com. 425 rooms. Set in 14 hectares (35 acres) of Balinese landscaped gardens and lagoons, the resort has a beautiful beach and is the ideal viewing spot for Bali's sunsets. Squash courts, spa, tennis courts, three swimming pools, water sports facilities, health club, bars. $$$$$ +

Four Seasons Resort, Jl. Bukit Permai, Jimbaran, Denpasar, tel: 701-010, fax: 701-020; www. fourseasons.com. Built on a terraced hillside amidst landscaped gardens, the resort has a spectacular view of the bay and Gunung Agung. 147 individual villas, most with plunge pools. Four restaurants; conference facilities; full-service spa, swimming pool, tennis pro and courts, water sports. $$$$$ +

Pan Sea Puri Bali, Jl. Uluwatu Jimbaran, tel: 701-605, fax: 701-320. 41 villas with private baths and a/c. Great view of the ocean. Pool, two restaurants, bar. $$$$$ +

Ritz-Carlton, Jl. Karang Mas Sejahtera, Jimbaran, tel: 702-222, fax: 701-555; www.ritzcarlton.com. 322 rooms in four-storey resort, club rooms and villas, all perched on bluff overlooking white-sand beaches and the ocean. A/c, television, pool, 18-hole golf putting course, tennis, kids' club, gym, sauna, nursery, spa, three restaurants. $$$$$ +

NUSA DUA

As the newcomer on the scene, Nusa Dua is at a bit of a disadvantage, as it is rather isolated from the rest of Bali. On the other hand, the hotels here have made up for this by providing a "total" hotel environment – everything you could possibly ask for is available on the premises. Restaurants and souvenir shops line the road outside the complex, and the Galleria Nusa Dua shopping complex has expanded

to feature 15 restaurants, 80 speciality shops, duty-free shopping, department stores and a supermarket. More upscale than Sanur and more inclusive than Jimbaran, this is a peaceful place but with little distinctive personality. Tanjung Benoa point, the northward continuation of Nusa Dua Beach, is lined with hotels catering to groups and watersports operations.

Amanusa, PO Box 33, Nusa Dua, tel: 772-333, fax: 772-335; www. amanresorts.com. 35 suites. Part of the Amanresorts chain in Indonesia, this resort overlooks Bali Golf and Country Club, the ocean and Bali's coastline. There is a spacious swimming pool and an Italian restaurant, tennis courts and golf facilities. $$$$$ +

Bali Hilton, PO Box 46, Nusa Dua, tel: 771-112, fax: 771-616; www. hiltonindonesia.com. 538 rooms. Health centre, tennis and squash courts, and watersports facilities. $$$$$ +

Bualu Village, Nusa Dua, PO Box 6, Denpasar, tel: 771-310, fax: 771-313. 50 rooms. Lush tropical gardens, a swimming pool about 100 metres from the beach. Transport to beach, tennis courts and sports available with instructors free of charge. $$$

Bali Gardenia, Jl. Dalem Tarukan 7, Taman Mumbul, PO Box 133, Nusa Dua, tel: 773-808, fax: 773-737. 353 suites with living room, kitchenette. Tennis, gym, pool. $$$$

Grand Hyatt Bali, PO Box 53, Nusa Dua, tel: 771-234, fax: 772-038; www.hyatt.com. 672 rooms. Designed by architect of the Hilton in Waikoloa, Hawaii. One of the most spectacular resorts in Asia. Four Balinese-style villages with five swimming pools. $$$$$ +

Melia Bali, PO Box 1048, Tuban, Kuta, tel: 771-510, fax: 771-360/2; www.meliabali.com. 510 rooms. Water sports facilities, four restaurants, swimming pool, gym and tennis courts. $$$$$

Nusa Dua Beach, PO Box 1028, Denpasar, tel: 771-210, fax: 771-229. 380 rooms. A hotel on a scale of grandeur worthy of Bali's rajas,

owned by the Sultan of Brunei. The choice for heads of state visiting Bali. Huge pool, three restaurants, squash courts, tennis courts, international spa, and large beachfront. $$$$$ +

Putri Bali, Nusa Dua, PO Box 1, Denpasar, tel: 771-020, fax: 771-139. 384 rooms. All rooms with a/c, balcony, television with two in-house video programmes, four restaurants, two bars, pool, tennis courts, water sports and recreation room. $$$$$

Sheraton Laguna, PO Box 77 Kuta, Nusa Dua, tel: 771-327, fax: 771-326. 270 rooms with butler service. Beautiful setting with cascading waterfalls and blue swimming lagoons. $$$$$ +

Sheraton Nusa Indah, PO Box 36, Nusa Dua, tel: 771-906, fax: 771-908. 315 rooms. Garden or ocean-view rooms, spectacular pool. Tuscany, seafood and bistro restaurants. Bali International Convention Centre. $$$$$ +

TANJUNG BENOA

Bali Tropic, Jl. Pratama 34A, PO Box 41, Tanjung Benoa, tel: 772-130, fax: 772-131. 106 rooms, private terraces overlooking the sea. All-inclusive resort. $$$$ +

Grand Mirage, Jl. Pratama 74, Tanjung Benoa, Nusa Dua, tel: 771-888, fax: 772-148; www. grandmirage.com. 310 comfortable rooms with all amenities, three restaurants, bar, tennis court, two pools and meeting room. French spa is attached to hotel. $$$$$ +

Klub Bali Mirage, Jl. Pratama 72, Tanjung Benoa, Nusa Dua, tel: 772-147, fax: 772-156. All-inclusive club with 98 rooms. Rate includes all meals, beverages, entertainment and non-motorised watersports. Balinese atmosphere. $$$$$

Novotel Benoa, Jl. Pratama, PO Box 39 Nusa Dua, Tanjung Benoa, tel: 772-239, fax: 772-237. 190 a/c rooms all in coconut wood. Three restaurants, room service, boutique and drugstore, kids' club, shuttle bus to Nusa Dua, satellite TV. $$$$ +

CENTRAL BALI

Ubud & Environs

The Ubud area has more rooms than one can count, as practically every month a new place is built. This used to be a budget traveller's dream but, even though cheap places abound, more and more *losmen* are upgrading by putting in swimming pools, tiled bathrooms and hot water.

Ubud encompasses a vast area, from Mas in the south, Andong, Sayan and Payangan in the north, Penestanan in the west and Peliatan in the east. Practically anywhere outside of Ubud town proper will give you more peace, although the availability of food and transport could be a problem.

Ubud proper can be divided into **Andong** (north, out of town, views of rice fields, road noise); **Tebesaya** (walking distance to town, quiet, intimate family inns); **Padang Tegal** (walking distance to town, some places in rice fields, quiet); **Padang Tegal Kaja** (in centre of town but off main road); **Monkey Forest Road** (close to everything, many with views or in rice fields, road noise if not set back); **Ubud Kaja** (centre of town, noisy but convenient); **Campuhan** (five-minute walk west of town, restful); **Penestanan** (up a long flight of stairs, rural feeling, very quiet, stunning panoramas of rice fields); **Sangginan** (further up the hill from Campuhan, tranquil, remote); **Sayan, Kedewatan** and **Payangan** (10–15-minute ride from Ubud, on a ridge that overlooks the Ayung River); **Pengoseken** (10–15 minutes' south of Ubud, quiet, many with views of rice fields, cheaper); **Peliatan** (village just south of Ubud, centre of music, dance and woodcarving; food can be difficult to obtain here and it's a 20 minute walk from Ubud).

Sayan/Kedewatan/Payangan

Amandari Hotel on Sayan Heights, 3 km (2 mi) west of Ubud, tel: 975-333, fax: 975-335; www.amandari.com. 30 pavilions. Designed by Peter Muller of Oberoi Bali fame, this hotel overlooking the Ayung River is on top of the world, both in beauty and in

price. Totally isolated from the village, it oozes solitude, relaxation and opulence. The main pool (filtered with salt, not chlorine) is modelled after a Balinese rice paddy and is worth a trip to see. The rooms are huge, a/c with large bathrooms, verandas, refrigerators and sound systems. 12 two-storey rooms have their own pool. Five-star restaurant. **$$$$$ +**

The Chedi, Desa Melinggih Kelod, Payangan, Gianyar, tel: 975-963, fax: 975-968. 64 rooms and villa suites about 15 minutes' north of Ubud in a spectacular setting with mountain, rice terrace and river-valley views. Pool, two restaurants, complete spa with traditional treatments. **$$$$$ +**

Price Guide

Price categories for standard rooms (or suites in larger hotels), usually without breakfast, are:

No $:	very cheap
$:	under $30
$$:	$30–$60
$$$:	$60–$100
$$$$:	$100–$150
$$$$$:	above $150, often hundreds of dollars

Four Seasons Bali, Sayan, Ubud, tel: 977-577, fax: 977-588; www.fourseasons.com. 54 luxury rooms, suites and villas nestled in 7 hillside hectares (17 acres) along the Ayung River. Two restaurants, bar, spa, three boutiques, meeting facilities, recreation, library and lounges, in-room safe, entertainment system, dual phone lines, mini-bar, room sevice. Not suitable for children. **$$$$$**

Kupu Kupu Barong, north in Kedewatan, tel: 975-478, fax: 975-079; www.balinetwork.com/hotel/kupukupubarong. Named for the butterflies that make this their home, this hotel's 19 bungalows all have sitting rooms and spectacular views. A/c, refrigerators in rooms, room service, whirlpool; traditional Balinese massage is available. The cuisine has been praised in several magazines. **$$$$$ +**

Sayan Terraces, 4 km (3 mi) west of Ubud, Sayan, tel: 975-384, fax: 975-384. 10 rooms. Set high above the Ayung River with breathtaking views. The rooms are standard *losmen* type with fine views. **$$ +**

Villa Indah, Kedewatan, PO Box 1, Ubud, 4 km (3 mi) from Ubud, tel/fax: 975-490. Six suites in three villas with kitchen and private staff. Meals prepared to order and served on wrap-around living terrace. Peaceful view over Sayan River valley. **$$$$**

Sangginggan & Campuhan

Ananda Cottages, Campuhan, PO Box 3205, Denpasar, tel: 975-376, fax: 975-375; email: anandaubud@denpasar.wasantra.net.id. 54 bungalows. This is a lovely hotel in the rice fields of Campuhan, where you can rent a "house" with three bedrooms, two baths and a huge sitting room or duplex rooms. All with hot water, fan. Pool, restaurant. **$$ +**

Ibah, Campuhan, tel: 976-225, fax: 974-466; www.ibahbali.com. 11 rooms. Owned by the Prince of Ubud. Great views of the Wos River valley and Gunung Lebah temple. Large baths, in-room *saes*, mini-bar, television and sound system. Roman bath-style pool and spa area. **$$$$$ +**

Campuhan Hotel, Campuhan, PO Box 198, Ubud, tel: 975-368/9, fax: 975-137. 67 bungalows. Once the only luxury hotel around, this is the former home of German artist Walter Spies, who strongly influenced Balinese painting. With a spectacular view, a large spring-fed swimming pool (open to the public) and restaurant, this is a quaint place to stay, although there are now many places which offer better service and rooms. 10-minute walk to the centre of Ubud. Badminton courts, two pools. **$$$**

Ulun Ubud, Jl. Sanggingan, along the main road 1.5 km (1 mi) west of Ubud, PO Box 3, Denpasar, tel: 975-024, 975-762, fax: 975-524. 23 rooms. Coming down the hill into Sanggingan village is this gem of a hotel carved into the hillside. Run by Ida Bagus Putu Suarta, brother of the famous woodcarver, the late Ida Bagus Tilem. Hotel grounds are filled with art. The swimming pool is down many steps and affords a stunning view of the paddy fields and ravine. Restaurant is OK. Located far from the centre of Ubud, so you will need transport (available at hotel) to go out. **$$$**

Penestanan

Melati Cottages, PO Box 129, Ubud, tel: 974-650, fax: 975-088. Set back in the paddy fields on a hilltop, this isolated hotel is a real charmer. Two villas and 20 huge rooms with two double beds, ceiling fan and large porch, en suite bath, hot water. Clean, breezy, tasteful, as well as quiet and idyllic. Pool. You have to be nimble to get here, as it's down a narrow pathway, but the serenity is worth it. **$ +**

Ubud Proper

Abangan Bungalows, Jl. Raya Ubud, tel: 975-977, fax: 975-082. 16 bungalows, some with ceiling fans, two with a/c and fabulous views of rice fields. All have hot water bathtubs, twin beds and screens. Small pool. Just west of town on the north side of the street, these bungalows offer peace and quiet as well as convenience. **$$ +**
Murni's House, east of her famous *warung*, is up the stairs at Andangan and overlooks the rice fields, tel: 975-165, fax: 975-282. Four rooms. This idyllic setting is perfect for those who want to rest. Murni's famous breakfasts are served here. Rooms range from a single room with bath and veranda to large house with two bedrooms and two baths (can sleep six). All rooms are screened, have hot water and fans. Babysitter available. Free transfers to and from airport for stays of one week or more. Credit cards accepted. **$$$ +**
Puri Saraswati, Jl. Raya Ubud, Ibu A. Agung Arimas Saraswati Bungalows, Ubud Kelod, tel/fax: 975-164. 21 bungalows in a garden. Smack in the middle of town, next to the Lotus Café. Pool, breakfast nook

Price Guide

Price categories for standard rooms (or suites in larger hotels), usually without breakfast, are:

No $:	very cheap
$:	under $30
$$:	$30–$60
$$$:	$60–$100
$$$$:	$100–$150
$$$$$:	above $150, often hundreds of dollars

(perfect for small to medium-sized groups). **$**
Puri Saren, Jl. Raya Ubud, across from the market, tel: 975-057, fax: 975-137. Eight rooms. This is the home of the former King of Ubud, and you too will feel regal in one of the pavilions, which sport antique Chinese beds and fabulously carved wood panels. **$$ +**

Ubud Kaja (North Ubud)

Rumah Roda, Jl. Kajeng, tel: 975-487, fax: 976-582. A "family-style" place which emphasises service to its guests. Some rooms in family compound itself, others out back. Concrete floor rooms with bathrooms.
Siti Bungalows, Jl. Kajeng No 3, PO Box 175, Ubud, tel: 975-699, fax: 975-643. Eight bungalows in the home of painter Hans Snel. Garden cottages in a quiet setting, five minutes' walk into town. One of area's few solar-heated hotels. **$$**

Jalan Wanara Wana (Monkey Forest Road)

Canderi's Homestay, Jl. Wanara Wana, tel: 975-054. Five rooms. Canderi's was one of the very first homestays in the early 1970s and the best place to eat. Today her rooms are upgraded and shifted to the back of her compound, and the restaurant still serves simple but delicious fare. Tiled rooms with screens, cold-water showers.
Fibra Inn, near the south end of Jl. Wanara Wana, tel/fax: 975-451. 16 rooms. Rooms are set back from the road; downstairs rooms have lovely garden bathrooms, upstairs

rooms a nice view of rice fields. Small swimming pool and bar. Good place for groups. **$$ +**
Oka Wati's Bungalows, off Jl. Wanara Wana, set in the rice fields, tel: 973-386, fax: 975-063. 19 rooms. Famous for her *warung* in the 1970s, she moved it here, started a restaurant and then a hotel. Small pool. Some rooms have hot-water showers. **$$**
Pertiwi, Jl. Wanara Wana, tel: 975-236, fax: 975-559. 56 rooms in two-storey bungalows with a lovely breeze and views of the paddy fields. Nice, simple rooms with tiled bathrooms and a/c, most have hot shower. Pool. **$$$**
Ubud Inn, Jl. Wanara Wana, tel: 975-071, fax: 975-188. 34 bungalows. Has a fantastic pool set by a cafe in the middle of lush greenery. The rooms have hot water and are screened, and those upstairs have a nice veranda overlooking the rice fields. **$$ +**
Ubud Village, Jl. Wanara Wana, tel: 975-571, 974-704, fax: 975-069; www.indo.com/hotels/ubud_village. 28 rooms (which need to be sound-proofed) with separate garden entrance. Full Western-style garden bathroom, ceiling fan, a/c, nice pool, restaurant, large pavilion suitable for group events. **$$ +**

Padang Tegal

Matahari Cottages, Jl. Jembawan (behind Neka Gallery), tel: 975-459. In a quiet and breezy setting, these very clean, tiled rooms have showers and western toilets. Some have hot water. Six single rooms which are quite small (but cheap!), plus one two-storey family house. Simple meals available all day. **$**
Nirwana Homestay, Padang Tegal Kaja, tel/fax: 975-415. Four rooms. Run by batik artist Nyoman Suradnya and his wife Rai. The rooms range from simple *losmen*-style to large, more isolated rooms with ceiling fan and hot water (can sleep three). All rooms are screened. Batik studio and gallery on premises. Nyoman speaks fluent English and teaches batik. **$**
Nuriani Guest House, Jl. Hanoman, tel/fax: 975-346. At the south end

of Padang Tegal Road and nestled far back off the road with a sweeping view of the rice fields. The feeling here is what Ubud was like 10 years ago. The 12 rooms are tastefully arranged around a central courtyard; parking is plentiful. Screened, clean rooms.

Pengoseken

Agung Raka Bungalows, Jl. Raya Mas, Pengoseken, tel: 975-757, fax: 975-546. 21 two-storey bungalows in the middle of rice fields. Marbled bathrooms with hot water and tub. Huge downstairs porch, small bedroom and veranda upstairs (stairs are extremely steep and not suitable for children). Large swimming pool. **$$$ +**

Bali Breeze Bungalows, Jl. Pengoseken, tel: 975-410, fax: 975-546. 13 rooms, all with mosquito nets on beds. Among the first cottages to go up in the rice fields in this village. Good value; great view. **$**

Dewi Sri Bungalows, Jl. Hanoman 69, Padangtegal, tel: 975-300, fax: 975-777. 20 rooms. A small hotel at the junction of Padang Tegal and Pengoseken, set in the middle of rice fields. You can stay in a simple but nice room with hot-water shower; in a poolside one-storey bungalow; in a two-storey cottage with a huge porch, outdoor bathroom and cramped upstairs bedroom; or opt for the larger bungalows with a decent-sized bedroom. Swimming pool, restaurant. **$ +**

Guci House, Jl. Raya Pengosekan, Pengoseken, tel/fax: 975-975. Quiet and in the midst of rice fields, there are two rooms and three bungalows for rent, tastefully decorated with owner Nyoman Wijaya's paintings and with an indoor bathroom (cold-water shower). **$$**

Kokokan Hotel, Jl. Pengoseken, tel: 975-742, fax: 975-332; www. nusantara.com/arma/. 15 rooms. Bills itself as exclusive bungalows. Set in the rice fields with a view of Gunung Agung, these large rooms with matching verandas are tastefully furnished. Large pool. All rooms have hot water, bathtubs,

mini-bar, fans and a/c. Free transport into Ubud for meals and performances. Part of Agung Rai Museum of Art with restaurants adjacent. Houses many artists. **$$$**

Tebesaya, Peliatan

Aji Bungalow, Jl. Tebesaya 11 (behind Pura Dalem Puri), tel: 973-255. Four rooms in a family compound, owner works for the Department of Education and Culture in Ubud and is a painter himself. All rooms are tiled and clean with shower and splash bath.

Homestay Tebesari, Jl. Tebesaya No 29. Six rooms in a garden setting. Tiled, clean shower, outdoor bathroom. Owner is a teacher and loves to go on walks. **$**

Oka Kartini's, Jl. Raya Ubud by Jl. Tebesaya, tel: 975-193, fax: 975-759. 15 rooms, set in the midst of gorgeous gardens. Rooms have fans and showers, some with hot water. Quiet location a short walk into town. **$$**

South Peliatan

Ketut Madra, Banjar Kalah, tel: 975-749. Six bungalows. Set right by a river and with a stunning view of rice fields, Madra's has been popular with groups for years, with Gamelan Sekar Jaya from California making this their base since 1985. Madra himself is a very fine painter of the *wayang* style. The cottages are made out of brick with squat and western-style toilets and showers; most of these are in need of a thorough cleaning.

Mandala Bungalows, main road in Peliatan, tel/fax: 975-026. 18 bungalows. Owned by the Peliatan-Sukawati royal family. All rooms have hot water. Legong performances held here. **$$**

Andong & Petulu

Andong Inn, Jl. Andong 26A, tel: 975-076. Set off from the road, there are four basic tiled rooms with cold-water shower and 10 bungalows with hot water. Large public pool in the front. Located behind Dr Siada's house.

Griya Loka Sari, Jl. Tegalalang, Petulu, tel/fax: 975-476. These 10

bungalows offer a relief from the standard rooms one finds all over Ubud and are quite reasonable. Extremely clean, each unit has its own simple kitchen, garden bathroom (with very creative decorating ideas) and ample bedrooms. Even though there's traffic noise in the daytime, a waterfall will lull you to sleep at night (and all day for that matter). Two bungalows with a downstairs and upstairs bedroom, veranda; two one-storey bungalows. **$$ +**

Kamandalu, Jl. Tegalalang, Banjar Nagi, PO Box 77, Ubud, tel: 975-825, fax: 975-851; www. kamandalu.com. 58 villas on the edge of the Petanu River valley, surrounded by rice fields. Deluxe and sensuous retreats. Full-range spa, international restaurant, pool, tennis, nature walks, conference facilities, swim up bar, private villa dining, shuttle to Ubud. **$$$$$ +**

Petulu Village Inn, Jl. Tegalalang, Petulu, tel: 975-209. Set far off the busy road, a complex of four rooms (two-up, two-down) with cold-water shower and western toilet. Rooms are cool and breeze comes off neighbouring rice fields. Even further off the road are so-called family rooms, with veranda. These are secluded and have a river view, but are a bit overpriced. **$**

Mas Village

Taman Harum , tel/fax: 975-567; email: tamanhrm@indosat.net.id. 17 rooms in duplexes with a sitting room and upstairs bedroom are tastefully furnished. Hot-water baths. Swimming pool. Restaurant is not great but there's nowhere else to eat in Mas. Breakfast included. **$$ +**

Bangli

There are two budget homestays in this town and both are part of *puris* or palaces. One of them, the **Homestay Darmaputra**, is a Youth Hostel and the rooms are dirt cheap but unfortunately they are full of dirt as well.

Artha Sastra Inn on the other hand is quite clean and full of antiques and exquisite carvings.

Kintamani Area
Telephone code 0366
Most of the accommodation at Gunung Batur is basic, with cold (very cold, actually) mountain-spring water and magnificent views. All room prices are subject to negotiation (most cost under $20) and generally reflect the market demand. Penelokan has the views, Kintamani is quieter and Toya Bungkah down at the lake gets great sunrises and sunsets.

On the rim
Lakeview Restaurant & Hotel, Penelokan, tel/fax: 514-64. 10 tiny, overpriced rooms without private bath. Popular stop-off spot and restaurant with a view. **$$**

In the caldera
Nyoman Mawa I (previously Under the Volcano I), Toya Bungkah, tel: 511-66. 12 clean, nice bungalows. Excellent dining room and service.
Nyoman Mawa II (previously Under the Volcano II), Songan, tel: 511-66. 16 rooms, some with hot water. Breakfast included.
Hotel Puri Berning, tel: 512-44, fax: 512-48. 38 rooms. Modern block of hotel rooms under the volcano; international standard. **$$$**
Surya Homestay, Kedisan, tel: 511-39. 10 bungalows on hillside, spacious and clean, some with hot water. Breakfast included.
Segara, left before Kedisan from Penelokan. 42 rooms with private baths, restaurant. Rooms with hot water; a bit overpriced, so best to bargain. VIP rooms have television. Rates include breakfast, laundry, tax and service. **$$**

THE EAST

Klungkung
Telephone Code 0363
The only decent place to stay here is the **Ramayana Hotel** on Jl. Diponegoro, on the eastern edge of town, tel/fax: 210-44. The new rooms have baths and western toilets; old rooms are sparse but

clean with shared bath and squat toilets. **$**

Nusa Penida/Nusa Lembongan
Arid Nusa Penida has only one place to stay, a government-run *losmen* in Sampalan. However, Nusa Lembongan, a surfing, snorkelling and diving paradise, has a number of *losmen* and resort options.
Hai Tide Huts, tel: 720-331, fax: 720-334. 12 traditional rice-barn style bungalows on stilts over the beach. King or twin beds, ceiling fans, a/c, veranda, outdoor day-bed. Some with private baths. Access to Bali Hai Cruise Beach Club facilities with pool, water sports, off-shore activities pontoon, bar, restaurant. **$$**
Nusa Lembongan Resort, tel: 725-864, fax: 725-866. 12 spacious, luxury villas on a cliffside; two adjoin to form family room. Private veranda, a/c, mini bar, phone, separate shower and bath. Pool, restaurant, bar, decks for sun or private dining, spa, gift shop. The Anchorage, the adjacent beach club, has pool, organised island excursions, buffet dining, water sports. **$$$$**
Waka Nusa, tel: 723-629, fax: 722-077. 10 spacious, twin-bed bungalows with mini bar, fan, private terrace. All inclusive resort with meals. Pool, restaurant, bar, shop. **$$$**

Padang Bai
Telephone code 0363
Padang Bai has a lovely white-sand beach, a few hotels and lots of boats, as this is one of the major ports on the island (the jumping-off point for Lombok, Nusa Penida and cruises).
Kerti Beach Inn, Jl. Selayukti, tel: 413-91. 18 rooms with fan in bungalows overlooking the ocean.
Hotel Madya, Jl. Pelabuan Padang Bai, tel: 413-93, is near the wharf and has simple rooms.
Rai Beach Inn, tel: 413-85/7, fax: 413-86, has a number of separate two-storey bungalows with a huge downstairs veranda. 30 rooms, 10 with a/c, hot water; pool. **$ +**

Topi Inn has five simple rooms in three-storey thatched bamboo structure and dormitory rooms over a restaurant. Beds with mosquito nets, squat toilets.

Balina Beach/Manggis/Buitan
Telephone code 0363
This is a spacious, gorgeous white-sand beach just 5 km (3 mi) from Candidasa. Currently, there is only a smattering of hotels and outrigger canoes here, going the gamut from luxury to basic. One of the major diving centres in Bali.
Amankila, Manggis, tel: 413-33, fax: 415-55; www.amankila.com. 35 luxurious suites, six with their own pool. Unsurpassed splendour but steep location. The main swimming pool has a fabulous view of Bali's east coast and of the Indian Ocean. The restaurant serves Asian and continental cuisine. **$$$$$ +**
Rama Ocean View Bungalows, PO Box 120, Karangasem, tel: 419-74, fax: 419-75. 70 rooms. A few hundred metres before Candidasa itself, these bungalows are set on the beach and have hot water, a/c and satellite television. **$$$ +**
The Serai, Desa Buitan, Manggis, tel: 410-11, fax: 410-15. 58 rooms facing pool and beach. Understated elegant decor in coconut wood and natural fibres. Shower only, a/c, satellite television, IDD phone. Great restaurant set in pond, spa, pool, watersports, bicycling, trekking. Peaceful and restful environment. A favourite getaway for expats. **$$$$**

Candidasa
Until the 1990s, this 2-km (1-mi) strip of exquisite beachfront was untouched paradise. A temple, Pura Pengumuman, was the only man-made fixture for miles around before an *ashram* was built in 1983. It was then that the tourists who were fed up with the growing commercialism of South Bali began to wander east and north for a more restful vacation.
     A string of hotels, restaurants and shops has since cropped up, making Candidasa a veritable "tourist spot", but one with a low profile. There are several low-key

discos in town, but most of the nightlife is confined to quiet walks on the beach at low tide; at high tide, there is no beach.

Being a two hour drive from Denpasar, it is the ideal place for a restful holiday.

Though the lack of indigenous village life lends a sort of open-ended, unrooted ambience to this community, it also keeps the clutter of arts and crafts down to a minimum. In short, the entire town exists for the sake of the tourist alone, and you will be treated graciously here.

The Ashram, Jl. Candidasa, tel/fax: 411-08. 12 rooms. Built in 1983 by Ibu Gedong as a pipedream in Gandhian self-sufficiency, the Ashram rents out rooms complete with three excellent semi-vegetarian meals a day. Ibu Gedong herself is a strong-willed, fascinating woman and an English teacher at Udayana University. If you want to volunteer as a worker here, then you pay a nominal charge for food and lodging. Regular guests' rates includes all meals. **$ +**

Bambu Garden Bungalows, non-oceanside. Has seven bungalows with a panoramic view of Lombok to Padang Bai and fully tiled sleeping and bathing areas. **$**

Candidasa Beach Cottage, Siengkidu, Candidasa, Amlapura, tel: 412-34, fax: 411-11. 64 cottages and hotel rooms in tropical gardens, a/c, private bath and shower, satellite television, pool, tennis, fitness centre. **$$$ +**

Candidasa Sunrise, Jl. Raya Candidasa, oceanside, west side of town, tel: 415-39, fax: 415-38. 20 bamboo bungalows, near the town centre, are set in a garden; cosy and classy. Some rooms have a/c and fan. **$$**

Homestay Segara Wangi, ocean-side, west end. Seven rooms with single beds. Some of the friendliest people in town here. **$**

Ida's Homestay, Jl. Raya Candidasa, Bubuk, on the east end of town, tel/fax: 410-96. Still one of the nicest places around. The owners did not try to cram as many rooms onto the land as possible,

and the six bungalows here are set in a huge coconut plantation next to the ocean. Also two-storey houses with garden bathrooms. No hot water. **$**

Pandawa Bungalows, Jl. Raya Candidasa, oceanside, on east end of lake, tel: 419-29. 10 bungalows with shower; breakfast, and coffee or tea all day.

The Water Garden, PO Box 26, Manggis, Amlapura, tel: 415-40, fax: 411-64. Run by the folks at TJs, this elegant hotel has 14 rooms (10 with a/c) built of teak in the midst of pools and gardens. Across the street from the beach. Swimming pool. **$$$**

Amlapura & Environs

There's really no reason to stay right in Amlapura, and there are only a few *losmen* here. Just east of town in Abian Soan is a cute little place in the middle of the paddyfields called **Homestay Lila**. A perfect place to get away from it all and just be. There's no electricity, but each bungalow has its own bath. And you can't beat the price. **Balai Kiran ($$)** has four rooms within the grounds of Amlapura's Puri Agung palace. Breakfast and dinner are provided. **Losmen Lahar Mas**, Jl. Gatot Subroto 1, tel: 213-45, has 20 rooms in a typical *losmen*, clean and friendly.

THE NORTH

Singaraja
Telephone code 0362
There's no real reason to stay in Singaraja, Bali's second largest

town, as the beach resorts are so close by.

Hotel Cendrawasih, Jl. Jen. A. Yani 21, tel/fax: 218-91. **$**

Losmen Dama Setu, Jl. A Yani 46, tel: 232-000.

Losmen Duta Karya, Jl. A. Yani 59, tel: 214-67. Nine fan-cooled or a/c rooms (it gets quite hot up here), television, breakfast included.

Air Sanih
These freshwater springs support a number of bungalows by the pools, themselves just by the ocean.

Apilan Beach Front Hotel, Bukti village, Buleleng. PO Box 188, Singaraja, tel: 811-13, fax: 211-08 (c/o Telcom Singaraja). Beach house with attached dining room. Private cottages with veranda and double beds. **$**

Sunset Graha Beach Hilltop Garden Bungalow, Jl. Raya Kubutambahan Singaraja, fax: 211-08. Six rooms on steep hill overlooking beach and springs, private bath, fan, mosquito net, restaurant adjacent. **$**

Lovina Beach
A northern beachfront alternative to Kuta and Sanur, this is a serene and frequently visited vacation spot 10 km (6 mi) west of Bali's original capital and port, Singaraja. Black-sand beaches and quiet waters protected by extensive coral reefs distinguish this idyllic spot. Snorkelling is superb here; the reef is close enough that even beginner swimmers feel comfortable.

Best news is that the local government has passed a moratorium on building, preventing any new hotel development along the non-ocean side of the main road, and limiting building on the oceanside. Rice paddies that currently separate the accom-modation into three major sections are required by law to stay put, ensuring an open and uncluttered beachfront for the future.

Don't be swayed by the condition of the signs you see on the road, for the quality and upkeep of an establishment often has little to do with its advertising skills. Most places don't include breakfast.

Higher-priced accommodation is on the ocean side of the main road, with private shower/tub, Western toilet, a/c, hot water and swimming pools. All of these are characterised by good management and cleanliness. Reasonably priced lodgings, with shower and private bathroom, are abundant. Nearly all include a simple breakfast.

Aditya Bungalow, Jl. Raya Lovina, west end, PO Box 134, Singaraja, tel: 410-59, fax: 413-42. 65 rooms, all with hot water. Restaurant and bar on premises, laundry services and snorkelling. **$$**

Banyualit Beach Inn, Jl. Raya Lovina, PO Box 116, Singaraja, tel: 417-89, fax: 415-63. 22 rooms, some with a/c, some fan-cooled. Isolated, quiet, and exquisitely managed. Advance reservations recommended. Excellent restaurant, money changer, laundry, tour services, water sports. **$**

Homestay Agung, east end, PO Box 124, Anturan. 10 rooms. Very friendly staff. Bamboo was used to build this hotel. Shared bathrooms. **Jati Reef Bungalows**, Jl. Raya Lovina, east end of beach, Tukad Mungga, tel: 410-52, fax: 411-60. 16 rooms. Thoughtful touches such as outdoor showers, safety deposit lockers, laundry service, towel, soap, and daily sheet changes. Four bungalows with four fan-cooled units in each, tiled floors, large garden bathrooms, thatched roofs, ideal location behind rice paddies, close to beach.

Nirwana Seaside Cottages, Jl. Pantai Binavia, centre of strip, Kalibukbuk, tel: 412-88, fax: 410-90. 37 rooms. Close to a popular section of the beach, yet also far from the road. Has its own restaurant and bar. Snorkel equipment and tours to Kintamani are available. All rooms have a/c or fans. **$**

Puri Tasik Madu, Jl. Seririt, tel: 413-76. 12 rooms. One of the original *losmen* in the area. Friendly staff, rooms have been renovated, restaurant.

Sol Inn Lovina, Jl. Raya Lovina, Lovina Beach, PO Box 131, Lovina, tel: 416-58, fax: 416-59. 129 rooms by the sea, complete with

Price Guide

Price categories for standard rooms (or suites in larger hotels), usually without breakfast, are:

No $:	very cheap
$:	under $30
$$:	$30–$60
$$$:	$60–$100
$$$$:	$100–$150
$$$$$:	above $150, often hundreds of dollars

a/c, TV, all amenities. Some villas have private pool. Fitness centre and pool. The only international chain hotel in Lovina. **$$$$ +**

WESTERN BEACHES

Telephone code 0362
Up along this coast north of Kuta and Legian lies a stretch of black sand beach beloved by surfers. With a dangerous reef and heavy undertow, these beaches are not ideal for swimming or beginner surfers and should be avoided by the inexperienced.

Tanah Lot
You can stay here – if you can stand all the hype surrounding this beautiful temple.

Dewi Sinta Cottage, Jl. Tanah Lot, Kediri, Tabanan, tel: 812-933, fax: 813-956. 27 rooms. Spacious suites and deluxe rooms, with mini bar, tub and shower, television. Original standard rooms with tub, shower and television. All with a/c. Block of fan and cold shower only rooms faces lovely pool and golf views. All rooms with terrace. Cottages have fan and hot water. Nice restaurant. Clean and friendly. Golf course nearby. **$$ +**

Le Meridien Nirwana Resort, PO Box 124, Kediri, Tanah Lot, Bali, tel: 815-900, fax: 815-907; www.balimeridien.com. 284 rooms. Luxury hotel set in the midst of 18-hole Greg Norman-designed golf course. Even most of the garden view rooms have partial ocean view. Rooms, suites,

bungalows, villas and one- to three-bedroom resort homes. Tennis, squash, fitness centre, swimming pools and lagoon with man-made white sand beach, museum, salon, kids' Pirate Club, amphitheatre. Five-minute walk to Tanah Lot temple. **$$$$$ +**

Losmen Artist, tel: 288-375. Six rooms. Small homestay compound operated by artist in residence, Putu Pagar. Pak Putu has his two-storey studio in front of the rooms, which have ensuite bathrooms with cold water. **$**

Mutiara Tanah Lot, Jl. Raya Tarah Lot, tel: 812-939, fax: 225-465. 12 rooms. Two blocks of simple rooms with carpet, a/c, television, patio with garden view, phone, mini-fridge, tub and shower with hot and cold water. Large restaurant frequented by tour groups.

West Coast
Balian Beach Bungalows, tel/fax: 813-017. Lalang Linggah Village, Selemadeg, Tabanan, 50 km (30 mi) west of Denpasar. 11 rooms and bungalows near surfing beach, coves and caves. Simple standard, superior and family rooms. Bar, restaurant. **$**

Sacred River Retreat, tel: 732-165, fax: 732-165. An alternative resort for the spiritually inclined. All-inclusive packages in 14 bungalows offer all meals and drinks, massages and body treatments, guided jungle treks and explorations, equinox, solstice and moon rituals, drumming circles and crystal bowl healing. Vegetarian restaurant, pool, yoga room, massage, waterfall cave; 200 metres from beach. **$$$**

Pemuteran & Menjangan
About 125 km (75 mi) north of Sanur lies the sizable Menjangan Island. Part of the West Bali National Park, this is a haven for all-season diving and snorkelling. Many stay at Pemuteran on the north shore and take a 30-minute boat ride to the island. Accommodation and professional dive facilities are available in Pemuteran.

Matahari Beach Resort,
Pemuteran, Singaraja, tel: 923-12,
fax: 923-13. 32 Balinese-style
bungalows with international hotel
facilities; a/c, garden shower,
watersports and dive centre, 200
metres off beach. **$$$$$ +**
Pondok Sari, Pemuteran, Grokgak,
Singaraja, tel/fax: 923-37. 30
bungalow rooms with a/c or fan,
restaurant. **$**
Taman Sari Hotel, Pemuteran,
Grokgak, Singaraja, tel: 926-24,
fax: 923-39. 23 a/c and fan rooms,
restaurant. **$$ +**

WESTERN INTERIOR

Bedugul
Telephone code 0368
This resort is famous for the
cleanliness of its air.
Bukit Permai, on main road,
Baturiti, tel: 214-43. 13 rooms.
There are fireplaces in all rooms.
Some bungalows face Bedugul's
Botanical Garden. Breakfast
included. **$**
Pacung Asri, Jl. Raya Baturiti, Desa
Pacung, 9 km (5 mi) south of
Bedugul, PO Box 3297, tel: 210-38,
fax: 210-43. 39 rooms with hot
water, very impressive views,
heated pool, three restaurants.
Choice Hotel chain affiliate. **$$$ +**
Strawbali Hill, south of Bedugul at
Bedugul Hotel turnoff, tel: 214-42,
212-65. 10 rooms. Blankets
provided. Clean and simple
restaurant. **$**

Negara
Telephone code 0365
In this western town, there are a
number of low-budget *losmen* costing
below $5. On the main road, you'll
find **Hotel Ana, Losmen**, tel: 414-
76, and **Rumah Makan Taman Sari**,
Jl. Nakula 18, tel:411-54.

Where to Eat

What to Eat

Centuries of contact with other
great civilisations have left their
mark on the wonderfully varied
cuisine of Indonesia, particularly in
Bali. Indian and Arab traders
brought not only merchandise,
Hinduism and Islam, but also a
variety of new spices such as
ginger, cardamon and turmeric.
Later the Chinese and (to a lesser
extent) the Dutch added their own
distinctive touch to the cooking pot.
    Spices abound in Balinese
cooking, and are often partnered by
coconut milk (the juice is made by
squeezing the grated flesh of the
coconut), which adds a rich flavour
and creamy texture to dishes
containing intriguing tropical
vegetables, poultry, meat and fish.
Happily for the unaccustomed
foreign palate, Balinese cooks (in
restaurants, that is) are light-
handed with both spices and
chilies. They are fond of using sugar
as well as fragrant roots and leaves
in their dishes, and the final result
is food that tastes subtle and
sophisticated.
    The basis of a Balinese meal is
rice. Everyone helps themselves to
a serving of steaming white rice
and then to a little of the three or
four dishes of vegetables or meat
(known as *lauk*), which are placed
in the centre of the table for all to
share. Balinese do not swamp their
plates with food on the first round,
but help themselves to a little more
of what they fancy as the meal
progresses.
    A side dish or *sambal*, made with
red-hot chilies ground with dried
shrimp paste and other seasonings
such as lime juice, should be
approached with caution. If you

scorch your mouth or throat with
chilies, don't rush for the nearest
water, as it aggravates the problem,
and cold beer or other fizzy drinks
are worse. The quickest relief
comes from plain boiled rice, bread,
cucumber or a banana. Common
side dishes are *tempe*, a protein-
rich savoury cake of fermented
soybeans, and small crisp cookies
(rempeyek) made of peanuts. Both
are delicious.
    The Dutch word *rijsttafel* (rice
table) is sometimes associated with
Indonesian food. The name was
originally given to gargantuan
banquets or rice and countless
dishes of vegetables and meats
accompanied by savoury offerings
such as *krupuk* (fried prawn or fish
crackers), *acar* (cucumber pickles),
fried banana, peanuts, chilies and
anything else capable of adding
fragrance and flavour to the spread.
Full-scale extravagances are seldom
witnessed (let alone eaten) these
days, although a few hotels make a
modest attempt at imitation, and all
of the individual dishes of the old
rijsttafel can still be found and
enjoyed.
    National favourites include *gado-
gado*, a lightly cooked vegetable
salad which includes beansprouts,
long beans, cabbage and potatoes
covered with a rich peanut sauce.
Saté, sometimes regarded as
Indonesia's national dish, is a
tempting assortment of meat,
chicken or seafood grilled on
skewers over a charcoal fire,
served with a spicy sauce. A tasty,
chicken soup known as *soto ayam*
is found everywhere.
    Chinese-influenced noodle
dishes such as *mie goreng* (fried
wheat-flour noodles) and *bakmi*
(wheat-flour noodles, either fried or
in soup) are also common. *Cap cai*
(previously *tjap tjai*) is very popular
and better than its Western name
"chop suey" would suggest.
    You will, of course, find *nasi
goreng* (fried rice) everywhere;
topped with a fried egg, it makes a
good and cheap meal for breakfast
or anytime. *Nasi campur* is the
name given to the daily staple: rice
with side dishes.

The speciality of Bali is *lawar*, usually made of minced pork, coconut and spices. There are other kinds of *lawar*: chicken, egg, green bean, jackfruit – the list goes on. If it's red, you know you've got pork *lawar* made with fresh raw blood: stay clear of it if you want to avoid running to the bathroom.

Saté lilit is another Balinese speciality: the meat and spices are rolled onto a stick and grilled (as opposed to barbecued chunks of skewered meat). For vegetarians, *jukut urab* is a taste sensation (long beans, bean sprouts, cabbage and green peas).

Something few foreigners get to try (mainly because they don't know about it) is *tupat*. Steamed rice in coconut-leaf packages, these are cut up into small pieces with *tofu*, cucumber, spinach and sprouts and then mixed with a fiery peanut sauce. (You can specify the number of chilies used, however, as each dish is made to order.) Just look for hanging packets of woven coconut leaves at a friendly *warung*.

For breakfast or dessert, don't miss *bubur injin* or black rice pudding. Black rice, which really is black, is cooked and then coconut milk and palm sugar are poured over the top. Delectable!

Fruits & Snacks

The tropical fruits of Bali are excellent: pineapples, bananas (ranging from tiny finger-sized *pisang mas* to the foot-long *pisang raja*; green bananas, *pisang kayu*, are ripe and very sweet), papayas and mangos are joined by even more unusual seasonal fruits. Some of the most outstanding are *rambutan* (hairy red skins enclosing sweet white meat, akin to a lichee), *mangosteen* (staining, purplish-black skins with a very sweet juicy white fruit inside – don't eat the seeds or skin), *jeruk Bali* (pomelo) and *markisa* (passion fruit). The best fruit of all is *salak*. This brown "snakeskin" fruit encloses crunchy white flesh with a pear-like flavour.

The huge spiky *durian* has (to most people) a revolting smell, but its butter-rich fruit is adored by local people and a few adventurous visitors. One fruit visitors often overlook is the *nangka* or jackfruit. Akin to the breadfruit, this large fruit has stringy yellow pulp inside – its smell is reminiscent of bubble gum but its taste is distinctive and sweet. Unripe and cooked, it is a great vegetable.

Drinking Notes

Most familiar Western drinks are available in Bali, though some take on an exciting new dimension.

Tea is usually very fragrant, and similar to Chinese tea in flavour. Served hot or cold, *manis* (with sugar, and *lots* of it) or *pahit* (without), it is both delicate and refreshing.

Coffee is a delight to real coffee lovers when it is served almost Turkish-style with grounds floating around (known as *kopi tubruk*). Otherwise, Balinese coffee is made like instant coffee and will keep you up all night. If you ask for it with milk, it's condensed milk and sweet. For all drinks, you must specify no sugar – if not, you'll end up with something extremely sweet.

Fresh fruit juices are popular. *Air jeruk*, as orange juice is called, is actually oranges or limes mixed with water. Drinking it hot is delightful, especially if you're feeling under the weather. There are also juices made from bananas, pineapples and other fruits, which are blender drinks made with ice. Westerners accustomed to regarding avocado as a vegetable will probably be amazed at the *apokat* drink, but it's wonderful. In the Ubud and Kuta area there is *lassi*, a yogurt drink nothing like the original in India. You can get it plain or with fruit.

Es kopyor is a favourite concoction of rose syrup, ice, scoops of jelly-like flesh from the inside of the *kopyor* coconut. You can ask for it without the rose syrup (no sugar). *Es campur*, a mixture of shaved ice with fruits and "jelly beans" made from tapioca (called *cendol*); *es tape*, made from fermented rice or sweet potato; and *es cendol*, akin to *es campur* but made with coconut milk, are all delicious.

The best thirst quencher, **water**, is widely available. Everyone these days is savvy enough to boil their water; all piping-hot drinks are perfectly safe. In most of the larger cafés and restaurants, ice drinks are safe as well. Bottled spring water, under the names of Aqua, Spring, Fresh, etc., is safe, but be sure the seal is still intact.

Locally manufactured **beer** (Anker, Bintang and Bali Hai) is similar to European lager and is excellent. It's moderately priced and found everywhere, but it won't be cold in outlying villages.

Wines and spirits: Try Balinese *brem*, a rose-coloured sweet rice wine, or *arak*, distilled palm liquor. A favourite drink in the bars is the potent combination of *brem*, arak and orange or lime juice. *Tuak* is fermented palm wine and on the sweet side. Imported alcohol has become scarce and expensive due to heavy taxation.

Eating Out

Note: For some reason, Indonesians love to cook with MSG (called Ajinomoto or Vetsin in Bali). So, if you're not fond of MSG, be sure to tell your waiter/waitress that you don't want any Ajinomoto: *tanpa ajinomoto*.

DENPASAR

Near the market are a number of eateries, most of them Chinese. The **Hawaii** in the Kumbasari Shopping Centre, 2nd floor, tel: 435-135, 437-752, is popular. **Rumah Makan Polaris**, Jl. Sulawesi 40, tel: 226-640, just south of the market, is a tiny hole in the wall but it has good chicken and vegetarian dishes, with a wide variety of cakes and baked goods. **Depot Mie 88**, Jl. Sumatra 88, has Chinese and Indonesian food at good prices in a clean restaurant. **Warung Wardani** in Tapak-gangsul, Jl. Yudistira 2, tel: 224-398, is a favourite with the

Balinese. Just north of the bank is a popular Chinese restaurant, **Siefu**.

The **Natour Bali Hotel**, Jl. Veteran 3, tel: 225-681, does a nice *rijstaffel*. A favourite of expatriates is **Rumah Makan Betty**, Jl. Sumatra 56, tel: 224-502, which has a not-so-spicy menu of Javanese and Chinese dishes. Try the *tahu goreng telur* (tofu and potato curry), *bubur ayam* (rice porridge with chicken) and their *nasi campur*.

If you can't get to Lombok, but want to try the famous Taliwang chicken, head down to **Ayam Bakar Taliwang** or **Rumah Makan Taliwang Baru** on Jl. Teuku Umar 8, near the Simpang Enam (six crossroads).

NUSA DUA & JIMBARAN

Galeria Nusa Dua's dining area has more than a dozen open-air restaurants with a good range of options. **Sendok**, tel: 772-850, has Swiss and German specialties. **Ole Ole** serves Mediterranean fare, while its sister eatery **Pica Pica** has an all-you-can-eat *churrasqueria* barbecue grill, tel: 774-208. Another place to browse a range of eateries is Jl. Pantai Peminge, outside the Nusa Dua complex's south gate. **Poco Loco** for Mexican fare and killer margaritas and **Ulam** for Balinese food are good choices. Bali's only real fine dining is at **Mayang Sari**, Sheraton Laguna Nusa Dua, tel: 771-327.

The Garuda Wisnu Kencana Cultural Centre on the Bukit has several restaurants. Notable are **Stiff Chili**, for Asian-Italian food and **Biu**, with a great view and a nice fusion of Asian and international cuisine, tel: 703-603. Four Seasons Bali, Jimbaran, has the island's best pizza, served right on the beach at **PJ's** terrace, tel: 701-010.

SANUR

For elegant as well as informal western dining, Sanur's **Bali Hyatt**, **Grand Bali Beach** and **Sanur Beach** hotels offer a wide choice of poolside lunches, buffets, barbecues, coffee shops and supper clubs often with evening dance performances and/or live musical entertainment. The menus are predominantly Western, Indonesian, Chinese and Japanese. These places are not cheap. Most Sanur restaurants provide transport to their establishments from your hotel. Alternatively, the night market has food stalls and a barbecue.

The **Tanjung Sari Hotel** restaurant, tel: 288-441 has a formidable reputation for Indonesian *rijsttafel* on Saturday and a sublime atmosphere. A bamboo *tingklink* orchestra provides the ideal accompaniment to dinner at 9pm in a cosy, antique-filled dining area by the beach.

The **Telaga Naga**, tel: 288-271 opposite the Bali Hyatt, is a stylish Cantonese and Sichuan restaurant under the stars overlooking a lotus pond. The food is good and the prices are non-hotel, even though the restaurant is owned and operated by the Bali Hyatt.

The nearby **Swastika Gardens**, tel: 288-573, is for those who are tired of paying hotel prices. The food is quite good and the menu varied enough to satisfy most tastes – order in advance the Balinese speciality, smoked duck (*bebek tutu*) and their grilled fish. The **Swastika I Restaurant**, tel: 288-373, up the road has some of the best grilled fish and chicken around at good prices. Open 11am–11pm.

Sadly, the **Trattoria Da Marco**, which used to serve some of the best Italian food on Bali, has gone downhill since the departure of the restaurateurs Reno and Diddit da Marco, and is no longer to be recommended.

La Taverna, tel: 288-497, is part of a Hong Kong-based chain of Italian restaurants in Asia. The Sanur branch has a nice bar and open dining area on the beach, with a menu that features imported cheese, French pepper steak, seafood and pizza from a real brick pizza oven.

In Banjar Semawang, right on the ocean, is **Terrazza Martini**, tel: 288-371, a tiny Italian restaurant that is always full of Italians. The food is good and the prices are quite reasonable.

For a meal by the seaside, try the inexpensive **Sanur Beach Market**, on Jl. Segara Ayu at the beach, tel: 289-374, a little outdoor restaurant run as a cooperative by Sanur's mayor. It is a great place for lunch (*saté, nasi goreng* and fresh grilled fish) or dinner (grilled lobster) with delicious Balinese desserts, all at reasonable prices. Once a week they have a dance performance and a special set dinner, though there is no cover charge and you may order from the regular menu.

For Chinese and European food at decent prices, try the restaurant at the **Leghawa Hotel** right on Jl. Danau Tamblingan, tel: 288-494. The **Sanur Food Market** on Jl. Bypass Ngurah Rai 70, has a variety of food stalls offering everything under the sun at reasonable prices.

If it's decent and cheap Indonesian food you're after, then head down to the **Rumah Makan "Mini"** on the bypass near Jl. Segara Ayu. Here you can get *nasi cap cay* and *saté* for less than $2. And the last *warung* (**Mak Beng's**) on the left on Jl. Hangtuah by the beach (just past the entrance to the Grand Bali Beach) serves tasty grilled fish.

Warung Ziro, Jl. Bypass Ngurah Rai 159, is a clean and efficient *warung* favoured by locals for its cheap lunches and fresh juices. **Mezzanine**, Jl. Mertasari, Sanur, tel: 270-624, serves Asian and international fare, and has a pastry bar. This is an open-air, two-level thatched-roof restaurant with patio dining, and the house band plays jazz nightly. **Spago Restaurant and Bar**, Jl. Danau Tamblingan 79, serves good Italian food. **Kafe Wayang**, Kompleks Sanur Raya on the bypass, tel: 287-591, has light and fresh options and delicious pastries, and is open for breakfast, lunch and dinner. **Sanur Deli**, Jl. Danau Poso 52, Blanjong, tel: 288-624, is a good place to pick up fresh-baked goods, light meals and snacks.

KUTA & LEGIAN

Kuta Beach and Legian Beach offer cuisines from all over the world at very reasonable prices. Most of the resident foreigners come to Kuta-Legian when dining out.

Made's Warung on Jl. Pantai, Kuta, tel: 755-297, hasn't missed a beat in its metamorphosis from one of only two foodstalls on the main street of a sleepy fishing village, to a hip "Café Voltaire" in this St Tropez of the East. It has great food (spare ribs, Thai salads, homemade ice cream and yogurt, chocolate cake, cappuccino, freshly squeezed juices, breakfast specials), great music and always a host of the young international Balinese *demi-monde*. Made also serves a fabulous *rijstaffel* on Saturday night. This is *the* place to see and be seen. **Made's Warung II**, Banjar Seminyak, tel: 732-130, is an upscale version in the quieter suburbs of Seminyak, with six fashionable boutiques and shops alongside.

Poppies Restaurant (tel: 751-059) on Gang Poppies I, a narrow lane parallel to Jl. Pantai Kuta, is another Kuta fixture. Avocado seafood salads, chicken liver pâté, *tacos*, grilled lobster, steaks, *kabobs* and tall mixed drinks pack this garden idyll to capacity during the peak tourist seasons. Get there early.

Nearby **TJ's Mexican Restaurant**, Gang Poppies I, tel: 751-093, serves the best *enchiladas*, *tacos*, *tostadas*, *nachos* and margaritas this side of the Pacific. Try the eggplant or *tahu*/bean dip with chips – great with a cold beer. Chocolate cake is a speciality.

For Indian food, go to **Goa 2001**, tel: 731-170, on Jl. Legian in Legian. Perhaps better known for its pre-disco hours bar than its food, it has wonderful tandoori dishes. Opens

7pm–3am. Another place serving Indian is **Warung Kopi**, Jl. Legian Tengah 427, tel: 753-602, where they serve inexpensive *falafels* and curries, not to mention delectable desserts.

New, up-market restaurants are springing up along Jl. Abimanyu (Gado-Gado Street). This is a good area to dine and continue into the evening with music and drinks. **Gateway to India**, tel: 732-940, serves authentic northern Indian food and has a tandoor oven. Nearby, the artistic flair of **Antique Restaurant**, tel: 730-907, is reflected in both the decor and the food. Other options on this street are the gay-friendly **Q Bar and Restaurant**, **Santa Fe** and **G-Land**.

Long-standing, reliable bets in Legian are **Glory**, Jl. Legian 445, tel: 751-091, a favourite restaurant with Australians; and **Cafe Luna**, Jl. Raya Seminyak, tel: 730-805, offering Italian food and rowdy nightlife after 10pm. **Hana** in Galeria Seminyak, tel: 732-778, is recommended for *sushi* and *tempura*. Across the street, **Fabio's**, tel: 730-805, is good for Italian.

Kori, Gang Poppies 2, tel: 758-605, is an up-scale option on the Kuta end, with a great atmosphere and presentation of a wide range of international and Indonesian dishes. For espresso and cappuccino, head to the nearby **Rainbow Cafe**, tel: 765-730.

KEROBOKAN/CANGGU

Kafe Warisan, Jl. Kerobokan Banjar Taman 68, tel: 731-1175, is a favourite on the island and has been featured widely in international press. French and Algerian restaurateurs dish up fresh, light and tasty fare with a French leaning. Pasta, salmon, salads, steak, daily specials, full bar. The prices are higher than Kuta but fair for the quality and presentation. Open for lunch and dinner. Reservations essential.

The best Mediterranean food and atmosphere combined are found at **La Lucciola Restaurant Bar and**

Beach Club, Jl. Laksmana, Petitenget, tel: 720-868. The big, two-level thatched structure looks out over Kayu Aya beach, offering beachfront chairs and service during the day. Great for sunset cocktails and packed for dinner. Reservations essential.

Warung Batavia, Jl. Seminyak, tel: 731-641, serves delightful *betawi* – Jakarta-style – fare, including *nasi campur* mixed rice with lots of side dishes, *soto* soup and *gado-gado* steamed vegetable salad with spicy peanut sauce.

Ku de Ta, Jl. Petitenget, Kerobokan, tel: 731-074, is the latest trendy spot with massive indoor and outdoor dining areas, plunge pool, beach chairs, cigar bar and large lounge. **The Living Room**, tel: 735-735, provides an atmosphere that lives up to its name, with Indonesian and Western dishes. Open from 7pm.

UBUD

Ubud's eateries are almost as varied as Kuta's with everything from egg *lawar* to yogurt shakes, to feta salads and brown bread, to some of the best *nasi campur* on the island.

Probably the most famous restaurant here is **Café Wayan**, Jl. Wana Warana, tel: 975-447, run by Ibu Wayan and her ever-smiling family, about a kilometre south on Jl. Wanara Wana. Her Wayan Special Salad is delicious with a bowl of soup and garlic toast to go along with it. The seafood here is scrumptious, as is the pizza. Sit at the table way in the back where rice fields still exist. Prices here are at the high end.

At the other end of the scale (and the north end of the road) is **Ibu Rai's**, the place where you can get home-cooked Indonesian cuisine at low prices. The grilled fish is one of their specialities.

The old stand-bys of Murni's and Lotus Café are being sidelined as more eateries co-run by Westerners are opening up. **Murni's**, tel: 975-233, located over the Campuhan river can't be beaten – there are now three levels of seating, the grill is open for scrumptious barbecues of fish, prawns and chicken. The **Lotus Café**, Jl. Ubud Raya, tel: 975-660, is located in a charming open-air courtyard. The menu includes fantastic homemade pastas, yummy cheesecake and brownies. You can dine al fresco right next to a huge lotus pond in front of the palace temple.

Ary's Warung, across the street and a bit east, tel: 975-053, has some of the best fare on the island. The food is of a high standard, and prices are reasonable. Taking in the neighbouring banjar, a two-level bar and dining terrace offers great breezes in a nice atmosphere. Nearby, **Casa Luna**, tel: 962-83, serves Balinese and vegetarian food, and has a kid's menu. Jungle Chicken is a favourite, as is the smoked duck feast, ordered a day in advance. Casa Luna holds Balinese cooking classes 10am–2pm Monday to Wednesday, with a minimum of five students.

One of the newer establishments is **Bebek Bengil** or The Dirty Duck, tel: 974-489, right at the Y junction between Padang Tegal and Pengoseken. An open-air café in the rice fields, with a spectacular view of Gunung Agung and a refreshing breeze, this is a fashionable hang-out, and the portions are on the small side. Often there's live bamboo music on weekends. **Mumbul Garden Terrace**, tel: 975-364, on the main road near Puri Lukisan Art Museum, is a small, intimate café with an extensive menu. The chefs have published a cookbook with their favourite recipes in it. Its sister restaurant, **Bumbu**, tel: 974-217, around the corner on Jl. Sueta 1, serves Balinese, Indian and vegetarian food. **Griya Barbecue**, tel: 975-428, has mouth-watering grilled tuna, chicken, and beef along with a regular menu. The room overlooking the gorge out the back has a breathtaking view. **Nomad's**, tel: 977-169, at the other end of the main street, serves steak and grilled fish, and their tzatzizi

skewers are out of this world (order one day ahead).

Down the road in Peliatan village is **Mudita Inn**, tel: 975-179, a tiny hole-in-the-wall that has the best fried noodles *(mie goreng)* and french fries this side of Lombok, and some of the best Balinese-style banana pancakes around. (You can change money and buy postcards while you're waiting for your lunch next door.) The most popular place to eat in Peliatan for the locals is **Ibu Made's Warung** (across the street from Banjar Tengah), where chicken dishes take on a new meaning. Hot and spicy, an incredible meal here costs around one dollar.

If you need to impress someone, then take them to the restaurant at the **Amandari Hotel**, tel: 975-333 for reservations, in Sayan, north of Ubud. Prices are high but the view of the Ayung River and the surrounding rice fields is superb. An even more spectacular view of the Ayung can be seen from the upstairs room at the **Kupu Kupu Barong** in Kedewatan, east of Sayan, tel: 975-478. A grand place for cocktails. More moderately priced, but with a million-dollar view, is **The Restaurant at The Chedi** in Payangan, tel: 975-963. Here you can get Indonesian, Asian and Continental cuisine, served by Bali's only female executive chef.

For those wanting a Balinese feast in a Balinese home, contact

Ketut Suartana at the **Suci Inn**, Jl. Sueta 40, tel: 975-304. For less than $10, Ketut will take you up to his parents' home for a truly scrumptious meal. Order on Saturday for a Sunday meal. Minimum of six people.

Red Rice, Jl. Raya Sayan, tel: 974-433. A warung with wine and eclectic fare that is open for lunch and dinner. Nearby **Gaya**, tel: 979-252, is a bar/restaurant featuring a primitive and contemporary art gallery. The elegant **Biji** restaurant and its private dining area **Kudus** at Begewan Giri Estate near Payangan is a wonderful dining experience, overlooking the river gorge, but take some extra cash with you.

THE EAST

Candidasa

It seems that every eatery here serves the same thing: grilled fish, french fries and vegetables, along with all the other standard Indonesian dishes. The most popular (and cheap) place for grilled fish is **Candra's**. **TJ's Café**, tel: (0363) 415-40, has a branch here; it doesn't specialise in Mexican food, but offers excellent salads and desserts served in an elegant atmosphere, with prices to match. **Pandan Restaurant**, tel: (0363) 415-41, right on the beach, serves Balinese food Tuesday and Friday, including fruit and a cocktail.

Notes for Vegetarians

With all the fresh vegetables and fruits and soybean products here, one would think it would be easy for vegetarians to find decent food. However, the Balinese are a meat-loving people and pork is a mainstay in their diet. Most soups are made with chicken stock (called kaldo) and often fish and chicken are not considered "meat" (daging in Indonesian). So you must always ask if there is any meat or fish in a dish or whether it's been cooked in meat – best to check

with the cook as often the waiting staff are ignorant of ingredients. The only pure meatless dish is gado-gado (steamed veggies with peanut sauce), although sometimes the peanut sauce is made with terasi or shrimp paste. Fried noodles and fried rice often are made with chicken, as are fried greens (sayur hijau), but these can be easily made without meat by request. Tempe is often fried with peanuts and tofu can be bought both plain and fried.

Pondok Bamboo, tel: 415-34, has excellent grilled fish and whopper iced juices.

For the best fresh seafood around, try the **Kubu Bali** hotel, which has an open kitchen and vast selection. The new **Kedai**, tel: 420-20, operated by the Ary's Warung clan of Ubud, specialises in vegetarian and Balinese dishes, served in a unique setting.

THE NORTH

In Singaraja, good eateries are few and far between. One of the most popular is the **Chinese Gandhi Restaurant**, tel: (0362) 211-63, which offers an extensive menu at moderate prices.

In the Lovina area, fresh seafood is the best choice. Most restaurants will offer a variety of Indonesian dishes, but the food here is like the life: simple and satisfying. One of the most popular tourist hang-outs in the Lovina area is **Badai Restaurant**, right over a river on the main road. Here you can find inexpensive yet delicious fish dishes. Vegetarian dishes are also available. The **Banyualit Hotel**, tel: (0362) 417-89, has the freshest fish and vegetables in town. The **Dhyana Bar and Restaurant** on the ocean side of the road is a well managed place that offers home-cooked food. The mixed seafood grill and yogurt *lassis* are house specialities.

THE WEST

Taman Sari restaurant in Negara, Jl. A. Yani 18, tel: (0365) 411-54, is reliable in this outback location. Simple, western-oriented dining can be found along Medewi Beach and at **Balian Beach** in Lalang Linggah Village. **Sacred River**, tel: (0361) 732-165, fax: (0361) 730-904, is more spiritually oriented and has vegetarian selections in a retreat atmosphere. It's near Suraberata village, 90 minutes from the airport.

Attractions

Most people come to Bali to experience the rich cultural heritage; some come for the beaches and the waves, others for pure relaxation. The major urban centres are Denpasar, Kuta and Sanur. Kuta has plenty of discotheques and there are a few good ones in Sanur as well. The major movie theatres are in Denpasar, and current videos are shown in Kuta at bars and restaurants. For culture-lovers, rituals abound all over the island. You can consult a Balinese calendar or pick up a calendar of events from the Tourism Office in Denpasar.

Many travel agencies also have information on rituals open to the public. Be wary of tour companies selling "tickets" to cremations and other rites. Dress and behave with decorum; you are welcome at cremations. Other life-cycle rites (weddings, tooth-filings, etc.) are by invitation only; don't attend if you don't know the host personally.

Amusements

Bali Butterfly Park: north of Tanah Lot temple, near Tabanan, tel: 814-282. The park is a huge aviary where butterflies fly free. Included are the large bird-wing butterfly, which lives for only two weeks. Open 8am–5pm.

Bali Ocean World: Under development in eastern Bali, the interactive marine park is scheduled to open in 2002. It will feature marine life exhibits and education centres, beach and diving areas, swims with dolphins, restaurants and retail outlets.

Elephant Safari Park: Taro Village, tel: 721-480, fax: 721-481. This 2.5 hectare (6-acre) park has 17 Sumatran elephants. Short treks, rides, conservation information and interactive experiences are all available. There is an elephant museum, gift shop, open-air restaurant and gardens. Transfers available by land or air from Bali Adventure Tours. Open 10am–4pm.

Garuda Wisnu Kencana Cultural Park: Jl. Raya Ubud, Bukit Unggasan, Jimbaran, tel: 703-603. The park features the giant bronze bust of the god Wisnu. Upon completion, it will sit on top of a mythical Garuda bird and be taller than the Statue of Liberty. Perched on the Bukit peninsula, the bust is visible from afar. The park has an art museum, several restaurants, cultural performances and a spectacular, panoramic view of Bali.

Rimba Reptile Park: Jl. Serma Cok Ngurah Gambir, Singapadu, tel: 299-252, fax: 299-614. Adjacent to the Taman Burung bird park is this smaller scale but impressive park with over 160 species. Visitors can hold iguanas, monitor lizards and an 8-metre (26-ft) reticulated python, said to be the largest in captivity. A combination ticket can be purchased for the bird and reptile park. Open 9am–6pm.

Taman Buaya & Reptil: Banjar Binong Werdi Bhuana, Mengwi, tel: 829-353. This crocodile and reptile park 25 km (15 mi) northwest of Denpasar houses 300 crocodiles from across Indonesia, four Komodo dragons and an variety of lizards and snakes. Daily crocodile and snake shows at 10.30am and 3pm. Open 9am–6pm.

Taman Burung-Bali Bird Park: Jl. Serma Cok Ngurah Gambir, Singapadu, tel: 299-352, fax: 299-614. With more than 250 species winging over the mountains and rice fields, Bali could be described as the "island of birds". The Bird Park is the first international-quality animal preserve on the island. The 2-hectare (5-acre) park at Singapadu contains more than 800 specimens of 250 bird species (a third of which are endangered) from Indonesia and around the world. Paths wander through gardens, leading to large aviaries in a natural setting. The landscape is populated with a tremendous selection of tropical plants from all over the world. The facilities are well signed for a self-guided tour. The park's breeding programme preserves rare and endangered species. Eggs and hatchlings, housed in a nursery, can be viewed through an observation window. Open 7am–6pm.

Waterbom Water Park: Jl. Kartika Plaza, Tuban, tel: 755-676, fax: 753-517. Centrally located in Tuban, south of Kuta, Waterbom Park has a fully certified staff of lifeguards, lockers and towels for rent. Main gate admission gives access to all park facilities, including water slides, numerous pools, lazy rivers, sun loungers, game areas, etc. Children under age 12 must be accompanied by an adult. Dining and bar facilities available. Open 9am–6pm daily.

Hiking & Outdoor Activities

An increasing range of interesting outdoor activities is available, allowing visitors to enjoy the "real Bali". Cycling through villages or walking through rice fields to view birds and life as it has been for centuries is relaxing and inform-ative. Among the latest additions to the island are 18 Sumatran elephants, which trek around the sacred village Taro, home of holy albino cows. Look for this niche of "eco" activities to expand.

Bali Bird Walks, Beggar's Bush, by the bridge, Campuhan, Ubud, tel: 975-009. See some of the many species of birds in Bali. Easy walk along trails, across rice fields and rivers, through coconut groves with experienced Balinese guides. Fee includes drinking water, binoculars, lunch, tea, coffee and a bird list.

Bali Adventure, Adventure House, Jl. Bypass Ngurah Rai, Suwung, tel: 721-4980, fax: 721-481. Bali

Cruises

A cruise can be a lovely way to see a different part of Bali. There are numerous yachts for hire; most offer a day cruise and a sunset cruise. The following are popular:

Adelaar offers tall ship adventures and scuba diving expeditions on charter. Based from Benoa harbour, tel: 723-604.

Aristocat is a sleek catamaran making scheduled daily excursions and available for charter or groups. Operated from Benoa Harbour by Bali Hai Cruises, tel: 720-331, fax: 720-334.

Bali Hai Cruises, tel: 720-331, fax: 720-334. Day cruises to Lembongan Island and and sunset harbour/dinner cruises aboard catamarans. Day cruises include hotel transfers, morning and after-noon tea, lunch, watersports, snorkel equipment, beach club or sea pontoon activities, island tours and diving optional; dinner cruise with transfers, buffet dinner and entertainment.

Barito, a 70-metre/230-ft, 925 passenger fast-ferry makes the 16-hour voyage to Bima, Sumbawa and Kupang, departing Benoa Harbour on Fridays at 6pm. Sunday departures midday reach Surabaya in seven hours. Gama Dewata Bali, tel: 263-568, 323-704.

Sail Sensations, Benoa Harbour, tel: 725-864, fax: 725-866. Daylight Sensations to The Anchorage day beach club on Nusa Lembongan island or overnight accommodation at Nusa Lembongan Resort. Twilight Sensations: gourmet dining aboard a luxurious sailing catamaran.

WakaLouka, tel: 484-085. Day cruise to Lembongan Island on a catamaran. Including continental breakfast, lunch with beer and wine, sunset cocktails, soft drinks all day, afternoon tea and coffee, all island facilities at WakaNusa resort, water sports, hotel transfers.

Traditional Fleet: A consortium of traditional wooden *pinisi* schooners, the Traditional Fleet based in Bali's Benoa Harbour sails to the Gili islands off Lombok, Komodo, the Lesser Sundas, Papua New Guinea and Sulawesi.

Divers are frequent passengers on these boats. All Traditional Fleet cruises support the Nature Conservancy Program of Indonesia. Staff and crew are knowledgeable, professional and dedicated to keeping the coves, waters and small ports to which they travel pristine and unspoiled long into the future. Ports of call follow the old trade routes, some so remote that they are rarely visited except by the occasional schooner. Onboard, passengers adjust to the rhythms of nature and explore a fascinating marine world, in comfort and safety. Among fleet members are:

Ombak Putih & Ombok Bira, Benoa Harbour, tel: 730-191, fax: 733-942. 36-metre/118-ft vessel, 12 private cabins with bath. Scheduled 4-, 7- and 12-day cruises around Bali, Lombok, Sulawesi and islands east of Bali

Perintis: Benoa Harbour, tel: 975-478, fax: 975-079. Tall-ship, 36 metres/118 ft in length, sails 3- and 4-night cruises from Bima, on Sumbawa, to Komodo, Flores and Rinca.

SeaTrek, Benoa Harbour, tel: 283-192, fax: 285-440. *Katharina* is handcrafted from ironwood in 19th century in design, 33 metres/118 ft with safety and navigation equipment, spacious, air-conditioned teak panelled cabins with a private bath. Choice of 4–12-day cruises to numerous destinations beyond Bali.

Songline Cruises: Benoa Harbour, tel: 283-192, fax: 286-985. Ratu Rima, a 22-metre/72-ft schooner, equipped for sailing and scuba diving, carries 12 passengers. Dormitory-style accommodation. Other boats are designed for the dedicated diver. Songline departs from Sulawesi.

Body Treats

How about a rub-down with exotic herbs and oils, followed by a steam bath? Or an hour-long facial to get rid of stress and city pollution. Or maybe a "cream bath" for your head and hair: an hour-long treatment including scalp and shoulder massage – the ultimate in relaxation?

Indonesians have used herbs and oils for centuries to cure and prevent ills. It's only in the last decade that these traditional healing techniques have been elevated to the "beautification and relaxation" level for international visitors, and Bali has become Asia's premier spa destination.

Jamu healing herbs are concocted from natural products and are available in pills, tea bags and bottles. The traditional form is a bitter powder mixed with lime juice and honey to make it more palatable. Originating from the Javanese royal palaces, there are recipes for everything from health tonics to post-partum purifiers to cough and slimming formulas, now made by several commercial *jamu* manufacturers in Java. The homeopathic blends are readily available in apothecaries, salons, at roadside carts or from roving potion vendors.

Massage is a routine part of daily life for Indonesians to treat and prevent an assortment of ailments. Among the most interesting is *masuk angin*, literally "the wind gets in" – or the common cold. For relief, a coin is scraped across the back, neck and shoulders, releasing the "wind". While this *kerok* treatment is not necessarily recommended, there are plenty of traditional massage parlours, *panti pijit*, all over the island that deliver a massage for about $5 an hour. In Kuta, you also can get a cheap, perfunctory massage on the beach.

Today, every star-rated hotel has a spa or massage facility. These are generally professional and hygienic operations, but with a menu in dollars and 21 percent tax and service charge added. Even the smallest *losmen* can summon a local masseuse to knead tired muscles at very little cost.

Treatments generally offered include traditional body scrubs, polishes and detoxifying wraps. The following are recommended from experience:

Mandara Spa, which manages spa centres at numerous hotels, including **The Chedi Ubud** (tel: 975-963); **The Serai Manggis** (tel: 0363-41011); **The Legian** (tel: 730-622); **Bali Padma**, Legian (tel: 752-111); **Bali Imperial**, Seminyak (tel: 730-730) and **Nikko Bali**, Nusa Dua (tel: 773-377). **Sheraton Laguna Nusa Dua** (tel: 771-327) has the most decadent spa on the island, offering a half-day private villa experience with champagne and lobster and massive floral bath for two. **Nusa Dua Beach Hotel**'s spa (tel: 771-210) was the forerunner on the island and still serves up the perfect treatment, either a la carte or with a villa experience. The advantage here is use of all facilities with any treatment, including gym, lap pool, sauna, Jacuzzi and Bodyworks classes.

Bali Hyatt, Sanur (tel: 281-234), has an exclusive enclave for its spa facilities, offering villas for package treatments, set apart from the hotel. **Bali Inter-Continental** (tel: 701-888) has a separate spa villa concept while the **Ritz-Carlton Bali** (tel: 702-222) offers a fully fledged Day Spa facility, paralleled by **Four Seasons Bali**, Jimbaran (tel: 701-010). **Kalaspa Health Retreat** (tel: 0828-361-034), overlooking the central mountain lakes, has total health retreats with daily spa treatments, meals and outdoor activities. **The Spa at the Villas**, Legian, managed by Jamu-Jamu, (tel: 730-840) delivers traditional treatments with a flair in an Middle Eastern environment – the only place of its kind in all of Indonesia. **Grand Mirage Bali**, Tanjung Benoa, has a French Thalasso Aquamedic Spa (tel: 771-888) with sea water treatments. Ubud has remarkable spa resorts such as **Ibah** (tel: 976-226).

Free-standing, much less costly but good quality, tried and true services can be found at:

Bodyworks, Jl. Raya Seminyak 63 and Jl. Petitenget, tel: 730-454, the oldest free-standing spa and salon on the island. **Nur's Salon**, Ubud (tel: 975-352) offers treatments on their premises or will come to you in Ubud for relaxing massage and salon treatments. **Martha Tilaar** has two spa outlets, Jimbaran (tel: 771-661) and Legian (tel: 731-463), which deliver treatments with a Javanese flair. One of the most intriguing options is *kendedes*, a cleansing of a woman's lower anatomy with the smoke of aromatic herbs.

Adventure started out with rafting on the Ayung River in 1990 but has recently expanded to include numerous soft adventure options, and will also package two or three activities together to provide a full day outdoors. Tandem paragliding off the Bukit near Ulu Watu temple; rice paddy treks; jungle treks; mountain cycling; rafting; elephant safaris. (Fees include transfers, insurance, equipment, tuition and a meal.)

Sobek Adventure Specialists, Jl. Tirta Ening 9, Bypass Ngurah Rai, Sanur, tel: 287-059. Sea kayaking; bird-watching; jungle trekking; rafting; mountain cycling.

Wakalouka, tel: 484-085, fax: 484-767, does two inner-island experiences. One, via Land Rover, cruises to the top of Mt Batukaru, through rainforests and villages with stops en route, including lunch in the rainforest. Waka Tangga is a hike up Bukit Tedung mountain, showing the spiritual side of Bali.

You can learn about temples, agriculture, fruit, coffee and rice along the way. Fee includes Balinese coffee and snacks, lunch and a massage.

Tour Packages

The tour companies listed below are reputable and can arrange island-wide tours; a guide is included (languages widely spoken are English, French, Japanese, German and Dutch; some companies have Italian-, Spanish- and Chinese-speaking guides).

There are many standard tour packages from which to choose, or you can design your own and hire a driver and a guide for the day (from $60–$125 per day; air-conditioned vehicles are more costly). For either type of tour, contact one of the agents below or inquire at the hotel travel desk. The most experienced agents for English-speaking travellers are BIL and Pacto.

Astrindo, Jl. Raya Kuta 109, Kuta, tel: 753-138; KCB, Jl. Raya Kuta 127, tel: 751-517; and Vayatour, 285-555. Good for cheap airline tickets.

Bali Ekawisata Tours (BEST), Jl. Ciung Wanara V/5A, Renon, tel: 238-260, 231-202, fax: 238-259. BEST offer wildlife safaris from $60 to $400, including airfare, to see Komodo dragons, to the Buluran Wild Game Reserve in East Java, and the Sukomade tour, continuing the above to Turtle Bay, renowned for surfing, diving and the impenetrable jungle of the Meru Betiri National Park. Tours are also available to Bali Barat National Park, home of the world's only remaining wild Rothschild Bali starling, which is white with a blue face.

Bali Indonesia (BIL), Jl. Danau Tamblingan 186, Sanur, tel: 288-464, fax: 288-261.

Golden Kris Tour, Jl. Bypass Ngurah Rai 7, Sanur, tel: 289-225, fax: 289-228.

Jan's Tour, Jl. Nusa Indah 11, Denpasar, tel: 234-930, 232-660, fax: 231-009.

Kuta Cemerlang Bali (KCB), Jl. Raya Kuta No 127, Kuta, tel: 751-517/8, fax: 752-777.

Natrabu, Jl. Bypass Ngurah Rai 63, Sanur, tel: 288-660, fax: 289-560.

Nitour, Jl. Veteran 5, Denpasar, tel: 234-742, fax: 235-832; counter at Grand Bali Beach Hotel, Sanur, tel: 288-562.

Pacto, Jl. Bypass, Sanur, tel: 288-247, fax: 288-240; counter at Grand Bali Beach Hotel, Sanur, tel: 288-511; counter at Bali Hyatt, tel: 288-271.

Rama Wira Perdana Tours, Jl. Bypass Ngurah Rai 100x, Kuta, tel: 752-321/7, fax: 752-320; or Bali Inter-Continental Hotel, tel: 701-888; Nikko, tel: 773-377; Grand Hyatt, tel: 771-234.

Satriavi Tours, Jl. Bypass Ngurah Rai 11A, Kuta, tel: 756-769, fax: 756-768.

Tunas Indonesia, Jl. Danau Tamblingan 107, Sanur, tel: 288-056, fax: 288-727.

Vayatour, Jl. Bypass Ngurah Rai 107, Sanur, tel: 285-55, 289-339, fax: 281-144.

WakaLouka, tel: 426-972, fax: 426-971, provides half-day land trips to the "secret soul of Bali" aboard four-wheel-drive vehicles. Travel grassy tracks through terraced rice fields, up mountain roads, see fruit growing, mineral hot springs, and wonderful scenery. Lunch in the WakaLouka Rainforest Camp. Rate includes transfers, soft drinks, lunch with beer and wine.

Museums

Bali has many museums with fine collections of traditional and modern art. The **Bali Museum**, tel: 235-059, 222-680, in Denpasar offers a vivid picture of Balinese life and art from prehistoric times up to modern times, with emphasis on the antique. Open 8am–4pm, Monday–Friday; 8am–2pm, Saturday–Sunday.

Museum Le Mayeur, just north of the Grand Bali Beach Hotel in Sanur, has the collection of the late Belgian painter, Le Mayeur. Open daily at 8am, Tuesday–Sunday to 2pm; tel: 286-764.

Museum Puri Lukisan, tel: 975-636, in Ubud displays works dating from the late 1920s, when Balinese painters first began to break away from the formality of traditional painting styles, up until the present. Many were gathered by Dutch painter Rudolph Bonnet, with the assistance of Ubud's prince. It contains excellent contemporary paintings and carvings, most created during the past 20 years by artists living in or around Ubud. A gallery has selected works of arts for sale. Open daily, 8am–4pm.

The **Lempad Museum** on the main street in Ubud houses the paintings of the famous I Nyoman Lempad, who died in 1978 at the age of 116. Noted for his pen-and-ink drawings (both erotic and otherwise), his style is quite unlike traditional Balinese painting and in a class of its own.

Nyoman Suradnya in Padang Tegal, Ubud (at the Nirwana Losmen) is a fine batik painter and has a gallery and studio at his home. Classes in batik are available. Tel: 975-415, fax: 975-052. Visit also the many private galleries in the homes of artists. One of the most lavish is the gallery/home of **Antonio Blanco**, tel: 975-502, fax: 975-551, up on the left after the bridge in Campuhan (Ubud). This old building is a well preserved example of Balinese architecture. Inside you can meet the late artist's family, and view his private collection of erotic paintings and collages. Open daily 8am–5pm.

Hans Snel, Jl. Kajeng 3, tel: 975-699, is another well-known foreign artist living in Ubud, a Dutchman painting in the Gauguin/Spies/ Bonnet tradition of native-modern art. His gallery has been expanded to include a guest house, bar and restaurant. After viewing his work, sit and have a cosy drink.

The **Neka Museum**, tel: 975-074, several kilometres to the west of Ubud, contains the finest collection of paintings on Bali, better than the Puri Lukisan. Neka is a Balinese art dealer known to all the great painters of Bali over the years, and this is his private collection. Paintings are sold in a gallery on Ubud's main street. Open daily 9am–4pm.

Down the road in Peliatan is the **Agung Rai Museum of Art** (ARMA), tel: 976-659, fax: 974-229, www.nusantara.com/arma/, which houses an impressive collection of traditional and modern Balinese paintings, as well as works of foreigners who have lived in Bali. The permanent collection, which has moved to Jl. Bima in Pengoseken, should not be missed. The gallery is open daily 8am–6pm.

The **Archaeological Museum** by the main road in Pejeng, tel: 942-354, 943-357, less than 1 km (½ mi) north of Bedulu on the Tampaksiring Road, contains a collection of Bronze Age remains found in this area, including huge stone sarcophagi and tiny Hindu lamps. Open 8am–3pm. Closed on Sunday.

In Mas, you can see the layout of a typical (but wealthy) Balinese compound at **Adil Gallery**, tel: 975-173, and Siadja & Son. The staff will explain what each structure is used for and how things are built according to the traditional system of architecture. Open 8am–5pm.

The late **Ida Bagus Tilem** was the most famous woodcarver in Mas. His house is on the main road just south of Ubud. His son, himself a talented carver, now manages a gallery exhibiting his father's work. Many contemporary carvings are also sold in adjoining showrooms. Open daily 8am–5pm.

The **Museum Mandala Wisata** in Mengwi, just across the moat from the Puri Taman Ayun Temple, was founded with the admirable idea of preserving, in a single collection, examples of the arts of Balinese temple offerings. Unfortunately, the museum has not been well kept and receives few visitors but, if you are fascinated by Balinese ritual life, this collection is well worth seeing. Exhibited are all sorts of offerings used for various rites of passage and temple ceremonies, and Manusia Yadnya ceremonial instruments. Open daily 9am–4pm.

Just before Tabanan town, on the right side of the road, is the **Subak Museum**, tel: 810-315, in the village of Sanggulan. Opened in the early 1980s, this museum houses a small but eclectic collection depicting the *subak* system used to irrigate paddy fields and a typical Balinese household, including all the implements used in a traditional wood-burning kitchen. Open daily 7am–6pm.

The **Gedong Kirtya** in Singaraja, tel: (0362) 251-41, is a unique library of old *lontar* (palm-leaf) manuscripts and scholarly Dutch books; it was founded by the colonial government in 1928. Open Monday–Friday 7am–3pm.

Performing Arts

The best way to see Balinese dance-dramas, *wayang kulit* (shadow puppet) and *gamelan* orchestras is to attend a village temple festival. There is one going on somewhere on the island almost every day. Ask at your hotel, or consult the *Bali Post* or Yayasan Bina Wisata in Ubud, tel: 973-285.

Public performances at various central locations are mainly for the benefit of tourists, but that doesn't mean they are inferior to genuine temple performances. Some of Bali's best dancers and musicians participate in tourist performances, a good source of additional income. The times and locations change constantly, but the following are fairly well established venues and schedules. The shows last no longer than 90 minutes and begin on time. (Camera flashes are normal in these performances, and can be distracting.)

Sunday: Kecak Fire & Trance, Padang Tegal, Ubud, 7pm or Bona Village, 6.30pm; Wayang Kulit, Oka Kartini Ubud, 8pm; Mahabharata Ballet, Ubud Palace, 7.30pm; Women's Gamelan, Peliatan, 7.30pm.

Monday: Legong, Ubud Palace, 7.30pm; Kecak Fire & Trance, Bona Village, 6.30pm; Ciwa Ratri with classical Gamelan Gebuyg, Pura Dalem Puri Ubud, 7.30pm; Barong & Keris, Jabu Pura Kerta, Padang Tegal Kelod, 7pm.

Tuesday: Mahabharata Dance, Teges village, 7.30pm; Ramayana Ballet, Ubud Palace, 7.30pm; Spirit of Bali, Jaba Pura Desa Kutuh, Ubud, 7.30pm.

Wednesday: Wayang Kulit, Oka Kartini Ubud, 8pm; Kecak Fire & Trance, Padang Tegal Ubud, 7pm; Legong & Barong, Banjar Tengah, Peliatan, 7pm.

Thursday: Gabor Dance, Ubud Palace, 7.30pm; Kecak, Puri Agung Peliatan, 7.30pm; Calonarang Dance, Mawang Village, 7pm;

Nightlife

The real night scene is to be found in **Kuta** and **Legian Beach**. Here the streets start to come alive after 10pm and pub-crawls happen nightly. This is not a Balinese scene at all; drinking establishments in Kuta cater mainly to holiday-making Australians. Discos are becoming more fashionable for young Indonesians, but drinking is still not a way of life here.

Kuta is full of Indonesian gigolos just waiting to go in for the kill; these slick operators offer romance and expect to be taken care of in return. It's prostitution by another name, and lots of foreign women fall for it.

Sanur is more sedate. Older Indonesian businessmen often frequent the discos, more for a place to relax than for the dancing.

Gambling is not legal in Indonesia; there are no casinos or other gambling establishments.

Discos: Kuta is the main disco scene. Discos in Kuta change clientele and popularity too often to make any listing reliable. In Sanur, the scene is more mellow. Hotel discos in Tuban and Nusa Dua are popular with locals, but sedate and expensive.

Legong, Jaba Pura Padang, Padang Tegel, Ubud, 7.30pm.
Friday: Barong, Ubud Palace, 6.30pm; Kecak Fire & Trance, Bona Village, 6.30pm; Pura Dalem Ubud, 7.30pm; Legong Dance, Peliatan Village, 7.30pm; Kecak Fire & Trance, Pura Dalem, Ubud, 7.30pm.
Saturday: Legong Dance, Pura Dalem Puri Ubud, 7.30am; Calonarang Dance, Mawang Village, 7pm; Kecak Fire & Trance, Padang Tegal Ubud, 7pm.

Many of the large hotels have regular evening dinner shows – call for information. It is also possible to charter performances. In Krambitan, at the Puri Anyar and Puri Gede, they perform a Calon Arang story accompanied by the unique *tektekan gamelan* or *joged* (flirtation dance). With a minimum of 10 people, guests will be met with a torch-lit procession, and you can feast on local Balinese food and be entertained by the dancers and musicians of this small village, in the west of Bali.

Other *gamelan* troupes can also be hired. The dance academies SMKI and STSI, in Batubulan and Jl. Nusa Indah in Denpasar respectively, frequently have student recitals; some of the best dancers on the island can be found there.

Festivals

Balinese Calendar

Trying to figure out the Balinese calendar requires mathematical genius, as three systems are in use simultaneously.

The indigenous *pawukon* **calendar** consists of a series of weeks, each numbering 1–10 days, which converge together after 210 days. The Balinese refer to this as the *wuku* system, *wuku* meaning a week (but not necessarily of seven days). The most important *wuku* are the three-day week (Pasah, Beteng and Kajeng), the five-day week (Umanis, Paing, Pon, Wage and Kliwon) and the seven-day week. The three-day week is based on the revolving market – large market days are held in the villages every three days. There are a number of holy days which occur when certain days fall together: Anggara Kasih, which is when a Tuesday and Kliwon fall together; Kajeng of the three-day week and Kliwon of the five-day week occur every 15 days, and this is a time considered to be conducive to the darker powers, a kind of Friday the 13th, if you will. Wednesdays are often days of special religious ritual and Saturdays are days of honour.

Another ancient system is the **lunar calendar**. Many of the temple festivals in the mountain villages occur on *tilem* (the new moon) or *purnama* (the full moon), and occur once a year instead of every 210 days. This system is called the Hindu *saka* calendar and is divided into 12 months, or *sasih*, of 29–30 days. Every two or three years, an additional month is added to bring the lunar calendar into accord with the solar calendar. This calendar is

named after the Indian Saka dynasty, which began in AD 78 – 1920 in the saka calendar is 1998 in the solar calendar.

The third calendar system is the **Gregorian**, which is used for national holidays. Balinese calendars hang in every home, as no one is able to memorise all the configurations. In the case of a large ceremony, a Brahman priest must be consulted to ascertain an auspicious day. These calendars are available in all the bookstores; they're quite interesting to look at and make intriguing gifts.

Balinese Holy Days

GALUNGAN

Every 210th day by the *wuku* calendar, the Balinese hold a great feast commemorating the victory of the people over the legendary demon-king Mayadanawa. According to myth, this king strictly forbade his subjects to worship their ancestors and deities. Assisted by the god Indra and his divine allies, the people revolted and, in a great battle, defeated the demon-king. Thus, they were free again to worship according to their own beliefs. On **Galungan**, it is believed that the supreme god, Sanghyang Widi Wasa, followed by other deities and ancestral spirits, descends from heavens to temples on earth to feast. For 10 days, they receive many offerings and processions, dances and songs. All the *barong* are marched from the temples and paraded from village to village, often stopping at the roadside and dancing on the spot. The 10th day, **Kuningan**, is the last day of their sojourn on earth and the spirits ascend.

TEMPLE FESTIVALS (ODALAN)

Each temple holds a festival on the anniversary of its consecration, either every 210th day or every lunar year. To the villagers, it means an all-day, all-night celebration.

Days of Honour

Besides national holidays and festivals, the Balinese set certain days *(tumpek)* aside to honour individual deities who are guardians of special disciplines.
● Once a year by the *wuku* calendar, a day is devoted to **Saraswati**, goddess of wisdom. Offerings are made to *lontar* manuscripts; no one is allowed to read or write on that day.
● Another day is dedicated to **Batara Sangkara**, the lord of all crops. Offerings are presented to coconut trees "dressed up" in wrappings of fine cloth – climbing them is prohibited on that day.
● On the day devoted to the divinity of **prosperity and financial success**, no business is done.
● The day honouring **weapons** forbids the use of any sharp objects.

● There is also a day of the **"golden blessing"**, when offerings are made to all objects of gold, silver and precious stones, and to the lord of gold, **Mahadewa**, guardian of the West.

Nature and the tools that serve the people are also honoured. One day is reserved for all offerings to domestic animals, another for all utensils and equipment used in rice farming (during which time no rice may be husked or sold), and still another for all musical instruments, dance costumes, puppets and even motor vehicles. In Bali, there are no off-seasons. Every day brings celebrations; no matter when you arrive, you are bound to encounter a celebration on the island.

(Some *odalan*, such as the one at Besakih, can go on for 35 days.) From early morning, the *pemangku* priest is on duty to receive and bless the offerings brought by the women. By afternoon, a cockfight is in full swing, vendors have set up their refreshments, a medicine man is laying out his paraphernalia for demonstrating cure-alls, processions of people in festival dress are arriving... and so it continues. In the evening, gods and mortals alike are entertained with dance-dramas and *gamelan* music, *wayang kulit* and sung poetry.

Many important temple festivals fall at much the same time as Galungan and Kuningan. Festivals also occur during the fourth month (September/October) and the tenth month (April).

NYEPI

The New Year by the *saka* calendar falls on the day after the new moon of the ninth month, usually in March. It is celebrated by a day of stillness, Nyepi, when no fires may be lit, no work done and no transport used. The Ngurah Rai International Airport is closed for 24 hours during Nyepi. On the day before Nyepi, the last day of the year *(pengerupuk)* and marking the end of the rainy season, a great purification offering is made by all the villages to cleanse the country of dark forces. Laid on the ground at every crossroad are huge offerings of wines and flesh from wild and domestic animals *(caru)*. These are to feed the ground spirits, while, from a raised platform, high priests recite powerful formulas to exorcise them. That night, everyone is out in the streets sounding gongs, cymbals and other noise-makers to chase the spirits away. In Denpasar, a huge parade *(ogoh-ogoh)* of papier-mâché monsters (some riding papier-mâché motorcycles) is held; at the end of the parade, some of them are burned. Although its roots are exorcistic, this ritual has become a competition between hamlets to see who can make the best *ogoh-ogoh*.

Outdoor Activities

The most recent boom in sports in Bali has been of the aquatic variety: the government is encouraging the development of watersports, and a wide variety is now available.

Bungee Jumping

Bungee jumping took Bali by storm in 1995 when several towers opened. The attraction to the sport here is that it is much cheaper and just as safe as elsewhere.
A.J. Hackett, Jl. Double Six, Legian, tel: 731-144.
Bali Bungy Co, Jl. Pura Puseh, Legian, tel: 752-658, fax: 755-425.

Golf

Bali Handara Country Club, Desa Pancasari, Bedugul, tel: 288-944. The serious golfer will want to visit this 18-hole championship course, designed by Peter Thompson. The only course in the world set inside a volcano, it is also gazetted among the world's top 50 most beautiful courses. If you stay at the adjoining hotel, there is a 30 percent discount on the green fees.
Bali Golf and Country Club, Nusa Dua, tel: 771-791. Within walking distance of Nusa Dua's main hotels. Exquisite course with 9 holes by the sea and 9 holes on the edge of the Bukit.
Bali Hilton, Nusa Dua, tel: 771-102. Nine-hole mini-golf course in landscaped gardens.
Grand Bali Beach, Sanur, tel; 288-511. A small 9-hole course that can be used for 18 holes. Guests of the hotel can use it for half price. Equipment and caddies are available. An 18-hole miniature golf course is also available.

Le Meridien Nirwana Golf Club and Resort, tel: 815-960. Greg Norman's challenging course set amidst working rice terraces with Tanah Lot temple as a back drop. Two spectacular holes overlooking the Indian Ocean.

Ritz-Carlton Bali, tel: 702-222, in Jimbaran has a unique 18-hole putting course.

River Rafting

White-water rafting adventures are offered down several rivers near Ubud. An all-day excursion (four persons minimum) usually includes lunch and a free cocktail up on the ridge afterwards, as well as transport to and from your hotel, insurance and professional guides.

Sobek Bina Utama, tel: 287-059, fax: 289-448.

Bali Adventure Rafting, Jl. Bypass Pesanggaran, tel: 721-480, fax: 721-461.

Bali Safari Rafting, tel: 235-196, fax: 221-316.

Sailing

For those who just want a ride in a *jukung*, an outrigger canoe with sails, Sanur, Candidasa and Lovina all have locals who will take you out for around $3/person. For more professional sailing, head on down to Benoa Harbour, where the **Bali International Yacht Club**, tel: 723-415, is building a modern 50-berth marina. Those who require permission to bring their own boats into Indonesian waters can contact them for assistance in obtaining documents.

Surfing

Kuta is the central location to rent/buy boards and find out surfing conditions. Tubes, Gang Poppies II, tel: 753-510, is probably

the best source of information. Dive & Ski, Bali Balance, The Curl and The Surf Shop all rent and sell surfboards. Aloha rents boards on the beach.

The best places for surfing are Kuta, Legian and Seminyak, for beginners. Intermediate surfers should go to Bingin, south of the airport reef in Kuta. Also Canggu, 20 minutes northwest of Legian. Much further west are Lalang Linggah village (Soka Beach) and Medewi Beach.

For expert surfers, there's Kuta Reef (accessible only by boat, in front of the Sunset Club), Uluwatu and Padang Padang. There is great surfing at Nusa Lembongan as well.

Swimming

For a fee ranging from $2 to $5 per day, the pools at some of the larger hotels in Denpasar, Sanur, Kuta and Nusa Dua are open to

Dive Sites

Sanur and Nusa Dua: Convenient access, dives at 2–12 metres (6–39 ft) deep are rewarded by beautiful underwater panoramas. Gigantic table and trophy-shaped coral and sponge grow for miles on barrier reef, but limited variety. Coral better at Nusa Dua.

Padangbai and the Gili Tepekong: Located about 60 km (40 mi) northeast of Sanur. Ideal for dives at 3–20 metres (9–66 ft) depths. Full growth of coral and fish. The Gili islands offer a variety of fish life and larger species. Water is cool; wetsuit essential. Strong, unpredictable currents.

Lembongan Island: About 20 km (12 mi) east of Sanur and two hours by motor boat, this is one of the three sister islands of Bali. White sandy bottom and crystal-clear, cool water offer assorted fish and marine vegetation. Underwater grottos are the wonders of this area.

Tulamben: Located about 100 km (60 mi) northeast of Sanur. On

location, 30 metres (100 ft) offshore are remnants of the US merchantman *Liberty* sunk during World War II. The wreck is fully grown with anemone, gorgonia, sponge, and coral; fish are tame.

Singaraja: Located about 80 km (50 mi) due north of Sanur, where the calm waters of the Bali Sea create pool-like conditions ideal for snorkelling. The best spots are around Lovina Beach, suitable for beginners, and Gondol Beach, with slight currents from 5–15 metre (16–50 ft) depths.

Menjangan: This tiny island, 120 km (70 mi) northwest of Sanur, and part of West Bali National Park, is accessible in 30 minutes by boat. All-season, undemanding diving where magnificent underwater vistas (visibility up to 50 metres/165 ft) will surprise even the most seasoned diver. It is rich with all kinds of sponges, sea plants, coral and fish.

This area is considered the diver's paradise in Bali. There is also an old shipwreck at 40

metres (130 ft), as well as superb coral at 5–7 metres (16–23 ft).

Pemuteran: The access point for Menjangan Island, a few minutes away by boat. Slight current, good variety of fish and abundant soft corals at 3–8 metres (10–26 ft) make this a good dive and snorkel area.

Tabuhan Islands: Coral reefs, tropical fish and shark sites are the main diving draws.

Amed: Located near Tulamben. Slope and drop-off between 3 and 40 metres (10–130 ft), has coral, plantation, sinall, large fish and drop-off. Mild current, best variety of hard coral in Bali, dense fish population on deep walls. Coral near the beach.

Nusa Penida: This is the adventure dive. Two hours by boat from Padangbai. Drift dive, flat slope and drop-off between 3 and 40 metres (10–130 ft). White sandy bottom, crystal-clear and cool water present assorted fish, crayfish and coral reef. The water is typically cool from the upswell. Currents can be strong.

non-guests. In Ubud, the pools open to the public are at Ubud Inn (great kiddy pool), Hotel Campuhan, tel: 976-368, Ubud Village Hotel, tel: 974-701, Oka Wati's Bungalow, tel: 973-86, Villa Rasa Sayang, tel: 975-491, Dewi Sri, tel: 975-300 and Fibra Inn, tel: 975-451.

One of the best-kept secrets (although it is becoming more widely known) in Ubud is the cave pool on the way to Pejeng. At the T-junction of Peliatan and Ubud, go east on the asphalt road. After around 200 metres there is a fabulous view of a gorge and river; there is a slippery path that goes down to the river. You can swim in crystal-clear water here, and if you are prepared to be adventurous, dive under a cave and come up in a private, natural pool.

Watersports

In recent years, surfing, snorkelling, scuba diving, spearfishing, windsurfing and deep-sea fishing have all become very popular in Bali. Nusa Lembongan, the small island directly opposite Sanur, has developed into a haven for surfers and divers alike.

Group charters and safari tours are available, together with equipment and instruction if needed. A complete scuba outfit and a ride out to the reef at Sanur is available. Ask about taking out insurance.

Baruna Water Sports, Jl. Bypass Ngurah Rai 300B, Tuban, tel: 753-820. They offer tours to all the main scuba diving attractions on the island. Also, parasailing, jetskiing, waterscooter, windsurfing, canoe and paddleboard, glass-bottom boat, waterskiing, trolling, coral/deep-sea fishing.

Bali Marine Sports, Jl. Bypass Ngurah Rai, Belanjong, Sanur, tel: 289-308, offers a number of different boating expeditions, including snorkelling and scuba diving.

Beluga, Benoa Harbour, Nusa Dua, tel: 771-997. Swimming

pool, diving and watersports, parasailing, dolphin tour, submarine, restaurant.

Dive Operators

Bali Marine Sports, Jl. Bypass Ngurah Rai, Belanjong, Sanur, tel: 287-872, 289-308.

Balina Diving in Balina (near Candidasa) offers snorkelling and scuba diving.

Reef Seen Aquatics Dive Centre, Desa Pemuteran, Gerokgak, Singaraja, Bali, fax: (0362) 923-39, e-mail: reefseen@denpasar. wasantara.net.id. Specialising in dives around Menjangan Island; Australian and US PADI instructors who have pioneered the area. Equipment rentals, dives and certification, cruises and sailing.

Bali Hai Diving Adventures, Bali Hai Cruises, in Benoa Harbour, tel: 720-331.

Stingray Diving at Puri Bali Homestay, tel: (0363) 412-68, fax: (0363) 410-62 in Candidasa.

Shopping

What to Buy

Thousands of artisans, crafts-people, seamstresses, wood-carvers, and painters are kept busy supplying the tourist demand. Swarms of vendors crowd the beaches and streets of Denpasar, offering friendship bracelets, necklaces and watches. Many shopkeepers have developed a hard-sell sales pitch reminiscent of Hong Kong or New York. Sometimes it is a bit overwhelming, but rare is the visitor who comes away without at least one bag of souvenirs. The variety is virtually endless. Most handicrafts and paintings can be found in the Gianyar district; textiles in Gianyar, Klungkung (Sideman), Karangasem (Tenganan), Kuta and Denpasar. Kuta has the best shopping, but you have to deal with the aggressive shopkeepers.

ANTIQUES

The "antique" business in Bali is booming. Carve a split piece of wood, paint it and bury it in the ground for a month and *voilà!* – an antique. Be very careful when buying antiques, as there's no guarantee as to age. However, intricately carved doors, doorways, huge ornate wedding beds, wavy ceremonial *keris*, textiles, old Dutch lamps, masks, Chinese ceramics and sculptures from many parts of Indonesia, as well as China and Japan, are available to the discriminating buyer.

The antique shops, adjacent to the Kerta Gosa in Klungkung, house collections of rare Chinese porcelains, old Kamasan *wayang*-style paintings, antique jewellery and Balinese weavings. Prices are reasonable. Singaraja has some of the best antique shops in Bali. They are on the main streets of the town.

CASSETTES

Cheap pirated cassettes are a thing of the past now, thanks to new trade agreements and government regulations. But there is still a great variety of cheap rock, pop, classical and folk music available. Probably the best selection is at **Mahogany** on Jl. Seminyak, Seminyak. **Ubud Music**, tel: 975-362, across from the Lotus Café, also has a good selection. For traditional Balinese and Indonesian music, you can't beat **Toko Melati**, Jl. Kartini 31, tel: 222-092, a block north of the main Denpasar market. The owner is knowledgeable about the latest releases and will play the tapes before you buy them.

Also try the **Lotus Music Cassette Centre**, Jl. Legian, Kuta, tel: 753-508.

CERAMICS

The village of **Pejaten** in Tabanan has whimsical and serious tiles, as well as stoneware plates, bowls and the like. Good quality stoneware can be found in **Kapal** (at the bend in the road just past Pura Sadah). Try **Jenggala Ceramics** in Jimbaran and in Ubud, just past the post office, on the south side of the street. All of these outlets sell lead-free pottery.

CLOTHES

Bali now has one of the biggest garment industries in Southeast Asia. There are perhaps 500 designers and exporters working out of Kuta and Legian (including many young foreigners). The clothes are ideal for casual summer wear in warm climates.

The best way to find a store that specialises in designs to your liking is to walk along Jl. Legian, or down Jl. Bakung Sari in Kuta. Overruns are available at **Mama and Leon**, Jl. Danau Tamblingan 99A, Sanur, tel: 288-044, on the west side of the street; and at **Bali Garments** on Jl. Bypass Ngurah Rai.

For more upscale sportswear, try **Kartini, Tao and Kingkong** in Legian. **Uluwatu** (on Jl. Danau Tamblingan), **Kekal** (Jl. Legian and Jl. Pantai Kuta) and **Bali High** on Jl. Semawang in Sanur offer lacy women's wear. Surfwear can be found all over, but the most popular shops are **The Curl** on Jl. Legian and **Ulu's Shop** on Jl. Melasti and **Bali Barrel** on Jl. Legian. For gorgeous *ikat* designer clothes, go to **Nogo's** on Jl. Danau Tamblingan in Sanur and Jl. Legian in Kuta.

Kuta Kid's is Bali's specialist for the small set, Jl. Legian, Kuta, tel: 756-327. Popular **Animale** now has outlets across the island, including Sanur, Kuta, Galeria Nusa Dua. Cool tropical fashions are widely exported. Famed local wordsmith Joger produces hilarious and collectible topical T-shirts, popular with domestic tourists or those who understand Indonesian; they're stocked at **Kata Kata Joger**, Jl. Raya Kuta, tel: 752-253

GOLD & SILVER

Inventive Balinese jewellers smelt, cast, forge and spin delicate flowers, bowls and images of demons studded with semi-precious stones. The centres for metal-working are **Celuk, Kamasan** in Klungkung, and **Bratan** in Buleleng, where all such ornaments are on sale at reasonable but negotiable prices. These craftsmen will also produce pieces and settings to order – bring them a drawing or a sample to copy. If you don't like it, they'll smelt it down and start over.

For traditional Balinese jewellery (and that means gold), visit the shops at Jl. Hasanudin (**Melati** is a reputable one – most of the gold is 22–24K) and Jl. Sulawesi. You'll see women sitting out in front of the shops buying and selling gold as well. If you want to take your chances with them, you can usually take the jewellery into one of the shops and have them test it to see how dense the gold is.

One of the best goldsmiths around is **Nyoman Sadia**, at Jl. Sersan Wayan Pugig No 5, in Sukawati. His prices are high but his work is exquisite. If coming from

Packing & Shipping

There are a number of ways to get things home. First, find yourself a reliable shipper. For a small fee, they'll do your packing. If you have something fragile, you might want to oversee the packing yourself.

Air cargo is charged by the kilo (minimum 10 kg/22 lbs) and can turn out to be pretty expensive. **Sea mail** is another option, taking two to three months to get to its destination. Packages less than 1 metre (3 ft) in length and under 10 kg (22 lbs) can be sent through the **postal service**. Insurance is highly recommended; read the fine print. If you have a lot of stuff, then send it by sea cargo – you can send a minimum of a cubic metre to Europe and the US for around $400, including packing. Insurance is 2 percent of the claimed value. Sea and air cargo go to the closest port and international airport, post goes to your door; therefore you have to think about how you'll get your goods home from the port/airport. Shippers will even pick things up from the shop or come to your hotel. All that remains is to be aware of what problems, restrictions or expenses you might encounter in your home country.

Alpha Sigma, Jl. Raya Kuta 139, tel: 752-872.

Angkasa Jaya, Jl. Raya Kuta 72, Kuta, tel: 751-390.

Bali Delta Express, Jl. Kartini 58, Denpasar, tel: 223-340.

Bintang Bali Cargo, Jl. Astasura 21X, Denpasar, tel: 410-939/40.

Pacific Express, Jl. Hangtuah 3X, Denpasar, tel: 235-181.

Denpasar, you'll see his placard on the right side of the road, past the police station. A new upscale shop in Ubud, **Treasures**, tel: 976-697, Jl. Ubud Raya next to Ary's Warung, features pricey jewels in gold settings by local designers-in-residence. In Ubud, go to **Putra's** for silver. Fixed prices here but it's a blessing as they aren't inflated (nor quoted in dollars like in Celuk). He has two shops on Monkey Forest Road, one across from Griya Restaurant on the main road; his wholesale outlet is in Puri Agung, in Peliatan. Kuta is a great place to shop for jewellery as the designs are quite contemporary. Try **Jonathan**, on Jl. Legian, Mirah, Jl. Majapahit 81, tel: 757-780; **Mario's**, Jl. Raya Seminak 19, tel: 730-977 and **Jusuf's**, Jl. Legian 182, tel: 758-442.

Mirah has popular silver designs, Jl. Majapahit 81, Kuta, tel: 757-780, as does **Suarti**, with outlets in Kuta, Jl. Legian 139, tel: 751-660, Sanur, Jl. Danau Tamblingan, and Sukawati, Jl. Raya Celuk, tel: 298-914. **Suardana** produces both gold and silver, Jl. Raya Celuk, Sukawati, tel: 298-648.

HANDICRAFTS

Bamboo implements, *wayang kulit* figures and ornaments made of coconut shell and teakwood are sold at most souvenir shops. Bone carvings can be bought at good prices at **Tampaksiring**, while plaited hats and baskets are the speciality of the women of **Bedulu** and **Bona**. **Pasar Seni Sukawati** and the row of stands opposite **Goa Gajah** (Elephant Cave) are the best places to buy baskets; to see them made (and sold, of course), go to **Pengoseken** near Ubud.

Wooden earrings (the animals and geometric-design styles) can be found at Tampaksiring and the kiosks at Gunung Kawi, as well as in shops in all the major tourist resort areas. Sandalwood fans can be ordered with your name on at **Toko Susila** on Jl. Hasanudin 29, tel: 221-978, near Jl. Sumatra in

Denpasar. Orders can be filled within a day. Specify real sandalwood, as most fans are coffeewood soaked in sandalwood perfume. Ebony nameplates can be ordered in Sanur in front of the Swastika II Restaurant.

The **Handicrafts Centre**, Sanggraha Karya Hasta, tel: 461-942, in Tohpati, Denpasar, has a collection of the handicrafts from Bali and the other islands of Indonesia, such as baskets and weavings. This centre is not really a museum, but a government-sponsored cooperative selling Indonesian and Balinese handi-crafts. Open 9am–5.30pm Monday–Friday, until 5pm on Saturday, closed on Sunday.

MUSICAL INSTRUMENTS

If it's gongs, xylophones, or drums you're after, head on out to the gong foundry in Blahbatuh and look up **Pande Gableran** and sons. They churn out instruments for *gamelan* clubs all over the world and always have some stock on hand. For bamboo flutes in the Ubud area, try **Cok Agung** in Banjar Teruna.

PAINTINGS

The classical *wayang* style has its origins in Kamasan, Klungkung. Cheap renditions can be bought in the parking lot across from Kerta Gosa in Klungkung. For traditional paintings, go to Batuan, Pengo-seken (fish and birds) and Peliatan, Ubud and Penestanan (Young Artist style). Visit major galleries, see which artist you like and then seek them out at their home.

STONECARVINGS

For traditional sandstone carvings, stop in at the workshops in Batubulan. **Wayan Cemul**, an Ubud stonecarver with an international following, has a house full of his weird and wonderful creations on Jl. Kajeng 28, tel: 964-49.

TEXTILES

The spiralling designs and geometric patterns of Javanese batik are seen everywhere on the island, as part of the daily dress of the Balinese. Most of what is being sold on the streets by vendors is not batik, but printed materials that the Balinese use for tablecloths. Be careful what you buy for "temple clothing", as a lot of it is inappropriate (not wrong, just funny to the Balinese sensibility). A good starting point for batik is **Batik Popiler**, Jl. W. R. Supratman 306, Denpasar, tel: 463-597. Here you can find everything from simple *cap* (stamped) batik to the glorious *tulis* (the batik artist uses a canting to make the designs) batiks.

For the Balinese hand-loomed *ikat* cloth, there are a number of "factories"; parts of the island specialise in certain motifs.

The most accessible and well-known factories are those in the town of Gianyar. **Cap Togog**, tel: 930-46, and **Cap Cili** are two showrooms which also have tours of the process. **Cap Anoman** in Beng (just north of Gianyar) doesn't provide a tour, but you're welcome to wander through the factory. Their showroom in Blahbatuh is fancy and overpriced. Other centres of *ikat* are **Sideman** and **Gelgel** in Klungkung, and **Singaraja** in the north.

Songket is another traditional Balinese cloth which has gold and silver threads in the weft. It is worn for rituals by both men and women. The villages of Blayu, Sideman, and Singaraja are known for *songket*.

Other types of weaving, such as *selendang* (temple sashes) are done in Batuan, Ubud, and Mengwi. The famous *geringsing* (double *ikat*) is made only in Tenganan, where *ikat* cloth from all over the Indo-nesian archipelago is for sale. Textiles such as the Sumbanese *hinggi* and Batak *ulos* may also be bought in many shops in Kuta and Denpasar.

Arts of Asia, Jl. Thamrin, tel: 423-350, has the highest quality.

Batik Kens outlets at Nusa Dua Galeria, tel: 771-303, the airport and Kuta, Jl. Raya Legian 133, also have quality selections.

WOODCARVINGS

You are sure to find good woodcarvings in the shops along the main road of Mas (particularly well known is **Ida Bagus Tilem's Gallery and Museum**, tel: 975-099, pricey but the work is gorgeous) and in the village of Kemenuh. For masks, try **Ida Bagus Anom** in Mas, **I Wayan Tangguh** in Singapadu and **I Wayan Regog** in Lantanghidung near Batuan. **Kemenuh**, on the way to Gianyar, also has fine exponents of ebony and other types of wood carvings. **Pujung** (past Tegalalang north of Ubud) is the banana-tree capital of the world (the wooden variety, that is). **Jati** is known as the home of "primitive" carving.

For exquisite work carved onto delicate roots, no one can surpass **Muja** in Singapadu. All sorts of indigenous woods are used, ranging from the butter-coloured jackfruit to inexpensive bespeckled coconut. Woods imported from other islands – such as buff hibiscus, rich brown Javanese teak and black Sulawesian ebony – are also hewn into delicate forms by the craftsmen.

Language

Although there are over 350 languages and dialects spoken in the archipelago, the one national tongue, Bahasa Indonesian, will take you from the northernmost tip of Sumatra through Java and across the string of islands to Irian Jaya. Unlike some Asian languages, is not tonal.

When speaking Bahasa Indonesian, you need to keep a few basic rules in mind. Adjectives always follow the noun: *rumah* (house) and *besar* (big) together are *rumah besar*, meaning big house. When constructing a sentence, the order is usually subject-verb-object: *saya* (I) *minum* (drink) *air* (water) *dingin* (cold). The possessive is made by putting the personal pronoun after the noun: *rumah saya* is my house.

Indonesians always show respect when addressing others, especially when a younger person speaks to elders. The custom is to address an older man as *bapak* or *pak* (father) and an older woman as *ibu* (mother), and even in the case of slightly younger people, who are obviously VIPs, this form of address is suitable and correct. *Nyonya* is polite when speaking with a married woman, *nona* with an unmarried woman.

General

thank you *terima kasih*
good morning *selamat pagi*
good day *selamat siang*
good evening *selamat sore*
good night *selamat malam*
goodbye (to person going) *selamat jalan*
goodbye (to person staying) *selamat tinggal*

I'm sorry *ma'af*
welcome *selamat datang*
please come in *silakan masuk*
please sit down *silakan duduk*
what is your name? *siapa nama saudara?*
my name is... *nama saya...*
where do you come from? *saudara datang dari mana?* or *dari mana?*
I come from... *saya datang dari...*

Forms of Address

I *saya*
you (singular) *saudara; anda/kamu* (to children)
he, she *dia*
we *kami* (excluding the listener)
we *kita* (including the listener)
you (plural) *saudara-saudara, anda*
Mr *Pak/Bapak*
Mrs *Ibu*
Miss *Nona*

Directions/Transport

left *kiri*
right *kanan*
straight *terus*
near *dekat*
far *jauh*
from *dari*
to *ke*
inside *didalam*
outside *diluar*
here *disini*
there *disana*
in front of *didepan, dimuka*
at the back *dibelakang*
next to *disebelah*
pedicab *becak*
car *mobil*
bus *bis*
train *kereta api*
bicycle *sepeda*
motorcycle *sepeda motor*
where do you want to go? *mau kemana?*
I want to go to... *saya mau ke...*
stop here *berhenti disini, stop disini*
train station *stasian kereta api*
petrol station *pompa bensin*
bank *bank*
post office *kantor pos*
Immigration Dept *Departemen Immigrasi*
tourist office *kantor pariwisata*
embassy *kedutaan*

Restaurants

restaurant *restoran, rumah makan*
food *makanan*
drink *minuman*
breakfast *makan pagi*
lunch *makan siang*
dinner *makan malam*
boiled water *air putih, air matang*
iced water *air es*
tea *teh*
coffee *kopi*
milk *susu*
rice *nasi*
noodles *mie, bihun, bakmie*
fish *ikan*
prawns *udang*
vegetables *sayur*
fruit *buah*
egg *telur*
sugar *gula*
salt *garam*
pepper *merica, lada*
cup *cangkir*
plate *piring*
glass *gelas*
spoon *sendok*
knife *pisau*
fork *garpu*

Shopping

shop *toko*
money *uang*
change (of money) *uang kembali*
to buy *beli*
price *harga*
expensive *mahal*
cheap *murah*
fixed price *harga pas*
How much is it? *Berapa?/Berapa harganya?*

Understanding Signs

open *buka, dibuka*
closed *tutup, ditutup*
entrance *masuk*
exit *keluar*
don't touch *jangan pegang*
no smoking *jangan merokok*
push *dorong*
pull *tarik*
gate *pintu*
ticket window *loket*
ticket *karcis*
information *keterangan*
city *kota*
market *pasar*

Planning the Trip

Lombok

Lombok is an excellent escape from the tourist scene of Bali. Those with only a few days on Bali should probably keep Lombok for the next trip. If, however, you have a few weeks on Bali and would like to see more of Indonesia, but without travelling great distances, consider visiting Lombok. For any traveller, a three-day excursion is a good sampler of Lombok's attractions – all of its sights are located within an hour or two of the old capital, Cakranegara. Diving at Gili Air or climbing to the summit of Mount Rinjani require at least three days.

Lombok's **telephone code 0370** precedes all phone numbers listed below, unless otherwise noted.

Tourist Information

The Ampenan-Mataram-Cakranegara stretch is the island's main business, administrative and shopping district. Call at the **West Nusa Tenggara Regional Tourist Office** (DIPARDA), Jl. Langko 70, Ampenan, tel: 631-829, 637-828, or fax: 637-828, for brochures and maps of the island. They haven't much information on cultural activities, unfortunately. The regional tourism ministry office, DIPARDA, also can be helpful: Jl. Singosari 2, West Lombok, tel: 632-723, fax: 637-233.

Women Travellers

Women should be aware that exposed thighs and plunging necklines are severely frowned upon, particularly by Lombok's Muslim majority (this applies especially to towns on the eastern and southern parts of the island, where the most staunch Muslims live). Cases of harassment have been reported – women thus attired are considered unworthy of respect – and women are advised not to travel alone outside of the urban areas. If you keep yourself discreetly covered, you should have no problems.

Getting There

To get from Bali to Lombok, you can choose between a quick 20-minute flight from Bali's Ngurah Rai to Lombok's **Selaparang Airport**, a leisurely cruise on the modern ferry that shuttles between Padang Bai, on Bali's eastern coast, and the port of Lembar, situated on Lombok's west coast, or a speedy hydrofoil from Bali's Benoa Harbour to Lembar.

BY AIR

Merpati Nusantara and **AirMark** from Denpasar, **Garuda** from Surabaya and **Silk Air** from Singapore serve Lombok. **Merpati** operates eastbound flights.
AirMark, Airport, tel: 646-847, 643-564.
Bouraq Airways, Jl Pejanggik 41/42, Cakranegara, tel: 633-370.
Garuda Indonesia, Hotel Lombok Raya, Jl. Panca Usaha 11, Cakranegara, tel: 637-950.
Merpati Nusantara, Jl. Pejanggik 69, Mataram, tel: 636-745, 632-226.
Silk Air, Airport, tel: 622-987, ext. 247.
Airport, tel: 640-784, 632-030.

BY SEA

The four-hour sea passage by ferry, with the majestic volcanic peaks of Bali and Lombok in the distance, is well worth the inconvenience of travelling to and from the ports. The ferry departs every 90 minutes, around the clock, from Padang Bai (Bali) to Lembar (Lombok). From

Medical Services

There are three hospitals in Mataram, one each in Praya and Selong. The **Mataram General Hospital**, Jl. Pejanggik 6, has a tourist clinic with an English-speaking doctor, Dr Felic, tel: 635-632.

Sanur or Kuta, it takes more than two hours to get to Padang Bai by private car, three hours or more by public transport, so get an early start. Better yet, go to East Bali the day before and spend the night in a beach bungalow at Candidasa, just 20 minutes from Padang Bai.

Ferry tickets are about $3 each way first-class, and $2 for economy. Cars are charged $25 for passage. The snack bar on board serves *nasi rawon*, soft drinks, beer, coffee and tea; or buy food from vendors at the port before departing.

Mabua Express, tel: (0361) 721-212 in Bali, (0370) 681-195 in Lombok, hydrofoil catamaran departs Benoa Harbour daily at 8.30am, and departs Lombok's Lembar harbour at 2.30pm. There are two classes of fares: $25 and $30.

Bounty Cruises, Senggigi, tel: 623-666; Gili Meno, tel: 642-363.

The port of Lembar, where the ferry and hydrofoil arrive from Bali, is about 20 km (12 mi) south of Mataram. Lombok's Selaparang Airport is right in Mataram and no more than 3 km (2 mi) from any hotel in the city area. A daily ferry departs for Alas on Sumbawa from the port of Labuhan Lombok, on Lombok's eastern shore. A trunk highway cuts right across the island, from Ampenan to Labuan Lombok, a distance of only 76 km (48 mi). Air-conditioned shuttle bus/ferry packages to Sumbawa depart daily for about $15 to $20, depending on destination, or $7 to $10 for the return trip to Bali.

On Arrival

Lombok's Selaparang Airport is right in Mataram, so the taxi fare to any hotel in urban Ampenan/

Mataram/Cakranegara will probably be no more than $3. Major hotels will pick up for free. Call from the airport or contact their representative in the arrival hall. Once in Lombok, transport is easy, though it is time-consuming to rely upon public transport. Taxis and minibuses *(bemos)* are available for charter.

Motorcycles

Bring a motorcycle from Bali on the ferry (rental cars cannot leave Bali). It is possible to rent motorcycles in Ampenan, Mataram and Senggigi for about $8 per day. Ask at your hotel, or at any motorcycle shop.

Taxis

Metered taxis can be ordered in advance directly to the depot, from hotel desks or from taxi stands in Senggigi. Flagfall is about $0.25 and about $0.12 per each kilometre thereafter. Taxies can also be chartered for the day from:
Lombok Taxi, Jl. Koperasi 102, Ampenan, tel: 627-000

Arranging a Tour

Tours of Lombok can be arranged by one of the following operators or agents. You could also use one of the English-speaking taxi drivers to be found at the airport; before setting off, agree a fee for a day trip around the island ($30–$80).
Bidy Tour, Jl. Ragigenap 17, Ampenan, tel: 632-129, 634-095, fax: 631-821
Citra Lombok Indah, BTN Griya Senggigi, Jl. Lumba Lumba 2/4, tel: 693-838, fax: 693-287.
Dewi Sri Murni Tours & Travel, Jl. Saleh Sungkar 70c, Ampenan, tel/fax: 634-807.
East Indies Company, Mayura Wisata, Galeria 67- Senggigi, tel/fax: 693-428
Express Rinjani Utama, Jl. Adi Sucipto 10, Mataram, tel: 359-68.
Kapitan Tour, Jl. Raya Senggigi km 8, Senggigi, tel: 693-054, fax: 693-055.

Lendang Express Taxi, Jl. Adi Sucipto 10, Mataram, tel: 635-968, 622-688.

Bemos & Buses

Bemos and buses service all towns on the island. Buy your *bemo* ticket at the snack bar on the ferry for the ride into Mataram from the port of Lembar. The central **bemo and bus terminal** is at the crossroads at Sweta, just to the east of Cakranegara; there is a signboard here displaying the official fares to all points on the island.

Chartering a Vehicle

You can charter a *bemo* for the day for between $25 and $30 and they will take you anywhere on the island. *Bemos* are slow and uncomfortable, so you are better off paying a bit more for a taxi (perhaps with an English-speaking driver). The best option for a comparable price is renting an air-conditioned car and driver by the day or hour. Choose from the

Mataram Vista Wisata, Jl. Cili-naya Blk. B/8 (complex APMH Cilinaya), tel: 622-314.
Perama Travel Club, Jl. Pejanggik 66, tel: 635-936; Senggigi, tel: 693-007, fax: 693-009.
Sunda Duta, Jl. Raya Senggigi 16, tel: 693-390, fax: 622-344, lombok@mataram.wasantara. net.id; www.vol.it/lombok.
Wannen Tours, Jl. Erlangga 4, Mataram, tel: 631-177, fax: 623-827.

To arrange an expedition up to the summit of Gunung Rinjani, Lombok's highest mountain, including food, tents, sleeping bags and a guide (to top, minimum two persons, $175; to Segara Anak, $130), contact **Mr Batubara** at Wisma Triguna, on Jl. Koperasi 76, Ampenan, tel: 631-705.

following (prices are approximate): Suzuki Jimny jeep, $25 daily without driver, $30 with driver; Mitsubishi minibus $35 without, $55 with; and Toyota Kijang, $45 without, $55 with driver. Hourly rates with driver are $5–10.
Four-Wheel Adventures: Most Lombok tour operators arrange four-wheel self-drive or chauffeured experiences off road or into remote locations. Opportunities include visiting agrotourism plantations, remote enclaves of indigenous leaf-eating monkeys and offshore islands to visit a pelican colony.

Car Rental

Lendang Express, Jl. Adi Sucipto 10, Mataram, tel: 635-968.
Rinjani Rent Car, Jl. Bung Karno 6B, tel: 632-259.
Surya Rent Car, Jl Panca Usaha, tel: 693-076; Jl. Raya Senggigi.

Where to Stay

Senggigi

The consistently best international-standard accommodation is centred along Senggigi Beach. A good mix of *losmen* and hotels, in all price ranges, suits every pocket.
Batu Bolong Cottages, Jl. Raya Senggigi km 12, Batu Bolong, Senggigi, tel/fax: 693-198. 37 rooms. **$$ +**
Graha Beach Senggigi, Jl. Raya Senggigi, Batu Layar, Gunung Sari, tel: 693-101, fax: 693-400. 39 air-conditioned, beachfront bungalows with expansion under way. **$$**
Hotel Hilberon, PO Box 1062, Mataram, Desa Pemenang Barat, Senggigi, tel: 693-898, fax: 693-252. 25 European-style bungalow villas with a/c, mini bar and television. Manicured gardens. Pool, restaurant, beach. **$$$**
Holiday Inn Resort, Mangsit, tel: 693-444, fax: 693-092. 159 international-standard a/c rooms in two-storey buildings, chalets and villas situated in coconut grove around pool. Mini-bar, satellite television, coffee/tea making facilities. Two restaurants, bar, pub, health club, tennis, clinic, beach shuttle to Senggigi. **$$$$**
Hotel Jayakarta, PO Box 1112, Jl. Raya Senggigi, tel: 693-045, 693-048, fax: 693-043. 171 a/c, international-standard rooms with mini-bar, sound system, television with in-house movies. Three restaurants, two bars and karaoke, tennis, conference centre, pool, jogging track, beach. **$$$**
Kebun Rohani Cottages, Jl. Raya Senggigi, tel: 693-018. Cool tropical garden setting, inviting and trendy restaurant, fans only. **$**

Hotel Lombok Intan Laguna, PO Box 1049, Mataram, Jl. Raya Senggigi, tel: 693-090, fax: 693-185. 123 a/c rooms and bungalows with satellite television and mini-bar. Restaurant, bar, room service, pool, tennis, beach. **$$$**
Mascot Berugan Elen Cottages, PO Box 1099, Mataram, Jl. Raya Senggigi, tel: 693-365, fax: 693-236. 19 rooms. **$$**
Hotel Nusa Bunga, PO Box 1118, Mataram, Jl. Raya Senggigi, Klui, tel: 693-035, fax: 693-036. 5 km (3 mi) north of Senggigi. 13 a/c bungalow rooms along beach with pool. Garden restaurant and room service. **$$**
Pantai Pacific, PO Box 1035, Jl. Raya Senggigi, Kerandangan, tel: 693-006, fax: 693-027. 26 a/c rooms and beachfront bungalows with restaurant, pool, room service, television, mini-bar. **$$ +**
Pondok Damai, Jl. Raya Senggigi, tel/fax: 693-019. **$**
Pondok Senggigi, Jl. Raya Senggigi, tel: 693-275, 693-273, fax: 693-276. 48 rooms. **$**
Hotel Puri Bunga, PO Box 51 Mataram, Senggigi Beach, tel: 693-013, 693-353, fax: 693-286. 50 a/c rooms with mini bar, television. Restaurant, bar, pool. Overlooking Senggigi. **$**
Hotel Puri Mas, PO Box 1123, Mataram, Jl. Senggigi Raya, Mangsit, tel/fax: 693-023. 17 beachfront villas and bungalows in homey surroundings. Must book two months in advance, many repeat and long-stay guests. Vegetarian restaurant, pool, library, room service. **$$**

Price Guide

Price categories for standard rooms (or suites in larger hotels), usually without breakfast, are:

No $:	very cheap
$:	under $30
$$:	$30–$60
$$$:	$60–$100
$$$$:	$100–$150
$$$$$:	above $150, often hundreds of dollars

Puri Saron, Desa Krandangan, Jl. Raya Senggigi, tel: 693-424, 693-425, fax: 693-266. 49 a/c, deluxe rooms and four beachfront bungalows with mini-bar, television, pool, restaurant and room service. Opened in late 1995, Lombok-style setting with manicured gardens. **$$$**

Hotel Senggigi Beach, PO Box 1001, Mataram, Jl. Raya Senggigi, tel: 693-210, fax: 693-200. 149 a/c rooms and 16 villas with satellite television, bar, room service, tennis, sports. The area's first hotel, set in mature grounds, on a point with two sweeping beaches. **$$$$ +**

Hotel Sheraton Senggigi Beach, PO Box 1154, Mataram, Jl. Raya Senggigi km 8, tel: 693-333, fax: 693-140. 156 international-standard, a/c rooms and suites with satellite television, mini-bar, balconies. Resort wraps around inviting lagoon pools with water slide, three restaurants, lounge, spa, room service, business centre, tennis, beach, airport departure lounge. **$$$$**

Mataram-Ampenan-Cakranegara

Hotel Lombok Raya in Mataram is the island's best hotel. The Selaparang Hotel is also very pleasant, near to the temples and markets in Cakra. Both hotels will pick you up at the airport on arrival, for a charge.

Hotel Granada, Jl. Bung Karno 7, Mataram, tel: 622-275, fax: 636-015. 97 a/c rooms. Pool, tropical gardens with birds and monkeys, restaurant.

Hotel Kertayoga, Jl. Pejanggik 64, Mataram, tel: 621-775. 15 rooms with private bath, fan, a/c and breakfast. **$**

Hotel Lombok Raya, Jl. Panca Usaha 11, Mataram, tel: 632-305, fax: 636-478. 135 large, clean rooms with a/c, mini-bar, television. Pool, restaurant, room service.

Losmen Pabean, Jl. Yos Sudarso 146, Komplek L. Yos Sudarso/M, Ampenan, tel: 621-758. 17 rooms.

Near the waterfront on the main street, opposite several restaurants. Popular with budget travellers.

Hotel Mataram, Jl. Pejanggik 105, Mataram, tel: 633-675, fax: 634-966. 32 a/c rooms with TV, minibar. Restaurant, pool. **$**

Nitour, Jl. Yos Sudarso 4, Ampenan, tel: 623-780, fax: 625-328. 20 a/c rooms with television, balcony. **$$**

Puri Indah, Jl. Sriwijaya 132, Gebang, Mataram, tel: 637-633, 637-609. 30 rooms.

Hotel Pusaka, Jl. S. Hassanudin 23, Cakranegara, tel: 633-119. 24 rooms. Centrally located. Rooms with private bath, a/c. **$$**

Hotel Ratih, Jl. Pejanggik 127, Cakranegara, tel: 631-096, fax: 624-685. 27 rooms with private bath, fan, a/c, television and hot water.

Sasaka Beach Hotel, Jl. Meniting, Ampenan. 24 rooms.

Selaparang Hotel, Jl. Pejanggik 40, Cakranegara, tel: 632-670. 16 rooms either a/c or fan-cooled, with hot water and television.

Wisma Triguna, Jl. Kopeorasi, Ampenan, tel: 631-705. A *losmen* near the airport. 22 rooms.

Hotel Zahir, Jl. Koperasi 9, Ampenan, tel: 634-248. 11 rooms.

Other Areas

Nestled high in the west Lombok hills, but only a 30-minute drive from the airport, is the old Suranadi Hotel dating from colonial times. The island's most exclusive resort for the rich and famous, The Oberoi Lombok, nestles along Medana Beach, between Pemanang and Tanjung in northwest Lombok.

South Lombok was targetted for development along the lines of Bali's Nusa Dua area but so far only the Novotel Lombok is open. Lombok's northwestern reefs are among the most spectacular in the world. Aquatic enthusiasts stay at the Sasaka Beach Hotel.

There are many *losmen* and homestays at Sira Beach and on the Gili islands at budget prices, but take your own mosquito net. *Losmen* on Gili Trawangan island

average only $5 a day with home-cooked meals. Gili Air's 29 places to stay range from $5 to $45, Mawar Bungalow being on the lower end and the air-conditioned Hotel Gili Air at the top.

Rinjani Country Club Resort, Golong, Desa Peresak, Narmada, tel: 633-488, fax: 633-839. 20 km (12 mi) east of Mataram. 20 rooms in blocks and villas surrounding 18-hole golf course. Clubhouse, restaurant, pool, tennis. **$$$**

Kuta Indah Hotel, Kuta, tel: 653-782, fax: 654-628. 43 a/c rooms with satellite television, fan, beach view. **$ +**

Matahari Inn, Kuta, tel: 654-832, fax: 654-909. 33 rooms, 6 bungalows and restaurant.

Novotel Coralia Lombok, Mandalika Resort, Pantai Putri Nyale, Kuta, tel: 653-333, fax: 653-555. 100 rooms and 23 bungalows on beachfront. Three pools, two restaurants, spa, and other mod-cons of a four-star resort. Recreates an ancient Sasak village with lovely thatched bungalows around water-garden pools with whimsical statuary. Nearby beaches and hills are excellent for walks. **$$$$ +**

The Oberoi Lombok, Medana Beach, Tanjung, tel: 638-444, fax: 632-496. 20 private villas and 30 terrace rooms along secluded Medana Beach, all with sunken baths, satellite television, CD systems, some with ocean views. Most villas have garden showers and private pool. Facilities include restaurants, bar, pool, health club, beach club and spa. **$$$$$ +**

Sasaka Beach Hotel, Meniting, 5 km (3 mi) north of Ampenan. A favourite with divers wanting to explore Lombok's spectacular northwestern reefs. Many travel daily from here to Pantai Sira or Pantai Pemenang beaches and Pulau Gili Air (cross to the islands from Bangsal harbour by motorboat or local sailing *prahu*).

Suranadi Hotel, PO Box 1009, Mataram, Jl. Raya Suranadi 1, Narmada, tel: 633-686, 636-411, fax: 635-630. 18 rooms with fans. Adjacent to the Suranadi temple at

300 metres (1,000 ft) above sea level and surrounded by a nature reserve, the hotel boasts spectacular views and cool, serene evenings. Its cottages wrap around a large spring-fed swimming pool and several tennis courts. The poolside restaurant, serving Chinese food, is excellent. **$$**
Wisma Sudjono, Tetebatu, is a delightful mountain resort with some bungalows attached to its restaurant complex; a simple alternative to the Suranadi Hotel. **$**

OTHER HOMESTAYS

Gili Air: Hotel Gili Air, Jl. Pemenang, Mataram, Gili Air, tel: 634-580, fax: 634-435. 29 rooms, a/c or fan, private showers, hot water, bar and restaurant. **$ +**
Gili Meno: Indah Ceman, Blue Coral and Ceman.
Gili Trawangan: Paradisa, Trawangan and Karin Homestay.

Price Guide

Price categories for standard rooms (or suites in larger hotels), usually without breakfast, are:

No $:	very cheap
$:	under $30
$$:	$30–$60
$$$:	$60–$100
$$$$:	$100–$150
$$$$$:	above $150, often hundreds of dollars

Where to Eat

The Balinese roast suckling pig, *babi guling*, done by the Lombok Balinese beats anything on the mother island. Arrange a feast (through hotel or driver) and ask if it can be served in one of the spacious courtyards of a Lombok Balinese home. Ask for *tuak* (palm toddy) to go with the pig, and a folk-dance performance (also easily arranged).

Mataram-Ampenan-Cakranegara

The Arab restaurants of Mataram often serve both Yemeni and Lombok dishes. **Kafe Espresso**, Mataram, tel: 693-148, has an Indonesian menu, sandwiches, soup and pasta. The **Taliwang** in the shopping centre on Jalan Pejanggik specialises in *ayam pelicing* – the searing hot curried chicken that is Lombok's speciality. The **Garden House Restaurant**, nearby on Jl. Pusat Pertokoan, tel: 632-233, serves both Indonesian and Chinese food.

The old Chinese restaurants on Jalan Pabean in Ampenan (the Tjirebon and the Pabean) are central and good, favourite hangouts of budget travellers. The **Tjirebon** has cold beer and steak with chips (don't eat the salad).

In Cakranegara, there are many restaurants along Jalan Selaparang. The **Asia** and the **Harum** serve Chinese food. The **Minang** has *nasi padang*. **Istimewa** has *saté* and, along with the **Hari Ini**, both serve *ayam pelicing*. **Restaurant Taliwang**, Jl. A. A. Ngurah, Cakranegara, tel: 682-530/15, is another good spot for *ayam pelicing*. Other Indonesian dishes can be had at **Siti Nurmaya**, Jl.

Palapa 34, and **Indonesia**, Jl. Selaparang 62. For western dishes, your best bet is at the hotels.

Senggigi Area

A wide range of cuisine is available from beachfront eateries at **Senggigi Art Market** *(Pasar Seni)*. **Alfredo** and **Putri Lombok** both have outlets along with **Café Coco Loco**, serving western and Lombok dishes; **Warung Lino**, a seafood grill; and **Kafe Senggigi Indah**, offering Italian, barbecue and Indonesian.

North of Senggigi, the hillside **Lombok Coconut** has spectacular sunset views across Lombok Strait to Gunung Agung. **Alang-Alang**, adjacent to Puri Mas, serves seafood.

Kafe Alberto, 6 km (4 mi) from Senggigi toward Ampenan, tel: 693-758, serves grilled seafood and homemade pasta in a tropical garden setting. **Dynasty**, just south of Senggigi Beach Hotel, tel: 693-039, offers Chinese food, pizza and international fare and **Marina Pub**, tel: 693-136, serves roadside western food, burgers and steaks.

In the heart of Senggigi, **Putri Lombok**, tel: 693-011, serves up steaks, Mexican food, barbecued and grilled food in an upstairs restaurant. The downstairs bar features a wide drinks list, billiards, darts and video. **Pacifik Restaurant**, at Pacifik Supermarket, has a menu offering Indonesian, Chinese, European and Italian food. The Blue Ocean bar is upstairs.

Other Areas

Both the **Suranadi Hotel** (in Suranadi) and the **Wisma Sudjono** (in Tetebatu) enjoy good reputations for tasty, fresh fish from their icy ponds. If staying in town, go there for lunch (and, at the Suranadi, for a swim). The main road from Batu Layar to Senggigi is lined with restaurants. Some offer transport within the Senggigi area if you telephone them ahead.

Sport

Diving

There are more than 15 mapped dive sites around the three Gili islands. Certified foreign and Indonesian dive instructors offer certification courses in Indonesian, English, German and other foreign languages. Introductory dive courses are available for approximately $65 to $80; two-day PADI open-water dive courses for certification are under $300; PADI advanced open-water certification costs around $300; rescue and other advanced courses vary in price.

Daily dive trips to the Gilis and beach dives start from about $25 for one-tank dives. Dive and snorkelling equipment rentals are available.

Golf

Rinjani Country Club Golf & Resort at Golong, Narmada, 12 mi (20 km) east of Mataram, tel: 633-488, fax: 633-839, is a Japanese joint-venture, 18-hole golf course and hotel. The simply landscaped par-72 course, designed by Shunji Ohno, is in a quiet setting under the shadow of Gunung Rinjani. A Japanese golf pro is in residence. Facilities include clubhouse and restaurant. Reasonable rates: weekdays $50 and weekends $90 for green fees, club rental Rp 30,000, shoes Rp 10,000, caddy fee included. Simple hotel rooms and villas around the course start at $60 per night. Guests may use the swimming pool free, others pay a nominal sum. Tennis and restaurant also on the grounds.

There's also the **Peluang Awal Sukses** golf course, Kebon Roik,

northwest Lombok. Sales office: Jl. Adisucipto, Ampenan, tel: 638-362.

For the less serious golfer, there is a miniature golf course is at Sandik, south of Senggigi.

Dive Centres

The following centres provide equipment and can arrange courses and trips.
Albatross Dive Centre & Pro Shop, Jl. Raya Senggigi km 8, Senggigi, PO Box 1066, Mataram, tel: 693-399, fax: 693-888. PADI English- and Indonesian-speaking instructors.
Blue Coral Diving Adventures, Jl. Raya Senggigi km 8, Senggigi, tel: 693-441, 693-032, fax: 693-251. On Trawangan island, tel: 634-496. PADI English-, Dutch- and German-speaking instructors. Dive equipment rental, sales and service.

Shopping

Traditional textiles and pottery are the best buys on the island.

Traditional Textiles

Visit the villages where the threads for traditional textiles are dyed and woven by hand: **Sukarare** (for *tenun Lombok*), **Pujung** (for *kain lambung*), **Purbasari** (for *kain Purbasari*) and **Balimurti** (for the sacred *beberut* cloth). **Labuhan Lombok** also produces fine blankets.

Contemporary Textiles

The best weaving factories for contemporary textiles are found in Cakranegara. Many of Bali's resident Italian couturiers buy fabrics from **Pak Abdullah** of C.V. Rinjani Handwoven, next door to the Hotel Selaparang (on Jl. Pejanggik, tel: 632-670). His stockroom often has leftovers from bolts of top designer fabrics. His silk sarongs and matching *selendang* scarves are highly regarded among the rag conscious of Bali and Jakarta.

The **Selamat Ryadi** weaving factory in the Arab quarter on Jl. Tenun (one block north and one block west of the Pura Mayura water palace) is another excellent source. The **Balimurti** factory nearby produces weavings in the Purbasari style.

Pottery

Three villages – **Banyumulek, Masbagik Timur** and **Penujak** – produce pottery. Wander behind the roadside stalls in any of the three villages to see pots being thrown and fired. Sofia, at the **Pottery Art Shop** in Banyumulek, worked five years with the New Zealand project and can provide concise information on methods.

The **Lombok Pottery Centre**, Jl. Sriwijaya IIIA, tel: 640-350, offers high-grade products for sale and offers information on the project. There is also an outlet in Singgigi. Lombok clay also is crafted into more contemporary ceramic tableware at **Citra Lombok Ceramics**, Jl. Brawijaya 26, Cakranegara, tel/fax: 634-502.

Baskets

Lombok's rattan and grass baskets are extremely fine and sturdy. Many are produced in the eastern Lombok villages of **Kotaraja** and **Loyok**. Baskets, pots and crafts are cheap and abundant at the main market by the bus and *bemo* terminal in **Sweta**, or in the **Cakranegara Market** to the west of the Pura Meru temple.

Antiques

Sudirman's Antiques is a few hundred metres down a side lane from Jalan Pabean in Ampenan (enter across from the *bemo* station, and ask for directions). Enterprising merchants of antiques will often call on you in your hotel. They have old Chinese ceramics, antique carvings and ceremonial weavings. Bargain hard and nonchalantly; never appear eager or rushed. A second outlet is along Jl. Raya Senggigi.

Parmour Antiques Oleh-Oleh collection also has two outlets, the original location at Jl. Montong Buwuh, km 13, in Ampenan and the large gallery at Jl. Raya Senggigi, in front of the post office, tel: 693-704. The gallery shop features fine antiques and furniture collected by owner Agus Heri Gomanthy, an excellent source of information on such arts. He also exports.

There are a few factories in Lombok doing a booming trade in primitive bottletops, wooden spoons and carved canisters – in some cases these are excellent

reproductions of traditional pieces. Most of what you see is new and made to look antique.

Sundries

The 6-km (4-mi) main street running through the centre of Ampenan, Mataram and Cakranegara (Langko/Pejanggik/ Selaparang street) is one long shopping mall. For sundries, basic necessities, groceries and drinks, especially for Gunung Rinjani treks, there are two supermarkets in the centre of Senggigi: Senggigi Abadi and Pacifik Supermarket.

Souvenirs

For general souvenirs, batiks, paintings and Lombok-produced pearls, visit **Kencana Gallery** near the airport, Jl. Adi Sucipto 12, tel: 635-727, or **Sari Kusuma Artshop**, Jl. Selaparang 45, Cakranegara, tel: 623-338, fax: 627-360. The **Senggigi Art Market** (Pasar Seni) has kiosk-style shops selling souvenirs, local clothing and artwork, along with eateries.

Further Reading

General

The Island of Bali by Miguel Covarrubias. Periplus, Singapore, 1999.
Bali: The Ultimate Island by Leonard Lueras. Times, Singapore, 1987.
The Balinese by Hugh Mabbett. January Books, Wellington, 1988.

History

A Tale from Bali by Vicki Baum. Periplus, Singapore, 1999.
Bali: A Paradise Created by Adrian Vickers. Periplus, Singapore, 1989.
Monumental Bali by A J Bernet Kempers and Van Goor Zonen. Periplus, Singapore, 1991.
Visible and Invisible Realms by Margaret J Wiener. University of Chicago Press, 1995.

Religion/Culture

Trance in Bali by Jane Belo. Columbia University Press, New York, 1960.
Offerings by Francine Brinkgreve and David Stuart-Fox. Image Network Indonesia, Sanur, 1992.

Art/Music/Dance

The Art and Culture of Bali by Urs Ramseyer. Oxford in Asia, Singapore, 1977.
Music in Bali by Colin McPhee. Yale University Press, 1966.
Balinese Music by Michael Tenzer. Periplus, Singapore, 1992.
Dance and Drama in Bali by Beryl de Zoete and Walter Spies. Oxford, Singapore, 1973.
Balinese Paintings (second edition) by A A M Djelantik. Oxford in Asia, Singapore, 1990.
The Development of Painting in Bali (second edition) by Suteja Neka and Garrett Kam. Yayasan Dharma Seni, Ubud, 1998.
Perceptions of Paradise by Garrett Kam. Yayasan Dharma Seni, Ubud, 1993.

Textiles in Bali by Brigitta Hauser-Schaublin, et al. Periplus, Singapore, 1991.

Other Insight Guides

Insight Guide: Indonesia. Apa Publications, Singapore, 2001. Comprehensive guide to the whole country, featuring stunning photography and useful maps.

Pocket Guide: Bali. Apa Publications, Singapore, 2000. Takes you straight to the best of the island in day-by-day itineraries specially created by a local host; includes a fold-out map which can be used independently of the book.

Compact Guide: Bali. Apa Publications, Singapore, 1996. A mini-encyclopaedia packed with facts, photos and maps, all carefully cross-referenced – the ideal easy-reference books for practical use on the spot.

Insight Flexi Map: Bali. Apa Publications, Singapore, 2000. These maps combine clear cartography with useful travel information and come in an easy-to-fold, rain-resistant laminated finish.

Feedback

We do our best to ensure the information in our books is as accurate and up-to-date as possible. The books are updated on a regular basis, using local contacts, who painstakingly add, amend and correct as required. However, some mistakes and omissions are inevitable and we are ultimately reliant on our readers to put us in the picture.

We would welcome your feedback on any details related to your experiences using the book "on the road". Maybe we recommended a hotel that you liked (or another that you didn't), as well as interesting new attractions, or facts and figures you have found out about the country itself. The more details you can give us (particularly with regard to addresses, e-mails and telephone numbers), the better.

We will acknowledge all contributions, and we'll offer an Insight Guide to the best letters received. Please write to us at:

Insight Guides
APA Publications
PO Box 7910
London SE1 1WE

Or send e-mail to: **insight@apaguide.demon.co.uk**

ART & PHOTO CREDITS

Amsterdam Institute 20, 21, 36R, 38, 39, 88, 91, 211T
Anderson, John 24
Begin Ende Voortgangh vande Oost-Indische Compagine 28, 29, 30
Bool, Dan 58, 77, 79R, 170T, 175T, 192T
Bowden, David 183, 251
Bruechman, P. 260T
Davis, James spine bottom
Diskin, D.A. 6/7
Evrard, Alain 86/87, 94
Gottschalk, Manfred 198R
Güler, Ara 59, 71, 73, 76, 80L, 155
Hahn, Werner 10/11
Heaton, D.J. 8/9
Hesselyn, Brent 112/113, 122, 186/187
Höfer, Hans 17, 22/23, 25, 31, 32/33, 41, 42/43, 44, 47, 49, 50, 52/53, 54/55, 56, 57, 62, 67, 68, 69R, 70, 74/75, 78L/R, 79L, 81, 82, 90, 93, 95, 97, 99, 100, 102/103, 106, 107L/R, 111, 114/115, 116, 118, 131, 132, 133, 134/135, 136/137, 140/141, 159T, 164/165, 168, 169, 172R, 173L, 174, 178R, 180, 181, 192L, 201T, 203, 207, 212, 213, 216, 220, 226, 232R, 242/243, 246, 248R, 250, 256, 262R, 270
Hollingsworth, Jack front flap, back flap, spine top, all back cover pictures, 14, 27, 51, 60, 61L/R, 63, 64/65, 72, 120, 121, 128, 130, 138/139, 142, 149, 150,

151T, 152, 153, 153T, 154, 156, 157, 158, 159, 160, 161, 162T, 163, 170, 171, 172L, 175, 176, 177, 178L, 179, 188, 189, 190, 192R, 193, 194L/R, 196, 197, 198L, 199, 200, 202, 202T, 206, 208, 209, 210, 210T, 211, 212T, 214/215, 217, 218, 218T, 221T, 227, 228, 230, 231, 233, 238, 239, 245, 248T, 249, 250T, 254/255, 259, 261, 264, 264T, 266, 267, 269
Indonesian Department of Information 48
Invernizzi Tettoni, Luca 26, 35, 258
Jezierski, Ingo 117, 123L, 161T, 182T, 195, 221, 234, 236
Kose – Bali 235
Lawrence, Max 18/19, 36L, 37, 45, 46R, 66, 83, 101, 124, 173R
Little, Philip 123R
Müller, Kal 12/13, 69L, 109, 119, 224/225, 232L, 252/253, 262L, 265, 268
Oey, Eric M. 125
Reichelt, G.P. 96, 98, 104, 129, 146/147, 162, 204/205, 223, 230T, 244
Rhodius, Hans 46L
Riedinger, H.H. 201
Ryan, David 80R
Strange, Morten 248L
Strange, Rick 92
University at Leiden, Amsterdam 34, 40
Van Riel, Paul 263
Waterfall, William 108
Wijaya, Made 105, 237

Picture Spreads

Pages 84/85: Top row, left to right: Andrea Pistolesi, Andrea Pistolesi, Rob Walls/Auscape, Andrea Pistolesi. Centre row, left to right: both Rio Helmi/Auscape. Bottom row, left to right: Rio Helmi/Auscape, Jim Holmes/Axiom.
Pages 126/127: Top row, left to right: Hutchison Library, Hutchison Library, Rio Helmi/Auscape, Jim Holmes/Axiom. Centre row, left to right: Hutchison Libary, Andrea Pistolesi. Bottom row, left to right: Jack Hollingsworth, Jack Hollingsworth, Andrea Pistolesi.
Pages 184/185: All by Hans Höfer except top left: G.P. Reichelt, bottom left Bill Wassman and bottom right Luca Invernizzi Tettoni.
Pages 240/241: Top row, left to right: Andrea Pistolesi, Jack Hollingsworth, Jim Holmes/Axiom. Bottom row, left to right: Jack Hollingsworth, Andrea Pistolesi, Jim Holmes/Axiom, Jim Holmes/Axiom.

Map Production Berndtson & Berndtson Productions

© 2002 Apa Publications GmbH & Co. Verlag KG (Singapore branch)

Cartographic Editor **Zoë Goodwin**
Production **Linton Donaldson**
Design Consultants
Klaus Geisler, Graham Mitchener
Picture Research **Hilary Genin**

Index